ANNUAL EDITIONS

Archaeology

Tenth Edition

EDITORS

Mari Pritchard Parker
Pasadena City College

Mari Pritchard Parker is a Registered Professional Archaeologist with more than 20 years of cultural resources management experience in coastal California, the Great Basin, and the Desert Southwest. Ms Pritchard Parker earned a Bachelor's degree in Anthropology from California State University, Fullerton, in 1986 and a Master's degree in Archaeology from the University of California at Riverside in 1995.

Her interest is primarily in ground stone analysis and replication, textile conservation, and ceramic studies. She has served as guest editor for the *Pacific Coast Archaeological Society Quarterly* on two special issues on ground stone analysis. She is also the founder of the Milford Archaeological Research Institute, a non-profit organization dedicated to educating the public and future archaeologists in the study of archaeology and past lifeways of the Desert Southwest.

Elvio Angeloni
Pasadena City College

Elvio Angeloni received his BA from UCLA in 1963, his MA in anthropology from UCLA in 1965, and his MA in communication arts from Loyola Marymount University in 1976. He has produced several films, including *Little Warrior,* winner of the Cinemedia VI Best Bicentennial Theme, and *Broken Bottles,* shown on PBS. He served as an academic adviser on the instructional television series *Faces of Culture.* He received the Pasadena City College Outstanding Teacher Award in 2006. He is also the academic editor of *Annual Editions: Physical Anthropology, Classic Edition Sources: Anthropology* and co-editor of *Annual Editions: Archaeology* and *Roundtable Viewpoints: Physical Anthropology.* His primary area of interest has been indigenous peoples of the American Southwest.

The McGraw·Hill Companies

ANNUAL EDITIONS: ARCHAEOLOGY, TENTH EDITION

Published by McGraw-Hill, a business unit of The McGraw-Hill Companies, Inc., 1221 Avenue of the Americas, New York, NY 10020.

Annual Editions is published by the **Contemporary Learning Series** group within the McGraw-Hill Higher Education division.

1 2 3 4 5 6 7 8 9 0 QDB/QDB 1 0 9 8 7 6 5 4 3 2

MHID: 0-07-805115-0
ISBN: 978-0-07-805115-9
ISSN: 1092-4760

Managing Editor: *Larry Loeppke*
Developmental Editor: *Debra A. Henricks*
Permissions Coordinator: *Lenny J. Behnke*
Senior Marketing Communications Specialist: *Mary Klein*
Senior Project Manager: *Joyce Watters*
Design Coordinator: *Margarite Reynolds*
Cover Designer: *Studio Montage, St. Louis, Missouri*
Buyer: *Susan K. Culbertson*
Media Project Manager: *Sridevi Palani*

Compositor: Laserwords Private Limited
Cover Image Credits: Victorio Castellani/Alamy (inset); MedioImages/Getty Images (background)

www.mhhe.com

Editors/Academic Advisory Board

Members of the Academic Advisory Board are instrumental in the final selection of articles for each edition of ANNUAL EDITIONS. Their review of articles for content, level, and appropriateness provides critical direction to the editors and staff. We think that you will find their careful consideration well reflected in this volume.

ANNUAL EDITIONS: Archaeology 12/13
10th Edition

EDITORS

Mari Pritchard Parker
Pasadena City College

Elvio Angeloni
Pasadena City College

ACADEMIC ADVISORY BOARD MEMBERS

Preface

In publishing ANNUAL EDITIONS we recognize the enormous role played by the magazines, newspapers, and journals of the public press in providing current, first-rate educational information in a broad spectrum of interest areas. Many of these articles are appropriate for students, researchers, and professionals seeking accurate, current material to help bridge the gap between principles and theories and the real world. These articles, however, become more useful for study when those of lasting value are carefully collected, organized, indexed, and reproduced in a low-cost format, which provides easy and permanent access when the material is needed. That is the role played by ANNUAL EDITIONS.

The tenth edition of *Annual Editions: Archaeology* has been compiled by its two editors with the intent of presenting a vivid overview of the field of archaeology as practiced today. It is our hope that these readings, in keeping with its previous editions will make the old bones, shards of pottery, and stone tools of the past pop into the present. The book's purpose is to present an approach in which archaeologists speak for themselves of their own special experiences. The student is shown that archaeology is a historical as well as a living, public science. The idea is to give the student the necessary basics in order to transform passive learning into active learning. This way, information is both perceived and conceptualized. Hopefully, the light bulb will go on when students read these articles.

This book is organized into six units, each of which contains several articles of various themes on "doing" archaeology. The *Table of Contents* provides a short synopsis of each article, while the *Topic Guide* assists students in finding other articles on a given subject within this edition. A list of *Internet References* offers the best sources of additional information on a topic.

Each unit is introduced by an overview that provides a commentary on the unit topic. It is highly recommended that the student read the unit overviews, as they are presented with humor and also contain challenges and puzzles to solve. *Learning Outcomes* preceding each overview provoke thought and discussion, and *Critical Thinking* questions at the end of each article allow students to test their understanding of key concepts.

The organization of this book is both suggestive and subjective. The articles may be assigned or read in any fashion that is deemed desirable. Each article stands on its own and may be assigned in conjunction with, or in contrast to, any other article.

Annual Editions: Archaeology may serve as a supplement to a standard textbook for both introductory and graduate archaeology courses. It may also be used in general, undergraduate, or graduate courses in anthropology. The lay reader in anthropology may also find the collection of readings insightful.

It is the desire of those involved in the production of this book that each edition be a valuable and provocative teaching and learning tool. Instructors will appreciate a password-protected online Instructor's Resource Guide, and students will find online quizzing to further test their understanding of the material. These tools are available at www.mhhe.com/cls via the Online Learning Center for this book.

We welcome your criticisms, advice, and suggestions in order to carefully hone new editions into finer artifacts of education. We would be most grateful for the time you take to give us your feedback.

Mari A. Pritchard Parker

Mari Pritchard Parker
Editor

Elvio Angeloni

Elvio Angeloni
Editor

The Annual Editions Series

VOLUMES AVAILABLE

Adolescent Psychology
Aging
American Foreign Policy
American Government
Anthropology
Archaeology
Assessment and Evaluation
Business Ethics
Child Growth and Development
Comparative Politics
Criminal Justice
Developing World
Drugs, Society, and Behavior
Dying, Death, and Bereavement
Early Childhood Education
Economics
Educating Children with Exceptionalities
Education
Educational Psychology
Entrepreneurship
Environment
The Family
Gender
Geography
Global Issues
Health
Homeland Security
Human Development
Human Resources
Human Sexualities
International Business
Management
Marketing
Mass Media
Microbiology
Multicultural Education
Nursing
Nutrition
Physical Anthropology
Psychology
Race and Ethnic Relations
Social Problems
Sociology
State and Local Government
Sustainability
Technologies, Social Media, and Society
United States History, Volume 1
United States History, Volume 2
Urban Society
Violence and Terrorism
Western Civilization, Volume 1
World History, Volume 1
World History, Volume 2
World Politics

Contents

UNIT 1
About Archaeologists and Archaeology

The concepts in bold italics are developed in the article. For further expansion, please refer to the Topic Guide.

UNIT 2
Problem Oriented Archaeology

The concepts in bold italics are developed in the article. For further expansion, please refer to the Topic Guide.

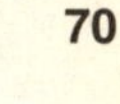

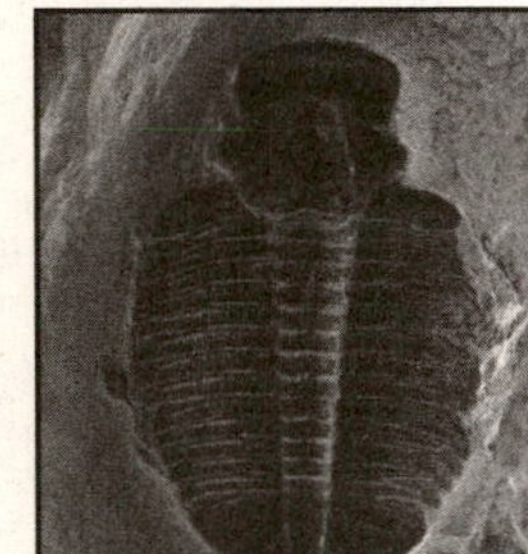

UNIT 3
Techniques in Archaeology

The concepts in bold italics are developed in the article. For further expansion, please refer to the Topic Guide.

UNIT 4
Pre-Historic Archaeology

The concepts in bold italics are developed in the article. For further expansion, please refer to the Topic Guide.

UNIT 5
Historical Archaeology

The concepts in bold italics are developed in the article. For further expansion, please refer to the Topic Guide.

UNIT 6
Contemporary Archaeology

The concepts in bold italics are developed in the article. For further expansion, please refer to the Topic Guide.

The concepts in bold italics are developed in the article. For further expansion, please refer to the Topic Guide.

Correlation Guide

The *Annual Editions* series provides students with convenient, inexpensive access to current, carefully selected articles from the public press. **Annual Editions: Archaeology, 10/e** is an easy-to-use reader that presents articles on important topics such as *epistemology, ethnographic analogy, historical archaeology,* and many more. For more information on *Annual Editions* and other *McGraw-Hill Contemporary Learning Series* titles, visit www.mhhe.com/cls.

This convenient guide matches the units in **Annual Editions: Archaeology, 10/e** with the corresponding chapters in two of our best-selling McGraw-Hill Archaeology textbooks by Ashmore/Sharer and Price/Feinman.

Annual Editions: Archaeology, 10/e	Discovering Our Past: A Brief Introduction to Archaeology, 5/e by Ashmore/Sharer	Images of the Past, 6/e by Price/Feinman
Unit 1: About Archaeologists and Archaeology	**Chapter 1:** Introduction **Chapter 2:** Archaeology's Past **Chapter 3:** Contemporary Approaches to Archaeology	**Chapter 1:** Principles of Archaeology
Unit 2: Problem Oriented Archaeology	**Chapter 4:** How Archaeology Works	**Chapter 2:** The First Humans **Chapter 3:** Out of Africa: Homo Erectus **Chapter 4:** The Hunters **Chapter 7:** Native North Americans **Chapter 8:** Ancient Mesoamerica **Chapter 10:** States and Empires in Asia and Africa
Unit 3: Techniques in Archaeology	**Chapter 5:** Fieldwork **Chapter 7:** Dating the Past **Chapter 8:** Reconstructing the Past	**Chapter 1:** Principles of Archaeology **Chapter 5:** Postglacial Foragers
Unit 4: Prehistoric Archaeology	**Chapter 8:** Reconstructing the Past	**Chapter 2:** The First Humans **Chapter 11:** Prehistoric Europe
Unit 5: Historical Archaeology	**Chapter 5:** Fieldwork **Chapter 6:** Analyzing the Past **Chapter 8:** Reconstructing the Past **Chapter 9:** Understanding the Past	
Unit 6: Contemporary Archaeology	**Chapter 3:** Contemporary Approaches to Archaeology **Chapter 10:** Archaeology Today	**Chapter 1:** Principles of Archaeology **Chapter 4:** The Hunters **Chapter 12:** The Past as Present and Future

Topic Guide

This topic guide suggests how the selections in this book relate to the subjects covered in your course. You may want to use the topics listed on these pages to search the Web more easily.

On the following pages a number of websites have been gathered specifically for this book. They are arranged to reflect the units of this Annual Editions reader. You can link to these sites by going to www.mhhe.com/cls

All the articles that relate to each topic are listed below the bold-faced term.

Internet References

The following Internet sites have been selected to support the articles found in this reader. These sites were available at the time of publication. However, because websites often change their structure and content, the information listed may no longer be available. We invite you to visit www.mhhe.com/cls for easy access to these sites.

Annual Editions: Archaeology 12/13

General Sources

Anthropology Resources on the Internet
www.socsciresearch.com/r7.html

This site provides extensive Internet links that are primarily of anthropological relevance. The Education Index rated it "one of the best education-related sites on the Web."

Archaeological Institute of America
www.archaeological.org

This home page of the AIA describes the purpose of the nonprofit organization. Review this site for information about AIA and AIA/IAA–Canada and other archaeological-research institutions and organizations around the world.

How Humans Evolved
www.wwnorton.com/college/anthro/bioanth

This site presents a good overview of human evolution, with links to *Science* and *Nature* magazines, access to e-mail chat groups, and other topics of archaeological interest.

Library of Congress
www.loc.gov

Examine this extensive website to learn about resource tools, library services/resources, exhibitions, and databases in many different subfields of archaeology.

The New York Times
www.nytimes.com

Browsing through the extensive archives of *The New York Times* will provide you with a wide array of articles and information related to archaeology.

Society for American Archaeology
www.saa.org

An international organization dedicated to the research, interpretation, and protection of the archaeological heritage of the Americas.

Society for Historical Archaeology
www.sha.org

The official website of the Society for Historical Archaeology. Historical Archaeology is the study of the material remains of past societies that also left behind historical documentary evidence. This subfield of archaeology studies the emergence, transformation, and nature of the Modern World.

USD Anthropology
www.usd.edu/anth

Many topics can be accessed from this site, such as South Dakota archaeology. Repatriation and reburial are just a few examples of the variety of information available.

UNIT 1: About Archaeologists and Archaeology

The Ancient Egyptian Pharaohs
www.ancient-egypt-online.com/ancient-egyptian-pharaohs.html

An introduction to the history of ancient Egypt, including the daily life of the people as well as that of the pharaohs.

Anthropology, Archaeology, and American Indian Sites on the Internet
http://dizzy.library.arizona.edu/library/teams/sst/anthro

This Web page points out a number of Internet sites of interest to archaeologists. Visit this page for links to electronic journals and more.

GMU Anthropology Department
www.gmu.edu/departments/anthro

Look over this site for current listings of scientific papers dealing with anthropological and archaeological studies. The site provides a number of interesting links, such as a listing of archaeological fieldwork opportunities.

Maya Archaeology Initiative
http://mayaarchaeology.org

A new, publicly funded NGO launched in February 2010 to fund cultural and archaeological programs having to do with Maya history and culture in northern Guatemala.

Smithsonian Institution Website
www.si.edu

This site, which will provide access to many of the enormous resources of the Smithsonian, will give you a sense of the scope of anthropological and archaeological inquiry today.

Society for American Archaeology
www.saa.org

An international organization dedicated to the research, interpretation, and protection of the archaeological heritage of the Americas.

UNIT 2: Problem Oriented Archaeology

Archaeology Links (NC)
www.arch.dcr.state.nc.us/links.htm#stuff

North Carolina Archaeology provides this site, which has many links to sites of interest to archaeologists, such as the paleolithic painted cave at Vallon-Pont-d'Arc (Ardeche).

***Archaeology* Magazine**
www.archaeology.org

This home page of *Archaeology* magazine, the official publication of the AIA, provides information about current archaeological events, staff picks of websites, and access to selected articles from current and past editions of the magazine.

Cahokia Mounds
http://cahokiamounds.org

The official web page of Cahokia Mounds State Historic Site offers information about the site as well as an interactive map and award-winning video.

UNIT 3: Techniques in Archaeology

American Anthropologist
www.aaanet.org

Check out this site—the home page of the American Anthropology Association—for general information about archaeology and anthropology as well as access to a wide variety of articles.

Internet References

GIS and Remote Sensing for Archaeology: Burgundy, France
www.informatics.org/france/france.html

This project has been an ongoing collaboration between Dr. Scott Madry from the Center for Remote Sensing and Spatial Analysis at Rutgers University and many other researchers. A period of over 2,000 years in the Arroux River Valley region of Burgundy is being analyzed to understand long-term interaction between the different cultures and the physical environment.

Radiocarbon Dating for Archaeology
www.rlaha.ox.ac.uk/orau/index.html

This website describes the advantages inherent in using radiocarbon dating to promote mass spectrometry over the older decay counting method.

Zeno's Forensic Page
http://forensic.to/forensic.html

A complete list of resources on forensics is here. It includes DNA/serology sources and databases, forensic-medicine anthropology sites, and related areas.

UNIT 4: Pre-Historic Archaeology

Bradshaw Foundation
www.bradshawfoundation.com/clottes/index.php

Read the article "Paleolithic Cave Art in France" by renowned authority, Jean Clottes, who provides a definitive and comprehensive analysis of the art, along with photos taken within such caves as Chauvet, Cosquer, and Niaux. At this site, you may also learn more about rock art around the world and take an interactive journey from Africa to the rest of the world, following the route used by our ancestors from 160,000 years ago to the present.

Department of Human Evolution/Max Planck Institute
www.eva.mpg.de/evolution

Provides an overview of the activities of paleoanthropologists, who study fossil material, archaeological scientists, who undertake biochemical analyses of the fossils, and Paleolithic archaeologists, who study the adaptive strategies of hominins to their environment, with links to publications dealing with Neanderthals and the Neanderthal Genome project.

Turkana Basin Institute
www.turkanabasin.org

The Turkana Basin Institute provides logistical support to researchers working in northern Kenya, provides online resources to the broader community interested in the region and is dedicated to safeguarding the extensive fossil deposits through engagement with the local communities.

UNIT 5: Historical Archaeology

NOVA Online/Pyramids—The Inside Story
www.pbs.org/wgbh/nova/pyramid

Take a virtual tour of the pyramids at Giza through this interesting site. It provides information on the pharaohs for whom the tombs were built and follows a team of archaeologists as they excavate a bakery that fed the pyramid builders.

Society for Historical Archaeology
www.sha.org

The official website of the Society for Historical Archaeology. Historical Archaeology is the study of the material remains of past societies that also left behind historical documentary evidence. This subfield of archaeology studies the emergence, transformation, and nature of the Modern World.

UNIT 6: Contemporary Archaeology

Al Mashriq-Archaeology in Beirut
http://almashriq.hiof.no/base/archaeology.html

At this site the links to the fascinating excavations taking place in Beirut can be explored. Reports from the site, background material, discussion of the importance of the site, and information on other Lebanese sites are included.

American Indian Ritual Object Repatriation Foundation
www.repatriationfoundation.org

Visit this home page of the American Indian Ritual Object Repatriation Foundation, which aims to assist in the return of sacred ceremonial material to the appropriate American Indian nation, clan, or family, and to educate the public.

Archaeology and Anthropology: The Australian National University
http://online.anu.edu.au/AandA

Browse through this home page of the Anthropology and Archaeology Departments of the Australian National University for information about topics in Australian and regional archaeology and to access links to other resource centers.

ArchNet—WWW Virtual Library
http://archnet.asu.edu/archnet

ArchNet serves as the World Wide Web Virtual Library for Archaeology. This site can provide you with access to a broad variety of archaeological resources available on the Internet, categorized by geographic region and subject.

Current Archaeology
www.archaeology.co.uk

This is the home page of *Current Archaeology,* Great Britain's leading archaeological magazine. Its various sections provide links about archaeology in Britain.

National Archaeological Database
www.cast.uark.edu/other/nps/nagpra/nagpra.html

Examine this site from the Archaeology and Ethnography Program of the NADB to read documents related to the Native American Graves Protection and Repatriation Act.

Past Horizons
www.pasthorizonspr.com

Society for Archaeological Sciences
www.socarchsci.org

The Society for Archaeological Sciences provides this site to further communication among scholars applying methods from the physical sciences to archaeology.

WWW Classical Archaeology
www.archaeology.org/wwwarky/classical.html

This site provides information and links regarding ancient Greek and Roman archaeology.

UNIT 1

About Archaeologists and Archaeology

Unit Selections

Learning Outcomes

After reading this Unit, you will be able to:

- Explain why modern archaeology is so different from archaeology of the nineteenth century and discuss the importance to modern archaeologists of archaeological methods, fieldwork, theory, and ethics.
- Discuss the anthropological view of culture.
- Using specific examples, outline the general relationship between anthropology and
- Discuss the importance of "action archaeology."
- Review the ways in which archaeologists could better convey to the public just what it is that they do and how it benefits the communities in which they work.
- Discuss the differeneces between academic and non-academic archaeologists and identify the roles they can, and should, play in their communities.
- Discuss the ways in which pharaohs such as Ramesses II did not fit the standard image.
- Outline some of the most significant achievements of the Maya at El Mirador and why their society ultimately failed.

Student Website

www.mhhe.com/cls

Internet References

The Ancient Egyptian Pharaohs
www.ancient-egypt-online.com/ancient-egyptian-pharaohs.html

Anthropology, Archaeology, and American Indian Sites on the Internet
http://dizzy.library.arizona.edu/library/teams/sst/anthro

GMU Anthropology Department
www.gmu.edu/departments/anthro

Maya Archaeology Initiative
http://mayaarchaeology.org

Smithsonian Institution Website
www.si.edu

Society for American Archaeology
www.saa.org

Ozymandias [1817]

I met a traveller from an antique land Who said: Two vast and trunkless legs of stone Stand in the desert. Near them, on the sand, Half sunk, a shattered visage lies, whose frown And wrinkled lip, and sneer of cold command Tell that its sculptor well those passions read Which yet survive, stamped on these lifeless things, The hand that mocked them and the heart that fed. And on the pedestal these words appear: "My name is Ozymandias, king of kings: Look on my works, ye Mighty, and despair!" Nothing beside remains. Round the decay Of that colossal wreck, boundless and bare The lone and level sands stretch far away.

—Percy Bysshe Shelley

© Digital Vision/Punchstock

So just who is an archaeologist? The job description presented by the mass media is very different from the reality of today's anthropological archaeologists. Archaeologists in the Americas, after all, are trained as anthropologists. Our goal is to reconstruct cultures of the past based on the material remains that managed to survive the "ravages of time." So today's archaeologists are concerned with the reconstruction of human behavior, not just with the collection of treasure objects.

If human behavior were a baseball game, the anthropologist would be in the broadcaster's booth. But long before the game was over, in a seeming paradox, the anthropologist would run into the stands to be a spectator, chow down on a good, fresh, steamy mustard-covered hot dog, and then rush onto the field to be a player and catch a high fly to left field. This is the eccentric nature of anthropology. This is why anthropology is so interesting.

If one compares anthropology, psychology, sociology, and history as four disciplines that study human nature, anthropology is the one that takes the giant step back and uses a 360-degree panoramic camera. The psychologist stands nose to nose with the individual person, the sociologist moves back for the group shot, and the historian goes back in time as well as space. However, the anthropologist does all these things, standing well behind the others, watching and measuring, using the data of all these disciplines, but recombining them into the uniqueness of the anthropological perspective: much the way meiosis generates novel genetic combinations.

Anthropology is the science of human behavior that studies all humankind, starting with our biological and evolutionary origins as cultural beings and continues with the diversification of our cultural selves. Humankind is the only species that has evolved culture as a way of adapting to the world. Academically, anthropology is divided into four major fields: cultural anthropology, physical anthropology, linguistics, and archaeology. Anthropologists hold in common a shared concept of culture. The ultimate goal shared by all anthropologists is to generate a behavioral science that can explain the differences and similarities between cultures. In order to achieve this, anthropologists view people from a cross-cultural perspective. This involves comparing the parts and parcels of all cultures, past and present, with each other. This is the holistic approach of anthropology: considering all things in their broader social and historical contexts. A grand task, indeed. One that requires, above all, learning to ask the "right" questions. If there is one thing that anthropologists have learned, it is that the kinds of answers you get depend upon the kinds of questions you ask.

What is culture? Culture is the unique way in which the human species adapts to its total environment. Total environment includes everything that affects human beings—the physical environment that includes plants, animals, the weather; beliefs; values; a passing insult; or an opportunistic virus. Everything that human beings learn is cultural.

Culture is the human adaptive system shaped by its particular time and space. It consists of learned ways to manipulate the environment by making and using tools and it involves shared values and beliefs which are passed down from one generation to the next by means of language. Cultures change and evolve over time. But whether they are high civilizations or small tribes, they do eventually cease to exist.

Archaeology is the subfield of anthropology that studies these extinct cultures. Archaeologists dig up the physical remains, the tools, the houses, the garbage, and the utensils of past cultures. And from this spare database, archaeologists attempt to reconstruct these past cultures in their material, social, and ideological aspects. Is this important to anthropology? Yes, this is anthropology. Because these once-living cultures represent approximately ninety-eight percent of all cultures that have ever existed. They tell us what we have been, what we are today, and what we might become in the future.

How do archaeologists do this? Today, the mass media, including the internet, is the major source of our understanding of the modern world, and it underscores the cultural values and cultural myths that all humans use to rationalize the way they live. The media is as much a response to our demands as we are to its manipulations. Its themes play a medley in our minds over and over again, until they fade into our unconscious only to be recycled again, pulled up, and laid before us like the ice cream man's musical chimes of our childhood. But the commercial media will also respond to a rational, skeptical, and articulate public, a public that has been educated to think scientifically with a very strict set of rules and regulations that test the veracity of conclusions. This is where anthropology in general and archaeology in particular have a role to play: spreading the word about the scientific method and the wonderful results that can be derived from its use in understanding our species.

Postmodernists may argue that knowledge is only knowable in a relative sense. But we know what we know in a very real pragmatic sense because we are, after all humans—the cultural animal. It is our way of knowing and surviving. Let us proceed now to see how archaeologists ply their magical trade.

Article 1

The Awful Truth about Archaeology

DR. LYNNE SEBASTIAN

"Ohhhh! You're an Archaeologist! That sounds soooo exciting!" Whenever I tell someone on a plane or at a dinner party what I do for a living, this is almost always the response that I get. Either that, or they want to talk to me about dinosaurs, and I have to explain gently that it is paleontologists who do dinosaurs; archaeologists study people who lived long ago.

The reason people think archaeology must be exciting is that they have spent WAY too much time watching *The Curse of the Mummy, Indiana Jones and the Temple of Doom,* and *Lara Croft, Tomb Raider* (do you suppose that she actually has that printed on her business cards?). Perhaps it is a flaw in my character or a lapse in my professional education, but I have never once recovered a golden idol or been chased through the jungle by thugs, and I appear to have been absent from graduate school on the day that they covered bullwhips, firearms, and the martial arts. I have not even, so far as I can tell, suffered from a curse, although I have had few nasty encounters with serpents, scorpions, and lightning.

I'm sure that members of every profession are exasperated by the way that they are portrayed in movies and on television, and archaeologists are no exception. Every time we see Sydney Fox (*Relic Hunter,* another great job title) fly off to an exotic country, follow the clues on the ancient map, and rip-off some fabulous object to bring home to the museum, we want to root for the bad guys who are trying to bring her career to an abrupt and permanent halt.

What would really happen if a mysterious man wearing an eye patch showed up at Sydney's university office and gave her the map, just before expiring as a result of slow-acting poison? Well, of course, first there would be a lot of unpleasantness with the campus police . . . but leaving that aside, she would spend months writing grant proposals to get funding for a research expedition and more months getting the needed permits and authorizations from the government of the exotic country. Then she would have to persuade the Dean and her department Chair to give her release time from teaching. And when she and her research team finally arrived in the exotic country, they would spend months meticulously mapping the site, painstakingly removing thin layers of soil from perfectly square holes, and recording every stone, every bit of stained earth, every piece of debris that they encountered, using photos, maps, sketches, and detailed written notes. Finally, at the end of the field season, the team would return to the university with 70 boxes of broken pottery, bits of stone, and all manner of scientific samples to be washed and cataloged and analyzed. And in the end, all that material would be returned to a museum in the exotic country.

Now, of course, nobody would want to watch a TV show where even the beauteous Sydney did all that, but this kind of tedious, detailed work is one important aspect of "real" archaeology. Just about every archaeologist that I know has a copy of an old Calvin and Hobbs cartoon somewhere in his or her office. In it, Calvin, who has spent an exhausting day doing a make-believe archaeological excavation in his backyard, turns to Hobbs in disgust and says, "Archaeology has to be the most mind-numbing job in the world!!" And some days it is. Worse yet, it is detailed work that involves a lot of paperwork and delicate instruments but has to be done outdoors in every sort of adverse weather. When it is 20 degrees and you are hunched down in a square hole in the ground trying to write a description of layers of dirt with a pen that keeps freezing solid or when the wind is blowing sheets of sand straight sideways into your face while you are lying on your stomach using a dental pick to expose a broken shell bracelet so you can photograph it before you remove it—these are experiences that can cause a person to question her career choice.

But you know what? Archaeology really IS exciting, and not for any of the reasons that Indy or Lara would suggest. Archaeology is exciting because it connects with the past in a way that nothing else can, and sometimes that connection can be stunningly immediate and personal. I worked one year on the Hopi Reservation in Arizona, excavating a site that was going to be destroyed by road construction. We found that one of the three "pithouses" or semi-subterranean structures on the site appeared to have been cleaned out and closed up, presumably in the expectation that someone would return to live in it again. A flat slab had been placed over the ventilator opening, perhaps to keep out dirt and debris and critters, and the slab was sealed in place with wet mud. But no one came back, and eventually the small pithouse burned.

When we excavated the pithouse, we found the imprint of human hands, perfectly preserved in the mud, which had been hardened by the fire. That little house was built in AD 805, but I could reach out and place my hands in those handprints left there by someone a thousand years before. And more important, the Hopi school children who visited the site could place their small hands in those prints made by one of their ancestors, 50 generations removed. We lifted each one of the children into the pithouse, and let them do just that—like children everywhere, they were astonished that they were being encouraged to touch rather than being forbidden to do so.

Afterward we sat together on the site and talked about what life was like for that Hisatsinom (the Hopi term for the people we call Anasazi) person. We talked about food and looked at the burned corn kernels and the squash seeds that we had found. We talked about shelter and tools and looked at the three houses and the broken bits of stone and bone and pottery that we were recovering from the trash areas at the site. One of the houses had burned while it was occupied, and we looked at the fragments of the rolled up sleeping mats and baskets of corn and other possessions that the people had lost. We talked about the family that had lived there, how much the parents loved their children and how they must have worried about providing for them after such a terrible loss. And we talked about the migration stories that are a central part of Hopi oral history, and about what the Hopi elders had told us about the place of this particular site in those stories. I like to think that those children, who reached back across the centuries and touched the hand of their fifty-times-great grandmother, came away with a stronger sense of who they were and where they came from and a richer understanding of the oral traditions of their people.

But what if I had been not me, Dr. Science, purveyor of meticulous and mind-numbing archaeological techniques, but rather Lara Croft, Tomb Raider? If Lara had been rooting about in this site, searching for "treasures," she would have quickly dismissed that small pithouse, although she might have smashed that burned mud with the handprints in order to rip away the slab and check for hidden goodies behind it.

No, she would have focused on the other house, the one that burned while it was being used. She would have pulled out all those burned roof beams whose pattern of rings enabled us to learn that the houses were built in AD 805, probably using them for her campfire. She would have crushed the remnants of the burned sleeping mats and baskets of corn. She would never have noticed the stone griddle still in place on the hearth or the grease stains left by the last two corn cakes cooking on it when the fire started. She would have kicked aside the broken pieces of the pottery vessels that were crushed when the burning roof fell, the same pots that we put back together in the lab in order to estimate the size of the family and to recover traces of the items stored and cooked in them.

No, Lara would have missed all that we learned about that site and the people who made their homes there. Instead, she would have seized the single piece of pottery that didn't break in the fire and clutching it to her computer enhanced bosom, she would have stolen away into the night, narrowly escaping death and destruction at the hands of the rival gang of looters.

Is archaeology the most mind-numbing pursuit in the world, as Calvin claims? Or is it "sooo exciting" as my airline seatmates always exclaim? Both. And much more. What Lara and Indy and the others don't know is that archaeology is not about things, it is about people. It is about understanding life in the past, about understanding who we are and where we came from—not just where we came from as a particular cultural group, but what we share with all people in this time and in all the time that came before.

Critical Thinking

1. Why do people think archaeology must be exciting?
2. Why wouldn't people watch a show about "real" archaeology?
3. Why does the author claim that archaeology "really is exciting"?
4. What made the author's work on the Hopi reservation meaningful?
5. What would the author have done if she were Lara Croft, Tomb Raider rather than "Dr. Science"?
6. What does the author think archaeology really is and why?

Lynne Sebastian is Director of Historic Preservation with the SRI Foundation, a private nonprofit dedicated to historic preservation, and an adjunct assistant professor of Anthropology at UNM. She is a former New Mexico State Archaeologist and State Historic Preservation Office, and she is currently the President of the Society for American Archaeology.

Annals of Archaeology

All the King's Sons

The biggest archaeological find in Egypt since King Tut's tomb is also the most unusual: it may explain the fate of most of Ramesses II's fifty-two sons, New Kingdom funerary practices, and pharaonic sex. What does it feel like to be the first person to enter such a place in three thousand years?

DOUGLAS PRESTON

On February 2, 1995, at ten in the morning, the archaeologist Kent R. Weeks found himself a hundred feet inside a mountain in Egypt's Valley of the Kings, on his belly in the dust of a tomb. He was crawling toward a long-buried doorway that no one had entered for at least thirty-one hundred years. There were two people with him, a graduate student and an Egyptian workman; among them they had one flashlight.

To get through the doorway, Weeks had to remove his hard hat and force his large frame under the lintel with his toes and fingers. He expected to enter a small, plain room marking the end of the tomb. Instead, he found himself in a vast corridor, half full of debris, with doorways lining either side and marching off into the darkness. "When I looked around with the flashlight," Weeks recalled later, "we realized that the corridor was tremendous. I didn't know *what* to think." The air was dead, with a temperature in excess of a hundred degrees and a humidity of one hundred per cent. Weeks, whose glasses had immediately steamed up, was finding it hard to breathe. With every movement, clouds of powder arose, and turned into mud on the skin.

The three people explored the corridor, stooping, and sometimes crawling over piles of rock that had fallen from the ceiling. Weeks counted twenty doorways lining the hundred-foot hallway, some opening into whole suites of rooms with vaulted ceilings carved out of the solid rock of the mountain. At the corridor's end, the feeble flashlight beam revealed a statue of Osiris, the god of resurrection: he was wearing a crown and holding crossed flails and sceptres; his body was bound like that of a mummy. In front of Osiris, the corridor came to a T, branching into two transverse passageways, each of them eighty feet long and ending in what looked like a descending staircase blocked with debris. Weeks counted thirty-two additional rooms off those two corridors.

The tomb was of an entirely new type, never seen by archaeologists before. "The architecture didn't fit any known pattern," Weeks told me. "And it was so *big*. I just couldn't make sense of it." The largest pharaonic tombs in the Valley contain ten or fifteen rooms at most. This one had at least sixty-seven—the total making it not only the biggest tomb in the Valley but possibly the biggest in all Egypt. Most tombs in the Valley of the Kings follow a standard architectural plan—a series of consecutive chambers and corridors like a string of boxcars shot at an angle into the bedrock, and ending with the burial vault. This tomb, with its T shape, had a warren of side chambers, suites, and descending passageways. Weeks knew from earlier excavations that the tomb was the resting place for at least four sons of Ramesses II, the pharaoh also known as Ramesses the Great—and, traditionally, as simply Pharaoh in the Book of Exodus. Because of the tomb's size and complexity, Weeks had to consider the possibility that it was a catacomb for as many as fifty of Ramesses' fifty-two sons—the first example of a royal family mausoleum in ancient Egypt.

Weeks had discovered the tomb's entrance eight years earlier, after the Egyptian government announced plans to widen the entrance to the Valley to create a bus turnaround at the end of an asphalt road. From reading old maps and reports, he had recalled that the entrance to a lost tomb lay in the area that was to be paved over. Napoleon's expedition to Egypt had noted a tomb there, and a rather feckless Englishman named James Burton had crawled partway inside it in 1825. A few years later, the archaeologist Sir John Gardner Wilkinson had given it the designation KV5, for Kings' Valley Tomb No. 5, when he numbered eighteen tombs there. Howard Carter—the archaeologist who discovered King Tutankhamun's tomb in 1922, two hundred feet farther on—dug two feet in, decided that KV5's entrance looked unimportant, and used it as a dumping ground for debris from his other excavations, thus burying it under ten feet of stone and dirt. The location of the tomb's entrance was quickly forgotten.

It took about ten days of channelling through Carter's heaps of debris for Weeks and his men to find the ancient doorway

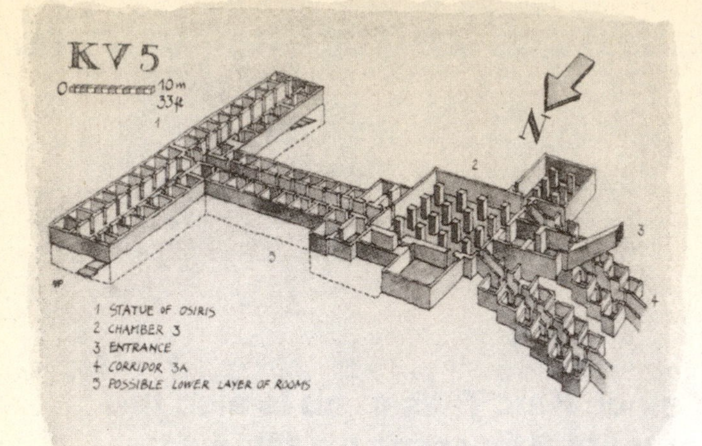

© Matteo Pericoli

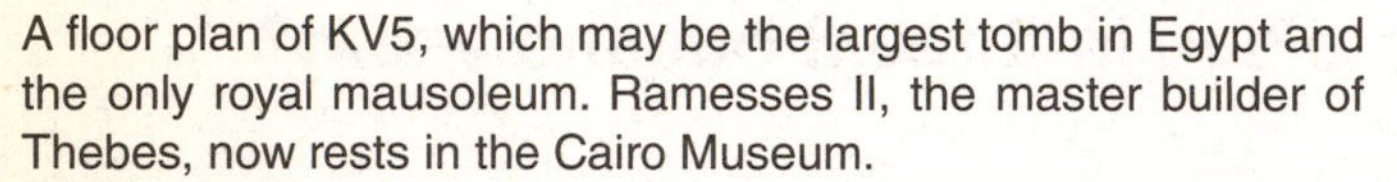

A floor plan of KV5, which may be the largest tomb in Egypt and the only royal mausoleum. Ramesses II, the master builder of Thebes, now rests in the Cairo Museum.

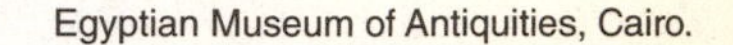

Egyptian Museum of Antiquities, Cairo.

of KV5, and it proved to be directly across the path from the tomb of Ramesses the Great. The entrance lay at the edge of the asphalt road, about ten feet below grade and behind the rickety booths of T-shirt venders and fake-scarab-beetle sellers.

Plans for the bus turnaround were cancelled, and, over a period of seven years, Weeks and his workmen cleared half of the first two chambers and briefly explored a third one. The tomb was packed from floor to ceiling with dirt and rocks that had been washed in by flash floods. He uncovered finely carved reliefs on the walls, which showed Ramesses presenting various sons to the gods, with their names and titles recorded in hieroglyphics. When he reached floor level, he found thousands of objects: pieces of faience jewelry, fragments of furniture, a wooden fist from a coffin, human and animal bones, mummified body parts, chunks of sarcophagi, and fragments of the canopic jars used to hold the mummified organs of the deceased—all detritus left by ancient tomb robbers.

The third chamber was anything but modest. It was about sixty feet square, one of the largest rooms in the Valley, and was supported by sixteen massive stone pillars arranged in four rows. Debris filled the room to within about two feet of the ceiling, allowing just enough space for Weeks to wriggle around. At the back of the chamber, in the axis of the tomb, Weeks noticed an almost buried doorway. Still believing that the tomb was like others in the Valley, he assumed that the doorway merely led to a small, dead-end annex, so he didn't bother with it for several years—not until last February, when he decided to have a look.

Immediately after the discovery, Weeks went back to a four-dollar-a-night pension he shared with his wife, Susan, in the mud village of Gezira Bairat, showered off the tomb dust, and took a motorboat across the Nile to the small city of Luxor. He faxed a short message to Cairo, three hundred miles downriver. It was directed to his major financial supporter, Bruce Ludwig, who was attending a board meeting at the American University in Cairo, where Weeks is a professor. It read, simply, "Have made wonderful discovery in Valley of the Kings. Await your arrival." Ludwig instantly recognized the significance of the fax and the inside joke it represented: it was a close paraphrase of the telegram that Howard Carter had sent to the Earl of Carnarvon, his financial supporter, when he discovered Tutankhamun's tomb. Ludwig booked a flight to Luxor.

"That night, the enormousness of the discovery began to sink in," Weeks recalled. At about two o'clock in the morning, he turned to his wife and said, "Susan, I think our lives have changed forever."

The discovery was announced jointly by Egypt's Supreme Council of Antiquities, which oversees all archaeological work in the country, and the American University in Cairo, under whose aegis Weeks was working. It became the biggest archaeological story of the decade, making the front page of the *Times* and the cover of *Time*. Television reporters descended on the site. Weeks had to shut down the tomb to make the talk-show circuit. The London newspapers had a field day: the *Daily Mail* headlined its story "PHARAOH'S 50 SONS IN MUMMY OF ALL TOMBS," and one tabloid informed its readers that texts in the tomb gave a date for the Second Coming and the end of the world, and also revealed cures for AIDS and cancer.

The media also wondered whether the tomb would prove that Ramesses II was indeed the pharaoh referred to in Exodus. The speculation centered on Amun-her-khopshef, Ramesses' firstborn son, whose name is prominent on KV5's wall. According to the Bible, in order to force Egypt to free the Hebrews from bondage the Lord visited a number of disasters on the land, including the killing of all firstborn Egyptians from the pharaoh's son on down. Some scholars believe that if Amun-her-khopshef's remains are found it may be possible to show at what age and how he died.

Book publishers and Hollywood producers showed great interest in Weeks's story. He didn't respond at first, dismissing inquiries with a wave of the hand. "It's all *kalam fadi,*" he said, using the Arabic phrase for empty talk. Eventually, however, so many offers poured in that he engaged an agent at William Morris to handle them; a book proposal will be submitted to publishers later this month.

In the fall, Weeks and his crew decided to impose a partial media blackout on the excavation site—the only way they could get any work done, they felt—but they agreed to let me accompany them near the end of the digging season. Just before I arrived, in mid-November, two mysterious descending corridors, with dozens of new chambers, unexpectedly came to light, and I had the good fortune to be the only journalist to see them.

The Valley of the Kings was the burial ground for the pharaohs of the New Kingdom, the last glorious period of Egyptian history. It began around 1550 B.C., when the Egyptians expelled the foreign Hyksos rulers from Lower Egypt and reestablished a vast empire, stretching across the Middle East to Syria. It lasted half a millennium. Sixty years before Ramesses, the pharaoh Akhenaten overthrew much of the Egyptian religion and decreed that thenceforth Egyptians should worship only one god—Light, whose visible symbol was Aten, the disk of the sun. Akhenaten's revolution came to a halt at his death. Ramesses represented the culmination of the return to tradition. He was an exceedingly conservative man, who saw himself as the guardian of the ancient customs, and he was particularly zealous in erasing the heretic pharaoh's name from his temples and stelae, a task begun by his father, Seti I. Because Ramesses disliked innovation, his monuments were notable not for their architectural brilliance but for their monstrous size. The New Kingdom began a slow decline following his rule, and finally sputtered to an end with Ramesses XI, the last pharaoh buried in the Valley of the Kings.

The discovery of KV5 will eventually open for us a marvellous window on this period. We know almost nothing about the offspring of the New Kingdom pharaohs or what roles they played. After each eldest prince ascended the throne, the younger sons disappeared so abruptly from the record that it was once thought they were routinely executed. The burial chambers' hieroglyphics, if they still survive, may give us an invaluable account of each son's life and accomplishments. There is a remote possibility—it was suggested to me by the secretary-general of the Supreme Council of Antiquities, Professor Abdel-Halim Nur el-Din, who is an authority on women in ancient Egypt—that Ramesses' daughters might be buried in KV5 as well. (Weeks thinks the possibility highly unlikely.) Before Weeks is done, he will probably find sarcophagi, pieces of funerary offerings, identifiable pieces of mummies, and many items with hieroglyphics on them. The tomb will add a new chapter to our understanding of Egyptian funerary traditions. And there is always a possibility of finding an intact chamber packed with treasure.

Ramesses the Great's reign lasted an unprecedented sixty-seven years, from 1279 to 1213 B.C. He covered the Nile Valley from Nubia to the delta with magnificent temples, statuary, and stelae, which are some of the grandest monuments the world has ever seen. Among his projects were the enormous forecourt at Luxor Temple; the Ramesseum; the cliffside temples of Abu Simbel; the great Hall of Columns at Karnak; and the city of Pi-Ramesse. The two "vast and trunkless legs of stone" with a "shattered visage" in Shelley's poem "Ozymandias" were those of Ramesses—fragments of the largest statue in pharaonic history. Ramesses outlived twelve of his heirs, dying in his early nineties. The thirteenth crown prince, Merneptah, became pharaoh only in his sixties.

By the time Ramesses ascended the throne, at twenty-five, he had fathered perhaps ten sons and as many daughters. His father had started him out with a harem while he was still a teenager, and he had two principal wives, Nefertari and Istnofret. He later added several Hittite princesses to his harem, and probably his sister and two daughters. It is still debated whether the incestuous marriage of the pharaohs were merely ceremonial or actually consummated. If identifiable remains of Ramesses' sons are found in KV5, it is conceivable that DNA testing might resolve this vexing question.

In most pharaonic monuments we find little about wives and children, but Ramesses showed an unusual affection for his family, extolling the accomplishments of his sons and listing their names on numerous temple walls. All over Egypt, he commissioned statues of Nefertari (not to be confused with the more famous Nefertiti, who was Akhenaten's wife), "for whose sake the very sun does shine." When she died, in Year 24 of his reign, Ramesses interred her in the most beautiful tomb yet discovered in the Valley of the Queens, just south of the Valley of the Kings. The tomb survived intact, and its incised and painted walls are nearly as fresh as the day they were fashioned. The rendering of Nefertari's face and figure perhaps speaks most eloquently of Ramesses' love for her. She is shown making her afterlife journey dressed in a diaphanous linen gown, with her slender figure emerging beneath the gossamer fabric. Her face was painted using the technique of chiaroscuro—perhaps the first known example in the history of art of a human face being treated as a three-dimensional volume. The Getty Conservation Institute recently spent millions restoring the tomb. The Getty recommended that access to the tomb be restricted, in order to preserve it, but the Egyptian government has opened it to tourists, at thirty-five dollars a head.

The design of royal tombs was so fixed by tradition that they had no architect, at least as we use that term today. The tombs were laid out and chiselled from ceiling to floor, resulting in ceiling dimensions that are precise and floor dimensions that can vary considerably. All the rooms and corridors in a typical royal tomb had names, many of which we still do not fully understand: the First God's Passage, Hall of Hindering, Sanctuaries in Which the Gods Repose. The burial chamber was often called the House of Gold. Some tombs had a Hall of Truth, whose murals showed the pharaoh's heart being weighed in judgment by Osiris, with the loathsome god Ammut squatting nearby, waiting to devour it if it was found wanting. Many of the reliefs were so formulaic that they were probably taken from copybooks. Yet even within this rigid tradition breathtaking flights of creativity and artistic expression can be found.

Most of the tombs in the Valley were never finished: they took decades to cut, and the plans usually called for something more elaborate than the pharaoh could achieve during his rule. As a result, the burial of the pharaoh was often a panicky, ad-hoc affair, with various rooms in the tomb being adapted for other purposes, and decorations and texts painted in haste or omitted completely. (Some of the most beautiful inscriptions were those painted swiftly; they have a spontaneity and freshness of line rivalling Japanese calligraphy.)

From the time of Ramesses II on, the tombs were not hidden: their great doorways, which were made of wood, could be opened. It is likely that the front rooms of many tombs were regularly visited by priests to make offerings. This may have been particularly true of KV5, where the many side chambers perhaps served such a purpose. The burial chambers containing treasure, however, were always sealed.

Despite all the monuments and inscriptions that Ramesses left us, it is still difficult to bridge the gap of thirty-one hundred years and see Ramesses as a person. One thing we do know: the standard image of the pharaoh, embodied in Shelley's "frown, and wrinkled lip, and sneer of cold command," is a misconception. One of the finest works from Ramesses' reign is a statue of the young king now in the Museo Egizio, in Turin. The expression on his face is at once compassionate and other-worldly, not unlike that of a Giotto Madonna; his head is slightly bowed, as if to acknowledge his role as both leader and servant. This is not the face of a tyrant-pharaoh who press-ganged his people into building monuments to his greater glory. Rather, it is the portrait of a ruler who had his subjects' interests at heart, and this is precisely what the archaeological and historical records suggest about Ramesses. Most of the Egyptians who labored on the pharaoh's monuments did so proudly and were, by and large, well compensated. There is a lovely stela on which Ramesses boasts about how much he has given his workers, "so that they work for me with their full hearts." Dorothea Arnold, the head curator of the Egyptian Department at the Metropolitan Museum, told me, "The pharaoh was *believed* in. As to whether he was beloved, that is beside the point: he was *necessary.* He was life itself. He represented everything good. Without him there would be nothing."

Final proof of the essential humanity of the pharaonic system is that it survived for more than three thousand years. (When Ramesses ascended the throne, the pyramids at Giza were already thirteen hundred years old.) Egypt produced one of the most stable cultural and religious traditions the world has ever seen.

Very little lives in the Valley of the Kings now. It is a wilderness of stone and light—a silent, roofless sepulchre. Rainfall averages a quarter inch per year, and one of the hottest natural air temperatures on earth was recorded in the surrounding mountains. And yet the Valley is a surprisingly intimate place. Most of the tombs lie within a mere forty acres, and the screen of cliffs gives the area a feeling of privacy. Dusty paths and sun-bleached, misspelled signs add a pleasant, ramshackle air.

The Valley lies on the outskirts of the ancient city of Thebes, now in ruins. In a six-mile stretch of riverbank around the city, there are as many temples, palaces, and monuments as anywhere else on earth, and the hills are so pockmarked with the yawning pits and doorways of ancient tombs that they resemble a First World War battlefield. It is dangerous to walk or ride anywhere alone. Howard Carter discovered an important tomb when the horse he was riding broke through and fell into it. Recently, a Canadian woman fell into a tomb while hiking and fractured her leg; no one could hear her screams, and she spent the days leading up to her death writing postcards. One archaeologist had to clear a tomb that contained a dead cow and twenty-one dead dogs that had gone in to eat it.

Almost all the tombs lying open have been pillaged. A papyrus now in Italy records the trial of someone who robbed KV5 itself in 1150 B.C. The robber confessed under torture to plundering the tomb of Ramesses the Great and then going "across the path" to rob the tomb of his sons. Ancient plunderers often vandalized the tombs they robbed, possibly in an attempt to destroy the magic that supposedly protected them. They smashed everything, levered open sarcophagi, ripped apart mummies to get at the jewelry hidden in the wrappings, and sometimes threw objects against the walls with such force that they left dents and smudges of pure gold.

Nobody is sure why this particular valley, three hundred miles up the Nile from the pyramids, was chosen as the final resting place of the New Kingdom pharaohs. Egyptologists theorize that the sacred pyramidal shape of el-Qurn, the mountain at the head of the Valley of the Kings, may have been one factor. Another was clearly security: the Valley is essentially a small box canyon carved out of the barren heart of a desert mountain range; it has only one entrance, through a narrow gorge, and the surrounding cliffs echo and magnify any sounds of human activity, such as the tapping of a robber's pick on stone.

Contrary to popular belief, the tombs in the Valley are not marked with curses. King Tut's curse was invented by Arthur Weigall, an Egyptologist and journalist at the *Daily Mail,* who was furious that Carnarvon had given the London *Times* the exclusive on the discovery. Royal tombs did not need curses to protect them. Priests guarded the Valley night and day, and thieves knew exactly what awaited them if they were caught: no curse could compete with the fear of being impaled alive. "There are a few curses on some private tombs and in some legal documents," James Allen, an Egyptologist with the Metropolitan Museum, told me. "The most extreme I know of is on a legal document of the Ramesside Period. It reads, 'As for the one who will violate it, he shall be seized for Amun-Ra. He shall be for the flame of Sekhmet. He is an enemy of Osiris, lord of Abydos, and so is his son, for ever and ever. May donkeys fuck him, may donkeys fuck his wife, may his wife fuck his son.' "

Some scholars today, looking back over the past two hundred years of archaeological activity, think a curse might have been a good idea: most of the archaeology done in the Valley has been indistinguishable from looting. Until the nineteen-sixties, those who had concessions to excavate there were allowed to keep a percentage of the spoils as "payment" for their work. In the fever of the treasure hunt, tombs were emptied without anyone bothering to photograph the objects found or to record their positions in situ, or even to note which tomb they came from. Items that had no market value were trashed. Wilkinson, the man who gave the tombs their numbers, burned three-thousand-year-old wooden coffins and artifacts to heat his house. Murals and reliefs were chopped out of walls. At dinner parties, the American lawyer Theodore M. Davis, who financed many digs in the Valley, used to tear up necklaces woven of ancient flowers and fabric to show how strong they were after three thousand years in a tomb. Pyramids were blasted open with explosives, and one tomb door was bashed in with a battering ram. Even Carter never published a proper scientific report on Tut's tomb. It is only in the last twenty-five years that real archaeology has come to Egypt, and KV5 will be one of the first tombs in the Valley of the Kings to be entirely excavated and documented according to proper archaeological techniques.

Fortunately, other great archaeological projects remain to be carried out with the new techniques. The Theban Necropolis is believed to contain between four thousand and five thousand tombs, of which only four hundred have been given numbers. More than half of the royal tombs in the Valley of the Kings have not been fully excavated, and of these only five have been properly documented. There are mysterious blocked passageways, hollow floors, chambers packed with debris, and caved-in rooms. King Tut's was by no means the last undiscovered pharaonic tomb in Egypt. In the New Kingdom alone, the tombs of Amosis, Amenhotep I, Tuthmosis II, and Ramesses VIII have never been identified. The site of the burial ground for the pharaohs of the entire Twenty-first Dynasty is unknown. And the richness and size of KV5 offer the tantalizing suggestion that other princely tombs of its kind are lying undiscovered beneath the Egyptian sands; Ramesses would surely not have been the only pharaoh to bury his sons in such style.

Work at KV5 in the fall season proceeds from six-thirty in the morning until one-thirty in the afternoon. Every day, to get to KV5 from my hotel in Luxor, I cross the Nile on the public ferry, riding with a great mass of fellaheen—men carrying goats slung around their necks, children lugging sacks of eggplants, old men squatting in their djellabas and smoking cigarettes or eating *leb* nuts—while the ancient diesel boat wheezes and blubs across the river. I am usually on the river in time to catch the sun rising over the shattered columns of Luxor Temple, along the riverbank. The Nile is still magical—crowded with feluccas, lined with date palms, and bearing on its current many clumps of blooming water hyacinths.

The ferry empties its crowds into a chaos of taxis, camels, donkeys, children begging for baksheesh, and hopeful guides greeting every tourist with a hearty "Welcome to Egypt!" In contrast to the grand hotels and boulevards of Luxor, the west bank consists of clusters of mud villages scattered among impossibly green fields of cane and clover, where the air is heavy with smoke and the droning prayers of the muezzin. Disembarkation is followed by a harrowing high-speed taxi ride to the Valley, the driver weaving past donkey carts and herds of goats, his sweaty fist pounding the horn.

On the first day of my visit, I find Kent Weeks sitting in a green canvas tent at the entrance to KV5 and trying to fit together pieces of a human skull. It is a cool Saturday morning in November. From the outside, KV5 looks like all the other tombs—a mere doorway in a hillside. Workmen in a bucket brigade are passing baskets filled with dirt out of the tomb's entrance and dumping them in a nearby pile, on which two men are squatting and sifting through the debris with small gardening tools. "Hmm," Weeks says, still fiddling with the skull. "I had this together a moment ago. You'll have to wait for our expert. He can put it together just like that." He snaps his fingers.

"Whose skull is it?"

"One of Ramesses' sons, I hope. The brown staining on it—here—shows that it might have come from a mummified body. We'll eventually do DNA comparisons with Ramesses and other members of his family."

Relaxing in the tent, Weeks does not cut the dapper, pugnacious figure of a Howard Carter, nor does he resemble the sickly, elegant Lord Carnarvon in waistcoat and watch chain. But because he is the first person to have made a major discovery in the Valley of the Kings since Carter, he is surely in their class. At fifty-four, he is handsome and fit, his ruddy face peering at the world through thick square glasses from underneath a Tilley hat. His once crisp shirt and khakis look like hell after an hour in the tomb's stifling atmosphere, and his Timberland shoes have reached a state of indescribable lividity from tomb dust.

Weeks has the smug air of a man who is doing the most interesting thing he could possibly do in life. He launches into his subject with such enthusiasm that one's first impulse is to flee. But as he settles back in his rickety chair with the skull in one hand and a glass of *yansoon* tea in the other, and yarns on about lost tombs, crazy Egyptologists, graverobbers, jackal-headed gods, mummies, secret passageways, and the mysteries of the Underworld, you begin to succumb. His conversation is laced with obscene sallies delivered with a schoolboy's relish, and you can tell he has not been to any gender-sensitivity training seminars. He can be disconcertingly blunt. He characterized one archaeologist as "ineffectual, ridiculously inept, and a wonderful source of comic relief," another as "a raving psychopath," and a third as "a dork, totally off the wall." When I asked if KV5 would prove that Ramesses was the Biblical Pharaoh, he responded with irritation: "I can almost guarantee you that we will *not* find anything in KV5 bearing on the Exodus question. All the speculation in the press assumed there *was* an exodus and that it was described accurately in the Bible. I don't believe it. There may have been Israelites in Egypt, but I sincerely doubt Exodus is an exact account of what occurred. At least I *hope* it wasn't—with the Lord striking down the firstborn of Egypt and turning the rivers to blood."

His is a rarefied profession: there are only about four hundred Egyptologists in the world, and only a fraction of them are archaeologists. (Most are art historians and philologists.) Egyptology is a difficult profession to break into; in a good year, there might be two job openings in the United States. It is the kind of field where the untimely death of a tenured figure sets the photocopying machines running all night.

"From the age of eight, I had no doubt: I wanted to be an Egyptologist," Weeks told me. His parents—one a policeman, the other a medical librarian—did not try to steer him into a sensible profession, and a string of teachers encouraged his interest. When Weeks was in high school, in Longview, Washington, he met the Egyptologist Ahmed Fakhry in Seattle, and Fakhry was so charmed by the young man that he invited him to lunch and mapped out his college career.

In 1963, Weeks's senior year at the University of Washington, one of the most important events in the history of Egyptology took place. Because of the construction of the High Dam at Aswan, the rising waters of the Nile began to flood Nubia; they would soon inundate countless archaeological sites, including the incomparable temples of Abu Simbel. UNESCO and the

Egyptian and Sudanese governments issued an international plea for help. Weeks immediately wrote to William Kelly Simpson, a prominent Egyptologist at Yale who was helping to coordinate the salvage project, and offered his services. He received plane tickets by return mail.

"The farthest I'd been away from home was Disneyland, and here I was going to Nubia," Weeks said. "The work had to be done fast: the lake waters were already rising. I got there and suddenly found myself being told, 'Take these eighty workmen and go dig that ancient village.' The nearest settlement was Wadi Halfa, ninety miles away. The first words of Arabic I learned were 'Dig no deeper' and 'Carry the baskets faster.' "

Weeks thereafter made a number of trips to Nubia, and just before he set out on one of them he invited along as artist a young woman he had met near the mummy case at the University of Washington museum—Susan Howe, a solemn college senior with red hair and a deadpan sense of humor.

"We lived on the river on an old rat-infested dahabeah," Susan told me. "My first night on the Nile, we were anchored directly in front of Abu Simbel, parked right in front of Ramesses' knees. It was all lit up, because work was going on day and night." An emergency labor force was cutting the temple into enormous blocks and reassembling it on higher ground. "After five months, the beer ran out, the cigarettes ran out, the water was really hot, the temperature was a hundred and fifteen degrees in the shade, and there were terrible windstorms. My parents were just *desperate* to know when I was coming home. But I thought, Ah! This is the life! It was so romantic. The workmen sang songs and clapped every morning when we arrived. So we wrote home and gave our parents ten days' notice that we were going to get married."

They have now been married twenty-nine years. Susan is the artist and illustrator for many of Kent's projects, and has also worked for other archaeologists in Egypt. She spends much of her day in front of KV5, in the green tent, wearing a scarf and peach-colored Keds, while she makes precise scale drawings of pottery and artifacts. In her spare time, she wanders around Gezira Bairat, painting exquisite watercolors of doorways and donkeys.

Weeks eventually returned to Washington to get his M.A., and in 1971 he received a Ph.D. from Yale; his dissertation dealt with ancient Egyptian anatomical terminology. He landed a plum job as a curator in the Metropolitan Museum's Egyptian Department. Two years later, bored by museum work, he quit and went back to Egypt, and was shortly offered the directorship of Chicago House, the University of Chicago's research center in Luxor. The Weekses have two children, whom they reared partly in Egypt, sending them to a local Luxor school. After four years at Chicago House, Weeks took a professorship at Berkeley, but again the lure of Egypt was too strong. In 1987, he renounced tenure at Berkeley, took a large pay cut, and went back to Egypt as a professor of Egyptology at the American University in Cairo, where he has been ever since.

While in Nubia, Weeks excavated an ancient working-class cemetery, pulling some seven thousand naturally desiccated bodies out of the ground. In a study of diet and health, he and a professor of orthodontics named James Harris X-rayed many of these bodies. Then Weeks and Harris persuaded the Egyptian government to allow them to X-ray the mummies of the pharaohs, by way of comparison. A team of physicians, orthodontists, and pathologists studied the royal X-rays, hoping to determine such things as age at death, cause of death, diet, and medical problems. They learned that there was surprisingly little difference between the two classes in diet and health.

One finding caused an uproar among Egyptologists. The medical team had been able to determine ages at death for most of the pharaohs, and in some cases these starkly contradicted the standard chronologies of the Egyptologists. The mystery was eventually solved when the team consulted additional ancient papyri, which told how, in the late New Kingdom, the high priests realized that many of the tombs in the Valley of the Kings had been robbed. To prevent further desecration, they gathered up almost all the royal mummies (missing only King Tut) and reburied them in two caches, both of which were discovered intact in the nineteenth century. "What we think happened is that the priests let the name dockets with some of the mummies fall off and put them back wrong," Weeks told me. It is also possible that the mixup occurred when the mummies were moved down the river to Cairo in the nineteenth century.

The team members analyzed the craniofacial characteristics of each mummy and figured out which ones looked most like which others. (Most of the pharaohs were related.) By combining these findings with age-at-death information, they were able to restore six of the mummies' proper names.

Weeks' second project led directly to the discovery of KV5. In 1979, he began mapping the entire Theban Necropolis. After an overview, he started with the Valley of the Kings. No such map had ever been done before. (That explains how KV5 came to be found and then lost several times in its history.) The Theban Mapping Project is to include the topography of the Valley and the three-dimensional placement of each tomb within the rock. The data are being computerized, and eventually Weeks will recreate the Valley on CD-s, which will allow a person to "fly" into any tomb and view in detail the murals and reliefs on its walls and ceilings.

Some Egyptologists I spoke with consider the mapping of the Theban Necropolis to be the most important archaeological project in Egypt, KV5 notwithstanding. A map of the Valley of the Kings is desperately needed. Some tombs are deteriorating rapidly, with murals cracking and falling to the floors, and ceilings, too, collapsing. Damage has been done by the opening of the tombs to outside air. (When Carter opened King Tut's tomb, he could actually hear "strange rustling, murmuring, whispering sounds" of objects as the new air began its insidious work of destruction. In other tombs, wooden objects turned into "cigar-ash.") Greek, Roman, and early European tourists explored the tombs with burning torches—and even lived in some tombs—leaving an oily soot on the paintings. Rapid changes in temperature and humidity generated by the daily influx of modern-day tourists have caused even greater damage, some of it catastrophic.

The gravest danger of all comes from flooding. Most of the tombs are now wide open. Modern alterations in the topography, such as the raising of the valley floor in order to build paths for the tourists, have created a highway directing floodwaters straight into the mouths of the tombs. A brief rain in November of 1994 generated a small flash flood that tore through the Valley at thirty miles an hour and damaged several tombs. It burst into the tomb of Bay, a vizier of the New Kingdom, with such force that it churned through the decorated chambers and completely ruined them. Layers of debris in KV5 indicate that a major flash flood occurs about once every three hundred years. If such a flood occurred tomorrow, the Valley of the Kings could be largely destroyed.

There is no master plan for preserving the Valley. The most basic element in such a plan is the completion of Weeks's map. Only then can preservationists monitor changes in the tombs and begin channelling and redirecting floodwaters. For this reason, some archaeologists privately panicked when Weeks found KV5. "When I first heard about it," one told me, "I thought, Oh my God, that's it, Kent will never finish the mapping project."

Weeks promises that KV5 will not interfere with the Theban Mapping Project. "Having found the tomb, we've got an obligation to leave it in a good, stable, safe condition," he says. "And we have an obligation to publish. Public interest in KV5 has actually increased funding for the Theban Mapping Project."

At 9 A.M., the workmen laboring in KV5—there are forty-two of them—begin to file out and perch in groups on the hillside, to eat a breakfast of bread, tomatoes, green onions, and a foul cheese called *misht.* Weeks rises from his chair, nods to me, and asks, "Are you ready?"

We descend a new wooden staircase into the mountain and enter Chamber 1, where we exchange our sun hats for hard hats. The room is small and only half cleared. Visible tendrils of humid, dusty air waft in from the dim recesses of the tomb. The first impression I have of the tomb is one of shocking devastation. The ceilings are shot through with cracks, and in places they have caved in, dropping automobile-size pieces of rock. A forest of screw jacks and timbers holds up what is left, and many of the cracks are plastered with "telltales"—small seals that show if any more movement of the rock occurs.

The reliefs in Chamber 1 are barely visible, a mere palimpsest of what were once superbly carved and painted scenes of Ramesses and his sons adoring the gods, and panels of hieroglyphics. Most of the damage here was the result of a leaky sewer pipe that was laid over the tomb about forty years ago from an old rest house in the Valley. The leak caused salt crystals to grow and eat away the limestone walls. Here and there, however, one can still see traces of the original paint.

The decorations on the walls of the first two rooms show various sons being presented to the gods by Ramesses, in the classic Egyptian pose: head in profile, shoulders in frontal view, and torso in three-quarters view. There are also reliefs of tables laden with offerings of food for the gods, and hieroglyphic texts spelling out the names and titles of several sons and including the royal cartouche of Ramesses.

A doorway from Chamber 2 opens into Chamber 3—the Pillared Hall. It is filled with dirt and rock almost to the ceiling, giving one a simultaneous impression of grandeur and claustrophobia. Two narrow channels have been cut through the debris to allow for the passage of the workmen. Many of the pillars are split and shattered, and only fragments of decorations remain—a few hieroglyphic characters, an upraised arm, part of a leg. Crazed light from several randomly placed bulbs throws shadows around the room.

I follow Weeks down one of the channels. "This room is in such dangerous condition that we decided not to clear it," he says. "We call this channel the Mubarak trench. It was dug so that President Mubarak could visit the tomb without having to creep around on his hands and knees." He laughs.

When we are halfway across the room, he points out the words "James Burton 1825" smoked on the ceiling with the flame of a candle: it represents the Englishman's farthest point of penetration. Not far away is another graffito—this one in hieratic, the cursive form of hieroglyphic writing. It reads "Year 19"—the nineteenth year of Ramesses' reign. "This date gives us a *terminus ante quem* for the presence of Ramesses' workmen in this chamber," Weeks says.

He stops at one of the massive pillars. "And here's a mystery," he says, "Fifteen of the pillars in this room were cut from the native rock, but this one is a fake. The rock was carefully cut away—you can see chisel marks on the ceiling—and then the pillar was rebuilt out of stone and plastered to look like the others. Why?" He gives the pillar a sly pat. "Was something very large moved in here?"

I follow Weeks to the end of the trench—the site of the doorway that he crawled through in February. The door has been cleared, and we descend a short wooden staircase to the bottom of the great central corridor. It is illuminated by a string of naked light bulbs, which cast a yellow glow through a pall of dust. The many doors lining both sides of the corridor are still blocked with debris, and the stone floor is covered with an inch of dust.

At the far end of the corridor, a hundred feet away, stands the mummiform statue of Osiris. It is carved from the native rock, and only its face is missing. Lit from below, the statue casts a dramatic shadow on the ceiling. I try to take notes, but my glasses have fogged up, and sweat is dripping onto my notebook, making the ink run off the page. I can only stand and blink.

Nothing in twenty years of writing about archaeology has prepared me for this great wrecked corridor chiselled out of the living rock, with rows of shattered doorways opening into darkness, and ending in the faceless mummy of Osiris. I feel like a trespasser, a voyeur, grazing into the sacred precincts of the dead. As I stare at the walls, patterns and lines begin to emerge from the shattered stone: ghostly figures and faint hieroglyphics; animal-headed gods performing mysterious rites. Through doorways I catch glimpses of more rooms and more doorways beyond. There is a presence of death in this wrecked tomb that goes beyond those who were buried here; it is the death of a civilization.

With most of the texts on the walls destroyed or still buried under debris, it is not yet possible to determine what function was served by the dozens of side chambers. Weeks feels it likely, however, that they were *not* burial chambers, because the doorways are too narrow to admit a sarcophagus. Instead, he speculates they were chapels where the Theban priests could make offerings to the dead sons. Because the tomb departs so radically from the standard design, it is impossible even to speculate what the mysterious Pillared Hall or many of the other antechambers were for.

Weeks proudly displays some reliefs on the walls, tracing with his hand the figure of Isis and her husband, Osiris, and pointing out the ibis-headed god Thoth. "Ah!" he cries. "And here is a *wonderful* figure of Anubis and Hathor!" Anubis is the jackal-headed god of mummification, and Hathor a goddess associates with the Theban Necropolis. These were scenes to help guide Ramesses' sons through the rituals, spells, and incantations that would insure them a safe journey through the realm of death. The reliefs are exceedingly difficult to see; Susan Weeks told me later that she has sometimes had to stare at a wall for long periods—days, even—before she could pick out the shadow of a design. She is now in the process of copying these fragmentary reliefs on Mylar film, to help experts who will attempt to reconstruct the entire wall sequence and its accompanying test, and so reveal to us the purpose of the room or the corridor. KV5 will only yield up its secrets slowly, and with great effort.

"Here's Ramesses and one of his sons," Weeks says, indicating two figures standing hand in hand. "But, alas, the name is gone. Very disappointing!" He charges off down the corridor, raising a trail of dust, and comes to a halt at the statue of Osiris, poking his glasses back up his sweating nose. "Look at this. Spectacular! A three-dimensional statue of Osiris is very rare. Most tombs depict him painted only. We dug around the base here trying to find the face, but instead we found a lovely offering of nineteen clay figs."

He makes a ninety-degree turn down the left transverse corridor, snaking around a cave-in. The corridor runs level for some distance and then plunges down a double staircase with a ramp in the middle, cut from the bedrock, and ends in a wall of bedrock. Along the sides of this corridor we have passed sixteen more partly blocked doors.

"Now, here is something new," Weeks says. "You're the first outsider to see this. I hoped that this staircase would lead to the burial chambers. This kind of ramp was usually built to slide the sarcophagi down. But look! The corridor just ends in a blank wall. Why in the world would they build a staircase and ramp going nowhere? So I decided to clear the two lowest side chambers. We just finished last week."

He ushers me into one of the rooms. There is no light; the room is large and very hot.

"They were empty," Weeks says.

"Too bad."

"Take a look at this floor."

"Nice." Floors do not particularly excite me.

"It happens to be the finest plastered floor in the Valley of the Kings. They went to enormous trouble with this floor, laying down three coats of plaster at different times, in different colors. Why?" He pauses. "Now stamp on the floor."

I thump the floor. There is a hollow reverberation that shakes not only the floor but the entire room. "Oh, my God, there's something underneath there!" I exclaim.

"*Maybe,*" Weeks says, a large smile gathering on his face. "Who knows? It could be a natural cavity or crack, or it might be a passageway to a lower level."

"You mean there might be sealed burial chambers below?"

Weeks smiles again. "Let's not get ahead of ourselves. Next June, we'll drill some test holes and do it properly."

We scramble back to the Osiris statue.

"Now I'm going to take you to our latest discovery," Weeks says. "This is intriguing. *Very* fascinating."

We make our way through several turns back to the Pillared Hall. Weeks leads me down the other trench, which ends at the southwest corner of the hall. Here, earlier in the month, the workmen discovered a buried doorway that opened onto a steep descending passageway, again packed solid with debris. The workmen have now cleared the passageway down some sixty feet, exposing twelve more side chambers, and are still at work.

We pause at the top of the newly excavated passageway. A dozen screw jacks with timbers hold up its cracked ceiling. The men have finished breakfast and are back at work, one man picking away at the wall of debris at the bottom of the passageway while another scoops the debris into a basket made out of old tires. A line of workmen then pass the basket up the corridor and out of the tomb.

"I've called this passageway 3A," Weeks says. He drops his voice. "The incredible thing is that this corridor is heading toward the tomb of Ramesses himself. If it connects, that will be extraordinary. No two tombs were ever deliberately connected. This tomb just gets curiouser and curiouser."

Ramesses' tomb, lying a hundred feet across the Valley, was also wrecked by flooding and is now being excavated by a French team. "I would dearly love to surprise them," Weeks says. "To pop out one day and say *'Bonjour! C'est moi!'* I'd love to beat the French into their own tomb."

I follow him down the newly discovered corridor, slipping and sliding on the pitched floor. "Of course," he shouts over his shoulder, "the sons might also be buried *underneath* their father! We clearly haven't found the burial chambers yet, and it is my profound hope that one way or another this passageway will take us there."

We come to the end, where the workmen are picking away at the massive wall of dirt that blocks the passage. The forty-two men can remove about nine tons of dirt a day.

At the bottom, Weeks introduces me to a tall, handsome Egyptian with a black mustache and wearing a baseball cap on backward. "This is Muhammad Mahmud," Weeks says. "One of the senior workmen."

I shake his hand. "What do you hope to find down here?"

"Something very nice, *inshallah.*"

"What's in these side rooms?" I ask Weeks. All the doorways are blocked with dirt.

Weeks shrugs. "We haven't been in those rooms yet."

"Would it be possible . . . " I start to ask.

He grins. "You mean, would you like to be the first human being in three thousand years to enter a chamber in an ancient Egyptian tomb? Maybe Saturday."

As we are leaving the tomb, I am struck by the amount of work still unfinished. Weeks has managed to dig out only three rooms completely and clear eight others partway—leaving more than eighty rooms entirely untouched. What treasures lie under five or ten feet of debris in those rooms is anyone's guess. It will take from six to ten more years to clear and stabilize the tomb, and then many more years to publish the findings from it. As we emerge from the darkness, Weeks says, "I know what I'll be doing for the rest of my life."

One morning, I find a pudgy, bearded man sitting in the green tent and examining, Hamlet-like, the now assembled skull. He is the paleontologist Elwyn Simons, who has spent decades searching the sands of the Faiyum for primate ancestors of human beings. Susan Weeks once worked for him, and now he is a close friend of the couple, dropping in on occasion to look over bones from the tomb. Kent and Susan are both present, waiting to hear his opinions about the skull's sex. (Only DNA testing can confirm whether it's an actual son of Ramesses, of course.)

Simons rotates the skull, pursing his lips. "Probably a male, because it has fairly pronounced brow ridges," he says. "This"—he points to a hole punched in the top of the cranium—"was made post mortem. You can tell because the edges are sharp and there are no suppressed fractures."

Simons laughs, and sets the skull down. "You can grind this up and put it in your soup, Kent."

When the laughter has died down, I venture that I didn't get the joke.

"In the Middle ages, people filled bottles with powdered mummies and sold it as medicine," Simons explains.

"Or mummies were burned to power the railroad," Weeks adds. "I don't know how many miles you get per mummy, do you, Elwyn?"

While talk of mummies proceeds, a worker brings a tray of tea. Susan Weeks takes the skull away and puts another bone in front of Simons.

"That's the scapula of an artiodactyl. Probably a cow. The camel hadn't reached Egypt by the Nineteenth Dynasty."

The next item is a tooth.

"Artiodactyl again," he says, sipping his tea. "Goat or gazelle."

The identification process goes on.

The many animal bones found in KV5 were probably from offerings for the dead: valley tombs often contained sacrificed bulls, mummified baboons, birds, and cats, as well as steaks and veal chops.

Suddenly, Muhammad appears at the mouth of the tomb. "Please, Dr. Kent," he says, and starts telling Weeks in Arabic that the workers have uncovered something for him to see. Weeks motions for me to follow him into the dim interior. We put on our hard hats and duck through the first chambers into Corridor 3A. A beautiful set of carved limestone steps has appeared where I saw only rubble a few days before. Weeks kneels and brushes the dirt away, excited about the fine workmanship.

Muhammad and Weeks go to inspect another area of the tomb, where fragments of painted and carved plaster are being uncovered. I stay to watch the workmen digging in 3A. After a while, they forget I am there and begin singing, handing the baskets up the long corridor, their bare feet white with dust. A dark hole begins to appear between the top of the debris and the ceiling. It looks as if one could crawl inside and perhaps look farther down the corridor.

"May I take a look in there?" I ask.

One of the workmen hoists me up the wall of dirt, and I lie on my stomach and wriggle into the gap. I recall that archaeologists sometimes sent small boys into tombs through holes just like this.

Unfortunately, I am not a small boy, and in my eagerness I find myself thoroughly wedged. It is pitch-black, and I wonder why I thought this would be exciting.

"Pull me out!" I yell.

The Egyptians heave on my legs, and I come sliding down with a shower of dirt. After the laughter subsides, a skinny man named Nubie crawls into the hole. In a moment, he is back out, feet first. He cannot see anything; they need to dig more.

The workmen redouble their efforts, laughing, joking, and singing. Working in KV5 is a coveted job in the surrounding villages; Weeks pays his workmen four hundred Egyptian pounds a month (about a hundred and twenty-five dollars), four times what a junior inspector of antiquities makes and perhaps three times the average monthly income of an Egyptian family. Weeks is well liked by his Egyptian workers, and is constantly bombarded with dinner invitations from even his poorest laborers. While I was there, I attended three of these dinners. The flow of food was limitless, and the conversation competed with the bellowing of a water buffalo in an adjacent room or the braying of a donkey tethered at the door.

After the hole has been widened a bit, Nubie goes up again with a light and comes back down. There is great disappointment: it looks as though the passageway might come to an end. Another step is exposed in the staircase, along with a great deal of broken pottery. Weeks returns and examines the hole himself, without comment.

As the week goes by, more of Corridor 3A is cleared, foot by foot. The staircase in 3A levels out to a finely made floor, more evidence that the corridor merely ends in a small chamber. On Wednesday, however, Weeks emerges from the tomb smiling. "Come," he says.

The hole in 3A has now been enlarged to about two feet in diameter. I scramble up the dirt and peer inside with a light, choking on the dust. As before, the chiselled ceiling comes to an abrupt end, but below it lies what looks like a shattered door lintel.

"It's got to be a door," Weeks says, excited. "I'm afraid we're going to have to halt for the season at that doorway. We'll break through next June."

Later, outdoors, I find myself coughing up flecks of mud.

"Tomb cough," Weeks says cheerfully.

On Thursday morning, Weeks is away on business, and I go down into the tomb with Susan. At the bottom of 3A, we stop to watch Ahmed Mahmud Hassan, the chief supervisor of the crew, sorting through some loose dirt at floor level. Suddenly, he straightens up, holding a perfect alabaster statuette of a mummy.

"Madame," he says, holding it out.

Susan begins to laugh. "Ahmed, that's beautiful. Did you get that at one of the souvenir stalls?"

"No," he says. "I just found it." He points to the spot. "Here."

She turns to me. "They once put a rubber cobra in here. Everyone was terrified, and Muhammad began beating it with a rock."

"Madame," Ahmed says. "Look, please." By now, he is laughing, too.

"I see it," Susan says. "I hope it wasn't too expensive."

"Madame, please."

Susan takes it, and there is a sudden silence. "It's real," she says quietly.

"This is what I was telling Madame," Ahmed says, still laughing.

Susan slowly turns it over in her hands. "It's beautiful. Let's take it outside."

In the sunlight, the statuette glows. The head and shoulders still have clear traces of black paint, and the eyes look slightly crossed. It is an *ushabti,* a statuette that was buried only with the dead, meant to spare the deceased toil in the afterlife: whenever the deceased was called upon to do work, he would send the *ushabti* in his place.

That morning, the workmen also find in 3A a chunk of stone. Weeks hefts it. "This is very important," he says.

"How?"

"It's a piece of a sidewall of a sarcophagus that probably held one of Ramesses' sons. It's made out of serpentine, a valuable stone in ancient Egypt." He pulls out a tape measure and marks off the thickness of the rim. "It's eight-point-five centimetres, which, doubled, gives seventeen centimetres. Add to that the width of an average pair of human shoulders, and perhaps an inner coffin, and you could not have fitted this sarcophagus through any door to any of the sixty side chambers in that tomb." He pauses. "So, you see, this piece of stone is one more piece of evidence that we have yet to find the burial chambers."

Setting the stone down with a thud on a specimen mat, he dabs his forehead. He proceeds to lay out a theory about KV5. Ramesses had an accomplished son named Khaemwaset, who became the high priest of an important cult that worshipped a god represented by a sacred bull. In Year 16, Khaemwaset began construction of the Serapeum, a vast catacomb for the bulls, in Saqqara. The original design of the Serapeum is the only one that remotely resembles KV5's layout, and it might have been started around the same time. In the Serapeum, there are two levels: an upper level of offering chapels and a lower level for burials. "But," Weeks adds, throwing open his arms, "until we find the burial chambers it's *all* speculation."

On Friday, Bruce Ludwig arrives—a great bear of a man with white hair and a white beard. Dressed like an explorer, he is lugging a backpack full of French wine for the team.

Unlike Lord Carnarvon and other wealthy patrons who funded digs in the Valley of the Kings, Ludwig is a self-made man. His father owned a grocery store in South Dakota called Ludwig's Superette. Bruce Ludwig made his money in California real estate and is now a partner in a firm managing four billion dollars in pension funds. He has been supporting Weeks and the Theban Mapping Project for twelve years.

Over the past three, he has sunk a good deal of his own money into the project and has raised much more among his friends. Nevertheless, the cost of excavation continually threatens to outstrip the funds at hand. "The thing is, it doesn't take a Rockefeller or a Getty to be involved," he told me over a bottle of Château Lynch-Bages. "What I like to do is show other successful people that it won't cost a fortune and that it's just hugely rewarding. Buildings crumble and fall down, but when you put something in the books, it's there forever."

Ludwig's long-term support paid off last February, when he became one of the first people to crawl into the recesses of KV5. There may be better moments to come. "When I discover that door covered with unbroken Nineteenth Dynasty seals," Weeks told me, joking, "you bet I'll hold off until Bruce can get here."

Saturday, the workers' taxi picks the Weekses and me up before sunrise and then winds through a number of small villages, collecting workers as it goes along.

The season is drawing to a close, and Susan and Kent Weeks are both subdued. In the last few weeks, the probable number of rooms in the tomb has increased from sixty-seven to ninety-two, with no end in sight. Everyone is frustrated at having to lock up the tomb now, leaving the doorway at the bottom of 3A sealed, the plaster floor unplumbed, the burial chambers still not found, and so many rooms unexcavated.

Weeks plans to tour the United States lecturing and raising more funds. He estimates that he will need a quarter of a million dollars per year for the indefinite future in order to do the job right.

As we drive alongside sugarcane fields, the sun boils up over the Nile Valley through a screen of palms, burning into the mists lying on the fields. We pass a man driving a donkey cart loaded with tires, and whizz by the Colossi of Memnon, two enormous wrecked statues standing alone in a farmer's field. The taxi begins the climb to a village once famous for tomb robbing, some of whose younger residents now work for Weeks. The houses are completely surrounded by the black pits of tombs. The fragrant smell of dung fires drifts through the rocky streets.

Along the way, I talk with Ahmed, the chief supervisor. A young man with a handsome, aristocratic face, who comes from a prominent family in Gezira Bairat, he has worked for Weeks for about eight years. I ask him how he feels about working in the tomb.

Ahmed thinks for a moment, then says, "I forget myself in this tomb. It is so vast inside."

"How so?"

"I feel at home there. I know this thing. I can't express the feeling, but it's not so strange for me to be in this tomb. I feel something in there about myself. I am descended from these people who built this tomb. I can feel their blood is in me."

When we arrive in the Valley of the Kings, an inspector unlocks the metal gate in front of the tomb, and the workers file in, with Weeks leading the way. I wait outside to watch the sunrise. The tourists have not yet arrived, and if you screen out some signs you can imagine the Valley as it might have appeared when the pharaohs were buried here three thousand years ago. (The venders and rest house were moved last year.) As dawn strikes el-Qurn and invades the upper reaches of the canyon walls, a soft, peach-colored lights fills the air. The encircling cliffs lock out the sounds of the world; the black doorways of the tombs are like dead eyes staring out; and one of the guard huts of the ancient priests can still be seen perched at the cliff edge. The whole Valley becomes a slowly changing play of light and color, mountain and sky, unfolding in absolute stillness. I am given a brief, shivery insight into the sacredness of this landscape.

At seven, the tourists begin to arrive, and the spell is dispersed. The Valley rumbles to life with the grinding of diesel engines, the frantic expostulations of venders, and the shouting of guides leading groups of tourists. KV5 is the first tomb in the Valley, and the tourists begin gathering at the rope, pointing and taking pictures, while the guides impart the most preposterous misinformation about the tomb: that Ramesses had four hundred sons by only two wives, that there are eight hundred rooms in the tomb, that the greedy Americans are digging for gold but won't find any. Two thousand tourists a day stand outside the entrance to KV5.

I go inside and find Weeks in 3A, supervising the placement of more screw jacks and timbers. When he has finished, he turns to me. "You ready?" He points to the lowest room in 3A. "This looks like a good one for you to explore."

One of the workmen clears away a hole at the top of the blocked door for me to crawl through, and then Muhammad gives me a leg up. I shove a caged light bulb into the hold ahead of me and wriggle through. I can barely fit.

In a moment, I am inside. I sit up and look around, the light throwing my distorted shadow against the wall. There is three feet of space between the top of the debris and the ceiling, just enough for me to crawl around on my hands and knees. The room is about nine feet square, the walls finely chiselled from the bedrock. Coils of dust drift past the light. The air is just breathable.

I run my fingers along the ancient chisel marks, which are as fresh as if they were made yesterday, and I think of workmen who carved out this room, three millennia ago. Their only source of light would have been the dim illumination from wicks burning in a bowl of oil salted to reduce smoke. There was no way to tell the passage of time in the tomb: the wicks were cut to last eight hours, and when they guttered it meant that the day's work was done. The tombs were carved from the ceiling downward, the workers whacking off flakes of limestone with flint choppers, and then finishing the walls and ceilings with copper chisels and sandstone abrasive. Crouching in the hot stone chamber, I suddenly get a powerful sense of the enormous religious faith of the Egyptians. Nothing less could have motivated an entire society to pound these tombs out of rock.

Much of the Egyptian religion remains a mystery to us. It is full of contradictions, inexplicable rituals, and impenetrable texts. Amid the complexity, one simple fact stands out: it was a great human bargain with death. Almost everything that ancient Egypt has left us—the pyramids, the tombs, the temples—represents an attempt to overcome that awful mystery at the center of all our lives.

A shout brings me back to my senses.

"Find anything?" Weeks calls out.

"The room's empty," I say. "There's nothing in here but dust."

Critical Thinking

1. What is unique about the tomb KV5?
2. What was the pharaoh traditionally known for?
3. In what ways was the tomb previously known and why was it quickly forgotten?
4. Why did the tomb become the "biggest archaeological story of the decade"?
5. How does the author describe the New Kingdom and the pharaoh Ramesses?
6. Describe the "new window" that may be opened with the excavation of KV5.
7. What were some of the unique accomplishments of Ramesses the Great?
8. In what ways was Ramesses unique in showing affection for his family?
9. In what sense was there no architect for the royal tombs?
10. Describe the Hall of Truth.
11. What is significant about the fact that most of the royal tombs were never finished?
12. What has been the standard image of the pharaoh and why is this a misconception? What is the "final proof" of the humanity of the pharaonic system?
13. What has happened to the tombs that lie open, and why?
14. What do Egyptologists think may be the reasons why this particular valley was chosen as the final resting place of the New Kingdom pharaohs?
15. What does the author say about the tombs being "marked with curses"? Why might curses have been a good idea?
16. Why do other great archaeological projects remain to be carried out?
17. What did the study of diet and health by Weeks and Harris reveal?
18. What kinds of damage have the tombs been subjected to and why? Why is the mapping project so important?
19. What are "tell-tales" and what are they for?
20. Why is it that there is so much work still unfinished in relation to KV5?
21. Why are there so many animal bones in KV5?
22. What is an *usbhabti* and what purposes was it supposed to serve?
23. What kind of misinformation is being spread by some of the tour guides?

Lost City of the Maya

Deep in the Guatemalan rain forest, an American archaeologist leads efforts to solve the mystery of El Mirador, a 2,500-year-old metropolis that's larger, more impressive and even older than the better-known Tikal.

CHIP BROWN

Had we been traveling overland, it would have taken two or three days to get from the end of the road at Carmelita to El Mirador: long hours of punishing heat and drenching rain, of mud and mosquitoes, and the possibility that the jungle novice in our party (that would be me, not the biologists turned photographers Christian Ziegler and Claudio Contreras) might step on a lethal fer-de-lance or do some witless city thing to provoke a jaguar or arouse the ire of the army ants inhabiting the last great swath of subtropical rain forest in Mesoamerica.

Mercifully, Itzamna, the supreme creator god of the ancient Maya, had favored us with a pilot named Guillermo Lozano, who was now easing his maroon-striped Bell helicopter into the air. It was a Sunday morning in northern Guatemala, late October. Next to him up front was the archaeologist Richard Hansen, the director and principal investigator of the Mirador Basin Project. About a half-hour's flying time due north was the Mirador basin itself—a 2,475-square-mile tract of jungle in northern Guatemala and Campeche, Mexico, filled with hidden ruins that Hansen and others refer to as "the cradle of Maya civilization."

We zipped away from the town of Flores at 140 knots. Off to the east were the spectacular Maya pyramids and ruins of Tikal National Park, which is now linked to Flores by road and draws between 150,000 and 350,000 visitors a year. We crossed a jungle-covered limestone ridge about 600 feet high. Hansen's voice crackled over the intercom.

"This is the southern tip of the Mirador basin," he said. "It's shaped like a heart. It's a self-contained ecosystem surrounded by these ridges. There are five kinds of tropical forest down there. Tikal has only two."

Visible below were clearings in the forest, the smoke of fires, a scattering of cattle, buildings and the occasional road.

"All this has been deforested in the last five years or so," Hansen said over the roar of the rotor. "Any use of this particular area of forest other than ecotourism would be, to me, the equivalent of using the Grand Canyon for a garbage dump."

After a few minutes there were no more roads or cows or any other signs of human settlement, just a few swampy open patches called avales breaking the great green quilt formed by the canopies of the 150-foot-tall ramón (breadnut) and sapodilla trees, whose trunks are slashed by skilled laborers known as chicleros for the sap used to make chewing gum. Hansen pointed out some of the sites that he and his colleagues have mapped in the Mirador basin, including the large lost cities of Tintai and Nakbe, which is one of the oldest known Maya settlements, dating from around 1000 to 400 B.C.

"See that there," he said, pointing to a slightly raised and darker line of trees. "That's a causeway. There's a plastered roadbed under there 2 to 6 meters high and 20 to 40 meters wide. Asacbe it's called—white road. It runs for about 12 kilometers from Mirador to Nakbe. It's part of the first freeway system in the world."

Suddenly clouds closed in, and Lozano began to climb, anxiously looking for a break in the skies. A tropical storm (named Richard, appropriately enough) was bearing down on northern Guatemala.

"There!" Hansen said. Lozano banked down toward what looked from afar to be a huge stone knoll, half swallowed in vines and trees. The pilots who first flew over the Mirador basin in the 1930s, among them Charles Lindbergh, were startled to see what they thought were volcanoes rising out of the limestone lowlands. In fact, they were pyramids built more than two millennia ago, and what we were circling was the largest of them all, the crown of the La Danta complex. At 230 feet, it is not as tall as the great pyramid at Giza, but, according to Hansen, it is more massive, containing some 99 million cubic feet of rock and fill.

We were hovering now over the heart of the ancient city of El Mirador, once home to an estimated 200,000 people and the capital of a complex society of interconnected cities and settlements that may have supported upwards of a million people. The last thing you would ever guess from a casual aerial overview was that virtually every topographical contour in the primordial forest was created not by geological and environmental forces but by the vanished inhabitants of one of the world's foundational civilizations.

"All this was abandoned nearly 2,000 years ago," Hansen said. "The whole thing developed before Tikal existed. It's like finding Pompeii."

A clearing appeared below us and we fluttered down onto a grassy strip, scattering a delegation of butterflies.

It's a dedicated archaeologist whose affection for a place increases even after he's gone into personal debt to keep his research and conservation work going, weathered death threats from irate loggers, had close encounters with fer-de-lances and falling trees, survived a jungle plane crash that nearly killed him, his wife and the oldest of his seven children and incinerated the only copies of his master's thesis. By the same token it's a versatile scientist who can enthrall audiences at Hollywood fundraisers and bargain in flawless Spanish with muleteers hauling sacks of specially formulated Preclassic Maya mortar.

"To do this you have to be a jack-of-all-trades or an absolute idiot," said Hansen as we sat around that first evening on the long log-and-plank benches of the dining hall, an opensided barnlike structure with a translucent plastic roof and special gutters that runnel rainwater into a 25,000—gallon cistern. Hansen was wearing a tan cap, a grungy off-white cotton shirt and stained off-white cotton pants—light-colored fabrics make it easier to see which exotic insects might be trying to attach themselves to flesh. (I was immediately regretting my choice of dark gray trousers.)

During the Mirador field-research season, which runs from May to September, there are as many as 350 people in the camp, including scientists from some 52 universities and institutions. The archaeological work could proceed year round but Hansen spends the off-months raising money (with the goal of maintaining a minimum annual budget of about $2.5 million) and preparing publications (now up to 177). He also teaches at Idaho State University in Pocatello, where he is an assistant professor in the department of anthropology and the senior scientist at the university's Institute for Mesoamerican Research.

"If I had five minutes for every hour I've spent chasing dollars, I'd have another 50 publications," he said with a sigh.

There was only a skeletal crew of workmen on hand now, along with guards Hansen had employed to ward off looters, and the camp cook, Dominga Soberanis, a short, powerfully built Maya woman who had fixed us all a supper of fried chicken and black beans on a steel sheet over a wood fire. Fresh tomatoes had come in on the helicopter, and there were pitchers of rice milk and tea brewed from the leaves of the allspice tree that grew in the ramón forest.

That afternoon, after Christian had amused himself at my expense by crying "Snake!" while fumbling in feigned horror with what looked like a fer-de-lance but proved to be a brown stick, Hansen had shown us around the camp. Tent sites, storage magazines, screening tables, a well equipped research building adjacent to the dining hall and guest bungalows where we had stashed our gear were linked by a web of root-riddled trails. Hansen was billeted in a bungalow that also served as his office. By some modern shamanism, it had Internet access.

We wandered out to the old helicopter landing strip where campsites had been established for tourists. Some 2,000 to 3,000 visitors a year either make the trek in from Carmelita or fly in by helicopter from Flores. Rangers stationed in the area were feeding an orphaned baby spider monkey creamed corn; dozens of ocellated turkeys—beautiful iridescent birds found only on the Yucatán Peninsula—were pecking at the grass. *Meleagris ocellata* is among the most photogenic of the 184 bird species recorded to date in the basin, which is also a key stopover for many migratory birds that travel the flyways of the eastern United States. The turkeys scrambled for cover under the trees when a pair of brown jays cried out. Their jaydar had spotted a raptor overhead—possibly an ornate hawkeagle (*Spizaetus ornatus*).

"The basin is a contained, enclosed, integrated cultural and natural system, unique in the world," Hansen said. And a veritable ark of biodiversity with some 300 species of trees (many festooned with orchids) and upwards of 200 animal species (many endangered or threatened), from tapirs and crocodiles to five of the six cats indigenous to Guatemala. In the past few years, researchers have found two bird species—the hooded oriole and the Caribbean dove—for the first time in Guatemala, and discovered nine previously unknown moth species. Efforts to preserve the basin's ancient ruins go hand in hand with conserving one of the world's living treasures.

When Hansen came to the Mirador basin as a graduate student in 1979, scientists had been studying the better known Maya sites in Mesoamerica—such as Palenque and Copan—for more than a century. El Mirador ("the lookout" in Spanish) was still largely unexplored. While some of the basin itself had been surveyed in 1885 by Claudio Urrutia, an engineer who noted the presence of ruinas grandes, the existence of El Mirador wasn't officially reported until 1926. And it would be another 36 years before an archaeologist, Harvard University's Ian Graham, would map and explore a portion of the area, partially revealing the extraordinary dimensions of the city.

What was most puzzling was the age of the site. Monumental architecture on the order of what had been found at El Mirador had always been associated with the Classic period of Maya history, from A.D. 250 to about A.D. 900; architecture of the Preclassic era, from 2000 B.C. to A.D. 150, was supposedly less sophisticated (as were, presumably, its political and economic systems). For nearly 40 years the only known Preclassic structure was a nearly nine-yard-high truncated pyramid excavated in the 1920s at Uaxactun, some 12 miles north of Tikal, by a Carnegie expedition. When the late William Coe of the University of Pennsylvania began excavating at Tikal in 1956, he was puzzled by the complexity of the earlier layers. In a 1963 article for the journal *Expedition*, he noted "things were not getting simpler" or more "formative."

Writing up his own research in 1967, Graham, who went on to found the Corpus of Maya Hieroglyphic Inscriptions at the Peabody Museum of Archaeology and Ethnology at Harvard, speculated that the poor condition of the ruins he examined at El Mirador might be attributed to an inferior brand of mortar rather than the sheer antiquity of the buildings. Examining pottery that Graham's colleague Joyce Marcus had collected at El Mirador in 1970, Donald Forsyth (now a professor at Brigham Young University) noted that the bulk of the ceramics were in the Chicanel style—monochrome red, black or cream, with thick bodies and the rims turned outward—that clearly dated the surrounding ruins to the Late Preclassic period (300 B.C. to A.D. 150). But could such monumental public architecture really have been built 700 to 1,000 years before the zenith of the Classic period, when, scholars supposed, the Maya had achieved the organizational, artistic and technical expertise to pull off such feats?

The dig Hansen joined was headed by his thesis adviser, Ray Matheny, from Brigham Young University, and Bruce Dahlin of Catholic University. "Hansen was a real go-getter," Matheny told me later. "I'm very proud of him." Twenty-six years old at the time, Hansen had grown up in Idaho in a Mormon family, the oldest of three brothers. He got a bug for archaeology at age 6 hunting arrowheads on his father's potato farm in Rupert. He planned to become a lawyer, but his undergraduate degree was delayed after he shattered his right leg in a ski accident. As all he needed for law school were good grades and test scores, he thought the fastest way to get them would be to major in Spanish, which he spoke, and archaeology, which he loved. Degrees in hand, he postponed law school for the chance to join an excavation north of Tel Aviv for two years, an experience that buried the lawyer and begot the archaeologist. It also turned up his wife, Jody, a scientific illustrator who first impressed him with her dogged work hauling buckets of sand. When they returned from Israel, Matheny invited Hansen to assist with a newly funded project at El Mirador.

So it was that Hansen found himself in March 1979 excavating a room on Structure 34, the Jaguar Paw Temple. The temple, one of the most intensively studied of all the ruins at El Mirador, is part of the Tigre complex in the western side of the city. Hansen had been given to understand it was most likely from the Classic period, but as he cleared the chamber, he came to the original plaster floor littered with pot fragments that had not been disturbed for centuries. "When the Maya walked away, they left everything in place," he said. "We've found flakes of a stone tool right around the tool." The potsherds had the colors and the waxy telltale feel of the Chicanel style, which dated the temple to two centuries before Christ. Hansen stared at them in disbelief.

"I realized at that moment the whole evolutionary model for the economic, cultural and social history of the Maya was wrong. The idea that the Maya slowly became more sophisticated was wrong. And I thought, 'Man, I'm the only person in the world at this moment who knows this.' "

By morning tropical storm Richard had eased, but the sky was still overcast and Hansen was surprised to hear the helicopter arriving out of the clouds. "You made it! Welcome!" he cried as three Californians scurried clear of the rotor: Andre Lafleur, an officer for a land trust in Santa Cruz; a travel consultant named Randy Durbin; and Joanna Miller, a board member of the Walt Disney Family Museum, established in San Francisco to commemorate her famous grandfather. They joined us at the dining hall for a breakfast of eggs, tortillas, beans and fried Spam. Dominga, the cook, tossed a few stale tortillas into the woods and called "Pancho! Pancho!" Duly summoned, a white-nosed coati appeared, wary and cute, striped tail high. He looked like a lanky raccoon.

Andre, Joanna and Randy had been invited by the Global Heritage Fund, a Palo Alto-based conservation group and one of several foundations that financially support Hansen's work in the basin, including the Foundation for Cultural and Natural Maya Heritage (PACUNAM) and Hansen's own Foundation for Anthropological Research and Environmental Studies (FARES). Its board includes actor Mel Gibson, who has given several million dollars to the cause and who hired Hansen as a consultant for his 2006 Maya chase film *Apocalypto*.

We headed east on a dirt track in two Kawasaki all-terrain vehicles. At more than 14 square miles, greater El Mirador is three times the size of downtown Los Angeles; for many years Hansen would routinely hike 10 to 12 miles a day to check on various sites. The ATVs, donated by a family of prominent Central American brewers, were much appreciated by his now 58-year-old knees. We were bound for La Danta, the pyramid complex we had circled on the flight in.

The trail climbed over what was once possibly a 60-foot-high perimeter wall surrounding a portion of the western part of the city—it was built in the Late Preclassic, Hansen said—and followed one of the elevated causeways to La Danta just over a mile east. We parked and started our ascent.

Hansen has excavated, mapped and explored 51 ancient cities in the Mirador basin. "What you had here was the first state-level society in the Western Hemisphere, a thousand years before anyone suspected," he said. It was not just the monumental architecture of La Danta and structures at sister cities like Nakbe and Tintai that were sophisticated. The achievements of the Preclassic Maya were reflected in the way they made the leap from clans and chiefdoms to complex societies with class hierarchies and a cohesive ideology; in the technical sophistication that enabled them to quarry huge limestone blocks without metal tools and move them to building sites without the wheel; how they collected rainwater off building roofs and stored it in reservoirs and cisterns; how they projected time in their calendars and preserved the records of their civilization in their still-enigmatic histories on stelae in images and glyphs that scholars have yet to decipher (unlike glyphs from the Classic period that have been decoded); how they constructed their homes with posts, stone and stucco; decorated their teeth with jade and brownish-red hematite inlays; imported exotic items such as obsidian, basalt and granite; wrapped the craniums of their infants to modify the shape of their skulls; and adorned themselves with shells from the Caribbean and Pacific Coast—as if civilization were keyed as much to aesthetic refinement as to written language, the specialization of labor or regimens of religious and social control.

To feed their burgeoning population, they terraced fields and carried mud up from swampy marshes to grow maize, beans, squash, cocoa, gourds and other crops. "What brought them here were the swamps," Hansen said. And in his view it was the destruction of the swamps with their nutrient-rich mud that caused the wholesale collapse of the society sometime between A.D. 100 and 200. What killed the swamps and crippled the farms, he believes, was the runoff of clay into the marshes after the massive deforestation of the surrounding area—deforestation caused by a demand for firewood the Maya needed to make lime plaster. They plastered everything, from major temples like La Danta to their plazas and house floors, which over time got thicker and thicker, an extravagance Hansen attributed to the temptations of "conspicuous consumption."

Hansen believes that El Mirador's inhabitants may have initially gone to the Caribbean coast and then migrated back inland, where they finally ended up in Mexico's Yucatán Peninsula at Calakmul, which emerged as a powerful city-state and rival to Tikal in the sixth and seventh centuries. "Mirador was known in the Preclassic as the Kan Kingdom—Kan meaning 'snake'—and the kings of Calakmul referred to themselves as the Lords of Kan, not as the Lords of Chiik Naab, which is the original name of Calakmul," Hansen said.

We came to the first tier of La Danta pyramid, a high forested platform of cut stone and rock fill that was some 980 feet wide and 2,000 feet long and covered nearly 45 acres.

"We calculate that as many as 15 million man-days of labor were expended on La Danta," Hansen said. "It took 12 men to carry each block—each one weighs about a thousand pounds. . . . We've excavated nine quarries where the stones were cut, some 600 to 700 meters away."

Before long we mounted another platform. It was about 33 feet high also and covered about four acres. The trail led to a set of steps that climbed to a third, 86-foot-high platform that served as the base for a triad of an impressive central pyramid flanked by two smaller pyramids—a formidable sight with its vertiginous staircase bisecting the west face.

"You don't find the triadic pattern before about 300 B.C." Hansen said of the three pyramids. Based upon conversations with present-day Maya spiritual leaders, researchers believe the three-point configuration represents a celestial hearth containing the fire of creation. The Maya thought three stars in the constellation Orion (Alnitak, Saiph and Rigel) were the hearth stones surrounding the fire—a nebula called M42, which is visible just below Orion's belt.

Archaeology at El Mirador is often less about bringing the past to light than keeping it from collapsing: Hansen spent three years just stabilizing the walls of La Danta. He had experimented to find the optimal mortar mix of finely sifted clay, organic compounds, lime, crushed limestone and a form of gritty, decomposed limestone called "sascab." And the archaeologists decided against clearing the trees entirely off the temples as had been done at Tikal because they had learned it was better to leave some shade to minimize the debilitating effects of the sun. Hansen and an engineer from Boeing had designed a vented polycarbonate shed roof that filtered ultraviolet light and protected some of the most delicate stucco carvings on the Jaguar Paw Temple from rain.

We hiked around the base of the upper platform and climbed a cantilevered wooden staircase that zigzagged up the near-vertical east face of La Danta, which plunged more than 230 feet to the jungle floor.

"Wow!" said Joanna.

The summit was the size of a decent home office. There was a surveyor's bench mark embedded in the limestone, a fence to keep you from tumbling off the east precipice and a big leafy tree that from afar stood out like a tasseled toothpick pinned to a club sandwich. After concentrating so long on the ground, verifying that roots weren't snakes, it was a great pleasure to lift my eyes to infinity. It was boggling to think we were standing on the labor of thousands of people from antiquity, and to imagine their vanished metropolis, the business of the city such as it might have been on a day like this; the spiritual and ideological imperatives that lifted these stones; the rituals that might have occurred at this sacred spot—everything from coronations to ceremonies in which priests and kings would draw blood from their genitals to spill onto paper and burn as a sacrifice to the gods.

To the west loomed the forested silhouettes of the Tigre Complex, where high on the pyramid Hansen and his team have found skeletons with obsidian arrow points in their ribs, possibly casualties of an Early Classic period battle that wiped out remnant inhabitants of the abandoned capital. Also visible were the outlines of the Monos and Leon pyramids, which along with Tigre and La Danta and the administrative complex known as the Central Acropolis, made up some of the oldest and largest concentrations of public architecture in all of Maya civilization.

I asked Hansen, if he could have anything, what would it be?

"Fifteen minutes," he answered immediately. "Fifteen minutes here when the city was in its glory. Just to walk around and see what it was like. I'd give anything for that."

In Maya cosmology the underworld is ruled by the Lords of Xibalba (shee-bal-ba). In April 1983, his fifth season at El Mirador, Hansen nearly met them. He boarded Professor Mathen's single-engine Helio Courier H395 with his wife, Jody, and their daughter Micalena; he was carrying the only two copies of his master's thesis, which he'd been working on at the camp, and cash for the camp workers' payroll.

When the plane cleared the trees it was suddenly running with the wind, not into it as a windsock had indicated, and struggling for lift. About two miles from the airstrip, the tail hit a tree, the nose pitched down, the wings sheared off, the propeller chewed through the canopy until it snapped and the plane cartwheeled across the floor of the jungle. The H395 crashed to a stop in a tree five feet off the ground, fuel leaking everywhere. Hansen sat in his seat thinking he was dead."Get out! Get out!" Jody yelled. As they scrambled clear, they heard a tremendous whoosh and were hurled to the ground as a fireball exploded behind them, cresting high above the trees. Everyone on board had survived.

"People say, 'Is your life like Indiana Jones?'" Hansen recalled as he showed us around the crash site. "I say my life isn't as boring. He always jumps out of the airplane before it crashes."

Hansen took us to see what is probably the most beautiful and significant artwork found so far at El Mirador: the Central Acropolis frieze. In 2009, an Idaho State student archaeologist named J. Craig Argyle unearthed two 26-foot carved stucco panels showing the hero twins of Maya cosmology, Hunahpu and his brother Xbalanque. They are the main protagonists in the Popol Vuh, a sacred book of myths, history, traditions and the Maya story of how the world was created. The Popol Vuh recounts the adventures of the supernaturally gifted twins, who resurrected their father Hun-Hunahpu (who had lost his head in a ball game against the evil lords of the underworld). The stucco frieze depicts Hunahpu in a jaguar headdress swimming with the head of his father.

"To find this story in the Preclassic period is beyond belief," Hansen said, pulling back a blue tarp that covered the frieze. "For many years it was thought that the Popol Vuh creation story had been contaminated by the Spanish priests who translated it—that the Indians had been influenced by Christianity. This frieze shows that the Maya account of creation was vibrantly established for thousands of years before the Spanish got here. It's like finding the original copy of the Constitution. I was stunned."

El Mirador today is part of the Mirador-Río Azul National Park, which itself is part of the Maya Biosphere Reserve, an 8,100-square-mile tract of rain forest in northern Guatemala. The reserve, established in 1990, has lost nearly half of its forests in just the past ten years. The protection afforded by the national park, which was set up at the same time, is marginal at best—it covers only a narrow swath of the northern basin along the Mexico border and includes only 3 or 4 of the 51 ancient Maya cities currently mapped. "The boundaries don't respect the hydrological, geological, geographic, botanical or cultural borders of the basin," Hansen said. "The park only saves a small area. We're trying to save the whole system."

Hansen and conservationists from Guatemala and around the world are hoping the government will declare the whole basin a roadless wilderness. Hansen hopes its ancient cities will attract ecotourism and provide livelihoods for local Guatemalans, who might otherwise turn to looting, poaching or the unsustainable promise of logging; despite short-term economic benefits, the industry undermines the long-term integrity of the ecosystem, as it leads to roads, cattle pastures and the destruction of habitat.

"We're trying to give the poor campesinos [peasants] more than they have now," Hansen said. "Every country needs wood and wood products. But the issue here is the potential for far greater economic benefits than can be generated [by logging]. There is a model that will work, and is far more lucrative economically, and has far better conservation results than anything in place now. It will need to be done right. If the area is declared a roadless wilderness, then tourists will be obligated to travel to the local communities rather than fly or drive directly to the sites. They will buy local artisan products, sandwiches, soft drinks and beers, and sleep in local microhotels, and hire local guides, cooks, mules, and rent local mountain bikes. The economic pie would get spread among the communities."

He supports those uses of the El Mirador forest that are sustainable, such as the harvesting of renewable plant products: allspice; xate, the Chamaedorea palm leaves used in floral arrangements; bayal, for wicker baskets; and chicle, for chewing gum.

And, of course, he supports archaeology, which has already pumped millions of dollars into the local communities of the Petén, as the region is called. Some of the guards Hansen has hired are former looters. Most of the workers hired to help excavate the ancient cities participate in literacy classes run by the Mirador Basin Project, which has also provided local schools with computers and computer training, helped install water-purification filters in villages and trained local residents to be guides. The future of the basin ultimately depends on the local people and communities.

My last evening in El Mirador I stopped in the forest not far from the Jaguar Paw Temple, where Hansen had his potsherd epiphany. It was unsettling to think how thoroughly the Preclassic capital of the Maya and hundreds of thousands of people had been silenced by time and rampant nature. The sun was hurrying away, darkness rising. Ocellated turkeys were ascending to the trees for the night, their wings laboring against the plush air. Red-eyed tree frogs were beginning to sing. Curassow birds fussed in the canopies. You could hear the cool interjections of a spectacled owl; cicadas droning; the croak of toucans; lineated woodpeckers running their jackhammers; the grunts of spider monkeys and the fantastic aspirated roar of howler monkeys, which seemed to cross the basso profundo of an African lion with the sound of metal grinding on a lathe. It always amazes me how unsentimental nature is, resoundingly here now, unbound by the past apart from what is secretly conserved in genes. It's left to us to listen for voices that can't be heard, to imagine the dead in that note between the notes, as in those moments when the jungle cacophony dies away and the almost-audible strains of the underworld echo in the stillness and silence of the night, until the clamor of the living starts up again.

Critical Thinking

1. How does the author describe the ancient city of El Mirador?
2. What has Richard Hansen had to do as a "dedicated archaeologist?"
3. Why was the age of the site so puzzling? How did Hansen come to realize that the evolutionary model for the Maya was wrong?
4. What is unique about El Mirador as the first state-level society in the Western Hemisphere?
5. In what ways are the achievements of the Preclassic Maya reflected?
6. How was the burgeoning population able to feed itself?
7. What killed the swamps and crippled the farms?
8. What is the significance of finding the Popol Vuh creation story at El Mirador?
9. Why does Hansen believe the National Park should be expanded to include the whole basin?

Chip Brown is a contributing writer for the *New York Times Magazine* and the author of two nonfiction books.

Article 4

Maya Archaeologists Turn to the Living to Help Save the Dead

To preserve ancient sites, pioneering archaeologists are trying to improve the lives of the Maya people now living near the ruins.

Michael Bawaya

Archaeologist Jonathan Kaplan tries to spend as much time as possible exploring Chocolá, a huge Maya site in southern Guatemala dating from 1200 B.C.E. So far his team has mapped more than 60 mounds, identified dozens of monuments, and found signs of the emergence of Maya civilization, including large, sophisticated waterworks that likely required social organization to build.

But today, instead of digging, Kaplan is lunching with the mayor of a municipality that includes the impoverished town of Chocolá. Kaplan, a research associate with the Museum of New Mexico's Office of Archaeological Studies in Santa Fe, is trying to enlist the mayor's support for a land swap that would give farmers land of no archaeological value in exchange for land that holds Maya ruins. The local people he's trying to help, many of them descended from the ancient Maya, are "clinging by their fingers to survival," says Kaplan. So, working with a Guatemalan archaeologist, he has established a trash-removal service, hired an environmental scientist to help improve the drinking water, and developed plans for two museums to attract tourists.

Kaplan and others are in the vanguard of a movement called community archaeology. From Africa to Uzbekistan, researchers are trying to boost local people's quality of life in order to preserve the relics of their ancestors. In the Maya region, the situation is urgent; the vestiges of the ancient Maya may be destroyed in 5 to 10 years unless something is done to curb looting, logging, poaching, and oil exploration, says Richard Hansen, president of the Foundation for Anthropological Research & Environmental Studies and an archaeologist at Idaho State University in Pocatello. Hansen, Kaplan, and others are using archaeology as an engine for development, driving associated tourism and education projects. The resultant intertwining of research and development is such that "I cannot accomplish the one without the other," says Kaplan, "because poverty is preventing the people from attending to the ancient remains in a responsible fashion."

It wasn't always that way. Until fairly recently, Maya researchers were solely focused on the hunt for "stones and bones," says Hansen. Archaeologist Arthur Demarest of Vanderbilt University in Nashville, Tennessee, says researchers often excavated a site with the help of local workers, only to abandon them when the project ended. Those who lost their income often resorted to looting and slash-and-burn agriculture to survive. "In the wake of every archaeological project is an economic and social disaster," says Demarest.

He offers one of his own projects as an example of what not to do. After employing about 300 people in the early 1990s at several sites in the Petén, the vast tropical forest in northern Guatemala, Demarest left the government with a continuing development plan for the region, much of it federal land. But the federal government brought in outsiders to implement it. Desperate at having lost their jobs, the local people plundered the sites.

"From that, I learned a lot of lessons," Demarest says. "Archaeology transforms a region." In his view, archaeologists themselves must take responsibility for helping the locals succeed. "The days of Indiana Jones, when archaeologists could go to a place, excavate, and then leave without concern about the impact that their actions are having on the people in the area, are gone," he has said.

Today, Demarest embraces this responsibility as he excavates part of the great trade route that ran through much of the Maya region, including along the Pasión River and through Cancuen, an ancient city in central Guatemala. He says his project is successful because it operates "bottom up—we're working through the village." Using ethnographic studies of the Maya people and working with leaders from several villages, Demarest designed a research and community development plan that enables the local people, rather than outsiders, to serve as custodians of their own heritage. The communities choose projects—archaeology, restoration, ecotourism, etc.—and run them with the guidance of experts, earning more than they would by farming.

One successful enterprise is a boat service, run by the Maya, that ferries tourists down the Pasión River from the village of La Union to Cancuen, now a national park. In addition to generating revenue, the service attracted a variety of agencies that provided potable water, electricity, and school improvements to La Union. The World Bank cited the boat service as one of the 10 most innovative rural development projects in the world in 2003.

Demarest also helped establish a visitor center, an inn, a guide service, and a campground at the park's entrance. Three nearby villages collaboratively manage these operations, and the profits pay for water systems, school expansions, and medical supplies. "The only way these things are going to succeed is if it's theirs," says Demarest, who has raised nearly $5 million for community development at Cancuen. Last year, he became the first U.S. citizen to be awarded the National Order of Cultural Patrimony by the Guatemalan government.

Other archaeologists are trying to achieve similar results in their own field areas. Hansen is exploring the origins, the cultural and ecological dynamics, and the collapse of the Preclassic Maya (circa 2000 B.C.E. to 250 C.E.) in the Mirador Basin. His project has a budget of $1.2 million, with about $400,000 going to development and $800,000 to archaeology. He raised roughly half of the funds from the Global Heritage Fund, a nonprofit organization that helps preserve cultural heritage sites in developing countries. The project employs more than 200 people who earn above-average wages while getting training; Hansen's team has also installed a new water system and bought 40 computers to boost locals' computer skills.

Looting in the basin has been devastating in the past, so Hansen has hired 27 guards—most of them former looters. They make good guards, he says, "because they know the tricks of the trade." The project has instilled "a sense of identity" in some residents, although Hansen acknowledges that others continue to loot. "It is a long battle to win the hearts and minds of these people," he says.

Although both Demarest and Hansen have won generous grants for their work, they agree that finding funding for community archaeology is "horrific," as Hansen puts it. Kaplan makes do with about $130,000 each year for his "terribly underfunded" project, although his ideal would be about $800,000. Traditional funders, such as the U.S. National Science Foundation (NSF), pay for research but not community development, says Demarest. NSF, with its modest budget of $5 million to $6 million, is most interested in the "intellectual merit" of a project, agrees archaeology program director John Yellen, although he adds that the foundation does consider "broader impacts," including community development. Demarest, who is financed by some 20 organizations including the United States Agency for International Development and the Solar Foundation, says a big budget is a must for community projects: "You've got to have about $400,000 a season to do ethical archaeology."

But other researchers say it's possible to run such projects without big budgets. Archaeologist Anabel Ford of the University of California, Santa Barbara, who has been practicing small-scale community archaeology while studying land-use patterns at a large site called El Pilar on the Belize-Guatemala border since 1983, says that she can achieve her community development goals for as little as $12,000 a year. "I actually think it's not about tons of money," she says. "It's about consistency."

Ford operates on an annual budget of $30,000 to $75,000, with funding sources ranging from the Ford and MacArthur Foundations to her own pocket. Within El Pilar's lush tropical forest are numerous temples and other buildings that stand as high as 22 meters. Over the years, Ford has built a cultural center and a caretaker house, and El Pilar now attracts hundreds of ecotourists annually. Ford started an annual festival to celebrate cultural traditions and foster community involvement, and she's organizing a women's collective to sell local crafts. "We've built the first infrastructure at El Pilar since 1000 [C.E.]," she says.

Whether they operate with big money or on the cheap, community archaeologists face a delicate juggling act between development and research. Ford believes her academic career has suffered because of the time and effort she's invested in development projects. "I would have written much more substantive work on my research at El Pilar," she says, lamenting that she has yet to finish a book about her work. Kaplan and Demarest say that they spend about half their time on community development, leaving only half for archaeology.

As impressive and well-intentioned as these and other community archaeology projects seem, at least a few researchers are concerned about unintended consequences. "If you don't understand the local politics, you can really do damage," says Arlen Chase of the University of Central Florida in Orlando, who has investigated Caracol, a major Maya site in Belize, since 1984. It's difficult to determine just what archaeologists owe the community they work in, he adds. "This is a new endeavor, and we're learning how best to do it," agrees archaeologist Anne Pyburn, outgoing chair of the Ethics Committee of the American Anthropological Association.

Despite these concerns, Hansen and his colleagues seem convinced that they're making progress. Guatemalans who were "dedicated to looting and destroying these sites," Hansen says, are "now dedicated to preserving them."

Critical Thinking

1. What is "community archaeology"?
2. What must be done to save the vestiges of the Ancient Maya from being destroyed and why?
3. What was Maya research focused on until recently? What were the consequences when the project was over?
4. How has Arthur Demarest exercised his responsibility to the community where he excavates? Describe his research and community development plan. In what ways has the community benefited?
5. What have been the benefits of Richard Hansen's community development efforts in the Mirador Basin and how has he achieved them?
6. Why is it that finding funding for community archaeology is "horrific," according to Demarest and Hansen?
7. Why does Anabel Ford believe that her academic career has suffered because of the development projects?
8. What concerns do some archaeologists have about community archaeology?

Michael Bawaya is the editor of *American Archaeology*.

Distinguished Lecture in Archaeology

Communication and the Future of American Archaeology

What follows is the revised text of the Distinguished Lecture in Archaeology, presented at the 95th Annual Meeting of the American Anthropological Association, held in San Francisco, California, November, 1996.

Jeremy A. Sabloff

I offer these remarks with somewhat ambivalent feelings. While it is an honor indeed to be asked to give the Archaeology Division's Distinguished Lecture, I nevertheless must admit that it is a daunting challenge. I have looked at many of the superb Distinguished Lectures that have been presented to you in recent years and subsequently published in the *American Anthropologist* and am very impressed with what our colleagues have had to say. Most of the recent talks have focused on aspects of the ongoing debates on modern archaeological theory and methods. I certainly could have continued this tradition, because, as many of you know, I have strong feelings about this topic. However, I decided to pursue a different, more general tack, which I hope you will agree is of equal importance.

In a few short years, we will be entering a new millennium. Will American archaeology survive in the twenty-first century? Of course it will. But will it continue to thrive in the new millennium? The answer to this question is a more guarded "yes." There are various causes for concern about the future health of archaeology. I would like to examine one of these concerns and offer some suggestions as to how this concern might be eased.

My theme will be archaeologists' communication with the public—or lack thereof—and, more specifically, the relevance of archaeology to non-professionals. In thinking about this theme, which has been a particular interest and concern of mine, it struck me how one of my favorite cartoons provided an important insight into the whole question of archaeological communication. I know that many of you have your office doors or bulletin boards festooned with a host of "Calvin and Hobbes," "Shoe," "Bloom County," "Doonesbury," or "Far Side" drawings that unerringly seem to pinpoint many of life's enduring paradoxes and problems. In particular, the "Far Side" cartoons by Gary Larson, who is now lamentably in early retirement like several of our master cartoonists, often resonate well with archaeologists' sensibilities. This cartoon, while not specifically targeting archaeologists or cultural anthropologists, as Larson often did pinpoint a central concern of my discussion.

While archaeologists may think they are talking clearly to the public, what the latter often hears, I believe, is "blah, blah, blah, *tomb,* blah, blah, blah *sacrifice,* blah, blah, blah, *arrowhead.*"

I will argue that the field of American archaeology, despite some significant progress in the past decade, is still failing to effectively tell the public about how modern anthropological archaeology functions and about the huge gains archaeologists have made in understanding the development of ancient cultures through time and space.

More than 25 years ago, John Fritz and Fred Plog ended their article on "The Nature of Archaeological Explanation" (1970:412) with the famous assertion that "We suggest that unless archaeologists find ways to make their research increasingly relevant to the modern world, the modern world will find itself increasingly capable of getting along without archaeologists." Although Fritz and Plog had a very particular definition of relevance in mind relating to the development of laws of culture change, as did Fritz in his important article on "Relevance, Archaeology, and Subsistence Theory" (1973), if one adopts a broader view of the term *relevance,* then the thrust of their statement is just as important today—if not more so—than it was in 1970.

How can this be true? Archaeology appears to be thriving, if one counts number of jobs, money spent on archaeological field research, course enrollments, publications, and public fascination with the subject as measured in media coverage. But is the public interest, or, better yet, the public's interest, being served properly and satisfied in a productive and responsible fashion? With some important exceptions, I unfortunately would answer "no." Why do I think this to be the case?

In the nineteenth century, archaeology played an important public and intellectual role in the fledgling United States. Books concerned wholly or in part with archaeology were widely read and, as Richard Ford has indicated clearly in his article on "Archaeology Serving Humanity" (1973), archaeology played an important part in overthrowing the then-dominant Biblical view of human development in favor of Darwinian evolutionary theory. Empirical archaeological research, which excited public interest and was closely followed by the public, was able to provide data that indicated that human activities had considerable antiquity and that archaeological studies of the past could throw considerable light on the development of the modern world.

As is the case in most disciplines, as archaeology became increasingly professionalized throughout the nineteenth century and as academic archaeology emerged in the late-nineteenth and early-twentieth centuries, the communications gap between professionals and the public grew apace. This gap was accentuated because amateurs had always played an important part in the archaeological enterprise. As late as the 1930s, before academic archaeology really burgeoned, the gap between most amateurs and professionals was still readily bridgeable, I believe. The first article in *American Antiquity,* for example, was written by an amateur, and, as I have discussed in detail elsewhere, the founders of the journal hoped that it "would provide a forum for communication between these two groups" (Sabloff 1985:228). However, even a quick look today at *American Antiquity* will indicate that those earlier hopes have been dashed. It may be a terrific journal for professionals, but much of it would be nearly incomprehensible to non-professionals, except perhaps to the most devoted amateurs.

In 1924, Alfred Vincent Kidder published his landmark book *An Introduction to the Study of Southwestern Archaeology.* This highly readable volume both made key advances in scholarly understanding of the ancient Southwest and was completely accessible to the general public. As Gordon Willey (1967:299) has stated: "It is a rarity in that it introduces systematics to a field previously unsystematized, and, at the same time, it is vitally alive and unpedantic.... He wrote a book that was romantic but not ridiculous, scrupulously close to the facts but not a boring recital of them." How many regional archaeological syntheses could have that said of them today? Happily, the answer is not "none," and there is some evidence of a positive trend in the publication of more popularly oriented regional and site syntheses (see, for instance, Kolata 1993; Plog 1997; or Schele and Freidel 1990, among others). Marcus and Flannery's (1996) recent book on Zapotec civilization is a superb example of how such accessible writing can be combined with a clear, theoretically sophisticated approach, as well.

Kidder also was deeply concerned about the relevance of archaeology to the contemporary world and was not shy about expressing his belief that archaeology could and should play an important social role in the modern world (a view which is paralleled today by some post-processual [e.g., Hodder et al. 1995] and feminist [e.g., Spector 1993] concerns with humanizing archaeological narratives). Kidder's views were most clearly expressed by him at a 1940 symposium at the American Philosophical Society on "Characteristics of American Culture and Its Place in General Culture." As Richard Woodbury (1973:171) notes: "Kidder presented one of his most eloquent pleas for the importance of the anthropological understanding of the past through the techniques of archaeology." Kidder (1940:528), for example, states: "it is good for an archaeologist to be forced to take stock, to survey his field, to attempt to show what bearing his delvings into the past may have upon our judgement of present day life; and what service, if any, he renders the community beyond filling the cases of museums and supplying material for the rotogravure sections of the Sunday papers." Lamentably, his prescription for the practitioners of archaeology has not been well filled in the past half century.

The professionalization of archaeology over the course of this century obviously has had innumerable benefits. In the most positive sense, the discipline has little resemblance to the archaeology of 100 years ago. With all the advances in method, theory, and culture historical knowledge, archaeologists are now in a position to make important and useful statements about cultural adaptation and development that should have broad intellectual appeal. Ironically, though, one aspect of the professionalization of the discipline, what can be termed the academization of archaeology, is working against such broad dissemination of current advances in archaeological understanding of cultures of the past. The key factor, I am convinced, is that since World War II, and especially in the past few decades as archaeology rapidly expanded as an academic subject in universities and colleges throughout this country, the competition for university jobs and the institutional pressures to publish in quantity, in general, and in peer review journals, in particular, has led in part to the academic devaluation of popular writing and communication with the general public. Such activities just don't count or, even worse, count against you.

In addition, I believe that it is possible that some archaeologists, in their desire to prove the rigor and scientific standing of the discipline within the academy and among their non-anthropological colleagues and university administrators, have rejected or denigrated popular writing because it might somehow taint archaeology with a nonscientific "softness" from which they would like to distance the field.

If popular writing is frowned upon by some academics, then popularization in other media, such as television, can be treated even more derisively by these scholars, and consequently too few archaeologists venture into these waters. Why should the best known "archaeologist" to the public be an unrepentant looter like Indiana Jones? Is he the role model we want for our profession? When I turn on the television to watch a show with archaeological content, why should I be more than likely to see Leonard Nimoy and the repeated use of the term *mysterious*? It should be professional archaeologists routinely helping to write and perhaps even hosting many of the archaeology shows on television, not just—at best—popular science writers and Hollywood actors. In sum, I strongly feel that we need more accessible writing, television shows, videos, CD-ROMs, and the like with archaeologists heavily involved in all these enterprises.

Forty years ago, Geoffrey Bibby, in his best-selling book *The Testimony of the Spade,* wrote in his foreword (1956:vii):

> It has long been customary to start any book that can be included under the comprehensive heading of "popular science" with an apology from the author to his fellow scientists for his desertion of the icy uplands of the research literature for the supposedly lower and supposedly lush fields of popular representation. This is not an apology, and it is not directed to archaeologists. In our day, when the research literature of one branch of knowledge has become all but incomprehensible to a researcher in another branch, and when the latest advances within any science can revolutionize—or end—our lives within a decade, the task of interpreting every science in language that can be understood by workers in other fields is no longer—if it ever was—a slightly disreputable sideline, but a first-priority duty.

Bibby was making a point that is similar to one made years ago by C. P. Snow (1959) that scholars in different disciplines do not read or are unable to read each others' works, but should! However, I believe that Bibby's argument can easily be expanded to include the lay public, which should be able to readily find out what archaeologists are doing. If they are interested in the subject, and they have no accessible professionally written sources to turn to—like *The Testimony of the Spade*—is it any surprise that they turn to highly speculative, non-professional sources? Unfortunately, Bibby's wise call has gone relatively unheeded. Where are all the *Testimony of the Spades* of this generation, or even the *Gods, Graves, and Scholars* (Ceram 1951)?

But even encouraging communication between archaeologists and the general public is not sufficient, I believe, to dispel the lack of popular understanding about the modern archaeological enterprise and the potential importance of archaeological knowledge. With all the problems that the world faces today, the conflicts and ethnic strife, the innumerable threats to the environment, and the inadequacy of food supplies in the face of rising populations, there never has been a more propitious time for archaeology's new insights into the nature of human development and diversity in time and space to be appreciated by people in all walks of life. In order for better communication to have a useful impact, I believe that the profession has to heed Fritz and Plog's call and strive to be relevant. Moreover, we should pursue relevance in both the general and specific senses of the term. In its broadest sense, *relevance* is "to the purpose; pertinent," according to *The American College Dictionary,* while in its more narrow definition, *relevance* according to *The Oxford English Dictionary,* means "pertinency to important current issues."

All things being equal, archaeology could be justified on the basis of its inherent interest. But all things are rarely equal, and therefore archaeological activities and their relevance to today's world do need justification. To what is archaeology pertinent? In the general sense, archaeology's main claim to relevance is its revelation of the richness of human experience through the study and understanding of the development of past cultures over the globe. Among the goals of such study is to foster awareness and respect of other cultures and their achievements. Archaeology can make itself relevant—pertinent—by helping its audiences appreciate past cultures and their accomplishments.

Why should we actively seek to fulfill such a goal? I firmly believe in the lessons of history. By appreciating the nature of cultures both past and present, their uniqueness and their similarities, their development, and their adaptive successes and failures, we have a priceless opportunity to better grapple with the future than is possible without such knowledge. For example, as many of you are aware, I have long argued that new understandings of the decline of Classic Maya civilization in the southern Maya lowlands in the eighth century A.D. can shed important light on the ability of the ancient Maya to sustain a complex civilization in a tropical rain-forest environment for over a millennium and the reasons why this highly successful adaptation ultimately failed (see Sabloff 1990). The potential implications for today's world are profound.

This form of striving for relevance is powerful and should have great appeal to the public, but it is not necessarily sufficient in terms of outreach goals for general audiences. Archaeology also needs to attempt to be relevant, where possible, in the narrower sense, too. As some of our colleagues in the Maya area, for instance, begin to take the new archaeological insights about sustainable agriculture and the potential for demographic growth and begin to directly apply them to modern situations, then archaeology clearly is becoming pertinent "to important current issues" (see, for example, Rice and Rice 1984).

In relation to this latter goal, I would argue that we need more "action archaeology," a term first coined by Maxine Klehidienst and Patty Jo Watson (1956) more than four decades ago (in the same year that *Testimony of the Spade* first appeared), but which I use in a more general way to convey the meaning of archaeology working *for* living communities, not just *in* them. One compelling example of such action archaeology is the field research of my colleague Clark Erickson, who has identified the remains of raised field agriculture in the Bolivian Amazon and has been studying the raised fields and other earthworks on the ground. He has been able to show that there was a complex culture in this area in Precolumbian times. Erickson also is working with local peasants in his field study area to show them how Precolumbian farmers successfully intensified their agricultural production and to indicate how the ancient raised field and irrigation techniques might be adapted to the modern situation so as to improve the current economic picture (see Erickson 1998). This is just one example of many that could be cited, including the close collaboration between archaeologists and Native American groups in, for example, the innovative research of my colleague Robert Preucel (1998) at Cochiti Pueblo, or in organizations like the Zuni Archaeological Project (see Anyon and Ferguson 1995), in the many pathbreaking modern garbage projects initiated by William L. Rathje and his colleagues (Rathje and Murphy 1992), in the thoughtful archaeological/environmental development project initiated by Anabel Ford and her collaborators at El Pilar in Belize and Guatemala (Ford 1998), or in cooperative projects between archaeologists and members of the local communities in locations such as Labrador or Belize that have been reported on by Stephen Loring and Marilyn Masson in recent Archaeology Division sections of the *AAA Newsletter* (October and November 1996). However, we need many more examples of such work. They should be the rule, not the exception.

This kind of work in archaeology parallels the continued growth of action anthropology among our cultural colleagues. The potential for collaboration among archaeologists and cultural anthropologists in this regard, as advocated, for example, by Anne Pybum and Richard Wilk (1995), is quite strong. Explorations of the possibilities of such cooperation should be particularly appropriate and of great importance to the Archaeology Division of the American Anthropological Association, which I know is interested in integrating archaeology within a general anthropological focus, and I urge the Division to pursue such an endeavor. Applied anthropology in its action form need not—and should not—be restricted to cultural anthropology.

It is depressing to note that the academic trend away from public communication appears to be increasing just as public interest in archaeology seems to be reaching new heights. Whatever the reasons for this growing interest, and clearly there are many potential reasons that could be and have been cited, including a turn to the past in times of current uncertainties, New Age ideological trends, or the growing accessibility of archaeological remains through travel, television, and video, there is no doubt that there is an audience out there that is thirsting for information about the past. But it does not appear that this interest is being well served, given the ratio of off-the-wall publications to responsible ones that one can find in any bookstore. I have written elsewhere (Sabloff 1982:7) that "Unfortunately, one of the prices we must pay for the privilege of sharing a free marketplace of ideas is the possibility that some writers will write unfounded speculation, some publishers will publish them, some bookstores will sell them, and some media will sensationalize them. In this way, unfounded speculations become widely spread among the general population of interested readers." I went on to suggest that "Perhaps the best solution to this problem is to help readers to become aware of the standards of scientific research so that scientific approaches can be better appreciated and pseudoscientific approaches can be read critically" (p. 7).

In order for this solution to work, however, archaeologists need to compete effectively in this free market. Why must we always run into the most outrageous pseudo-archaeology books (what Stephen Williams [1991] has termed "fantastic archaeology") in such visible places as airport news shops? I simply refuse to believe that among the large pool of professional archaeological writing talent that there aren't some of our colleagues who can write books that can replace *Chariots of the Gods?* (Von Däniken 1970). If we abandon much of the field of popular writing to the fringe, we should not be surprised at all that the public often fails to appreciate the significance of what we do. So what? Why does it matter if many archaeologists don't value public communication and much of the public lacks an understanding of archaeology and what archaeologists do and accomplish? There are two principal answers to this question, I believe. First, I strongly feel that we have a moral responsibility to educate the public about what we do. Good science and public education not only are compatible but should go hand in hand. The overwhelming majority of us, whether in the academic, government, or business world, receive at least some public support in our work. I believe that we have a responsibility to give back to the public that provides us with grants, or contracts, or jobs. We need to share with them our excitement in our work and our insights into how peoples of the past lived and how our understandings of the past can inform us about the present and future; and we need to share all this in ways that everyone from young schoolchildren to committed amateur archaeologists can understand and appreciate.

Moreover, the better the public understands and appreciates what we do, what we know, and how we come to know it, the better it can assess the uses and—unfortunately—the abuses of archaeology, especially in political contexts. In this age of exploding ethnic conflicts, a public that has been educated to understand the nature of archaeological research and is thus able to cast a critical eye on how archaeological findings are used in modern political arenas clearly is preferable to people who lack such understanding. On a global scale, the use of archaeological myths in some of the former Soviet republics by various ethnic groups to justify repression of others is just one example—unfortunately!—of many kinds of abuses of archaeological data that could be cited (see Kohl and Fawcett 1995).

Second, there are eminently practical reasons for emphasizing and valuing public communication. Namely—and obviously—it is in our enlightened self-interest! As governmental, academic, and corporate budgets grow tighter and tighter, we are increasingly vying with innumerable groups and people, many with very compelling causes and needs, for extremely competitive dollars. If we don't make our case to the public about the significance of our work, then, in Fritz and Plog's (1970) words, we will surely find our public increasingly capable of getting along without us. How many of our representatives in Congress or in state legislatures really understand what archaeologists do and what they can contribute to the modern world? How many of them get letters from constituents extolling the virtues of the archaeological enterprise and urging them to support archaeological research both financially and through legislation? Unless we educate and work with our many publics, we are certain to find our sources of support, many of which have been taken for granted in recent years, rapidly drying up.

Let's turn our attention from the general problem to potential solutions. How can American archaeologists rectify the situation just described and particularly promote more popular writing by professional scholars? One answer is deceptively simple: we need to change our value system and our reward system within the academy. Just as Margaret Mead and other great anthropological popularizers have been sneered at by some cultural anthropologists, so colleagues like Brian Fagan, who has done so much to reach out to general readers (see, for example, Fagan 1977, 1984, 1987, 1991, and 1995, among many others), are often subject to similar snide comments. We need to celebrate those who successfully communicate with the public, not revile them. Ideally, we should have our leading scholars writing for the public, not only for their colleagues. Some might argue that popular writing would be a waste of their time. To the contrary, I would maintain that such writing is part of our collective academic responsibility. Who better to explain what is on the cutting edge of archaeological research than the field's leading practitioners? Moreover, we need to develop a significant number of our own Stephen Jay Goulds or Stephen Hawkings, not just a few.

Why do some scholars look down at archaeologists who are perceived as popularizers? There are probably a host of reasons, but one of them definitely is pure jealousy. Some archaeologists are jealous of their colleagues who successfully write popular books and articles because of the latter's writing skills. They also are jealous, I believe, of the visibility that popular communication brings those who enter this arena, and they are jealous of the monetary rewards that sometimes accompany popular success. But since such jealousy is not socially acceptable, it tends to be displaced into negative comments on the scholarly abilities of the popularizers.

Not only do we need to change our value system so that public communication is perceived in a positive light, more particularly, we need to change the academic evaluation and reward system for archaeologists (and others!), so that it gives suitable recognition to popular writing and public outreach. Clearly, these activities also can be counted as public service. But they further merit scholarly recognition. I also would include the curation of museum exhibits in this regard, especially ones that include catalogs or CD-ROMs that are accessible to broad audiences. Effective writing for general audiences requires excellent control of the appropriate theoretical, methodological, and substantive literature and the ability to comprehend and articulate clearly the core issues of the archaeology of an area, time period, or problem, and therefore should be subject to the same kind of qualitative academic assessment that ideally goes on today in any academic tenure, promotion, or hiring procedure. However, such a development would go against the current pernicious trend that features such aspects as counting peer-review articles and use of citation indices. I strongly believe that the growing reliance on numbers of peer-review articles and the denigration of both popular and non-peer-review writing needs to be reversed. As in so many areas of life, quantity is being substituted for quality, while the measurement of quality becomes increasingly problematic. As the former editor of a major peer-review journal, as well as the editor of many multi-author volumes, I can assure you that the quality of chapters in edited books—often discounted as non-peer-reviewed writings—can be and frequently are of as high or higher quality than peer-reviewed articles. However, many faculty and administrators appear to be looking for formulae that shortchange the qualitative evaluation of research and writing, no matter what form of publication. The whole academic system of evaluation for hiring, tenure, promotion, and salary raises needs to be rethought. In my opinion it is headed in the wrong direction, and the growing trend away from qualitative evaluation is especially worrisome.

As a call to action, in order to encourage popular writing among academics, particularly those with tenure, all of us need to lobby university administrators, department chairs, and colleagues about the value and importance of written communication with audiences beyond the academy. Academics should be evaluated on their popular as well as their purely academic writings. Clearly, what is needed is a balance between original research and popular communication. In sum, evaluations should be qualitative, not quantitative.

Concerning non-academic archaeologists, we need to raise the perceived value of general publications and public outreach in the cultural resource management arm of the profession and work toward having public reporting be routinely included in scopes of work of as many cultural resource management contracts as is feasible. In some areas, fortunately, such as in the National Parks Service or in some Colonial archaeological settings, such outreach already is valued. Positive examples like this need to be professionally publicized and supported.

I would be remiss if I didn't point out that there clearly is a huge irony here. The academic world obviously is becoming increasingly market-oriented with various institutions vying for perceived "stars" in their fields with escalating offers of high salaries, less teaching, better labs, more research funds, and so on, and most academics not only are caught up in this system but have bought into it. At the same time, those scholars who are most successful in the larger marketplace of popular ideas and the popular media and who make dollars by selling to popular audiences are frequently discounted and denigrated by the self-perceived "true scholars," who often have totally bought into the broad academic market economy and are busy playing this narrower market game!

To conclude, I hope that I have been able to stimulate some thought about what might appear to be a very simple problem but which in reality is quite complicated. In order to fulfill what I believe is one of archaeology's major missions, that of public education, we need to make some significant changes in our professional modes of operation. The Archaeology Division can form a common cause with many other units of the American Anthropological Association to realize this goal. This is a four-field problem with four-field solutions! The Society for American Archaeology has just endorsed public education and outreach as one of the eight principles of archaeological ethics. This Division can also play a key role in such endeavors by working within the American Anthropological Association and using its influence to help change the emphases of our professional lives and the reward systems within which we work. To reiterate, I strongly believe that we must change our professional value system so that public outreach in all forms, but especially popular writing, is viewed and supported in highly positive terms. We need to make this change. There are signs that the pendulum of general communication in the field of American archaeology is starting to swing in a positive direction. Let us all work to push it much further!

I am sure that we all have heard the clarion call to the American public—"will you help me to build a bridge to the twenty-first century"—many, many times. It is my belief that, unfortunately, the bridge to the twenty-first century will be a shaky one indeed for archaeology and anthropology—perhaps even the proverbial bridge to nowhere!— unless we tackle the communication problem with the same energy and vigor with which we routinely debate the contentious issues of contemporary archaeological theory that past lecturers to this group have delineated for you. The fruits of our research and analyses have great potential relevance for the public at large. The huge, exciting strides in understanding the past that anthropological archaeology has made in recent years need to be brought to the public's attention both for our sakes and theirs.

References

Anyon, Roger, and T. J. Ferguson 1995 Cultural Resources Management at the Pueblo of Zuni, N.M., U.S.A. Antiquity 69 (266):913–930.

Bibby, Geoffrey 1956 The Testimony of the Spade. New York: Alfred A. Knopf.

Ceram, C. W. 1951 Gods, Graves, and Scholars: The Story of Archaeology. New York: Alfred A. Knopf.

Erickson, Clark L. 1998 Applied Archaeology and Rural Development: Archaeology's Potential Contribution to the Future. In Crossing Currents: Continuity and Change in Latin America. M. Whiteford and S. Whiteford, eds. pp. 34–45. Upper Saddle, NJ: Prentice-Hall.

Fagan, Brian M. 1977 Elusive Treasure: The Story of Early Archaeologists in the Americas. New York: Scribners. 1984 The Aztecs. New York: W. H. Freeman. 1987 The Great Journey: The Peopling of Ancient America. London: Thames and Hudson. 1991 Kingdoms of Gold, Kingdoms of Jade: The Americas before Columbus. London: Thames and Hudson. 1995 Time Detectives: How Archaeologists Use Technology to Recapture the Past. New York: Simon and Schuster.

Ford, Anabel, ed. 1998 The Future of El Pilar: The Integrated Research and Development Plan for the El Pilar Archaeological Reserve for Flora and Fauna, Belize-Guatemala. Department of State Publication 10507, Bureau of Oceans. and International Environmental and Scientific Affairs, Washington, DC.

Ford, Richard I. 1973 Archaeology Serving Humanity. In Research and Theory in Current Archaeology. Charles L. Redman, ed. Pp. 83–94. New York: John Wiley.

Fritz, John M. 1973 Relevance, Archaeology, and Subsistence Theory. In Research and Theory in Current Archaeology. Charles L. Redman, ed. Pp. 59–82. New York: John Wiley.

Fritz, John M., and Fred Plog 1970 The Nature of Archaeological Explanation. American Antiquity 35:405–12.

Hodder, Ian, Michael Shanks, Alexandra Alexandri, Victor Buchli, John Carman, Jonathan Last, and Gavin Lucas, eds. 1995 Interpreting Archaeology: Finding Meaning in the Past. New York: Routledge.

Kidder, Alfred V. 1924 An Introduction to the Study of Southwestern Archaeology, with a Preliminary Account of the Excavations at Pecos. Papers of the Southwestern Expedition, No. 1. Published for the Department of Archaeology, Phillips Academy, Andover. New Haven, CT: Yale University Press. 1940 Looking Backward. Proceedings of the American Philosophical Society 83:527–537.

Kleindienst, Maxine R., and Patty Jo Watson 1956 'Action Archaeology': The Archaeological Inventory of a Living Community. Anthropology Tomorrow 5:75–78.

Kohl, Philip L., and Clare Fawcett, eds. 1995 Nationalism, Politics, and the Practice of Archaeology. Cambridge: Cambridge University Press.

Kolata, Alan L. 1993 The Tiwanaku: Portrait of an Andean Civilization. Cambridge: Blackwell.

Marcus, Joyce, and Kent V. Flannery 1996 Zapotec Civilization: How Urban Society Evolved in Mexico's Oaxaca Valley. New York: Thames and Hudson.

Plog, Stephen 1997 Ancient Peoples of the American Southwest. London: Thames and Hudson.

Preucel, Robert W. 1998 The Kotyiti Research Project: Report of the 1996 Field Season. Report submitted to the Pueblo of Cochiti and the USDA Forest Service, Santa Fe National Forest, Santa Fe, NM.

Pyburn, Anne, and Richard Wilk 1995 Responsible Archaeology Is Applied Anthropology. In Ethics in American Archaeology: Challenges for the 1990s. Mark J. Lynott and Alison Wylie, eds. Pp. 71–76. Washington, DC: Society for American Archaeology.

Rathje, William L., and Cullen Murphy 1992 Rubbish!: The Archaeology of Garbage. New York: HarperCollins.

Rice, Don S., and Prudence M. Rice 1984 Lessons from the Maya. Latin American Research Review 19(3):7–34.

Sabloff, Jeremy A. 1982 Introduction. In Archaeology: Myth and Reality. Jeremy A. Sabloff, ed. Pp. 1–26. Readings from Scientific American. San Francisco: W. H. Freeman. 1985 American Antiquity's First Fifty Years: An Introductory Comment. American Antiquity 50:228–236. 1990: The New Archaeology and the Ancient Maya. A Scientific American Library Book. New York: W. H. Freeman.

Schele, Linda, and David A. Freidel 1990 A Forest of Kings: The Untold Story of the Ancient Maya. New York: Morrow.

Snow, C. P. 1959 The Two Cultures and the Scientific Revolution. Cambridge: Cambridge University Press.

Spector, Janet 1993 What This Awl Means: Feminist Archaeology at a Wahpeton Dakota Village. St. Paul: Minnesota Historical Society Press.

Von Däniken, Erich 1970 Chariots of the Gods? New York: G. P. Putnam's Sons.

Willey, Gordon R. 1967 Alfred Vincent Kidder, 1885–1963. In Biographical Memoirs, vol. 39. Published for the National Academy of Sciences. New York: Columbia University Press.

Williams, Stephen 1991 Fantastic Archaeology: The Wild Side of North American Prehistory. Philadelphia: University of Pennsylvania Press.

Woodbury, Richard B. 1973 Alfred V. Kidder. New York Columbia University Press.

Critical Thinking

1. What is the theme of these remarks?
2. Describe the important and public role of archaeology in the nineteenth century.
3. How and when did the gap between amateurs and professionals become unbridgeable?
4. What have been some of the benefits of the professionalization of archaeology? How and why has this worked against the dissemination of current advances in archaeological understanding of cultures of the past?
5. Why have some archaeologists rejected or denigrated popular writing in archaeology?
6. Why is it not a surprise that people turn to speculative, nonprofessional sources for their interest in archaeology?
7. To what is archaeology pertinent and why, according to the author?
8. Why do we need more "action archaeology"? What is one "compelling example"?
9. What is the evidence for increasing public interest in archaeology? Why should archaeologists take responsibility for educating the public?
10. How can American archaeologists rectify the situation, according to the author?
11. Why do some scholars look down at archaeologists who are perceived as popularizers, according to the author?
12. What changes does the author recommend with respect to the academic evaluation and reward system?
13. What does the author recommend with respect to the non-academic archaeologists?
14. What is the "huge irony," according to the author?

Jeremy A. Sabloff is from the University of Pennsylvania Museum of Archaeology and Anthropology Philadelphia, PA 19104.

Acknowledgments—I am honored that I was asked to deliver the Archaeology Division's 1996 Distinguished Lecture and grateful to the Archaeology Division for its kind invitation to deliver this important talk. I wish to acknowledge the growing list of colleagues, only a few of which have been cited above, who have accepted the crucial challenge of writing for general public. May your numbers multiply! I also wish thank Paula L. W. Sabloff, Joyce Marcus, and the reviewer for this journal for their many insightful and helpful comments and suggestions, only some of which I have been able to take advantage of, that have certainly improved the quality of paper.

UNIT 2

Problem Oriented Archaeology

Unit Selections

Learning Outcomes

After reading this Unit, you will be able to:

- Explain the causes of primitive warfare. Is warfare endemic to the human species?
- Compare the major theories as to when modern humans migrated to the New World. Cite the archaeological evidence.
- Develop your own theories as to why the society of Cahokia existed in the time and place that it did and why it eventually disappeared.
- Explain why the development of agriculture often leads to poor health for some.
- Review the evidence for and against cannibalism among the Ancestral Puebloans.
- Discuss the role that women played in hunting and gathering in Ice-Age Europe and contrast what we know now with what was once thought.
- Discuss the anthropological evidence regarding women as toolmakers in Ice-Age Europe.
- Define "garbology" and discuss its importance as a science.
- Using the example of the Bushmen, show how archaeological investigation can reveal details of the past.
- Discuss the factors that were involved in the collapse of the Mayan civilization as well as the lessons they hold for the modern world.

Student Website

www.mhhe.com/cls

Internet References

Archaeology Links (NC)
www.arch.dcr.state.nc.us/links.htm#stuff

Archaeology Magazine
www.archaeology.org

Cahokia Mounds
http://cahokiamounds.org

What are the goals of archaeology? What kinds of things motivate well-educated people to go out and dig square holes in the ground and sift through their diggings like sifting flour for a cake? How do they know where to dig? What are they looking for? What do they do with the things they find? Let us drop in on an archaeology class at Metropolis University.

"Good afternoon, class. I'm Dr. Penny Pittmeyer. Welcome to Introductory Archaeology. Excuse me, young lady. Yes, you in the back, wearing the pith helmet. I don't think you'll need to bring that shovel to class this semester. We aren't going to be doing any digging."

A moan like that of an audience who had just heard a bad pun sounded throughout the classroom. Eyes bugged out, foreheads receded, sweat formed on brow ridges, and mouths formed into alphabet-soup at this pronouncement.

"That's right, no digging. You are here to learn about archaeology."

"But archaeology is digging. So what are we going to do all semester? Sheesh!" protested a thin young man with stern, steel granny glasses and a straight, scraggly beard, wearing a stained old blue work shirt and low slung 501's with an old, solid, and finely tooled leather belt and scuffed cowboy boots. A scratched trowel jutted from his right back pocket where the seam was half torn away.

Dr. Pittmeyer calmly surveyed the class and quietly repeated, "You are here to learn about archaeology." In a husky, compelling voice, she went on. "Archaeology is not *just* digging, nor is it just about Egyptian ruins or lost civilizations. It's a science. First you have to learn the basics of that science. Digging is just a technique. Digging comes later. Digging comes after you know why you are going to dig."

"No Egyptian ruins . . . ," a plaintive echo resonated through the still classroom.

"You can have your ruins later. Take a class in Egyptian archaeology—fine, fine! But this class is the prerequisite to all those other classes. I hate to be the one to tell you this, people, but there ain't no Indiana Jones! I would have found him by now if there were." Dr. Pittmeyer said this with a slightly lopsided smile. But a veiled look in her light eyes sent an "uh-oh" that the students felt somewhere deep in their guts. They knew that the woman had something to teach them. And teach them she would!

Dr. Pittmeyer half sat on the old desk at the front of the classroom. Leaning one elbow on the podium to her right, she picked up a tall, red, opaque glass, and took a long and satisfying drink from it. Behind her large-framed black glasses, her eyes brightened noticeably. She wiped away an invisible mustache from her upper lip and settled onto the desk, holding the red glass in her left hand and letting it sway slightly as she unhurriedly looked over the students. Her left eyebrow rose unconsciously.

The quiet lengthened so that the students filling out the Day-Glo-orange drop cards stopped writing, conscious of the now loud silence in the room.

"OK! Let's go!" Dr. Pittmeyer said with a snap like a whip swinging over their heads. The startled students went straight backed in unison.

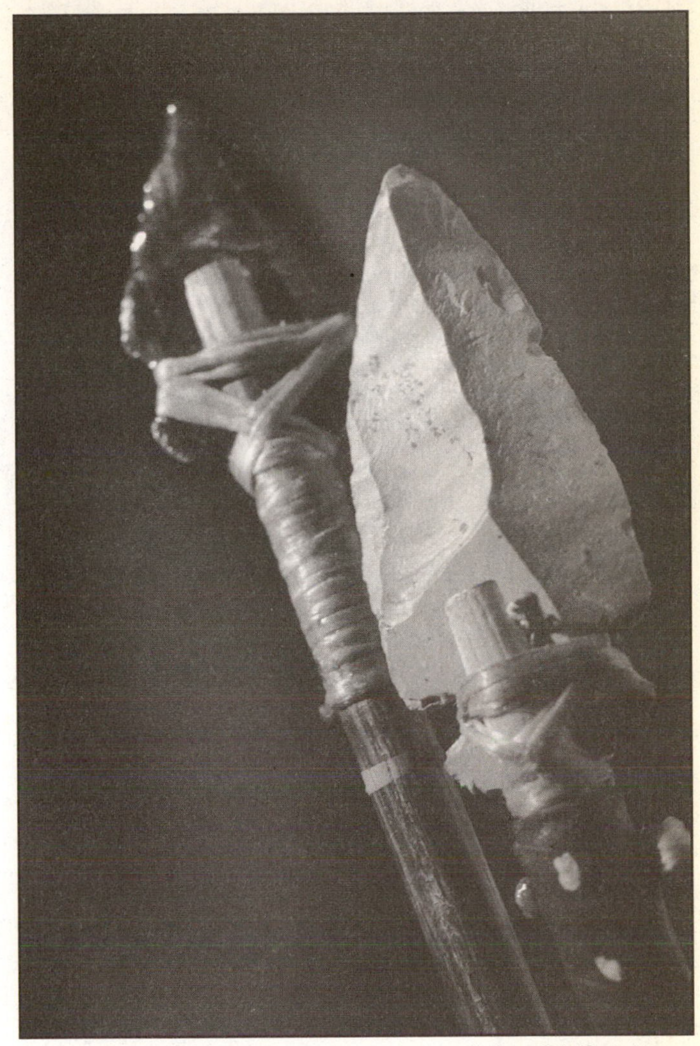

"Archaeology is a science, ladies and gentlemen. It's part of the larger science of anthropology. The goals of both are to understand and predict human behavior. Let's start by looking at an area, or subfield, of archaeology that we may designate as problem-oriented archaeology. Humans evolved in Africa, Asia, and Europe, or what we refer to as the Old World."

Dr. Pittmeyer simultaneously turned out the lights and clicked on the PowerPoint projector. On the whiteboard, she wrote rapidly with a harshly bright, purple pen in a hieroglyphic-like scrawl. Dangling from her neck was a microphone that was plugged into a speaker that was then plugged back into an old, cracked socket, the single electric outlet offered by the ancient high-ceilinged room.

Doubtful students suddenly felt compelled to take notes in the dim light provided by the irregularities of old-fashioned thick blinds that did not quite close completely.

"In the New World, in the Americas, from Alaska down to the tip of Tierra del Fuego, we only have well documented evidence that the first people lived here about 15,000–11,000 years ago. In contrast, people have been living in the Old World for 200,000 years or more—people in the sense of *Homo sapiens*.

"So what took them so long to get here?" a perplexed female voice asked.

"Please let me point out that your question contains a very telling assumption. You said, what took them so long to get here. The question is moot because these early peoples were not trying to get here. We're talking about the Paleolithic era—people were migratory. They hunted and collected their food every day. They followed their food resources, usually in seasonal patterns but within fairly local areas. If they moved at all, it was because they were successfully expanding in population. So it is a non-question. Let me explain, please.

"In archaeology, you have to ask the right questions before you can get any useful answers. That is why archaeologists dig—not to make discoveries, but to answer questions. Now, here's what I want you to do. Go home and try to think yourself back into the Paleolithic. Its 35,000 years ago, and mostly you hang out with your family and other close relatives. You get your food and shelter on a daily basis, and you have some free time, too. Everyone cooperates to survive. The point is that wherever you are, you are there. There is no place to try to get to. There is no notion of private property or ownership of land. Nobody needs to conquer anybody. There are no cities, no freeways, no clocks, and no rush. Think about it. It's a concept of life without measurements or urgencies."

"But they must have been pretty stupid back that long ago!" the young man with the beard, now nibbling his trowel, protested.

"Please think about that assumption! No, these were people just like you and me. If they were here today, they probably could program their DVRs. These were people with many skills and accomplishments. They met their needs as we meet ours. But they had something we might envy. They were already there no matter where they were! There's a lot to be learned from our prehistoric ancestors."

"But, frankly, tomorrow's another day." Alone in the classroom, Dr. Penny Pittmeyer finished her soda and allowed her eyes to glaze over as the forgotten Day-Glo-orange drop cards fluttered to the floor. She stared far back in time where she saw intelligent people living a simple life in peace—or so she hoped.

Prehistory *of* Warfare

Humans have been at each others' throats since the dawn of the species.

STEVEN A. LEBLANC

In the early 1970s, working in the El Morro Valley of west-central New Mexico, I encountered the remains of seven large prehistoric pueblos that had once housed upwards of a thousand people each. Surrounded by two-story-high walls, the villages were perched on steep-sided mesas, suggesting that their inhabitants built them with defense in mind. At the time, the possibility that warfare occurred among the Anasazi was of little interest to me and my colleagues. Rather, we were trying to figure out what the people in these 700-year-old communities farmed and hunted, the impact of climate change, and the nature of their social systems—not the possibility of violent conflict.

One of these pueblos, it turned out, had been burned to the ground; its people had clearly fled for their lives. Pottery and valuables had been left on the floors, and bushels of burned corn still lay in the storerooms. We eventually determined that this site had been abandoned, and that immediately afterward a fortress had been built nearby. Something catastrophic had occurred at this ancient Anasazi settlement, and the survivors had almost immediately, and at great speed, set about to prevent it from happening again.

Thirty years ago, archaeologists were certainly aware that violent, organized conflicts occurred in the prehistoric cultures they studied, but they considered these incidents almost irrelevant to our understanding of past events and people. Today, some of my colleagues are realizing that the evidence I helped uncover in the El Morro Valley is indicative warfare endemic throughout the entire Southwest, with its attendant massacres, population decline, and area abandonments that forever changed the Anasazi way of life.

When excavating eight-millennia-old farm villages in southeastern Turkey in 1970, I initially marveled how similar modern villages were to ancient ones, which were occupied at a time when an abundance of plants and animals made warfare quite unnecessary. Or so I thought. I knew we had discovered some plaster sling missiles (one of our workmen showed me how shepherds used slings to hurl stones at predators threatening their sheep). Such missiles were found at many of these sites, often in great quantities, and were clearly not intended for protecting flocks of sheep; they were exactly the same size and shape as later Greek and Roman sling stones used for warfare.

The so-called "donut stones" we had uncovered at these sites were assumed to be weights for digging sticks, presumably threaded on a pole to make it heavier for digging holes to plant crops. I failed to note how much they resembled the round stone heads attached to wooden clubs—maces—used in many places of the world exclusively for fighting and still used ceremonially to signify power. Thirty years ago, I was holding mace heads and sling missiles in my hands, unaware of their use as weapons of war.

We now know that defensive walls once ringed many villages of this era, as they did the Anasazi settlements. Rooms were massed together behind solid outside walls and were entered from the roof. Other sites had mud brick defensive walls, some with elaborately defended gates. Furthermore, many of these villages had been burned to the ground, their inhabitants massacred, as indicated by nearby mass graves.

Certainly for those civilizations that kept written records or had descriptive narrative art traditions, warfare is so clearly present that no one can deny it. Think of Homer's *Iliad* or the Vedas of South India, or scenes of prisoner sacrifice on Moche pottery. There is no reason to think that warfare played any less of a role in prehistoric societies for which we have no such records, whether they be hunter-gatherers or farmers. But most scholars studying these cultures still are not seeing it. They should assume warfare occurred among the people they study, just as they assume religion and art were a normal part of human culture. Then they could ask more interesting questions, such as: What form did warfare take? Can warfare explain some of the material found in the archaeological record? What were people fighting over and why did the conflicts end?

Today, some scholars know me as Dr. Warfare. To them, I have the annoying habit of asking un-politic questions about their research. I am the one who asks why the houses at a particular site were jammed so close together and many catastrophically burned. When I suggest that the houses were crowded behind defensive walls that were not found because no one was looking for them, I am not terribly appreciated. And I don't win any popularity contests when I suggest that twenty-mile-wide zones with no sites in them imply no-man's lands—clear evidence for warfare—to archaeologists who have explained a region's history without mention of conflict.

Scholars should assume warfare occurred among the people they study, just as they assume religion was a normal part of human culture. Then they would ask more interesting questions, such as: What form did warfare take? Why did people start and stop fighting?

Virtually all the basic textbooks on archaeology ignore the prevalence or significance of past warfare, which is usually not discussed until the formation of state-level civilizations such as ancient Sumer. Most texts either assume or actually state that for most of human history there was an abundance of available resources. There was no resource stress, and people had the means to control population, though how they accomplished this is never explained. The one archaeologist who has most explicitly railed against this hidden but pervasive attitude is Lawrence Keeley of the University of Illinois, who studies the earliest farmers in Western Europe. He has found ample evidence of warfare as farmers spread west, yet most of his colleagues still believe the expansion was peaceful and his evidence a minor aberration, as seen in the various papers in Barry Cunliffe's *The Oxford Illustrated Prehistory of Europe* (1994) or Douglas Price's *Europe's First Farmers* (2000). Keeley contends that "prehistorians have increasingly pacified the past," presuming peace or thinking up every possible alternative explanation for the evidence they cannot ignore. In his *War Before Civilization* (1996) he accused archaeologists of being in denial on the subject.

Witness archaeologist Lisa Valkenier suggesting in 1997 that hilltop constructions along the Peruvian coast are significant because peaks are sacred in Andean cosmology. Their enclosing walls and narrow guarded entries may have more to do with restricting access to the *huacas,* or sacred shrines, on top of the hills than protecting defenders and barring entry to any potential attackers. How else but by empathy can one formulate such an interpretation in an area with a long defensive wall and hundreds of defensively located fortresses, some still containing piles of sling missiles ready to be used; where a common artistic motif is the parading and execution of defeated enemies; where hundreds were sacrificed; and where there is ample evidence of conquest, no-man's lands, specialized weapons, and so on?

A talk I gave at the Mesa Verde National Park last summer, in which I pointed out that the over 700-year-old cliff dwellings were built in response to warfare, raised the hackles of National Park Service personnel unwilling to accept anything but the peaceful Anasazi message peddled by their superiors. In fact, in the classic book *Indians of Mesa Verde,* published in 1961 by the park service, author Don Watson first describes the Mesa Verde people as "peaceful farming Indians," and admits that the cliff dwellings had a defensive aspect, but since he had already decided that the inhabitants were peaceful, the threat must have been from a new enemy—marauding nomadic Indians. This, in spite of the fact that there is ample evidence of Southwestern warfare for more than a thousand years before the cliff dwellings were built, and there is no evidence for the intrusion of nomadic peoples at this time.

Of the hundreds of research projects in the Southwest, only one—led by Jonathan Haas and Winifred Creamer of the Field Museum and Northern Illinois University, respectively—deliberately set out to research prehistoric warfare. They demonstrated quite convincingly that the Arizona cliff dwellings of the Tsegi Canyon area (known best for Betatakin and Kiet Siel ruins) were defensive, and their locations were not selected for ideology or because they were breezier and cooler in summer and warmer in the winter, as was previously argued by almost all Southwestern archaeologists.

For most prehistoric cultures, one has to piece together the evidence for warfare from artifactual bits and pieces. Most human history involved foragers, and so they are particularly relevant. They too were not peaceful. We know from ethnography that the Inuit (Eskimo) and Australian Aborigines engaged in warfare. We've also discovered remains of prehistoric bone armor in the Arctic, and skeletal evidence of deadly blows to the head are well documented among the prehistoric Aborigines. Surprising to some is the skeletal evidence for warfare in prehistoric California, once thought of as a land of peaceful acorn gatherers. The prehistoric people who lived in southern California had the highest incident of warfare deaths known anywhere in the world. Thirty percent of a large sample of males dating to the first centuries A.D. had wounds or died violent deaths. About half that number of women had similar histories. When we remember that not all warfare deaths leave skeletal evidence, this is a staggering number.

There was nothing unique about the farmers of the Southwest. From the Neolithic farmers of the Middle East and Europe to the New Guinea highlanders in the twentieth century, tribally organized farmers probably had the most intense warfare of any type of society. Early villages in China, the Yucatán, present-day Pakistan, and Micronesia were well fortified. Ancient farmers in coastal Peru had plenty of forts. All Polynesian societies had warfare, from the smallest islands like Tikopia, to Tahiti, New Zealand (more than four thousand prehistoric forts), and Hawaii. No-man's lands separated farming settlements in Okinawa, Oaxaca, and the southeastern United States. Such societies took trophy heads and cannibalized their enemies. Their skeletal remains show ample evidence of violent deaths. All well-studied prehistoric farming societies had warfare. They may have had intervals of peace, but over the span of hundreds of years there is plenty of evidence for real, deadly warfare.

When farmers initially took over the world, they did so as warriors, grabbing land as they spread out from the Levant through the Middle East into Europe, or from South China down through Southeast Asia. Later complex societies like the Maya, the Inca, the Sumerians, and the Hawaiians were no less belligerent. Here, conflict took on a new dimension. Fortresses, defensive walls hundreds of miles long, and weapons and armor expertly crafted by specialists all gave the warfare of these societies a heightened visibility.

Demonstrating the prevalence of warfare is not an end in itself. It is only the first step in understanding why there was so much of it, why it was "rational" for everyone to engage in it all the time. I believe the question of warfare links to the availability of resources.

There is a danger in making too much of the increased visibility of warfare we see in these complex societies. This is especially true for societies with writing. When there are no texts, it is easy to see no warfare. But the opposite is true. As soon as societies can write, they write about warfare. It is not a case of literate societies having warfare for the first time, but their being able to write about what had been going on for a long time. Also, many of these literate societies link to European civilization in one way or another, and so this raises the specter of Europeans being warlike and spreading war to inherently peaceful people elsewhere, a patently false but prevalent notion. Viewing warfare from their perspective of literate societies tells us nothing about the thousands of years of human societies that were not civilizations—that is, almost all of human history. So we must not rely too much on the small time slice represented by literate societies if we want to understand warfare in the past.

The Maya were once considered a peaceful society led by scholarly priests. That all changed when the texts written by their leaders could be read, revealing a long history of warfare and conquest. Most Mayanists now accept that there was warfare, but many still resist dealing with its scale or implications. Was there population growth that resulted in resource depletion, as throughout the rest of the world? We would expect the Maya to have been fighting each other over valuable farmlands as a consequence, but Mayanist Linda Schele concluded in 1984 that "I do not think it [warfare] was territorial for the most part," this even though texts discuss conquest, and fortifications are present at sites like El Mirador, Calakmul, Tikal, Yaxuná, Uxmal, and many others from all time periods. Why fortify them, if no one wanted to capture them?

Today, more Maya archaeologists are looking at warfare in a systematic way, by mapping defensive features, finding images of destruction, and dating these events. A new breed of younger scholars is finding evidence of warfare throughout the Maya past. Where are the no-man's lands that almost always open up between competing states because they are too dangerous to live in? Warfare must have been intimately involved in the development of Maya civilization, and resource stress must have been widespread.

Demonstrating the prevalence of warfare is not an end in itself. It is only the first step in understanding why there was so much, why it was "rational" for everyone to engage in it all the time. I believe the question of warfare links to the availability of resources.

During the 1960s, I lived in Western Samoa as a Peace Corps volunteer on what seemed to be an idyllic South Pacific Island—exactly like those painted by Paul Gauguin. Breadfruit and coconut groves grew all around my village, and I resided in a thatched-roof house with no walls beneath a giant mango tree. If ever there was a Garden of Eden, this was it. I lived with a family headed by an extremely intelligent elderly chief named Sila. One day, Sila happened to mention that the island's trees did not bear fruit as they had when he was a child. He attributed the decline to the possibility that the presence of radio transmissions had affected production, since Western Samoa (now known as Samoa) had its own radio station by then. I suggested that what had changed was not that there was less fruit but that there were more mouths to feed. Upon reflection, Sila decided I was probably right. Being an astute manager, he was already taking the precaution of expanding his farm plots into some of the last remaining farmable land on the island, at considerable cost and effort, to ensure adequate food for his growing family. Sila was aware of his escalating provisioning problems but was not quite able to grasp the overall demographic situation. Why was this?

The simple answer is that the rate of population change in our small Samoan village was so gradual that during an adult life span growth was not dramatic enough to be fully comprehended. The same thing happens to us all the time. Communities grow and change composition, and often only after the process is well advanced do we recognize just how significant the changes have been—and we have the benefit of historic documents, old photographs, long life spans, and government census surveys. All human societies can grow substantially over time, and all did whenever resources permitted. The change may seem small in one person's lifetime, but over a couple of hundred years, populations can and do double, triple, or quadruple in size.

The consequences of these changes become evident only when there is a crisis. The same can be said for environmental changes. The forests of Central America were being denuded and encroached upon for many years, but it took Hurricane Mitch, which ravaged most of the region in late October 1998, to produce the dramatic flooding and devastation that fully demonstrated the magnitude of the problem: too many people cutting down the forest and farming steep hillsides to survive. The natural environment is resilient and at the same time delicate, as modern society keeps finding out. And it was just so in the past.

From foragers to farmers to more complex societies, when people no longer have resource stress they stop fighting. When climate greatly improves, warfare declines. The great towns of Chaco Canyon were built during an extended warm—and peaceful—period.

These observations about Mother Nature are incompatible with popular myths about peaceful people living in ecological balance with nature in the past. A peaceful past is possible only if you live in ecological balance. If you live in a Garden of Eden surrounded by plenty, why fight? By this logic, warfare is a sure thing when natural resources run dry. If someone as smart as Sila couldn't perceive population growth, and if humans all over Earth continue to degrade their environments, could people living in the past have been any different?

A study by Canadian social scientists Christina Mesquida and Neil Wiener has shown that the greater the proportion of a society is composed of unmarried young men, the greater the likelihood of war. Why such a correlation? It is not because the young men are not married; it is because they cannot get married. They are too poor to support wives and families. The idea that poverty breeds war is far from original. The reason poverty exists has remained the same since the beginning of time: humans have invariably overexploited their resources because they have always outgrown them.

There is another lesson from past warfare. It stops. From foragers to farmers, to more complex societies, when people no longer have resource stress they stop fighting. When the climate greatly improves, warfare declines. For example, in a variety of places the medieval warm interval of ca. 900–1100 improved farming conditions. The great towns of Chaco Canyon were built at this time, and it was the time of archaeologist Stephen Lekson's *Pax Chaco*—the longest period of peace in the Southwest. It is no accident that the era of Gothic cathedrals was a response to similar climate improvement. Another surprising fact is that the amount of warfare has declined over time. If we count the proportion of a society that died from warfare, and not the size of the armies, as the true measure of warfare, then we find that foragers and farmers have much higher death rates—often approaching 25 percent of the men—than more recent complex societies. No complex society, including modern states, ever approached this level of warfare.

If warfare has ultimately been a constant battle over scarce resources, then solving the resource problem will enable us to become better at ridding ourselves of conflict.

There have been several great "revolutions" in human history: control of fire, the acquisition of speech, the agricultural revolution, the development of complex societies. One of the most recent, the Industrial Revolution, has lowered the birth rate and increased available resources. History shows that peoples with strong animosities stop fighting after adequate resources are established and the benefits of cooperation recognized. The Hopi today are some of the most peaceful people on earth, yet their history is filled with warfare. The Gebusi of lowland New Guinea, the African !Kung Bushmen, the Mbuti Pygmies of central Africa, the Sanpoi and their neighbors of the southern Columbia River, and the Sirionno of Amazonia are all peoples who are noted for being peaceful, yet archaeology and historical accounts provide ample evidence of past warfare. Sometimes things changed in a generation; at other times it took longer. Adequate food and opportunity does not instantly translate into peace, but it will, given time.

The fact that it can take several generations or longer to establish peace between warring factions is little comfort for those engaged in the world's present conflicts. Add to this a recent change in the decision-making process that leads to war. In most traditional societies, be they forager bands, tribal farmers, or even complex chiefdoms, no individual held enough power to start a war on his own. A consensus was needed; pros and cons were carefully weighed and hotheads were not tolerated. The risks to all were too great. Moreover, failure of leadership was quickly recognized, and poor leaders were replaced. No Hitler or Saddam Hussein would have been tolerated. Past wars were necessary for survival, and therefore were rational; too often today this is not the case. We cannot go back to forager-band-type consensus, but the world must work harder at keeping single individuals from gaining the power to start wars. We know from archaeology that the amount of warfare has declined markedly over the course of human history and that peace can prevail under the right circumstances. In spite of the conflict we see around us, we are doing better, and there is less warfare in the world today than there ever has been. Ending it may be a slow process, but we are making headway.

Critical Thinking

1. Be familiar with the evidence cited by the author for prehistoric warfare.
2. What happened when farmers took over the world?
3. How did conflict take on a new dimension in more complex societies?
4. What is the relationship between literacy and our perception of warfare?
5. Did Europeans spread warfare to inherently peaceful people elsewhere?
6. What evidence is there for warfare among the Maya?
7. Why does the author think there is a link between warfare and the availability of resources?
8. When do the consequences of population growth become evident?
9. What did Christina Mesquida and Neil Wiener find with respect to the likelihood of warfare?
10. What is significant about the fact that warfare stops?
11. What is another "surprising fact"? Explain.
12. How does the author compare war in traditional societies versus today?

© 2003 by **Steven A. LeBlanc.** Portions of this article were taken from his book *Constant Battles,* published in April 2003 by St. Martin's Press. LeBlanc is director of collections at Harvard University's Peabody Museum of Archaeology and Ethnology. For further reading visit www.archaeology.org.

The Origin of War: New ^{14}C Dates from Ancient Mexico

KENT V. FLANNERY AND JOYCE MARCUS

War is well documented in ancient states and empires. Tracing its origins back to earlier societies has proven more challenging. Data from Stone Age Nubia[1] show that even hunting–gathering groups occasionally massacred their neighbors. Studies of more recent agricultural tribes and chiefdoms by Carneiro,[2] Keeley,[3] and Redmond[4] reveal high frequencies of raiding, high per capita death rates, torture, and headhunting. On the other hand, groups like the Mbuti and !Kung appear warless to many anthropologists. Why do some societies display armed conflict and others not?

A recent cross-cultural study by Kelly,[5] Warless Societies and the Origin of War, takes on this question and in so doing, provides a framework for prehistorians. Kelly found the highest incidence of warlessness among unsegmented societies: hunter–gatherers with no level of organization beyond the local group, relatively impermanent extended families, and little tendency to form segments like lineages and clans. While such societies may have individual homicide (and capital punishment for it), group violence is rare.

The case was different among societies divided into equivalent segments, such as patrilineal, matrilineal, or ancestor-based cognatic descent groups, which combine into progressively more inclusive units. Such segmentary societies (which are usually agricultural, but can include foragers) display a principle Kelly calls social substitutability. The killing of any member of another segment is considered a group offense, and can be avenged by killing any member of the offender's segment. Raiding thus begins as group vs. group social action, and can escalate into war as societies grow in scale and complexity.

A significant observation by Kelly is that raiding often begins in the richest environments, where societies "can afford to have enemies for neighbors"; conditions of scarcity encourage mutually beneficial cooperation. The higher the population, the greater the storage facilities, and the more reliable the surplus, the greater the likelihood for segmentary organization and war.

Kelly's model can be tested in the Valley of Oaxaca, 400 km south of Mexico City, owing to collaborative research by the Universities of Michigan,[6] Purdue,[7] Georgia, and Wisconsin,[8] and the American Museum of Natural History.[9] Armed conflict in Oaxaca seems to have begun as raiding, involving killing, burning, and captive taking but no permanent acquisition of territory. By the time sixteenth-century Spanish eyewitnesses arrived, the Zapotec-speaking inhabitants of the valley had armies with noble officers and commoner footsoldiers, waging wars that produced tribute from conquered territories.[10,11]

We present ^{14}C dates for the origin of Zapotec war three ways. "B.P." refers to conventional radiocarbon years before the present. "B.C." refers to the 2 σ range of each date when converted to calendar years B.C. (before Christ) by dendrocalibration. Lowercase "b.c." refers to conventional radiocarbon years B.C.E. (before the Christian era), derived by the 50-year tradition of subtracting 1950 from the B.P. date. (It is necessary to do this because Mexico's pre-Hispanic chronology is still heavily based on such b.c. dates.)

Warless Societies: The Archaic Period, 10,000–4,000 B.P.

The Archaic period in Oaxaca was a time of hunting, gathering, and early attempts at agriculture.[6] Human populations were small and nomadic, coalescing into groups of 25–30 at times of resource abundance and dispersing into family bands of 4–6 persons in other seasons.[12] Even the domestication of maize before 5420 ± 60 B.P.[13] did not lead immediately to village life. As recently as 4000 B.P.[14] there is evidence only for temporary camps. The Archaic has produced no evidence for segmentary societies or group conflict.

Sometime before 3600 B.P. village life was established at San José Mogote, overlooking a river in the northern part of the valley.[6] The site occupied a piedmont spur in one of the richest environments in the valley, surrounded on three sides by high-water-table alluvium.

By the start of the Tierras Largas phase (3500–3100 B.P.), there were at least 19 villages in the valley.[8] San José Mogote, the largest, had a population numbering in the hundreds. There were nuclear family houses of wattle-and-daub; subterranean storage pits, collectively holding up to 1,000 kg of maize per household; and ritual "men's houses" like those known ethnographically from segmentary societies.[6] House 19, one of the earliest of this phase, had been burned, possibly during a raid by a rival village. Charcoal from one of its posts yielded a date of 3490 ± 80 B.P., or 1540 b.c. (Beta Analytical laboratory no. β173807).

It appears that during this time, the western periphery of San José Mogote was defended by a palisade. This palisade took the form of a double line of posts, spaced in such a way that posts of the second line faced the gaps between posts in the first line. Palisades of this type were used by the eighteenth-century Maori.[15]

We do not know whether the palisade at San José Mogote protected the entire village or only one part. Its postholes could be mapped only where bedrock was firm and level; where bedrock sloped down, the holes were lost. Posts could be traced intermittently for 30–40 m, until they disappeared under modern cattle pens. Several posts in Feature 21, the best-preserved section of palisade, had been burned. ^{14}C dates on charcoal from three posts gave dates of 3260 ± 60 B.P., or 1310 b.c. (β177623); 3160 ± 130 B.P., or 1210 b.c. (β175895); and 3250 ± 80 B.P., or 1300 b.c. (β175896). Feature 21 is the oldest directly dated defensive work in ancient Mexico. It meets Kelly's expectations by occurring at a village (i) in a relatively rich environment, (ii) with abundant storage facilities for agricultural surplus, and (iii) with a population high enough to be divided into social segments.

During the subsequent San José phase (3100–2800 B.P.) San José Mogote's population grew to more than 1,000 persons, evidently making it secure enough to expand beyond the palisade. We have no clear evidence of raiding during this period, but evidence for social segments is strong. Different residential wards at the village maintained separate public buildings, and there is iconographic evidence for ancestor-based descent groups[6]. Sumptuary goods in houses and graves also indicate that a hereditary elite had emerged.

The Escalation of Raiding: 2800–2450 B.P.

During the Guadalupe phase (2800–2650 B.P.) San José Mogote remained the largest community in the valley, but other chiefly centers were arising only a day's journey away. None of these new centers were yet in a position to challenge San José Mogote; however, some of the latter's satellite villages were vulnerable. One of those satellites was Fábrica San José, a salt-producing village 5 km to the east.

At least three Guadalupe phase houses at Fábrica San José were burned, leaving masses of burned clay from their wattle-and-daub walls. House LG-1 yielded 828 pieces of daub totaling 41 kg; House LG-3 had a charcoal stripe 90 cm long from a burned roof beam; and the destruction of House LG-5 resulted in "enormous quantities of burned daub".[16] All three houses may have been burned during raids.

Intervillage raiding, presumably increased by competition among rival chiefs for land, water, and manpower, reached its peak during the Rosario phase (2650–2450 B.P.). There were now 75–85 communities in the valley, and chunks of burned daub appear on the surface of Rosario phase sites with 7 times the frequency observed at typical Valley of Oaxaca sites.[8] Each of the three main parts of the valley was controlled by a chiefly center, with an intervening 80-km^2 buffer zone left virtually unoccupied. San José Mogote in the northern valley was still the largest center, at 60–65 hectares (ha); San Martín Tilcajete in the southern valley, at 25 ha, was probably its main rival.[17,18]

Midway through the Rosario phase, San José Mogote was attacked and its main temple, Structure 28, burned. So intense was the fire that the clay of the temple walls was reduced to vitrified cinders. Charcoal from a fallen roof beam among those cinders has been dated to 2550 ± 60 B.P., or 600 b.c. (β177624).

Chiefly Warfare and the Origin of Writing: 2650–2450 B.P.

Structure 28 was never rebuilt. Instead a new Rosario temple, Structure 37, was built only a few meters to the north. Charcoal from a burned post in one wall of Structure 37 has recently been dated to 2540 ± 90 B.P., or 590 b.c. (β177626). This date suggests no great lapse of time between the burning of the old temple and the building of the new one.

Both Structures 28 and 37 rested on stone masonry platforms separated by a narrow corridor. At some point after the construction of the new temple, a carved stone was set in place as a threshold for this corridor. The carving, known as Monument 3, depicts the naked corpse of a captive whose heart has been removed. Between his feet is the Zapotec hieroglyph for his name. This stone would appear to commemorate the sacrifice of a chiefly rival taken in combat. The fact that his name is given may provide another analogy with Maori warfare. As Buck says, "No matter how great the casualty list after an engagement, if there were no chiefs killed, there was nothing much to talk about. If there was no chiefly name to connect the engagement with a tribal genealogy, the battle was without a name."[19]

Because Monument 3 is our first record of captive taking and hieroglyphic writing, its date is of some importance. We have previously indicated that its stratigraphic context and associated ceramics date it to the Rosario phase.[6] However, the fact that a stone monument cannot be directly ^{14}C dated has encouraged a few attempts to date it to later periods (e.g., ref. 20). Such attempts are contradicted by the stratigraphy, and, fortunately, dates from the overlying level now provide us with a terminus ante quem for this carved stone.

The dates come from two well made stone-lined hearths, Features 18 and 19, which were dug into the humic layer of a soil horizon that formed above Monument 3 after it (and the buildings flanking it) fell into disuse. Charcoal from Feature 18 dated to 2510 ± 40 B.P., or 560 b.c. (β173808). Charcoal from Feature 19 dated to 2580 ± 40 B.P., or 630 b.c. (β175898). Because Monument 3 was sealed stratigraphically below the layer to which these hearths belong, it can date no later than 2580–2510 B.P. We conclude that (i) by that time it had become important to record the sacrifice of elite captives in stone, and (ii) one of the earliest uses of writing was to give the captive's name.[21]

Military Consolidation of the Valley of Oaxaca: 2450–2000 B.P.

Some time before 2450 B.P., presumably seeking a more defensible location, the occupants of San José Mogote and its satellite communities moved to the summit of a 400-m mountain. This mountain, known as Monte Albán, lay in the former buffer zone between rival polities.[7] The new arrivals, at least 2,000 strong, began building 3 km of defensive walls along the more easily climbed western slopes of the mountain. They also began work on a building with more than 300 carved stones depicting slain captives. For the next 400 years they would fight relentlessly to subjugate their political rivals, and raiding would give way to full-scale war.

During the period known as Early Monte Albán I (2450–2250 B.P.) the population of the Valley of Oaxaca grew to an estimated 8,000–10,000 persons, distributed through 261 communities.[8] Nearly a third of the valley's population lived on the defended mountaintop at Monte Albán. They had the support of the entire northern and central valley, the region from which their founding populations had come. A day's journey to the south, however, lay Tilcajete, an unyielding rival. One of the most interesting stories to emerge from recent research is Monte Albán's use of military force to subjugate Tilcajete. Details and ^{14}C dates have been provided by Spencer and Redmond.[9,17,18]

Tilcajete's response to the founding of Monte Albán was to double its own size, from 25 ha to 52.8 ha; future research may show that it drew in manpower from satellite villages for defense. Tilcajete built a civic-ceremonial plaza with an astronomical orientation different from Monte Albán's. Its defiance deprived it of luxury goods that Monte Albán supplied to its allies. Then, toward the end of Early Monte Albán I, Tilcajete was attacked by Monte Albán and its plaza was burned.[18] Charcoal from this conflagration[9] has been dated to 2280 ± 40 B.P., or 330 b.c. (β147541).

Tilcajete refused to capitulate. During the period known as Late Monte Albán I (2250–2000 B.P.), it grew to 71.5 ha and built a new plaza on a more easily defended ridge. The new civic-ceremonial center retained the astronomical orientation of its predecessor, and added defensive walls on its most easily climbed southern flanks.

Monte Albán, however, was prepared for a long campaign; it concentrated thousands of farmers, artisans, and warriors in 155 satellite villages within 15 km of its plaza[8]. Eventually it attacked Tilcajete again, burning both the ruler's palatial residence and a nearby temple.[9] Charcoal from the burned residence (currently our oldest dated Zapotec palace) came out 1970 ± 60 B.P., or 20 b.c. (β143355). Charcoal from the burned temple dated to 1980 ± 70 B.P., or 30 b.c. (β143353).

Tilcajete did not survive this second attack. It was abandoned, and on a mountaintop nearby, its conquerors commissioned an administrative center subordinate to Monte Albán.[22] At this point Monte Albán controlled the entire 2,150-km^2 Valley of Oaxaca and had become the capital of a Zapotec state.[18]

Military Expansion Outside the Valley of Oaxaca: 2000–1700 B.P.

Over the next 200 years, the Zapotec state expanded 150 km beyond the limits of the Valley of Oaxaca. One building in the civic-ceremonial plaza at Monte Albán displayed hieroglyphic names for more than 40 places claimed as provinces. Only a handful of these places have been identified, but that identification has provided evidence for Zapotec expansion. One of the best-studied places is the Cuicatlán Cañada, an arid tropical river canyon 80 km north of Monte Albán. Both the details of conquest and the ^{14}C dates are provided by Spencer and Redmond.[11,17,23]

The Zapotec military encountered little resistance in Cuicatlán, burning villages on the river alluvium and moving the population to the piedmont to make way for new irrigation canals. At one village, La Coyotera, the conquerors erected a feature the Zapotec called yàgabetoo, a wooden rack displaying the skulls of 61 of the vanquished. A carbonized postmold from this rack[17] dated to 1960 ± 100 B.P., or 10 b.c. (β143344). The Zapotec then built a major fortress near the region's northern gateway. Charcoal from construction fill in this fortress[17] provides a date of 1910 ± 70 B.P., or A.D. 40 (β147535).

By this period, known as Monte Albán II, Zapotec armies were so professionalized that celebrated warriors were given helmets depicting pumas, coyotes, or raptorial birds. It is likely that by 2000 B.P., only 1,200 years since the first palisaded village, the Zapotec were already waging war on the scale witnessed by the 16th-century Spaniards.

Note

Abbreviations: B.C., calendar years before Christ; b.c., conventional radiocarbon years before the Christian era; ha, hectare.

References

1. Wendorf, F. (1968) *Prehistory of Nubia* (Southern Methodist Univ. Press, Dallas), Vol. 2, pp. 954–995.
2. Carneiro, R. L. (1991) *Anthropol. Pap. Mus. Anthropol. Univ. Mich.* 85, 167–190.
3. Keeley, L. H. (1996) *War Before Civilization* (Oxford Univ. Press, New York).
4. Redmond, E. M. (1994) *Tribal and Chiefly Warfare in South America* (Museum of Anthropology, Univ. of Michigan, Ann Arbor).
5. Kelly, R. C. (2000) *Warless Societies and the Origin of War* (Univ. of Michigan Press, Ann Arbor).
6. Marcus, J. & Flannery, K. V. (1996) *Zapotec Civilization* (Thames and Hudson, New York).
7. Blanton, R. E. (1978) *Monte Albán: Settlement Patterns at the Ancient Zapotec Capital* (Academic, New York).
8. Kowalewski, S. A., Feinman, G. M., Finsten, L., Blanton, R. E. & Nicholas, L. M. (1989) *Monte Albán's Hinterland, Part II* (Museum of Anthropology, Univ. of Michigan, Ann Arbor).
9. Spencer, C. S. & Redmond, E. M. (2003) *Social Evol. Hist.* 2, 25–70.

10. de Burgoa, F. (1934) *Publ. del Archivo Gen. Nación* (Talleres Gráficos de la Nación, México D.F., México), Vols. 24–26.
11. Redmond, E. M. (1983) *A Fuego y Sangre: Early Zapotec Imperialism in the Cuicatlán Cañada* (Museum of Anthropology, Univ. of Michigan, Ann Arbor).
12. Flannery, K. V. (1986) *Guilá Naquitz: Archaic Foraging and Early Agriculture in Oaxaca, Mexico* (Academic, Orlando, FL).
13. Piperno, D. R. & Flannery, K. V. (2001) *Proc. Natl. Acad. Sci. USA* 98, 2101–2103. [PMC free article] [PubMed]
14. Lorenzo, J. L. (1958) *Inst. Nac. Antropol. Hist. Dir. Prehist.* No. 6.
15. Fox, A. M. (1976) *Prehistoric Maori Fortifications in the North Island of New Zealand* (Longman Paul, Auckland, NZ), Fig. 106.
16. Drennan, R. D. (1976) *Fábrica San José and Middle Formative Society in the Valley of Oaxaca* (Museum of Anthropology, Univ. of Michigan, Ann Arbor), p. 99.
17. Spencer, C. S. & Redmond, E. M. (2001) *Latin Am. Antiq.* 12, 182–202.
18. Spencer, C. S. & Redmond, E. M. (2001) *J. Anthropol. Archaeol.* 20, 195–229.
19. Buck, P. H. (1949) *The Coming of the Maori* (Whitcombe and Tombs, Wellington, NZ), p. 400.
20. Pohl, M. E. D., Pope, K. O. & von Nagy, C. (2002) *Science* 298, 1984–1987. [PubMed]
21. Marcus, J. (1992) *Mesoamerican Writing Systems: Propaganda, Myth, and History in Four Ancient Civilizations* (Princeton Univ. Press, Princeton, NJ), p. 441.
22. Elson, C. (2003) Ph.D. dissertation (Univ. of Michigan, Ann Arbor).
23. Spencer, C. S. (1982) *The Cuicatlán Cañada and Monte Albán: A Study of Primary State Formation* (Academic, New York).

Critical Thinking

1. For what kinds of society is war well documented?
2. How are warless societies described by the authors?
3. What is "social substitutability" and how does it relate to segmentary societies?
4. Why does raiding occur in rich environments and yet scarcity promotes beneficial cooperation?
5. What is the evidence for armed conflict and violence in Oaxaca over time? How does it seem to correlate with social complexity?

Acknowledgments—We thank the Office of the Vice President for Research, University of Michigan, for providing us with funds to run an extensive series of ^{14}C dates from Oaxaca. All new dates were run by Beta Analytic of Miami, FL.

Article 8

Who Were the First Americans?

MICHAEL D. LEMONICK AND ANDREA DORFMAN

It was clear from the moment Jim Chatters first saw the partial skeleton that no crime had been committed—none recent enough to be prosecutable, anyway. Chatters, a forensic anthropologist, had been called in by the coroner of Benton County, Wash., to consult on some bones found by two college students on the banks of the Columbia River, near the town of Kennewick. The bones were obviously old, and when the coroner asked for an opinion, Chatters' off-the-cuff guess, based on the skull's superficially Caucasoid features, was that they probably belonged to a settler from the late 1800s. Then a CT scan revealed a stone spear point embedded in the skeleton's pelvis, so Chatters sent a bit of finger bone off to the University of California at Riverside for radiocarbon dating. When the results came back, it was clear that his estimate was dramatically off the mark. The bones weren't 100 or even 1,000 years old. They belonged to a man who had walked the banks of the Columbia more than 9,000 years ago.

In short, the remains that came to be known as Kennewick Man were almost twice as old as the celebrated Iceman discovered in 1991 in an Alpine glacier, and among the oldest and most complete skeletons ever found in the Americas. Plenty of archaeological sites date back that far, or nearly so, but scientists have found only about 50 skeletons of such antiquity, most of them fragmentary. Any new find can thus add crucial insight into the ongoing mystery of who first colonized the New World—the last corner of the globe to be populated by humans. Kennewick Man could cast some much needed light on the murky questions of when that epochal migration took place, where the first Americans originally came from and how they got here.

U.S. government researchers examined the bones, but it would take almost a decade for independent scientists to get a good look at the skeleton. Although it was found in the summer of 1996, the local Umatilla Indians and four other Columbia Basin tribes almost immediately claimed it as ancestral remains under the Native American Graves Protection and Repatriation Act (*see box*), demanding that the skeleton be reburied without the desecration of scientific study. A group of researchers sued, starting a legal tug-of-war and negotiations that ended only last summer, with the scientists getting their first extensive access to the bones. And now, for the first time, we know the results of that examination.

What the Bones Revealed

It was clearly worth the wait. The scientific team that examined the skeleton was led by forensic anthropologist Douglas Owsley of the Smithsonian Institution's National Museum of Natural History. He has worked with thousands of historic and prehistoric skeletons, including those of Jamestown colonists, Plains Indians and Civil War soldiers. He helped identify remains from the Branch Davidian compound in Texas, the 9/11 attack on the Pentagon and mass graves in Croatia.

In this case, Owsley and his team were able to nail down or make strong guesses about Kennewick Man's physical attributes. He stood about 5 ft. 9 in. tall and was fairly muscular. He was clearly right-handed: the bones of the right arm are markedly larger than those of the left. In fact, says Owsley, "the bones are so robust that they're bent," the result, he speculates, of muscles built up during a lifetime of hunting and spear fishing.

An examination of the joints showed that Kennewick Man had arthritis in the right elbow, both knees and several vertebrae but that it wasn't severe enough to be crippling. He had suffered plenty of trauma as well. "One rib was fractured and healed," says Owsley, "and there is a depression fracture on his forehead and a similar indentation on the left side of the head." None of those fractures were fatal, though, and neither was the spear jab. "The injury looks healed," says Owsley. "It wasn't a weeping abscess." Previous estimates had Kennewick Man's age as 45 to 55 when he died, but Owsley thinks he may have been as young as 38. Nothing in the bones reveals what caused his demise.

But that's just the beginning of an impressive catalog of information that the scientists have added to what was already known—all the more impressive given the limitations placed on the team by the U.S. Army Corps of Engineers, which is responsible for the skeleton because the Corps has jurisdiction over the federal land on which it was found. The researchers had to do nearly all their work at the University of Washington's Burke Museum, where Kennewick Man has been housed in a locked room since 1998, under the watchful eyes of representatives of both the Corps and the museum, and according to a strict schedule that had to be submitted in advance. "We only had 10 days to do everything we wanted to do," says Owsley. "It was like a choreographed dance."

Perhaps the most remarkable discovery: Kennewick Man had been buried deliberately. By looking at concentrations of

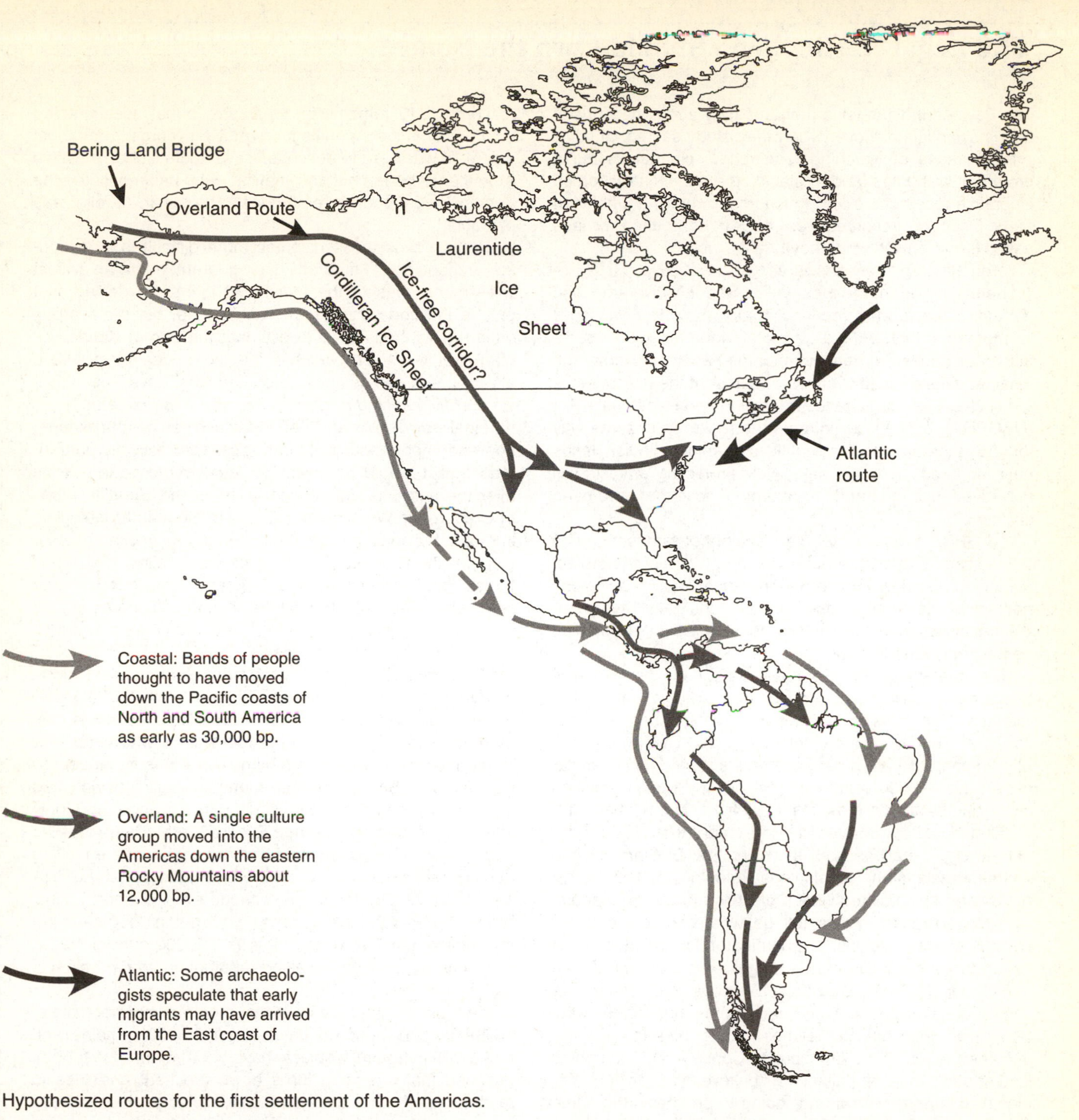

Hypothesized routes for the first settlement of the Americas.

calcium carbonate left behind as underground water collected on the underside of the bones and then evaporated, scientists can tell that he was lying on his back with his feet rolled slightly outward and his arms at his side, the palms facing down—a position that could hardly have come about by accident. And there was no evidence that animal scavengers had been at the body.

The researchers could also tell that Kennewick Man had been buried parallel to the Columbia, with his left side toward the water: the bones were abraded on that side by water that eroded the bank and eventually dumped him out. It probably happened no more than six months before he was discovered, says team member Thomas Stafford, a research geochemist based in Lafayette, Colo. "It wouldn't have been as much as a year," he says. "The bones would have been more widely dispersed."

The deliberate burial makes it especially frustrating for scientists that the Corps in 1998 dumped hundreds of tons of boulders, dirt and sand on the discovery site—officially as part of a project to combat erosion along the Columbia River, although some scientists suspect it was also to avoid further conflict with

The Legal Battle: Who Should Own the Bones?

The Pawnee Indians tell a mordant story about the kinds of things scientists discover when they study sacred remains. After decades of watching researchers plunder its burial grounds for bodies and artifacts, the tribe finally forced Nebraska researchers and museums to return the items in 1989. Once the treasures were back in hand, the Pawnees asked the scientists what they had learned.

"You ate corn," they answered.

Kennewick Man, the most talked-about Native American remains uncovered in recent memory, may be revealing a lot more than that. But if it's a mother lode for scientists, it's also been a massive headache for the Federal Government, local tribes and the lawyers who represent them. At issue is the Native American Graves Protection and Repatriation Act (NAGPRA), a 1990 law intended to make up in some way for the generations of scientific strip-mining Indian lands have endured, by either selectively protecting artifacts still in Native American hands or returning those that have been carried off.

NAGPRA probably seemed straightforward enough to the legislators' eyes. It requires Indians who want to protect an artifact to show by a preponderance of archaeological, geological, historical or other evidence that they have some cultural affiliation to it. But what appears clear to lawyers can be devilishly hard to apply.

For one thing, the older an artifact is, the harder it becomes to show the neat nexus of affiliations that the law requires. "The evidence collapses as you go back in time," says Pat Barker, an archaeologist for the Bureau of Land Management (BLM) in Nevada, who is working on a similar case. "The first 500 years is pretty solid, by 1,000 it's getting dicey, and by 10,000 most of that stuff you just can't get at."

That would put Kennewick Man—more than 9,000 years old—firmly in the hands of the scientists. But lawyers and archaeologists aren't theologians, and for a lot of Native Americans, spirituality is what protecting artifacts is all about.

"Archaeologists always tell us where we came from," says Rochanne Downs, a coordinator for the dozens of Indian tribes that have banded together in the Great Basin Inter-Tribal NAGPRA Coalition. "Well, we know where we came from. Our people were made from mud, and then the tribes were sent out. Sometimes people think that's funny, but when I look at the immaculate Conception, that seems kind of odd to me." Not all Indians believe in the ancient-clay idea, but if those who do are going to be shown the same respect as the adherents of any other faith, then the age of the find becomes immaterial. "We don't have a prehistory," says Downs. "We have one continuous history."

Human remains that are returned to tribes are treated reverently. Several weeks ago, the Umatilla tribe in Washington reinterred 240 remains in a massive burial accompanied by traditional ceremonies and moving words from tribal elders. "It was hard to describe," says Audie Huber, a Native American—though not an Umatilla—who has monitored the Kennewick case for several tribes. "The sense of relief was palpable."

What makes these disputes more difficult is that modern archaeological methods often guarantee that an artifact will—in the eyes of the Indians at least—be defiled. Not only is the find seized from sacred land, but radiocarbon dating (which was used to estimate the age of Kennewick Man) requires that a portion of the find be destroyed. "We're always presented as antiscience Luddites," says Huber. "But we don't like seeing remains pulverized and irradiated."

Finally, ticklish as any NAGPRA case can be, the extreme age and importance of Kennewick Man practically guaranteed that it would be beset by legal maneuvering. Soon after the find was announced in 1996, the Umatilla tribes of Oregon and Washington claimed it. Eight anthropologists immediately sued for the right to study it, and archaeologists for the National Park Service were called in to study the skeleton and help settle the dispute. They found in favor of the Umatillas, but a federal district court disagreed, as did a circuit court, citing a lack of cultural and genetic evidence to link the bones to the claimants.

That stunned the tribes, since NAGPRA does not include a DNA requirement. Last year Senator John McCain proposed an amendment that might have smoothed things over by broadening NAGPRA to include Indians who were ever indigenous to a particular region. The measure appeared headed for approval until the Interior Department objected to it—a move that helped scuttle the change and only inflamed the situation further. Even if the McCain measure had passed, the Indians see it as merely a first step, citing another recent case in which the BLM ignored a NAGPRA committee recommendation without even a court ruling. "With NAGPRA," says Downs, "you get a judgment but no enforcement." With as many as 118,000 sets of Native American remains still awaiting repatriation, that problem is not going away.

The pity is that even in its current, imperfect state, NAGPRA can work (to date, about 30,000 remains and half a million funerary objects have been returned to tribes), provided that everyone turns down the heat and tries to reach consensus. However much knowledge scientists pry from the Kennewick bones, the goodwill lost and the contentious precedents set may make the next generation of NAGPRA cases a lot less friendly than the last.

—Jeffrey Kluger.
Reported by Dan Cray/Los Angeles.

the local tribes. Kennewick Man's actual burial pit had already been washed away by the time Stafford visited the site in December 1997, but a careful survey might have turned up artifacts that could have been buried with him. And if his was part of a larger burial plot, there's now no way for archaeologists to locate any contemporaries who might have been interred close by.

Still, the bones have more secrets to reveal. They were never fossilized, and a careful analysis of their carbon and nitrogen composition, yet to be performed, should reveal plenty about Kennewick Man's diet. Says Stafford: "We can tell if he ate nothing but plants, predominantly meat or a mixture of the two." The researchers may be able to determine whether he preferred meat or fish. It's even possible that DNA could be extracted and analyzed someday.

While the Corps insisted that most of the bones remain in the museum, it allowed the researchers to send the skull fragments and the right hip, along with its embedded spear point, to a lab in Lincolnshire, Ill., for ultrahigh-resolution CT scanning. The process produced virtual slices just 0.39 mm (about 0.02 in.) thick—"much more detailed than the ones made of King Tut's mummy," says Owsley. The slices were then digitally recombined into 3-D computer images that were used to make exact copies out of plastic. The replica of the skull has already enabled scientists to clear up a popular misconception that dates back to the initial reports of the discovery.

Was Kennewick Man Caucasian?

Thanks to Chatters' mention of Caucasoid features back in 1996, the myth that Kennewick Man might have been European never quite died out. The reconstructed skull confirms that he was not—and Chatters never seriously thought otherwise. "I tried my damnedest to curtail that business about Caucasians in America early," he says. "I'm not talking about today's Caucasians. I'm saying they had 'Caucasoid-like' characteristics. There's a big difference." Says Owsley: "[Kennewick Man] is not North American looking, and he's not tied in to Siberian or Northeast Asian populations. He looks more Polynesian or more like the Ainu [an ethnic group that is now found only in northern Japan but in prehistoric times lived throughout coastal areas of eastern Asia] or southern Asians."

That assessment will be tested more rigorously when researchers compare Kennewick Man's skull with databases of several thousand other skulls, both modern and ancient. But provisionally, at least, the evidence fits in with a revolutionary new picture that over the past decade has utterly transformed anthropologists' long-held theories about the colonization of the Americas.

Who Really Discovered America?

The conventional answer to that question dates to the early 1930s, when stone projectile points that were nearly identical began to turn up at sites across the American Southwest. They suggested a single cultural tradition that was christened Clovis, after an 11,000-year-old-plus site near Clovis, N.M. And because no older sites were known to exist in the Americas, scientists assumed that the Clovis people were the first to arrive. They came, according to the theory, no more than 12,000 years B.P. (before the present), walking across the dry land that connected modern Russia and Alaska at the end of the last ice age, when sea level was hundreds of feet lower than it is today. From there, the earliest immigrants would have made their way south through an ice-free corridor that geologists know cut through what are now the Yukon and Mackenzie river valleys, then along the eastern flank of the Canadian Rockies to the continental U.S. and on to Latin America.

That's the story textbooks told for decades—and it's almost certainly wrong. The first cracks in the theory began appearing in the 1980s, when archaeologists discovered sites in both North and South America that seemed to predate the Clovis culture. Then came genetic and linguistic analyses suggesting that Asian and Native American populations diverged not 12,000 years ago but closer to 30,000 years ago. Studies of ancient skulls hinted that the earliest Americans in South America had different ancestors from those in the North. Finally, it began to be clear that artifacts from Northeast Asia dating from just before the Clovis period and South American artifacts of comparable age didn't have much in common with Clovis artifacts.

Those discoveries led to all sorts of competing theories, but few archaeologists or anthropologists took them seriously until 1997. In that year, a blue-ribbon panel of researchers took a hard look at evidence presented by Tom Dillehay, then at the University of Kentucky, from a site he had been excavating in Monte Verde, Chile. After years of skepticism, the panel finally affirmed his claim that the site proved humans had lived there 12,500 years ago. "Monte Verde was the turning point," says David Meltzer, a professor of prehistory at Southern Methodist University in Dallas who was on the panel. "It broke the Clovis barrier."

Why? Because if people were living in southern Chile 12,500 years ago, they must have crossed over from Asia considerably earlier, and that means they couldn't have used the ice-free inland corridor; it didn't yet exist. "You could walk to Fairbanks," says Meltzer. "It was getting south from Fairbanks that was a problem." Instead, many scientists now believe, the earliest Americans traveled down the Pacific coast—possibly even using boats. The idea has been around for a long time, but few took it seriously before Monte Verde.

One who did was Jon Erlandson, an archaeologist at the University of Oregon, whose work in Daisy Cave on San Miguel Island in California's Channel Island chain uncovered stone cutting tools that date to about 10,500 years B.P., proving that people were traveling across the water at least that early. More recently, researchers at the Santa Barbara Museum of Natural History redated the skeletal remains of an individual dubbed Arlington Springs Woman, found on another of the Channel Islands, pushing her age back to about 11,000 years B.P. Farther south, on Cedros Island off the coast of Baja California, U.C. at Riverside researchers found shell middens—heaps of kitchen waste, essentially—and other materials that date back to the same period as Daisy Cave. Down in the Andes, researchers have found coastal sites with shell middens dating to about 10,500 years B.P.

And in a discovery that offers a sharp contrast to the political hoopla over Kennewick Man, scientists and local Tlingit and Haida tribes cooperated so that researchers could study skeletal remains found in On Your Knees Cave on Prince of Wales Island in southern Alaska. "There's no controversy," says Erlandson, who has investigated cave sites in the same region. "It hardly ever hits the papers." Of about the same vintage as Kennewick Man and found at around the same time, the Alaskan bones, along with other artifacts in the area, lend strong support to the coastal-migration theory. "Isotopic analysis of the human remains," says James Dixon, the University of Colorado at Boulder anthropologist who found them, "demonstrates that the individual—a young male in his early 20s—was raised primarily on a diet of seafood."

Cruising Down the Kelp Highway

Erlandson has found one more line of evidence that supports the migration theory. While working with a group of marine ecologists, he was startled to learn that there were nearly continuous kelp forests growing just offshore all the way from Japan in the western Pacific to Alaska and down the West Coast to Baja California, then (with a gap in the tropics) off the coast of South America. In a paper presented three weeks ago, he outlined the potential importance to the earliest Americans of what he calls the "kelp highway."

"Most of the early sites on the west coast are found adjacent to kelp forests, even in Peru and Chile," he says. "The thing about kelp forests is they're extremely productive." They not only provide abundant food, from fish, shellfish, seals and otters that thrive there, but they also reduce wave energy, making it easier to navigate offshore waters. By contrast, the inland route along the ice-free corridor would have presented travelers with enormous ecological variability, forcing them to adapt to new conditions and food sources as they traveled.

Unfortunately, the strongest evidence for the coastal theory lies offshore, where ancient settlements would have been submerged by rising seas over the past 10,000 years or so. "Artifacts have been found on the continental shelves," says Dixon, "so I'm quite confident there's material out there." But you need submersible craft to search, and, he says, that type of research is a very hard sell to the people who own and operate that kind of equipment. "The maritime community is interested in shipwrecks and treasures. A little bit of charcoal and some rocks on the ocean floor is not very exciting to them."

Multiple Migrations

Even if the earliest Americans traveled down the coast, that doesn't mean they couldn't have come through the interior as well. Could there have been multiple waves of migration along a variety of different routes? One way scientists have tried to get a handle on that question is through genetics. Their studies have focused on two different types of evidence extracted from the cells of modern Native Americans: mitochondrial DNA, which resides outside the nuclei of cells and is passed down only through the mother; and the Y chromosome, which is passed down only from father to son. Since DNA changes subtly over the generations, it serves as a sort of molecular clock, and by measuring differences between populations, you can gauge when they were part of the same group.

Or at least you can try. Those molecular clocks are still rather crude. "The mitochondrial DNA signals a migration up to 30,000 years ago," says research geneticist Michael Hammer of the University of Arizona. "But the Y suggests that it occurred within the last 20,000 years." That's quite a discrepancy. Nevertheless, Hammer believes that the evidence is consistent with a single pulse of migration.

Theodore Schurr, director of the University of Pennsylvania's Laboratory of Molecular Anthropology, thinks there could have been many migrations. "It looks like there may have been one primary migration, but certain genetic markers are more prevalent in North America than in South America," Schurr explains, suggesting secondary waves. At this point, there's no definitive proof of either idea, but the evidence and logic lean toward multiple migrations. "If one migration made it over," Dillehay, now at Vanderbilt University, asks rhetorically, "why not more?"

Out of Siberia?

Genetics also points to an original homeland for the first Americans—or at least it does to some researchers. "Skeletal remains are very rare, but the genetic evidence suggests they came from the Lake Baikal region" of Russia, says anthropologist Ted Goebel of the University of Nevada at Reno, who has worked extensively in that part of southern Siberia. "There is a rich archaeological record there," he says, "beginning about 40,000 years ago." Based on what he and Russian colleagues have found, Goebel speculates that there were two northward migratory pulses, the first between 28,000 and 20,000 years ago and a second sometime after 17,000 years ago. "Either one could have led to the peopling of the Americas," he says.

Like just about everything else about the first Americans, however, this idea is open to vigorous debate. The Clovis-first theory is pretty much dead, and the case for coastal migration appears to be getting stronger all the time. But in a field so recently liberated from a dogma that has kept it in an intellectual straitjacket since Franklin Roosevelt was President, all sorts of ideas are suddenly on the table. Could prehistoric Asians, for example, have sailed directly across the Pacific to South America? That may seem far-fetched, but scientists know that people sailing from Southeast Asia reached Australia some 60,000 years ago. And in 1947 the explorer Thor Heyerdahl showed it was possible to travel across the Pacific by raft in the other direction.

At least a couple of archaeologists, including Dennis Stanford of the Smithsonian, even go so far as to suggest that the earliest Americans came from Europe, not Asia, pointing to similarities between Clovis spear points and blades from France and Spain dating to between 20,500 and 17,000 years B.P. (Meltzer, Goebel and another colleague recently published a paper calling this an "outrageous hypothesis," but Dillehay thinks it's possible.)

All this speculation is spurring a new burst of scholarship about locations all over the Americas. The Topper site in South Carolina, Cactus Hill in Virginia, Pennsylvania's Meadowcroft, the Taima-Taima waterhole in Venezuela and several rock shelters in Brazil all seem to be pre-Clovis. Dillehay has found several sites in Peru that date to between 10,000 and 11,000 years B.P. but have no apparent links to the Clovis culture. "They show a great deal of diversity," he says, "suggesting different early sources of cultural development in the highlands and along the coast."

It's only by studying those sites in detail and continuing to search for more evidence on land and offshore that these questions can be fully answered. And as always, the most valuable evidence will be the earthly remains of the ancient people themselves. In one 10-day session, Kennewick Man has added immeasurably to anthropologists' store of knowledge, and the next round of study is already under way. If scientists treat those bones with respect and Native American groups acknowledge the importance of unlocking their secrets, the mystery of how and when the New World was populated may finally be laid to rest.

Critical Thinking

1. What did the bones reveal about Kennewick Man and his burial? What further secrets are yet to be revealed?
2. What was the preliminary assessment regarding his ancestral origins?
3. Why were the Clovis people assumed to be the first Americans for so long? What does the genetic, linguistic, and archaeological evidence now say?
4. What is the "kelp highway" and why does it appear to be the most plausible route to the Americas?
5. What evidence is there for multiple migrations?

Uncovering America's Pyramid Builders

Karen Wright

When U.S. 40 reaches Collinsville, Illinois, the land is flat and open. Seedy storefronts line the highway: a pawnshop, a discount carpet warehouse, a taco joint, a bar. Only the Indian Mound Motel gives any hint that the road bisects something more than underdeveloped farmland. This is the Cahokia Mounds State Historic Site, a United Nations World Heritage Site on a par with the Great Wall of China, the Egyptian pyramids, and the Taj Mahal. The 4,000-acre complex preserves the remnants of the largest prehistoric settlement north of Mexico, a walled city that flourished on the floodplain of the Mississippi River 10 centuries ago. Covering an area more than five miles square, Cahokia dwarfs the ancient pueblos of New Mexico's Chaco Canyon and every other ruin left by the storied Anasazi of the American Southwest. Yet despite its size and importance, archaeologists still don't understand how this vast, lost culture began, how it ended, and what went on in between.

A thousand years ago, no one could have missed Cahokia—a complex, sophisticated society with an urban center, satellite villages, and as many as 50,000 people in all. Thatched-roof houses lined the central plazas. Merchants swapped copper, mica, and seashells from as far away as the Great Lakes and the Gulf of Mexico. Thousands of cooking fires burned night and day. And between A.D 1000 and 1300, Cahokians built more than 120 earthen mounds as landmarks, tombs, and ceremonial platforms. The largest of these monuments, now called Monks Mound, still dominates the site. It is a flat-topped pyramid of dirt that covers more than 14 acres and once supported a 5,000-square-foot temple. Monks Mound is bigger than any of the three great pyramids at Giza outside Cairo. "This is the third or fourth biggest pyramid in the world, in terms of volume," says archaeologist Tim Pauketat of the University of Illinois at Urbana-Champaign. It towers 100 feet over a 40-acre plaza that was surrounded by lesser mounds and a two-mile-long stockade. The monument was the crowning achievement of a mound-building culture that began thousands of years earlier and was never duplicated on this continent.

Why Cahokia crumbled and its people vanished is unknown. Malnutrition, overcrowding, a dwindling resource base, the raids of jealous trade partners—any or all of these reasons may have contributed to the city's demise. No one knows whether the populace cleared out all at once or dispersed gradually, but by A.D 1300 Cahokia was a ghost town. By the time Europeans arrived in the Mississippi bottomland, the region was only sparsely settled, and none of the native residents could recount what had happened there centuries before. So far, archaeologists have uncovered no evidence of invasion, rampant disease, overpopulation, deforestation, or any of the other hallmarks of the decline and fall of civilization. Cahokia abounds in artifacts, but archaeologists have not yet made sense of them in a meaningful way. "It actually becomes quite scary," says John Kelly of Washington University in St. Louis. "After a while you begin to realize that you're dealing with rituals that had a great deal of meaning 800 years ago and that you're kind of clueless."

Intellectual frustration is not the only reason for Cahokia's obscurity. Pauketat complains that the region is geographically challenged. It has the look and feel of a place "like Buffalo, except warmer," he says. Cahokia doesn't exactly lure others away from more exotic digs in Turkey, Mexico, or Peru, he says. "That's the problem with this site." Another reason for its lack of popularity is the ordinary, perishable building materials used by the residents. "Cahokians are discounted because they built with dirt—dirt and wood, things they valued," says Pauketat. "I get tired of hearing people say, 'We have civilization and you guys don't.'"

Meanwhile, developers see Cahokia as ripe for expansion; strip malls and subdivisions threaten on every side. "It's developing faster than we can survey," Pauketat says. "We don't know what we're losing out there." Although a good portion of the central city is now protected, archaeologists are discovering related sites throughout a six-county region on both sides of the nearby Mississippi—an area 3,600 miles square. Indeed, digs are under way in such unlikely places as a railroad yard eight miles west in East St. Louis, where a new bridge is scheduled. "If you want to find out the archaeology of an area," says Brad Koldehoff of the Illinois Department of Transportation's archaeology team, "build a road through it."

One morning last September, a warm red sun rose behind Monks Mound, inching above the level terrace where a tribal palace once stood, burning the mist off the flat green expanses of former plazas. To the west of the mound, in a circle more than 400 feet in diameter, several dozen cedar posts rise to the height of telephone poles. The woodhenge, as the structure is known, is a reconstruction of a series of circles found in the 1960s and '70s when excavations to build a mammoth cloverleaf joining three interstate highways unearthed the remains of several hundred houses and dozens of post pits. (The findings persuaded the Federal Highway Administration to relocate the cloverleaf a few miles north.)

At the autumnal equinox, the rising sun aligns exactly with one post when viewed from the center of the circle, just as it does at the spring equinox and the solstices. William Iseminger, assistant site manager for the Cahokia Mounds State Historic Society, takes these alignments as evidence that the posts may have functioned as a kind of calendar, marking the turn of the seasons. Other woodhenges may have been part of lesser mounds, but, says Iseminger, they are nearly impossible to find because the post pits are so far apart, and wood rarely survives centuries underground.

Many archaeologists point to the size and ambition of structures like the woodhenge as evidence of Cahokia's sophistication. The construction of Monks Mound, for example, used between 15 billion and 20 billion pounds of soil, which were lugged to the site in woven baskets that held 50 to 60 pounds of dirt each. Grading and draining the 40-acre plaza in front of it meant moving just as much earth. The stockade walls consumed 20,000 trees. Subsidiary mounds in the city "grid" seem to be placed according to a rational design. These accomplishments imply organized feats of labor and planning enacted by a central authority.

In many excavations, the number of artifacts and the amount of refuse indicate the population spiked sharply around A.D 1100, jumping from hundreds to perhaps tens of thousands of people. Large homes and mounds appeared where villages of small houses had existed just a generation before. In the mid-1990s, excavations by Pauketat, Kelly, and others showed that the hills east of Cahokia were far more populous than anyone had suspected. A wooded rise among farmhouses in the city of O'Fallon marks the site of an ancient acropolis that probably served more than 500 people. At a site south of O'Fallon, Pauketat found remnants of 80 houses, three temples, clay pots, hoe blades, ax heads, and carved redstone statues. On a tree-lined street in Lebanon, a flagpole is planted in the center of a former platform mound marking another temple center.

Based on these findings, Pauketat estimates that as many as 50,000 people may have lived in Cahokia's greater metropolitan area at the settlement's peak. They seem to have appeared as if from nowhere. "Cahokia had to be created by large-scale migration from other places," says Tom Emerson, director of the state transportation department's archaeological program. "Nobody can breed that fast."

Why did migrants come to Cahokia? Past theories suggested that the dual forces of nature and commerce drove the city's rapid growth. The fertile bottomland was ripe for cultivation by farmers skilled in raising corn, squash, and sunflowers. The nearby confluence of the Illinois, Missouri, and Mississippi rivers could have put Cahokia at the nexus of trade networks that spanned much of the continent. But American Indians had been building modest mounds in the Mississippi River valley since 3500 B.C.; they'd been growing corn with much the same tools for hundreds of years, and the rivers and flood-plains had been there for thousands. Economic and geographic felicities alone cannot account for the sudden concentration of people in the area at a particular moment.

Pauketat has come to believe that charismatic leaders created a dynamic social movement with Cahokia at the epicenter, luring inhabitants of far-flung communities away from their home-steads to the fast urban action. Pauketat resists the term *cult,* but it evokes the phenomenon he envisions. "There were certainly individuals who were movers and shakers, but they weren't consciously, deliberately exploiting people," he asserts.

"Cahokia is a political construct," Emerson adds. "It's not due to some massive change in subsistence, it's not archaeological, it's not technological. It's the kind of place that results from changes in how you conduct yourself socially and politically. What happened at Cahokia is politics, probably in the guise of religion."

Not all scholars see a burgeoning statehood in Cahokia's remains. Anthropologist George Milner of Pennsylvania State University believes there were at most 8,000 people at Cahokia, and he calculates that with even half that population one person per household working just a few weeks a year could have built Monks Mound. The construction would have proceeded at a desultory pace, he concedes; it may have required hundreds of years to complete. Only if the woodhenges and mounds were rapidly constructed would they require full-time laborers or engineers. And he is skeptical that the ecology of the region, abundant as it was, could have supported a community as vast as that supposed by Pauketat and others.

The trump card for Milner and other minimalists is the fact that, unlike the ancient Mesopotamians, Maya, Egyptians, and Chinese, Cahokians never developed a written counterpart to their spoken language. Writing is generally considered a prerequisite for the kind of record keeping typical of organized governments. (The names "Cahokia" and "Monks Mound" were applied long after the fact: Cahokia was the name of an Illini tribe that occupied the area in the 1600s, and Monks Mound was named for French Trappists who settled on one of its terraces in the 1800s.)

But champions of an advanced Cahokian civilization would rather make their case with numbers than with language anyway. Even Milner admits that if Cahokia was as populous or expansive as some claim, it would have exerted statelike control over its citizens. To support his theory, Pauketat is looking for evidence that the settlements outside of Cahokia follow a planned pattern—a support network of communities allied with the power center, perhaps communicating with the capital using runners and smoke signals. He found traces of buildings at the intersection of Routes 159 and 64, now home to a Toys 'R' Us and a Ramada Inn, and he believes they may have faced Cahokia, a six-hour walk away. That orientation would bolster his contention that the outlying villages were all part of one big polity.

Early in his career at the state department of transportation, Tom Emerson found an eight-inch statuette at the site of a temple two or three miles from Cahokia. Five pounds of distinctive redstone called flint clay had been carved into a kneeling female figure sinking a hoe into the back of a serpent. The serpent's tail climbs up the woman's back, bearing squash and gourds like a vine. The images echo familiar pre-Columbian themes of reproductive and agricultural fertility. As similar figures were discovered in the Cahokian environs, a pattern emerged.

Around A.D 1100, Emerson says, the elite of Cahokia seem to have co-opted or codified the fertility symbol, raising it to an unprecedented stature that became a kind of brand identity for the budding metropolis. "They're taking a symbolism that exists across the entire hemisphere and selectively emphasizing parts of it to their own benefit," Emerson says.

Some archaeologists have taken the emphasis on the bucolic feminine as a sign that Cahokian society was peaceful, egalitarian, and possibly matriarchal. There is, in fact, no evidence that the city was ever invaded, and no indication of bellicose tendencies other than the robust stockade surrounding the city center. But Emerson warns against this interpretation. For one thing, he says, war wasn't necessary, because it would have been clear from the city's size alone that it could mount raiding parties with more members than the total of men, women, and children in any of the surrounding villages. "Nobody could stand against Cahokia. I don't know that they had to do much actual conflict. It was mostly intimidation."

Cahokia's downfall has been blamed on a variety of culprits. A corn-based, protein-poor diet might have sent urban dwellers west in search of buffalo. A centuries-long cold spell could have crippled the region's agricultural productivity. Deforestation of the uplands would have choked downstream water supplies with silt and exacerbated flooding. Or the cause could have been those same intangibles invoked by latter-day theorists to describe Cahokia's rise: a shift in belief systems or the balance of power. Certainly the sprawling pacts that Cahokian chiefs may have forged with nearby villages would have challenged any lasting centralization of power.

"The typical life history of a chiefdom is that it comes together, it has its heyday, and it falls apart, all within a couple of generations," says Emerson. "The interesting thing about Cahokia is that it managed to hang together. The fact that it didn't go on forever isn't unusual at all."

One of Cahokia's chiefs appears to be buried in Mound 72, which lies a half mile south of Monks Mound. It is a modest hillock by comparison, but the site holds far grimmer implications about Cahokian society. During excavations there in the late 1960s, Melvin Fowler of the University of Wisconsin at Milwaukee uncovered the remains of more than 250 people. One middle-aged male had been laid on a shelf of 20,000 seashell beads arranged in the shape of a bird. Near him were the bones of six other people, a cache of more than 800 flint arrowheads, a rolled-up sheet of copper, and several bushels of unprocessed mica—all seemingly placed in tribute to the Beaded Birdman.

In other parts of the mound, skeletons of more than 100 young women clearly indicate human sacrifice, and another grouping of four men with no hands or heads denotes the same. Another 40 bodies seemed to have been tossed into a grave haphazardly. Other mass burials in Mound 72 show varying degrees of respect and carelessness—and seem to reflect some sort of social hierarchy as yet undeciphered. Human sacrifice, for example, can be a sign of a coercive society or of a cult-like mentality. "Mound 72 is an ancient text with its own set of Rosetta stones and is slow to give up its secrets," Fowler wrote in *Cahokia,* a book he coauthored with Biloine Whiting Young.

The cause of Cahokia's demise is no more certain, but at least one expert links it to the Toltec civilization of south-central Mexico some 1,400 miles away. Although no Mexican artifacts have ever been found at Cahokia, similarities in the monumental and ornamental styles are conspicuous—and far from accidental, according to anthropologist Stephen Lekson of the University of Colorado at Boulder. Lekson and anthropologist Peter Peregrine of Lawrence University in Wisconsin believe that the mound cultures of the American East, the pueblo cultures of the American Southwest, and the pyramid cultures of the Mexican highlands were not only familiar but possibly even integrated with one another. There's plenty of evidence for such an exchange at Chaco Canyon, where copper bells, macaw feathers, pyrite mirrors, and other Mexican goods turn up. But Chaco was a wannabe compared with Cahokia—much smaller, far less populous, and without a centuries-long tradition preceding its development. Cahokia, with its central location, entrenched culture, and extensive trade network, didn't need Mexican trinkets to bolster its stature, Lekson says. "If someone from Cahokia showed up in any major town in Mexico, he'd be taken seriously," says Lekson. "But if someone from Chaco wandered in, they'd ask him if he had an appointment."

The Toltec, Chaco, and Cahokian societies all collapsed at very nearly the same moment, and Lekson believes that that, too, is no accident. Events in Mexico may have rippled up the Gulf Coast to the Mississippi and thence to Cahokia. "I'm not saying that Mexico is pulling everybody's strings," says Lekson. "But [the cultures] are more alike than not, and it's interesting to ask why."

Interesting as it might be, a continental perspective doesn't yield an explanation, because no one's sure what caused the Toltec regime to fall, either. It may be that if scientists ever determine why Cahokia fell, they may be able to help explain what happened elsewhere in the Americas. At present it's still anyone's guess. "We are telling stories that will fall apart in the future," says Pauketat. "But we can't ignore the evidence, either. You could make the mistake of saying this is a coercive society, based on Mound 72. Or you could look at the outlying villages and say, 'This is a peaceful community.' They must have *wanted* to build Cahokia. The truth may be somewhere in between. We don't really know what happened here."

Critical Thinking

1. Why is Cahokia on a par with the other World Heritage Sites?
2. What is it that archaeologists still don't understand about it?
3. Why does the author describe Cahokia as a "complex, sophisticated society" that "no one could have missed a thousand years ago"?
4. Why is it still unknown as to why Cahokia crumbled and its people vanished?
5. Why is it difficult to lure archaeologists there?
6. Why is economic development a concern?
7. What is the significance of the woodhenge?

8. What are the implications regarding the amount of work devoted to building Cahokia?
9. Why might migrants have come to Cahokia? Why are these theories insufficient, according to the author?
10. What do archaeologists Pauketat, Kelly, and Emerson suggest as an explanation? Why is George Milner skeptical of these views?
11. What "pattern emerged" with respect to the female figurines? How can this be variously interpreted?
12. What theories have been put forth regarding Cahokia's downfall?
13. What seems to be the significance of the burials?
14. Why does there seem to be a connection to the Toltecs of Mexico, which might help to explain Cahokia's downfall? Why would there still be no explanation even if there were a connection?
15. Why is it still as easy to say that Cahokia was peaceful as it is to say that it was a coercive society?

Disease and Death at Dr. Dickson's Mounds

ALAN H. GOODMAN AND GEORGE J. ARMELAGOS

Clustered in west-central Illinois, atop a bluff near the confluence of the Illinois and Spoon rivers, are twelve to thirteen poorly defined earthen mounds. The mounds, which overlap each other to some extent, cover a crescent-shaped area of about an acre. Since at least the middle of the nineteenth century, local residents have known that prehistoric Native Americans built these mounds to bury their dead. But it was not until the late 1920s that Don Dickson, a chiropractor, undertook the first systematic excavation of the mounds located on farmland owned by his father. Barely into his thirties at the time, Dickson became so involved in the venture that he never returned to his chiropractic practice. Apparently, he was intrigued by the novel undertaking of unearthing skeletons and trying to diagnose the maladies of long-dead individuals. Later on, he became more concerned with the patterns of disease and death in this extinct group in order to understand how these people lived and why they often died at an early age.

The "Dickson Mounds" (the site also includes two early, unmounded burial grounds) quickly attracted the attention of professional anthropologists. In the early 1930s, a team of University of Chicago archeologists exposed about 200 of the estimated 3,000 burials and identified a number of settlement sites in a 100-square-mile area. A second phase of excavation at Dickson began in the 1960s under the direction of Alan Harn, an archeologist working for the state of Illinois, whose crew excavated many of the local living sites and more than 800 additional burials. The archeological research revealed that these prehistoric people had taken part in an important transition, from hunting and gathering to an agricultural way of life.

About A.D. 950, hunter-gatherers lived along the Illinois River valley area near Dickson, subsisting on a wide range of local plants and animals, including grasses and seeds, fruits and berries, roots and tubers, vines, herbs, large and small mammals, migratory waterfowl and riverine birds, and fish. The moderate climate, copious water supply, and rich soil made this a bountiful and attractive area for hunter-gatherers. Groups occupied campsites that consisted of a few small structures, and the debris scattered around these sites suggests seasonal use. The population density was low, perhaps on the order of two to three persons per square mile. Then, about 1050, broken hoes and other agricultural tools, as well as maize, began to form part of village refuse, evidence of the introduction of maize agriculture. At the same time, the population grew. By 1200 the population density may have increased by a factor of ten, to about twenty-five persons per square mile. Living sites became larger and more permanent. The largest settlement in the area, Larson, was a residential and ceremonial center where some 1,000 inhabitants lived, many behind a palisaded wall.

Trade also flourished. Dickson became part of what archeologists call the Mississippian tradition, a network of maize-growing, mound-building societies that spread throughout most of the eastern United States. More and more, items used at the village sites or deposited as grave offerings were not of local origin. Some, such as marine shell necklaces, came from as far away as the Gulf of Mexico and Florida, one thousand miles to the south. Everyday objects such as spoons and jars were received from peoples of the eastern plains and the western prairies, while luxury items of ceremonial or decorative value arrived in trade from the south, probably coming upriver to Dickson through Cahokia, a Mississippian center some 110 miles away. Cahokia is a massive site that includes some 120 mounds within a six-square-mile area. As many as 30,000 persons lived at Cahokia and in the surrounding villages.

What we know about Dickson might have ended at this point, but continues because the skeletal remains that Harn excavated have been used to evaluate how the health of these prehistoric people fared following the adoption of agriculture and other changes in their life style. Interest in this issue stems from the writings of the eminent British archeologist V. Gordon Childe (1892–1957), who believed that the development of agriculture prompted the first great revolution in human technology, ushering in fundamental changes in economy, social organization, and ideology. Archeologists continue to debate the causes of agricultural revolutions. For example, some believe that in various regions of the world, increased population pressure, leading to food shortages and declining health, spurred the switch to agricultural food production. Others believe population increase was one of the consequences of agricultural revolutions. More important to us are the effects of an agricultural revolution on the health of people who lived at the time of such change.

Three circumstances have made it possible to test the effects agriculture had upon health at Dickson. First, Harn and those working with him valued the potential information to be gained from skeletons and therefore paid close attention to their excavation. Ultimately, the skeletal remains were sent to the University of Massachusetts at Amherst for analysis by George Armelagos and many of his graduate students (this is how we became involved). Second, the recovered remains include both individuals who lived before the development of maize agriculture (Late Woodland, or pre-Mississippian) and after (Mississippian). The two groups of individuals could be distinguished according to the mounds they were buried in, their placement within each mound, and their burial position (in earlier burials the bodies tend to be in a flexed or semiflexed position; in later burials they tend to be extended). The third enabling condition was provided by Janice Cohen, one of Armelagos's graduate students. Her analysis of highly heritable dental traits showed that although Dickson was in contact with persons from outside the central Illinois River valley area during the period of rapid cultural change, outside groups did not replace or significantly merge with the local groups. It is therefore possible to follow the health over time of a single population that, for all intents and purposes, was genetically stable.

As a doctoral student working under Armelagos in the early 1970s, John Lallo, now at Cleveland State University, set out to test whether health at Dickson improved, got worse, or remained the same with the advent of agriculture and its accompanying changes. Lallo argued that intensification of maize agriculture most likely resulted in a poorer diet. Although a common assumption is that the adoption of agriculture should have provided a prehistoric people with a better diet, there are good reasons to predict just the opposite. Heavy reliance on a single crop may lead to nutritional problems. Maize, for example, is deficient in lysine, an essential amino acid. Furthermore, agricultural societies that subsist on a few foodstuffs are more vulnerable to famines brought about by drought and other disasters. Finally, increased population density, a more sedentary life style, and greater trade, all of which are associated with agriculture, provide conditions for the spread and maintenance of infectious diseases.

The skeletons of individuals who lived before and after the introduction of maize agriculture were examined for a number of different health indicators, in order to provide a balanced picture of the pattern of stress disease, and death that affected the Dickson population. The indicators that proved most sensitive to health differences were: bone lesions (scars) due to infection, nutritional deficiencies, trauma, and degenerative conditions; long bone growth; dental developmental defects; and age at death. To avoid unconscious bias, we and the other researchers involved measured these seven traits without knowing in advance which skeletons came from each of the two cultural periods.

Persistent bacterial infection leaves its mark on the outer, or periosteal, layer of bone. Tibias (shinbones) are the most frequently affected bones because they have relatively poor circulation and therefore tend to accumulate bacteria. Toxins produced by bacteria kill some of the bone cells; as new bone is produced, the periosteal bone becomes roughened and layered. Lallo and his co-workers found that following the introduction of agriculture there was a threefold increase in the percentage of individuals with such lesions. Eighty-four percent of the Mississippian tibias had these "periosteal reactions," as compared with only 26 percent of pre-Mississippian tibias. The lesions also tended to be more severe and to show up in younger individuals in the Mississippian population.

A second type of lesion, more easily seen in the thinner bones of the body (such as those of the skull), is a sign of anemia. In response to anemia, the body steps up its production of red blood cells, which are formed in the bone marrow. To accomplish this the marrow must expand at the expense of the outer layer of bone. In severe cases, this expansion may cause the outer layer of bone to disappear, exposing the porous, sieve-like inner bone. This lesion, called porotic hyperostosis, can occur with any kind of anemia. In the Dickson Mounds populations, the lesions are not severe, are restricted to the eye sockets and crania, and occur mainly in children and young adult females. This pattern suggests anemia resulting from a nutritional deficiency, specifically an iron deficiency. (A hereditary anemia, such as sickle-cell anemia, would have been more severe in its manifestation and would have affected all ages and both sexes in the population.)

There is a significant increase in the frequency of porotic hyperostosis during the Mississippian period. Half the Mississippian infants and children had porotic hyperostosis, twice the rate found for pre-Mississippian infants and children. Individuals with both periosteal reactions and porotic hyperostosis tend to have suffered more severely from each condition. This may be evidence of a deadly synergism of malnutrition and infection, like that often reported among contemporary populations.

Traumatic lesions were measured by diagnosis of healed fractures of the long bones of the legs and arms. Adult males had the highest frequency of such fractures. Approximately one out of three Mississippian males had at least one fracture, twice the frequency of their predecessors. These fractures often occurred at the midshaft of the ulna and radius, the bones of the lower arm. Fractures at this location are called parry fractures because they are typically the result of efforts to ward off a blow.

The frequency of degenerative pathologies, including arthritic conditions found on joints and the contacting surfaces of the vertebral column, also increased through time. One or more degenerative conditions were diagnosed in 40 percent of pre-Mississippian adults but in more than 70 percent of Mississippian adults.

In addition to the studies of the changing pattern of disease and trauma, we, along with Lallo and Jerome Rose, now at the University of Arkansas, assessed differences in skeletal growth and developmental timing. Skeletal growth and development are susceptible to a wide variety of stressful conditions and therefore reflect overall health. We found that in comparison to pre-Mississippians of the same age, Mississippian children between the ages of five and ten had significantly shorter and narrower tibias and femurs (the major long bones of the legs).

This difference may be explained by a decreased rate of growth before the age of five. The Mississippians apparently were able to catch up in growth after age ten, however, since adult Mississippians are only slightly smaller than pre-Mississippians.

A more detailed exploration of developmental changes came from studying defects in enamel, the hard white coating of the crowns of teeth. Ameloblasts, the enamel-forming cells, secrete enamel matrix in ringlike fashion, starting at the biting surface and ending at the bottom of the crown. A deficiency in enamel thickness, called a hypoplasia, may result if the individual suffers a systemic physiological stress during enamel formation. Since the timing of enamel secretion is well known and relatively stable, the position of such a lesion on a tooth corresponds to an individual's age at the time of stress.

We examined the permanent teeth—teeth that form between birth and age seven. For skeletons with nearly complete sets of permanent teeth, 55 percent of pre-Mississippians had hypoplasias, while among Mississippians the figure rose to 80 percent. In both groups, hypoplasias were most frequently laid down between the ages of one and one-half and four. However, the hypoplasias in the Mississippian group peak at age two and one-half, approximately one-half year earlier than the pre-Mississippian peak. The peak is also more pronounced. This pattern of defects may indicate both an earlier age at weaning and the use of cereal products as weanling foods.

The repeated occurrence of hypoplasias within individuals revealed an annual cycle of stress. Most likely there was a seasonal food shortage. This seems to have worsened in the period just before the population becomes completely "Mississippianized," suggesting that it provided a rationale for intensifying agriculture.

All the above six indicators point toward a decrease in health associated with cultural change at Dickson. However, they are not meaningful apart from an analysis of the pattern of death in these populations. Healthy-looking skeletons, for example, may be the remains of young individuals who died outright because their bodies were too weak to cope in the face of disease, injury, and other forms of stress. Conversely skeletons that show wear and tear may be those of individuals who survived during stressful times and lived to a ripe old age.

At Dickson, however, the trend is unambiguous. Individuals whose skeletons showed more signs of stress and disease (for example, enamel hypoplasias) also lived shorter lives, on average, than individuals with fewer such indications. For the population as a whole, life expectancy at birth decreased from twenty-six years in the pre-Mississippian to nineteen years in the Mississippian. The contrast in mortality is especially pronounced during the infant and childhood years. For example, 22 percent of Mississippians died during their first year as compared to 13 percent of the pre-Mississippians. Even for those who passed through the dangerous early years of childhood, there is a differential life expectancy. At fifteen years of age, pre-Mississippians could expect to live for an average of twenty-three more years, while Mississippians could expect to live for only eighteen more years.

What caused this decline in health? A number of possibilities have been proposed. Lallo and others have emphasized the effect of agriculture on diet. Most of the health trends may be explained by a decline in diet quality. These include the trends in growth, development, mortality, and nutritional disease, all four of which have obvious links to nutrition. The same explanation may be offered for the increase in infectious diseases, since increased susceptibility may be due to poor nutrition. Furthermore, a population subject to considerable infectious disease would be likely to suffer from other conditions, including increased rates of anemia and mortality and decreased growth rates.

The link between diet and infectious disease is bolstered by an analysis of trace elements from tibial bone cores. Robert Gilbert found that the Mississippian bones contain less zinc, an element that is limited in maize. Building on this research, Wadia Bahou, now a physician in Ann Arbor, Michigan, showed that the skeletons with the lowest levels of zinc had the highest frequency of infectious lesions. This is strong evidence that a diet of maize was relied on to a point where health was affected.

The population increase associated with the changeover to agriculture probably also contributed to the decline in health. We do not believe that the population ever threatened to exceed the carrying capacity of the bountiful Dickson area (and there are no signs of the environmental degradation one would expect to find if resources were overexploited). However, increased population density and sedentariness, coupled with intensification of contact with outsiders, create opportunities for the spread of infectious disease. George Milner of the University of Kentucky, while still a graduate student at Northwestern University, argued this point in comparing Dickson with the Kane Mounds populations. Kane is located near Cahokia, the major center south of Dickson. Despite Kane's proximity to this large center, its population density was much lower than at Larson, the major agricultural village of the Dickson population. Of the two, Kane had the lower rate of infectious diseases.

While the "agricultural hypothesis," including the effects of population pressure, offers an explanation for much of the health data, it doesn't automatically account for the two remaining measures: degenerative and traumatic pathologies. Poor nutrition and infectious disease may make people more susceptible to degenerative disease. However, the arthritic conditions found in the Dickson skeletons, involving movable joints, were probably caused by strenuous physical activity. The link, then, is not with the consumption of an agricultural diet but, if anything, with the physically taxing work of agricultural production. An explanation for the increase in traumatic injuries is harder to imagine. Possibly, the increased population density caused social tension and strife to arise within communities, but why should this have happened?

A curious fact makes us think that explanation based only on agricultural intensification and population increase are missing an important contributing factor. Recent archeological research at Dickson suggests that hunting and gathering remained productive enterprises and were never completely abandoned. Many of the local Mississippian sites have a great concentration of animal bones and projectile points used for hunting. A balanced diet apparently was available. The health and trace element data, however, suggest that the Mississippian diet was deficient. There is a disparity between what was available and what was eaten.

At present our search for an explanation for this paradox centers on the relationship between Dickson and the Cahokia population. The builders of the Dickson Mounds received many items of symbolic worth from the Cahokia region, such as copper-covered ear spools and marine shell necklaces. Much of the health data would be explained if Dickson had been trading perishable foodstuffs for these luxury items. In particular, the diversion of meat or fish to Cahokia would explain the apparent discrepancy between diet and resources.

To have a food surplus to trade, individuals from the Dickson area may have intensified their agricultural production while continuing to hunt and gather. The increase in degenerative conditions could have resulted from such a heavy workload. The system may also have put social strain on the community, leading to internal strife. And the accumulation of wealth in terms of ceremonial or other luxury items may have necessitated protection from outside groups. This would explain why the Larson site was palisaded. Both internal and external strain may have led to the increase in traumatic pathologies.

To test the validity of this scenario, we are hoping to gather additional evidence, concentrating on an analysis of trade. The flow of perishable goods such as meat is hard to trace, but we can study the sets of animal bones found at Cahokia and at Dickson village and butchering sites. The distribution of animal bones at the archeological sites can then be compared with examples of bone distributions in areas where trading has been ethnographically recorded. Further evidence is provided by data such as Milner's, which showed that health at Kane—a community that shared in Cahokia's power—was better than at Dickson.

The trading of needed food for items of symbolic value, to the point where health is threatened, may not seem to make sense from an objective outsider's perspective. But it is a situation that has been observed in historic and modern times. An indigenous group learns that it can trade something it has access to (sugar cane, alpacas, turtles) for something it greatly admires but can only obtain from outside groups (metal products, radios, alcohol). The group's members do not perceive that the long-term health and economic results of such trade are usually unfavorable. Nor are all such arrangements a result of voluntary agreement. The pattern of health observed at Dickson is seen in most situations where there is a decline in access to, and control over, resources. For example, lower classes in stratified societies live shorter lives and suffer more from nearly all major diseases.

Agriculture is not invariably associated with declining health. A recent volume edited by Mark N. Cohen and George J. Armelagos, *Paleopathology and the Origins of Agriculture,* analyzed health changes in twenty-three regions of the world where agriculture developed. In many of these regions there was a clear, concurrent decline in health, while in others there was little or no change or slight improvements in health. Perhaps a decline is more likely to occur when agriculture is intensified in the hinterland of a political system. Groups living far away from the centers of trade and power are apt to be at a disadvantage. They may send the best fruits of their labors to market and receive little in return. And during times of economic hardship or political turmoil, they may be the ones to suffer the most, as resources are concentrated on maintaining the central parts of the system.

Critical Thinking

1. Why was the area around Dickson suitable for hunter-gatherers? How does the author describe their circumstances?
2. How did Dickson become part of the "Mississippian tradition"?
3. Of the issues surrounding the agricultural revolution, which is the most important to the authors?
4. What three circumstances made it possible to test the effects of agriculture upon health at Dickson?
5. Why might one predict that the development of agriculture would lead to a poorer diet?
6. What health indicators were used? How was bias avoided?
7. What are the symptoms of persistent bacterial infection and why? What did Lallo and his co-workers find?
8. Why was there an increase in porotic hyperostosis?
9. To what extent did Mississippian males suffer fractures of the ulna and radius? Why are these called "parry fractures"?
10. To what extent were there degenerative pathologies such as arthritis?
11. What was found with respect to skeletal growth and development?
12. How do the authors explain the increased hypoplasia?
13. What are the relationships between decrease in health and rates of life expectancy?
14. Why do the authors think diet caused the decline in health?
15. How is the link between diet and infectious disease bolstered?
16. How do the authors explain the link between population increase and infectious disease?
17. What hypotheses do the authors put forth to explain the degenerative and traumatic pathologies such as arthritis?
18. Is agriculture invariably associated with declining health? Under what circumstances might there be such a relationship, according to the authors?

Article 11

A Coprological View of Ancestral Pueblo Cannibalism

Debate over a single fecal fossil offers a cautionary tale of the interplay between science and culture.

KARL J. REINHARD

As the object of my scientific study, I've chosen coprolites. It's not a common choice, but to a paleonutritionist and archaeoparasitologist, a coprolite—a sample of ancient feces preserved by mineralization or simple drying—is a scientific bonanza. Analysis of coprolites can shed light on both the nutrition of and parasites found in prehistoric cultures. Dietary reconstructions from the analysis of coprolites can inform us about, for example, the origins of modern Native American diabetes. With regard to parasitology; coprolites hold information about the ancient emergence and spread of human infectious disease. Most sensational, however, is the recent role of coprolite analysis in debates about cannibalism.

Most Americans know the people who lived on the Colorado Plateau from 1200 B.C. onward as the Anasazi, a Navajo (or Dine) word. The modern Pueblo people in Arizona and New Mexico, who are their direct descendants, prefer the description Ancestral Pueblo or Old Ones. Because the image of this modern culture could be tainted by the characterization of their ancestors, it's especially important that archaeologists and physical anthropologists come to the correct conclusion about cannibalism. This is the story of my involvement in that effort.

When a coprolite arrived in my laboratory for analysis in 1997, I didn't imagine that it would become one of the most contentious finds in archaeological history. Banks Leonard, the Soil Systems archaeologist who directed excavation of the site at Cowboy Wash, Utah, explained to me that there was evidence of unusual dietary activity by the prehistoric individual who deposited the coprolite. He or she was possibly a cannibal.

I had been aware of the cannibalism controversy for a number of years, and I was interested in evaluating evidence of such activity. But from my scientific perspective, it was simply another sample that would provide a few more data points in my reconstruction of ancient diet from a part of the Ancestral Pueblo region that was unknown to me.

The appearance of the coprolite was unremarkable—in fact, it was actually a little disappointing. It looked like a plain cylinder of tan dirt with no obvious macrofossils or visible dietary inclusions. I have analyzed hundreds of Ancestral and pre-Ancestral Pueblo coprolites that were more interesting. Indeed, I have surveyed tens of thousands more that, to my experienced eye, held greater scientific promise. Yet this one coprolite, when news of it hit the media, undid 20 years of my research on the Ancestral Pueblo diet. On a broader scale, it caused the archaeological community to rethink our perception of the nature of this prehistoric culture and to question what is reasonable scientific proof.

Cannibalism, Without Question

In the arid environment of the U.S. Southwest, feces dried in ancient times provide a 9,000-year record of gastronomic traditions. This record allows me and a few other thick-skinned researchers to trace dietary history in the deserts. (I say "thick-skinned," because analysts generally don't last long in this specialty. Many have done one coprolite study, only to move on to a more socially acceptable archaeological specialty.)

From the mid-1980s to the mid-'90s, I had characterized the Ancestral Pueblo lifestyle as a combination of hunting and gathering mixed with agriculture based on the analysis of about 500 coprolites from half a dozen sites. Before me, Gary Fry, then at Youngstown State University, had come to the same conclusion in work he published during the '70s and '80s, based on the analysis of a large number of Ancestral Pueblo coprolites from many sites. These people were finely attuned to the diverse and complicated habitats of the Colorado Plateau for plant gathering, as well as for plant cultivation. The Ancestral Pueblo certainly ate meat—many kinds of meat—but never had there been any indication of cannibalism in any coprolite analysis from any site.

The evidence for cannibalism at Cowboy Wash has been widely published. A small number of people were undoubtedly killed, disarticulated and their flesh exposed to heat and boiling. This took place in a pit house typical of the Ancestral Pueblo circa 1200 A.D. At the time of the killings, the appearance of the pit house must have been appallingly gruesome. Human blood residue was found on stone tools, and I imagine that the disarticulation of the corpses must have left a horrifying splatter of blood around the room. But the most conclusive evidence of cannibalism did not come from the room where the corpses were dismembered. It came from a nearby room where someone had defecated on the hearth around the time that the killings took place. The feces was preserved as a coprolite and would turn out to be the conclusive evidence of cannibalism.

My analysis of the coprolite was not momentous. I could determine from its general morphology that it was indeed from a human being. However, the tiny fragment that I rehydrated and examined by several microscopic techniques contained none of the typical plant foods eaten by the Ancestral Pueblo. Background pollen of the sort that would have been inhaled or drunk was the only plant residue that I found. Thus, I concluded that the coprolite did not represent normal Ancestral Pueblo diet. It seemed to represent a purely meat meal, something that is unheard of from Ancestral Pueblo coprolite analyses.

After analyzing the Cowboy Wash coprolite, I took a half-year sabbatical as a Fulbright scholar in Brazil. When I returned, I learned that my analysis had been superseded by a new technology. Richard Marlar from the University of Colorado School of Medicine and colleagues had taken over direct analysis of the coprolite using an enzyme-linked immunosorbent assay to detect human myoglobin, and their work had confirmed and expanded my analysis. The coprolite was from a human who had eaten another human. The technical paper appeared in *Nature* and was followed by articles in the *New Yorker, Discover, Southwestern Lore* and the *Smithsonian,* among many others. The articles became the focus of a veritable explosion of media pieces in the press, on radio and television, and on the Internet, amounting to an absolute attack on Ancestral Pueblo culture.

Initially, I sat and watched the media feeding frenzy and Internet chat debates with a sense of awe and post-sabbatical detachment. My original report suggesting the coprolite was not of Ancestral Pueblo origin went largely unnoticed. The few journalists who did call me for an opinion proved uninterested in publishing it. In some cases it was too far to fly to Nebraska to film; in others my opinion didn't fit into the context of the debate. Well, I have looked at more Ancestral Pueblo feces than any other human being, and I do have an opinion: The Ancestral Pueblo were not cannibalistic. Cannibalism just doesn't make sense as a pattern of diet for people so exquisitely adapted to droughts by centuries of hunting-gathering traditions and agricultural innovation.

Then a media quote knocked me out of my stupor. Arizona State University anthropologist (emeritus) Christy G. Turner II, commenting in an interview about a book he co-authored on Ancestral Pueblo cannibalism, said, "I'm the guy who brought down the Anasazi." Perhaps to temper Turner's broad generalization, Brian Billman (a coauthor of the Marlar *Nature* paper) of the University of North Carolina at Chapel Hill, suggested that a period of drought brought on emergency conditions that resulted in cannibalism. Beyond the scientific quibbling about who ate whom and why, I am amazed at the vortex of debate around the Coyote Wash coprolite. The furor over that one coprolite represents a new way of thinking about the Ancestral Pueblo and archaeological evidence.

What Did the Ancestral Pueblo Eat?

To me, a specialist in Ancestral Pueblo diet, neither Turner's nor Billman's explanation made sense. So, in the years since the *Nature* paper appeared in 2000, I have renewed my analyses of Ancestral Pueblo coprolites to understand just what they did eat in times of drought. And let me say emphatically that Ancestral Pueblo coprolites are not composed of the flesh of their human victims. Some of their dietary practices were, perhaps, peculiar. I still recall in wonderment the inch-diameter deer vertebral centrum that I found in one sample. It was swallowed whole. The consumption of insects, snakes and lizards brought the Ancestral Pueblo notice in the children's book *It Was Disgusting and I Ate It.* But looking beyond such peculiarities, their diet was delightfully diverse and testifies to the human ability to survive in the most extreme environments. To me, diet is one of the most fundamental bases of civilization, and the Ancestral Pueblo possessed a complicated cuisine. They were gastronomically civilized.

Widespread analysis of coprolites by "paleoscatologists" began in the 1960s and culminated in the '70s and '80s when graduate students worked staunchly on their coprological theses and dissertations. From Washington State University to Northern Arizona University to Texas A & M and many more, Ancestral Pueblo coprolites were rehydrated, screened, centrifuged and analyzed. Richard Hevly, Glenna Williams-Dean, John Jones, Mark Stiger, Linda Scott-Cummings, Kate Aasen, Gary Fry, Karen Clary, Molly Toll and Vaughn Bryant, Jr., to name a few, joined me in puzzling over Ancestral Pueblo culinary habits. In their conscientious and rigorous research, the same general theme emerged. The Ancestral Pueblo were very well adapted to the environment, both in times of feast and in times of famine.

In general, the Ancestral Pueblo diet was the culmination of a long period of victual tradition that began around 9,000 years ago, when people on the Colorado Plateau gave up hunting big animals and started collecting plants and hunting smaller animals. Prickly pear cactus, yucca, grain from dropseed grass, seeds from goosefoot and foods from 15 other wild plants dominated pre-Ancestral Pueblo life. One of the truly interesting dietary patterns that emerged in the early time and continued through the Ancestral Pueblo culture was the consumption of pollen-rich foods. Cactus and yucca buds and other flowers were the sources of this pollen. Rabbit viscera probably provided a source of fungal spores of the genus *Endogane,* although I doubt that these people knew they were eating the spores when they ate the rabbits. The pre-Ancestral Pueblo people adapted to starvation from seasonal food shortages by eating yucca leaf bases and prickly pear pads and the few other plants that were available in such lean times.

Prey for the pre-Ancestral Pueblo people included small animals such as rabbits, lizards, mice and insects. In tact, most pre-Ancestral Pueblo coprolites contain the remains of small animals. My analysis of these remains shows that small animals, especially rabbits and mice, were a major source of protein in summer and winter, good times and bad.

The Ancestral Pueblo *per se* descended from this hunter-gatherer tradition. Coprolite analysis shows that they were largely vegetarian, and plant foods of some sort are present in every Ancestral Pueblo coprolite I have analyzed. But these later people also expanded on their predecessors' cuisine. They cultivated maize, squash and eventually beans. Yet they continued to collect a wide diversity of wild plants. They actually ate more species of wild plants—more than 50—than their ancestors who were totally dependent on wild species.

Adapting to the Environment

In 1992, I presented a series of hypotheses addressing why the Ancient Pueblo ate so many species of wild plants. Later, Mark Stiger of Western State College and I went to work on the problem using a statistical method that he devised. We determined that the Ancestral Pueblo encouraged the growth of edible weedy species in the disturbances caused by cultivation and village life. In doing so, they increased the spectrum of wild edible plants available to them, often using them to spice cultivated plants. Rocky Mountain beeweed, purslane and groundcherry were especially important in conjunction with maize. Corn smut was another important condiment. In fact, maize, purslane, beeweed and corn smut appear as the earliest components of a distinct cuisine in the earliest Ancestral Pueblo coprolites I have analyzed, from Turkey Pen Cave, Utah. These coprolites are about 1,500 years old. The maize-beeweed-corn smut-purslane association remained a central feature of Ancestral Pueblo cuisine at most sites to the latest periods of the culture. Importantly, they also ate wild plants to offset seasonal shortages, especially in winter when their stores of cultivated food were exhausted. Thus, retaining a diverse array of wild plants in the mix helped them adapt to food shortages.

Paul Minnis of the University of Oklahoma applied a different statistical test to address a different problem. He analyzed coprolite findings from Arizona, New Mexico, Utah and Colorado to see if people in different regions had distinct dietary traditions. Paul showed that the Ancient Pueblo adapted to the environmental variability of the Colorado Plateau by adjusting their agricultural, hunting and gathering habits to the natural resources available. Ancient Pueblo from Glen Canyon, Utah, had a slightly different dietary tradition from those of Inscription House, Arizona; those of Mesa Verde, Colorado; and those of Chaco Canyon, New Mexico. Later, in separate work, he identified how these people adapted to bad times. He found that the Ancestral Pueblo had "starvation foods," such as yucca and prickly pear, to get through poor times. These were a legacy from their hunter-gatherer ancestors.

Sometimes Ancestral Pueblo groups developed dietary traditions that required trade or foraging in areas remote from their home. Sara LeRoy-Toren, with the Lincoln High School Science Focus Program, and I are analyzing coprolites from Salmon Ruin, which was built along the San Juan River between the modern towns of Farmington and Bloomfield, New Mexico. It was abandoned by its original occupants and reoccupied by people from the San Juan River Valley. Our analysis is from the San Juan occupation, which was generally a time of abundance for both agriculture and gathered foods.

These coprolites reflect the Ancestral Pueblo tradition and contain juniper berries and cactus buds from areas local to the site, but they also contain piñon nuts that must have been harvested some miles away. We also calculated the number of pollen grains per gram of Salmon Ruin coprolites and found both maize and beeweed pollen in quantities as large as millions of grains per gram. Importantly, the maize pollen is shredded in a manner consistent with pollen eaten in corn meal, so maize was eaten both fresh off the cob and in the form of stored flour, although most of the macroscopic remains from Salmon Ruin are in the ground form.

One of my former graduate students, Dennis Danielson, now at the Central Identification Laboratory at the Joint POW/MIA Accounting Command, found phytoliths—microscopic crystals produced in plant cells—in the Salmon Ruin coprolites. More than half of the Salmon Ruin coprolites contain phytoliths from yucca-type plants and cactus, a legacy of pre-Ancestral Pueblo gathering adaptation to the desert. Denny eventually found phytoliths from these wild plants in coprolites from other Ancestral Pueblo sites. These gathered plants predominated in his analyses and reaffirmed that the Ancestral Pueblo could adapt to drought by turning to edible desert plants that were adapted to extremely dry conditions.

But were these plants actually what the Ancestral Pueblo ate in times of drought, rather than just a routine part of their diet? Denny and I analyzed coprolites from the last occupation of Antelope House in Canyon de Chelly, Arizona. All archaeological, climatological and biological analyses indicate that the last occupation was a time of ecological collapse. The level of anemia in skeletons from this time and region is the highest known among the Ancestral Pueblo. Archaeological surveys show that the mesas around the canyon were abandoned as people moved into the canyon to have access to water. The levels of parasitism, especially with crowd diseases, elevated; parasites were present in one-quarter of the 180 Antelope House coprolites I studied.

The coprolites at Antelope House record the adaptation to this environmental collapse and drought. Phytoliths from prickly pear and yucca leaf bases were present in 92 percent of the coprolites. The Ancestral Pueblo at Antelope House had clearly resorted to reliance on desert starvation foods. Yet their diet still lacked desperate monotony, as they ate wild plants from moist areas. Pollen occurs at concentrations in the hundreds of thousands to tens of millions of pollen grains per gram in the Antelope House coprolites. The main sources of pollen and spores were cattail, horsetail, beeweed and maize, but the diet at Antelope House included the greatest diversity of wild plants—27 species—ever recorded in Ancestral Pueblo coprolite studies. By contrast, only 16 wild species were identified in Salmon Ruin coprolites.

As for meat, my colleagues Mark Sutton, with California State University, Bakersfield, and Richard Marlar have found chemical signals in Ancestral Pueblo coprolites of bighorn sheep, rabbits, dogs and rodents. But as for cannibalism, Richard looked for human muscle indicators in the Salmon Ruin coprolites and found none. At Antelope House, Mark found protein residue of rabbit, rodents, dog, big horn sheep and pronghorn. There were also human protein residues present, but they were from intestinal cells shed by the body. The Ancestral Pueblo at Antelope House suffered parasitism from hookworms and hookworm-like organisms that would have resulted in excess shedding of intestinal cells. In fact, one Antelope House coprolite I analyzed was a mass of excreted parasitic worms mixed with seeds. Stable carbon and stable-nitrogen isotope analyses of the bones of these people from many sites indicate that, although they did eat meat, they were 70 percent herbivorous.

Every coprolite researcher who has worked with Ancestral Pueblo material has found animal bone. Kristin Sobolik of the University of Maine has shown that these people ate a particularly large number of lizard- and mouse-sized animals. This reliance on small animals was a remarkable adaptation to the Southwestern deserts, where small animals are most numerous and therefore a reliable source of protein—something the Ancestral Pueblo relied on feast or famine, just as their predecessors had.

Life on the Edge

Compared with other agricultural traditions I have studied in other parts of the world, the Ancestral Pueblo were rarely far from agricultural failure. My students and I have examined coprolites from the most primitive and advanced cultures in the Andes, from the earliest Chinchorros to the latest Incas. In the Andes, too, there is a long history of hunting and gathering that preceded agriculture. Once agriculture was established, however, 90 percent of the food species of Andean peoples were cultivated. This stands in meaningful contrast to the Ancestral Pueblo, whose food species remained predominantly wild. I think this is because they were on the very northern fringe of the region conducive to agriculture and couldn't rely on consistent productivity of their cultivated plots from year to year. Therefore, they maintained the hunter-gatherer dietary traditions to supplement, or replace if necessary, cultivated plants. Complete caloric dependence on cultivated plants, as took place in the Andes, was simply impossible for the Ancestral Pueblo.

Furthermore, these people often survived times of drought without cultural perturbations such as cannibalism. In my experience, the most poignant example of drought adaptation was seen in the analysis of a partially mummified child from Glen Canyon, Arizona. The child was buried during a long drought period, from 1210 to 1260 A.D. Archaeologist Steve Dominguez of the Midwest Archaeological Center directed the analysis of many specialists including myself and my students, Danielson and Kari Sandness. Burial offerings included a wide variety of ceramic, gourd and basketry artifacts. Compared with burial goods of other Ancestral Pueblo, these were consistent with those of average-status individuals. The drought did not disrupt the standard burial traditions for this three-to-four-year-old, yet x rays showed that this child survived seven episodes of starvation. The cause of death is unknown for this otherwise healthy child.

Analysis of the intestinal contents of the child provided insights into adaptation to drought. About 20 coprolites were excavated, and all of them were composed of a wild grass known as "rice grass." In the absence of cultivated foods, the child was provided with an alternative, and equally nutritious, wild food. Dominguez summarized the findings from the research succinctly:

> Investigations in nearby areas indicate that this was a period of environmental degradation and that Anasazi populations may have experienced nutritional stress or other consequent forms of physiological stress. Studies of both prehistoric populations and living populations suggest that a number of methods were employed to support individuals through periods of stress, and to promote the well-being of the group.

Was the Cannibal Ancestral Pueblo?

Work by numerous investigators thus shows that the Ancestral Pueblo possessed remarkable ecological adaptability; if they resorted to cannibalism because of environmental stress, it was a highly atypical response. Further, burial excavations demonstrate that they maintained their traditions even in times of drought. Besides, beyond a single sample, hundreds of coprolite analyses find not even a hint of cannibalism. Overwhelmingly, the Ancestral Pueblo were primarily herbivorous. Why, then, does one coprolite from the northern reaches of the Ancestral Pueblo domain come to characterize an entire culture? A number of researchers were incredulous at the hysteria created by the Cowboy Wash cannibal coprolite. Vaughn Bryant, Jr., at Texas A & M, e-mailed his disbelief to our small specialist community. From his experience in the study of Western diets, cannibalism was simply not plausible. Karen Clary, with the University of Texas at Austin, also e-mailed her concerns with the findings as well as with the unbridled sensationalism.

Both coprolite and skeletal evidence examined by Utah State University bio-archaeologist Patricia Lambert do show that Ancestral Pueblo of Cowboy Wash were victims of violence and cannibalism—there's little question about it. But that doesn't mean that the cannibal(s) were Ancestral Pueblo. Mark Sutton and I found that these people invariably ate plant foods when they ate meat; it was a feature of their cuisine. The complete lack of plant matter in the Cowboy Wash coprolite tells me that it was not from an individual who observed the Ancestral Pueblo dietary tradition. To date, none of the principal investigators involved in the Cowboy Wash analysis have implicated residents or even Ancestral Pueblo from another location as the perpetrators of the violence. In short, I don't know who killed and ate the residents of Cowboy Wash, but I am sure the cannibal wasn't an Ancestral Pueblo.

The Peaceful People Concept

Christy Turner's quote in the popular media puzzled me. Why would anyone want to bring down an ancient culture, especially Turner, whose work is characterized by attention to detail, meticulous analytical procedures and, most of all, accumulation of mountains of data to support his conclusions? One of my most striking memories of any scientist was an afternoon chat I had with Turner regarding his work with dental traits to trace migrations to the New World. His office was packed with neat columns of computer printouts from data collected from thousands of skulls. That same afternoon, the conversation turned to his study of cannibalism. I asked him specifics about his methods and found that he approached this area of research with the same exhaustive thoroughness he applied to his dental work. At no time did he indicate that he intended to "bring down the Anasazi."

Then I read the book that Turner cowrote, *Man Corn,* and I realized that it was not the Ancestral Pueblo culture that he brought down. He was after our archaeological biases in how we reconstruct the nature of Ancestral Pueblo culture. To understand how that one coprolite came to be considered ironclad evidence of cannibalism among the Ancestral Pueblo, it's necessary to understand how these people have been characterized by anthropologists and archaeologists at various times over the past 50 or so years.

The view of the Ancestral Pueblo as peaceful people took root in the 1960s and '70s. Earlier work had shown that violence, and perhaps even cannibalism, had taken place among the Ancestral Pueblo. But in the '60s and '70s—a time of social volatility, seemingly suffused in the violence of combat and revolt—modern American culture was searching for examples of nonviolent social systems. Academia sought out paradigms of peacefulness from other regions, other times and even other species. The Ancestral Pueblo became one of those "paragons of peace," as did the San Bushmen and wild chimpanzees. Elizabeth Marshall Thomas published her book about the bushmen, *The Harmless People,* in 1959, and anthropologists took to highlighting the nonviolence of hunter-gatherers. This was when the "New Archaeology" emerged as a replacement for previous approaches. Students were discouraged from reading archaeological research that dated from before 1960; thus the earlier work that described evidence of violence was ignored.

Excavations during the 1970s were very counter-cultural in appearance and philosophy. Scholarly excavation camps often had the flavor of hippie communes. In that atmosphere, evidence of violence was largely dismissed both in the field and during the analysis phase. I recall participating in three excavations in which houses had burned and people perished within them. This seemed like pretty good evidence that all was not tranquil with the peaceful people, but such fires were explained as accidental. Once, when we discovered arrow points in a skeleton in a burned house, the evidence of violence was not deemed conclusive because the arrow points had not penetrated bone. At the time, I wondered whether we were being a little too quick to dismiss the possibility of violence; the alternative was that these people were remarkably negligent with their hearths and weapons. I began to think of the Ancestral Pueblo as peaceful but fatally accident prone.

Those claiming evidence of cannibalism among ancient American cultures were excluded from presenting their findings at the Pecos Conference, the regional meeting for Southwestern archaeologists. This caused quite a furor. A symposium on the subject of violence and cannibalism had been scheduled for the meeting, and the participants arrived, but the symposium was canceled at the last minute. In 20 years of participating in scientific meetings, this is the only instance I can recall of a scheduled event being canceled for purely political reasons.

In the '80s and '90s, the paragons of peaceful society began to fall—and fall in a big way. First, violence was acknowledged among the Maya, held as the Mesoamerican counterweight to the undoubtedly violent and cannibalistic Aztec prior to ascendance of the peaceful people. Violence and cannibalism were then documented among wild chimpanzees, the behavioral analogues to ancestral human beings. The evidence of conflict among the Ancestral Pueblo became so overwhelming that it was the focus of a 1995 Society of American Archaeology symposium, the proceedings of which were published in the book, *Deciphering Anasazi Violence.* The Ancestral Pueblo cannibalism argument was formalized in University of California, Berkeley anthropologist Tim White's 1992 book *Prehistoric Cannibalism at Mancos 5Mtumr2346.* In each case, physical anthropology alone, or in combination with scientific archaeology, brought down the peaceful paradigm with the weight of scientific evidence. Turner produced much of that evidence.

Cannibalism at Other Sites?

In *Man Corn,* Turner carefully stated that he thought the Ancestral Pueblo were victims of terrorism imposed on them by a more violent and cannibalistic culture. The book reviews skeletal evidence of violence at more than 76 sites in the Ancestral Pueblo region. He believes that violence and cannibalism were introduced by migrants from central Mexico, where there is a long tradition of violence, human sacrifice and cannibalism.

Of the sites Turner discusses, I have first-hand experience with one, Salmon Ruin, where I spent three seasons excavating and later reconstructing the parasite ecology and diet of this large pueblo's occupants as part of my thesis and dissertation research. He focuses on a high structure called a kiva at the center of the three-story pueblo. Initially it was thought that the bodies of two adults and 35 children were burned in the tower kiva. His analysis indicates that these bodies were disarticulated and cannibalized. However, there are other interpretations.

In 1977, I discussed the tower kiva finds with the excavation director, the late Cynthia Irwin-Williams, who was then with Eastern New Mexico State University. She believed that the children were sent to the highest place in the pueblo with two adults when the structure caught fire. As the fire went out of control, they were trapped there.

Another explanation was offered to me by Larry Baker, director of the Salmon Ruin Museum. He told me that a new analysis of the bones showed that the people in the tower kiva were long dead when their bodies burned. Furthermore, there is evidence in the burned bones that the bodies had at least partly decomposed. It may be that the bodies were placed in the tower as part of a mortuary custom after the pueblo was abandoned. When the pueblo burned, so did the bodies.

More recently, Nancy Akins, with the Museum of New Mexico, reanalyzed the human remains and stratigraphy of the tower kiva. She found that only 20 children and 4 adults were represented. Some of the bodies were deliberately cremated and others partially burned. Some remains showed that the bodies were dry before they were burned. This analysis suggests a complex series of mortuary events preceding the burning of the tower kiva and surrounding rooms. Analysis of the stratigraphy shows that they were not burned simultaneously but were deposited in different episodes. In this view, the evidence suggests a previously unknown mortuary practice rather than trauma and cannibalism.

I conclude that when analyzing the remains of the Ancestral Pueblo, it is important to consider that recent work shows that their mortuary practices were more complicated than we previously thought—and that complex mortuary practices should come as no surprise and constitute ambiguous evidence. Prehistoric people in Chile, the Chinchorros, not only disarticulated the dead, but also rearticulated the cleaned bones in vegetation and clay "statues." In Nebraska, disarticulation and burning of bones was done as a part of mortuary ritual. Closer to the Ancestral Pueblo, the Sinagua culture of central Arizona cremated their dead. Thus disarticulated skeletal remains and burning fall short of proving cannibalism.

What We Can Learn

Because the members of extinct cultures cannot speak for themselves, the nature of cultural reconstruction easily becomes colored by the projections of the archaeological community and the inclination of the media to oversimplify or even sensationalize. The Ancestral Pueblo, once thought to be peaceful, have now become, especially in the lay mind, violent cannibals. Neither depiction is fair. They had a level of violence typical of most human populations—present but not excessive. Is that really so surprising?

Perhaps more astonishing is how unquestioning our culture can be in tearing down its icons. Much as we scientists may prefer to stick to the field or the laboratory, shunning the bright lights, we bear a responsibility to present our data in a way that reduces the opportunity for exaggeration. Our findings must be qualified in the context of alternative explanations. As such, the Cowboy Wash coprolite offers us a cautionary tale.

Bibliography

Billman, B. R., P. M. Lambert and L. B. Leonard. 2000. Cannibalism, warfare, and drought in the Mesa Verde Region during the Twelfth Century A.D. *American Antiquity* 65:145–178.

Bryant, V. M., Jr., and G. Williams-Dean. 1975. The coprolites of man. *Scientific American* 232:100–109.

Dongoske, K. K., D. L. Martin and T. J. Ferguson. 2000. Critique of the claim of cannibalism at Cowboy Wash. *American Antiquity* 65:179–190.

Fry, G. F. 1980. Prehistoric diet and parasites in the desert west of North America. In: *Early Native Americans,* ed. F. L. Browman. The Hague: Mouton Press, pp. 325–339.

Fry, G. F., and H. J. Hall. 1986. Human coprolites. In: *Archaeological Investigations at Antelope House,* ed. D. P. Morris. Washington, D. C.: U.S. Government Printing Office, pp. 165–188.

Lambert, P. M., L. B. Leonard, B. R. Billman, R. A. Marlar, M. E. Newman and K. J. Reinhard. 2000. Response to the critique of the claim of cannibalism at Cowboy Wash. *American Antiquity* 65:397–406.

Marlar, R., B. Billman, B. Leonard, P. Lambert and K. Reinhard. 2000. Fecal evidence of cannibalism. *Southwestern Lore* 4:14–22.

Reinhard, K. J. 1992. Patterns of diet, parasitism, anemia in prehistoric west North American. In: *Diet, Demography, and Disease: Changing Perspectives on Anemia,* ed. P. Stuart-Macadann and S. Kent. New York: Aldine de Gruyter, pp. 219–258.

Reinhard, K. J., and V. M. Bryant, Jr. 1992a. Coprolite analysis: A biological perspective on archaeology. In: *Advances in Archaeological Method and Theory 4,* ed. M. D. Schiffer. Tucson: University of Arizona Press, pp. 245–288.

Reinhard, K. J., and D. R. Danielson. 2005. Pervasiveness of phytoliths in prehistoric southwestern diet and implications for regional and temporal trends for dental mircowear. *Journal of Archaeological Science* 32:981–988.

Scott, L. 1979. Dietary inferences from Hoy House coprolites: A palynological interpretation. *The Kiva* 44:257–281.

Sobolik, K. 1993. Direct evidence for the importance of small animals to prehistoric diets: A review of coprolite studies. *North American Archaeologist* 14:227–243.

Sutton, M. Q., and K. J. Reinhard, 1995. Cluster analysis of coprolites from Antelope House:. Implications for Anasazi diet and culture. *Journal of Archaeological Science* 22:741–750.

Critical Thinking

1. What is a coprolite? What can we learn from analyses of coprolites?
2. What is the evidence for cannibalism at Cowboy Wash? What did the author's analysis of the coprolite show?
3. What part of the author's report went largely unnoticed by the media? What is the author's opinion about Ancestral Pueblo cannibalism?
4. How does the author describe the Ancestral Pueblo diet?
5. How were "starvation foods" important?
6. How does the author describe the health and diet of the Ancestral Pueblo at the time of the last occupation in Canyon de Chelly? What about cannibalism at this time?
7. How does the author compare and contrast Ancestral Pueblo agriculture with that of the Andes?
8. How did the analysis of the partially mummified child serve as an example of drought adaptation?
9. How does the author answer the question of cannibalism among the Ancestral Pueblo people?
10. How did the author come to understand the Christy Turner intention to "bring down the Anasazi"?
11. Be familiar with the rise and fall of the "peaceful people" concept.
12. How might disarticulated bones be interpreted in other ways than as cannibalism?

Karl J. Reinhard is a professor in the School of Natural Resources at the University of Nebraska and a Fulbright Commission Senior Specialist in Archaeology for 2004–2009. The main focus of his career since earning his Ph.D. from Texas A&M has been to find explanations for modern patterns of disease in the archaeological and historic record. He also developed a new specialization called archaeoparasitology, which attempts to understand the evolution of parasitic disease.

Article 12

New Women of the Ice Age

Forget about hapless mates being dragged around by macho mammoth killers. The women of Ice Age Europe, it appears, were not mere cavewives but priestly leaders, clever inventors, and mighty hunters.

HEATHER PRINGLE

The Black Venus of Dolní Vestonice, a small, splintered figurine sensuously fashioned from clay, is an envoy from a forgotten world. It is all soft curves, with breasts like giant pillows beneath a masked face. At nearly 26,000 years old, it ranks among the oldest known portrayals of women, and to generations of researchers, it has served as a powerful—if enigmatic—clue to the sexual politics of the Ice Age.

Excavators unearthed the Black Venus near the Czech village of Dolní Vestonice in 1924, on a hillside among charred, fractured mammoth bones and stone tools. (Despite its nickname, the Black Venus is actually reddish—it owes its name to the ash that covered it when it was found.) Since the mid-nineteenth century, researchers had discovered more than a dozen similar statuettes in caves and open-air sites from France to Russia. All were cradled in layers of earth littered with stone and bone weaponry, ivory jewelry, and the remains of extinct Ice Age animals. All were depicted naked or nearly so. Collectively, they came to be known as Venus figurines, after another ancient bare-breasted statue, the Venus de Milo. Guided at least in part by prevailing sexual stereotypes, experts interpreted the meaning of the figurines freely. The Ice Age camps that spawned this art, they concluded, were once the domain of hardworking male hunters and secluded, pampered women who spent their days in idleness like the harem slaves so popular in nineteenth-century art.

Over the next six decades, Czech archeologists expanded the excavations at Dolní Vestonice, painstakingly combing the site square meter by square meter. By the 1990s they had unearthed thousands of bone, stone, and clay artifacts and had wrested 19 radiocarbon dates from wood charcoal that sprinkled camp floors. And they had shaded and refined their portrait of Ice Age life. Between 29,000 and 25,000 years ago, they concluded, wandering bands had passed the cold months of the year repeatedly at Dolní Vestonice. Armed with short-range spears, the men appeared to have been specialists in hunting tusk-wielding mammoths and other big game, hauling home great mountains of meat to feed their dependent mates and children. At night men feasted on mammoth steaks, fed their fires with mammoth bone, and fueled their sexual fantasies with tiny figurines of women carved from mammoth ivory and fired from clay. It was the ultimate man's world.

Or was it? Over the past few months, a small team of American archeologists has raised some serious doubts. Amassing critical and previously overlooked evidence from Dolní Vestonice and the neighboring site of Pavlov, Olga Soffer, James Adovasio, and David Hyland now propose that human survival there had little to do with manly men hurling spears at big-game animals. Instead, observes Soffer, one of the world's leading authorities on Ice Age hunters and gatherers and an archeologist at the University of Illinois in Champaign-Urbana, it depended largely on women, plants, and a technique of hunting previously invisible in the archeological evidence—net hunting. "This is not the image we've always had of Upper Paleolithic macho guys out killing animals up close and personal," Soffer explains. "Net hunting is communal, and it involves the labor of children and women. And this has lots of implications."

Many of these implications make her conservative colleagues cringe because they raise serious questions about the focus of previous studies. European archeologists have long concentrated on analyzing broken stone tools and butchered big-game bones, the most plentiful and best preserved relics of the Upper Paleolithic era (which stretched from 40,000 to 12,000 years ago). From these analyses, researchers have developed theories about how these societies once hunted and gathered food. Most researchers ruled out the possibility of women hunters for biological reasons. Adult females, they reasoned, had to devote themselves to breast-feeding and tending infants. "Human babies have always been immature and dependent," says Soffer. "If women are the people who are always involved with biological reproduction and the rearing of the young, then that is going to constrain their behavior. They have to provision that child. For fathers, provisioning is optional."

To test theories about Upper Paleolithic life, researchers looked to ethnography, the scientific description of modern and historical cultural groups. While the lives of modern hunters do not exactly duplicate those of ancient hunters, they supply valuable clues to universal human behavior. "Modern ethnography cannot be used to clone the past," says Soffer. "But people have always had to solve problems. Nature and social relationships present problems to people. We use ethnography to look for theoretical insights into human behavior, test them with ethnography, and if they work, assume that they represent a universal feature of human behavior."

But when researchers began turning to ethnographic descriptions of hunting societies, they unknowingly relied on a very incomplete literature. Assuming that women in surviving hunting societies were homebodies who simply tended hearths and suckled children, most early male anthropologists spent their time with male informants. Their published ethnographies brim with descriptions of males making spears and harpoons and heaving these weapons at reindeer, walruses, and whales. Seldom do they mention the activities of women. Ethnography, it seemed, supported theories of ancient male big-game hunters. "When they talked about primitive man, it was always 'he,'" says Soffer. "The 'she' was missing."

Recent anthropological research has revealed just how much Soffer's colleagues overlooked. By observing women in the few remaining hunter-gatherer societies and by combing historical accounts of tribal groups more thoroughly, anthropologists have come to realize how critical the female half of the population has always been to survival. Women and children have set snares, laid spring traps, sighted game and participated in animal drives and surrounds—forms of hunting that endangered neither young mothers nor their offspring. They dug starchy roots and collected other plant carbohydrates essential to survival. They even hunted, on occasion, with the projectile points traditionally deemed men's weapons. "I found references to Inuit women carrying bows and arrows, especially the blunt arrows that were used for hunting birds," says Linda Owen, an archeologist at the University of Tübingen in Germany.

The revelations triggered a volley of new research. In North America, Soffer and her team have found tantalizing evidence of the hunting gear often favored by women in historical societies. In Europe, archeobotanists are analyzing Upper Paleolithic hearths for evidence of plant remains probably gathered by women and children, while lithics specialists are poring over stone tools to detect new clues to their uses. And the results are gradually reshaping our understanding of Ice Age society. The famous Venus figurines, say archeologists of the new school, were never intended as male pornography: instead they may have played a key part in Upper Paleolithic rituals that centered on women. And such findings, pointing toward a more important role for Paleolithic women than had previously been assumed, are giving many researchers pause.

Like many of her colleagues, Soffer clearly relishes the emerging picture of Upper Paleolithic life. "I think life back then was a hell of a lot more egalitarian than it was with your later peasant societies," she says. "Of course the Paleolithic women were pulling their own weight." After sifting through Ice Age research for nearly two decades, Soffer brings a new critical approach to the notion—flattering to so many of her male colleagues—of mighty male mammoth hunters. "Very few archeologists are hunters," she notes, so it never occurred to most of them to look into the mechanics of hunting dangerous tusked animals. They just accepted the ideas they'd inherited from past work.

But the details of hunting bothered Soffer. Before the fifth century B.C., no tribal hunters in Asia or Africa had ever dared make their living from slaying elephants; the great beasts were simply too menacing. With the advent of the Iron Age in Africa, the situation changed. New weapons allowed Africans to hunt elephants and trade their ivory with Greeks and Romans. A decade ago, keen to understand how prehistoric bands had slaughtered similar mammoths, Soffer began studying Upper Paleolithic sites on the Russian and Eastern European plains. To her surprise, the famous mammoth bone beds were strewn with cumbersome body parts, such as 220-pound skulls, that sensible hunters would generally abandon. Moreover, the bones exhibited widely differing degrees of weathering, as if they had sat on the ground for varying lengths of time. To Soffer, it looked suspiciously as if Upper Paleolithic hunters had simply camped next to places where the pachyderms had perished naturally—such as water holes or salt licks—and mined the bones for raw materials.

If one of these Upper Paleolithic guys killed a mammoth, and occasionally they did, they probably didn't stop talking about it for ten years.

Soffer began analyzing data researchers had gathered describing the sex and age ratios of mammoths excavated from four Upper Paleolithic sites. She found many juveniles, a smaller number of adult females, and hardly any males. The distribution mirrored the death pattern other researchers had observed at African water holes, where the weakest animals perished closest to the water and the strongest farther off. "Imagine the worst time of year in Africa, which is the drought season," explains Soffer. "There is no water, and elephants need an enormous amount. The ones in the worst shape—your weakest, your infirm, your young—are going to be tethered to that water before they die. They are in such horrendous shape, they don't have any extra energy to go anywhere. The ones in better shape would wander off slight distances and then keel over farther away. You've got basket cases and you've got ones that can walk 20 feet."

To Soffer, the implications of this study were clear. Upper Paleolithic bands had pitched their camps next to critical resources such as ancient salt licks or water holes. There the men spent more time scavenging bones and ivory from mammoth carcasses then they did risking life and limb by attacking 6,600-pound pachyderms with short-range spears. "If one of these Upper Paleolithic guys killed a mammoth, and occasionally they did," concedes Soffer dryly, "they probably didn't stop talking about it for ten years."

But if Upper Paleolithic families weren't often tucking into mammoth steaks, what were they hunting and how? Soffer found the first unlikely clue in 1991, while sifting through hundreds of tiny clay fragments recovered from the Upper Paleolithic site of Pavlov, which lies just a short walk from Dolní Vestonice. Under a magnifying lens, Soffer noticed something strange on a few of the fragments: a series of parallel lines impressed on their surfaces. What could have left such a regular pattern? Puzzled, Soffer photographed the pieces, all of which had been unearthed from a zone sprinkled with wood charcoal that was radiocarbon-dated at between 27,000 and 25,000 years ago.

When she returned home, Soffer had the film developed. And one night on an impulse, she put on a slide show for a visiting colleague, Jim Adovasio. "We'd run out of cable films," she jokes. Staring at the images projected on Soffer's refrigerator, Adovasio, an archeologist at Mercyhurst College in Pennsylvania and an expert on ancient fiber technology, immediately recognized the impressions of plant fibers. On a few, he could actually discern a pattern of interlacing fibers—weaving.

Without a doubt, he said, he and Soffer were gazing at textiles or basketry. They were the oldest—by nearly 7,000 years—ever found. Just how these pieces of weaving got impressed in clay, he couldn't say. "It may be that a lot of these [materials] were lying around on clay floors," he notes. "When the houses burned, the walked-in images were subsequently left in the clay floors."

Soffer and Adovasio quickly made arrangements to fly back to the Czech Republic. At the Dolní Vestonice branch of the Institute of Archaeology, Soffer sorted through nearly 8,400 fired clay pieces, weeding out the rejects. Adovasio made positive clay casts of 90. Back in Pennsylvania, he and his Mercyhurst colleague David Hyland peered at the casts under a zoom stereomicroscope, measuring warps and wefts. Forty-three revealed impressions of basketry and textiles. Some of the latter were as finely woven as a modern linen tablecloth. But as Hyland stared at four of the samples, he noted something potentially more fascinating: impressions of cordage bearing weaver's knots, a technique that joins two lengths of cord and that is commonly used for making nets of secure mesh. It looked like a tiny shred of a net bag, or perhaps a hunting net. Fascinated, Soffer expanded the study. She spent six weeks at the Moravian Museum in Brno, sifting through the remainder of the collections from Dolní Vestonice. Last fall, Adovasio spied the telltale impression of Ice Age mesh on one of the new casts.

The mesh, measuring two inches across, is far too delicate for hunting deer or other large prey. But hunters at Dolní Vestonice could have set nets of this size to capture hefty Ice Age hares, each carrying some six pounds of meat, and other furbearers such as arctic fox and red fox. As it turns out, the bones of hares and foxes litter camp floors at Dolní Vestonice and Pavlov. Indeed, this small game accounts for 46 percent of the individual animals recovered at Pavlov. Soffer, moreover, doesn't rule out the possibility of turning up bits of even larger nets. Accomplished weavers in North America once knotted mesh with which they captured 1,000-pound elk and 300-pound bighorn sheep. "In fact, when game officials have to move sheep out west, it's by nets," she adds. "You throw nets on them and they just lie down. It's a very safe way of hunting."

Illustration by Ron Miller

Nets made Ice Age hunting safe enough for entire communities to participate, and they captured everything from hares and foxes to deer and sheep.

In many historical societies, she observes, women played a key part in net hunting since the technique did not call for brute strength nor did it place young mothers in physical peril. Among Australian aborigines, for example, women as well as men knotted the mesh, laboring for as much as two or three years on a fine net. Among native North American groups, they helped lay out their handiwork on poles across a valley floor. Then the entire camp joined forces as beaters. Fanning out across the valley, men, women, and children alike shouted and screamed, flushing out game and driving it in the direction of the net. "Everybody and their mother could participate," says Soffer. "Some people were beating, others were screaming or holding the net. And once you got the net on these animals, they were immobilized. You didn't need brute force. You could club them, hit them any old way."

People seldom returned home empty-handed. Researchers living among the net-hunting Mbuti in the forests of Congo report that they capture game every time they lay out their woven traps, scooping up 50 percent of the animals encountered. "Nets are a far more valued item in their panoply of food-producing things than bows and arrows are," says Adovasio. So lethal are these traps that the Mbuti generally rack up more meat than they can consume, trading the surplus with neighbors. Other net hunters traditionally smoked or dried their catch and stored it for leaner times. Or they polished it off immediately in large ceremonial feasts. The hunters of Dolní Vestonice and Pavlov, says Soffer, probably feasted during ancient rituals. Archeologists unearthed no evidence of food storage pits at either site. But there is much evidence of ceremony. At Dolní Vestonice, for example, many clay figurines appear to have been ritually destroyed in secluded parts of the site.

Soffer doubts that the inhabitants of Dolní Vestonice and Pavlov were the only net makers in Ice Age Europe. Camps stretching from Germany to Russia are littered with a notable abundance of small-game bones, from hares to birds like ptarmigan. And at least some of their inhabitants whittled bone tools that look much like the awls and net spacers favored by historical

Illustration by Ron Miller

Once animals were caught in the nets, hunters could beat them to death with whatever was handy.

net makers. Such findings, agree Soffer and Adovasio, reveal just how shaky the most widely accepted reconstructions of Upper Paleolithic life are. "These terribly stilted interpretations," says Adovasio, "with men hunting big animals all the time and the poor females waiting at home for these guys to bring home the bacon—what crap."

In her home outside Munich, Linda Owen finds other faults with this traditional image. Owen, an American born and raised, specializes in the microscopic analysis of stone tools. In her years of work, she often noticed that many of the tools made by hunters who roamed Europe near the end of the Upper Paleolithic era, some 18,000 to 12,000 years ago, resembled pounding stones and other gear for harvesting and processing plants. Were women and children gathering and storing wild plant foods?

Most of her colleagues saw little value in pursuing the question. Indeed, some German archeologists contended that 90 percent of the human diet during the Upper Paleolithic era came from meat. But as Owen began reading nutritional studies, she saw that heavy meat consumption would spell death. To stoke the body's cellular engines, human beings require energy from protein, fat, or carbohydrates. Of these, protein is the least efficient. To burn it, the body must boost its metabolic rate by 10 percent, straining the liver's ability to absorb oxygen. Unlike carnivorous animals, whose digestive and metabolic systems are well adapted to a meat-only diet, humans who consume more than half their calories as lean meat will die from protein poisoning. In Upper Paleolithic times, hunters undoubtedly tried to round out their diets with fat from wild game. But in winter, spring, and early summer, the meat would have been very lean. So how did humans survive?

Owen began sifting for clues through anthropological and historical accounts from subarctic and arctic North America. These environments, she reasoned, are similar to that of Ice Age Europe and pose similar challenges to their inhabitants. Even in the far north, Inuit societies harvested berries for winter storage and gathered other plants for medicines and for fibers. To see if any of the flora that thrived in Upper Paleolithic Europe could be put to similar uses, Owen drew up a list of plants economically important to people living in cold-climate regions of North America and Europe and compared it with a list of species that botanists had identified from pollen trapped in Ice Age sediment cores from southern Germany. Nearly 70 plants were found on both lists. "I came up with just a fantastic list of plants that were available at that time. Among others, there were a number of reeds that are used by the Eskimo and subarctic people in North America for making baskets. There are a lot of plants with edible leaves and stems, and things that were used as drugs and dyes. So the plants were there."

The chief plant collectors in historical societies were undoubtedly women. "It was typically women's work," says Owen. "I did find several comments that the men on hunting expeditions would gather berries or plants for their own meals, but they did not participate in the plant-gathering expeditions. They might go along, but they would be hunting or fishing."

Were Upper Paleolithic women gathering plants? The archeological literature was mostly silent on the subject. Few archeobotanists, Owen found, had ever looked for plant seeds and shreds in Upper Paleolithic camps. Most were convinced such efforts would be futile in sites so ancient. At University College London, however, Owen reached a determined young archeobontanist, Sarah Mason, who had analyzed a small sample of charcoal-like remains from a 26,390-year-old hearth at Dolní Vestonice.

The sample held more than charcoal. Examining it with a scanning electron microscope, Mason and her colleagues found fragments of fleshy plant taproots with distinctive secretory cavities—trademarks of the daisy and aster family, which boasts several species with edible roots. In all likelihood, women at Dolní Vestonice had dug the roots and cooked them into starchy meals. And they had very likely simmered other plant foods too. Mason and her colleagues detected a strange pulverized substance in the charred sample. It looked as if the women had either ground plants into flour and then boiled the results to make gruel or pounded vegetable material into a mush for their babies. Either way, says Soffer, the results are telling. "They're stuffing carbohydrates."

Owen is pursuing the research further. "If you do look," she says, "you can find things." At her urging, colleagues at the University of Tübingen are now analyzing Paleolithic hearths for botanical remains as they unearth them. Already they have turned up more plants, including berries, all clearly preserved after thousands of years. In light of these findings, Owen suggests that it was women, not men, who brought home most of

Illustration by Ron Miller

The clay figurines at Dolní Vestonice may have been used in divination rituals.

the calories to Upper Paleolithic families. Indeed, she estimates that if Ice Age females collected plants, bird eggs, shellfish, and edible insects, and if they hunted or trapped small game and participated in the hunting of large game—as northern women did in historical times—they most likely contributed 70 percent of the consumed calories.

Moreover, some women may have enjoyed even greater power, judging from the most contentious relics of Ice Age life: the famous Venus figurines. Excavators have recovered more than 100 of the small statuettes, which were crafted between 29,000 and 23,000 years ago from such enduring materials as bone, stone, antler, ivory, and fired clay. The figurines share a strange blend of abstraction and realism. They bare prominent breasts, for example, but lack nipples. Their bodies are often minutely detailed down to the swaying lines of their backbones and the tiny rolls of flesh—fat folds—beneath their shoulder blades, but they often lack eyes, mouths, and any facial expression. For years researchers viewed them as a male art form. Early anthropologists, after all, had observed only male hunters carving stone, ivory, and other hard materials. Females were thought to lack the necessary strength. Moreover, reasoned experts, only men would take such loving interest in a woman's body. Struck by the voluptuousness of the small stone, ivory, and clay bodies, some researchers suggested they were Ice Age erotica, intended to be touched and fondled by their male makers. The idea still lingers. In the 1980s, for example, the well-known American paleontologist Dale Guthrie wrote a scholarly article comparing the postures of the figurines with the provocative poses of *Playboy* centerfolds.

But most experts now dismiss such contentions. Owen's careful scouring of ethnographic sources, for example, revealed that women in arctic and subarctic societies did indeed work stone and ivory on occasion. And there is little reason to suggest the figurines figured as male erotica. The Black Venus, for example, seems to have belonged to a secret world of ceremony and ritual far removed from everyday sexual life.

The evidence, says Soffer, lies in the raw material from which the Black Venus is made. Clay objects sometimes break or explode when fired, a process called thermal-shock fracturing. Studies conducted by Pamela Vandiver of the Smithsonian Institution have demonstrated that the Black Venus and other human and animal figurines recovered from Dolní Vestonice—as well as nearly 2,000 fired ceramic pellets that litter the site—were made from a local clay that is resistant to thermal-shock fracturing. But many of the figurines, including the celebrated Black Venus, bear the distinctive jagged branching splinters created by thermal shock. Intriguingly, the fired clay pellets do not.

Curious, Vandiver decided to replicate the ancient firing process. Her analysis of the small Dolní Vestonice kilns revealed that they had been fired to temperatures around 1450 degrees Fahrenheit—similar to those of an ordinary hearth. So Vandiver set about making figurines of local soil and firing them in a similar earthen kiln, which a local archeological crew had built nearby. To produce thermal shock, she had to place objects larger than half an inch on the hottest part of the fire; moreover, the pieces had to be so wet they barely held their shape.

To Vandiver and Soffer, the experiment—which was repeated several times back at the Smithsonian Institution—suggests that thermal shock was no accident. "Stuff can explode naturally in the kiln," says Soffer, "or you can make it explode. Which was going on at Dolní Vestonice? We toyed with both ideas. Either we're dealing with the most inept potters, people with two left hands, or they are doing it on purpose. And we reject the idea that they were totally inept, because other materials didn't explode. So what are the odds that this would happen only with a very particular category of objects?"

These exploding figurines could well have played a role in rituals, an idea supported by the location of the kilns. They are situated far away from the dwellings, as ritual buildings often are. Although the nature of the ceremonies is not clear, Soffer speculates that they might have served as divination rites for discerning what the future held. "Some stuff is going to explode. Some stuff is not going to explode. It's evocative, like picking petals off a daisy. She loves me, she loves me not."

Moreover, ritualists at Dolní Vestonice could have read significance into the fracturing patterns of the figurines. Many historical cultures, for example, attempted to read the future by a related method called scapulimancy. In North America, Cree ceremonialists often placed the shoulder blade, or scapula, of a desired animal in the center of a lodge. During the ceremonies, cracks began splintering the bone: a few of these fractures leaked droplets of fat. To Cree hunters, this was a sign that they would find game if they journeyed in the direction indicated by the cracks.

Venus figurines from other sites also seem to have been cloaked in ceremony. "They were not just something made to look pretty," says Margherita Mussi, an archeologist at the University of Rome–La Sapienza who studies Upper Paleolithic figurines. Mussi notes that several small statuettes from the Grimaldi Cave carvings of southern Italy, one of the largest troves of Ice Age figurines ever found in Western Europe, were carved from rare materials, which the artists obtained with great difficulty, sometimes through trade or distant travel. The statuettes were laboriously whittled and polished, then rubbed with ocher, a pigment that appears to have had ceremonial significance, suggesting that they could have been reserved for special events like rituals.

The nature of these rites is still unclear. But Mussi is convinced that women took part, and some archeologists believe they stood at the center. One of the clearest clues, says Mussi, lies in a recently rediscovered Grimaldi figurine known as Beauty and the Beast. This greenish yellow serpentine sculpture portrays two arched bodies facing away from each other and joined at the head, shoulders, and lower extremities. One body is that of a Venus figurine. The other is a strange creature that combines the triangular head of a reptile, the pinched waist of a wasp, tiny arms, and horns. "It is clearly not a creature of this world," says Mussi.

The pairing of woman and supernatural beast, adds Mussi, is highly significant. "I believe that these women were related to the capacity of communicating with a different world," she says. "I think they were believed to be the gateway to a different dimension." Possessing powers that far surpassed others in their communities, such women may have formed part of a spiritual elite, rather like the shamans of ancient Siberia. As intermediaries between the real and spirit worlds, Siberian shamans were said to be able to cure illnesses and intercede on behalf of others for hunting success. It is possible that Upper Paleolithic women performed similar services for their followers.

Although the full range of their activities is unlikely ever to be known for certain, there is good reason to believe that Ice Age women played a host of powerful roles—from plant collectors and weavers to hunters and spiritual leaders. And the research that suggests those roles is rapidly changing our mental images of the past. For Soffer and others, these are exciting times. "The data do speak for themselves," she says finally. "They answer the questions we have. But if we don't envision the questions, we're not going to see the data."

Critical Thinking

1. What do the Venus figurines have in common? How was Ice Age life perceived and why?
2. How has recent anthropological research such views?
3. What do archaeologists of the "new school" say about the Venus figures?
4. Why does Soffer think that life was more "egalitarian"?
5. What evidence is there in the archaeological record and in historical societies that women have played a key role in food-getting? Be familiar with all that this has involved.
6. Why does the author claim that women may have "enjoyed even greater power"?
7. What is the significance of the way the Venus figures were produced?

Heather Pringle lives in Vancouver, British Columbia. "I love how this article overturns the popular image of the role of women in the past," says Pringle, who specializes in writing about archaeology. "It was fun to write and a delight to research." Pringle is the author of *In Search of Ancient North America.*

Article 13

Woman the Toolmaker

A day in the life of an Ethiopian woman who scrapes hides the old-fashioned way.

Steven A. Brandt and Kathryn Weedman

On the edge of the western escarpment of the Ethiopian Rift Valley, we sit in awe, not of the surrounding environment—some of the world's most spectacular scenery—but of an elderly woman deftly manufacturing stone scrapers as she prepares food, answers an inquisitive child, and chats with a neighbor. She smiles at us, amused and honored by our barrage of questions and our filming of her activities.

In our world of electronic and digital gadgetry, it is surprising to meet someone who uses stone tools in their everyday life. Yet, over the past three decades, researchers have identified a handful of ethnic groups in Ethiopia's southern highlands whose artisans live by making stone scrapers and processing animal hides.

In 1995, with colleagues from Ethiopia's Authority for Research and Conservation of Cultural Heritage and the University of Florida, we surveyed the highlands and, much to our surprise, identified hundreds of stone tool makers in ten different ethnic groups.

The Konso, one group we surveyed, grow millet and other crops on terraces and raise livestock that provide the skins for the hide workers. While hide working in virtually all of the other groups is conducted by men who learn from their fathers, among the Konso the hide workers are women, taught by their mothers or other female relatives.

In archaeological writings, scholarly and popular, stone toolmaking has generally been presented as a male activity; *Man the Toolmaker* is the title of one classic work. This is despite the fact that Australian Aboriginal, North American Inuit (Eskimo), and Siberian women, among others, have been reported in recent times to have made flaked-stone artifacts. The Konso hide workers are probably the only women in the world still making stone tools on a regular basis. They provide a unique opportunity for ethnoarchaeology, the study of the material remains of contemporary peoples. In the past two summers, our team returned to study the women hide workers, following them with our notebooks and cameras, and observing them as they went through their daily lives.

One Konso woman we studied is Sokate, a respected and energetic grandmother now in her 70s. Our many questions amuse Sokate, but she is polite and patient with us. When we ask why only 31 of the 119 Konso hide workers are men, she can only laugh and say that hide working has always been women's work.

After an early morning rain, Sokate strides through her village's terraced millet fields to the same riverbed in which her mother and grandmother searched for chert, a flakeable stone similar to flint. She uses a digging stick to pry stones loose. After almost an hour, Sokate picks up a small nodule of chert. She places it on a large, flat basalt rock. Lifting another large piece of basalt, she brings it down onto the nodule several times, striking off many pieces. Sokate selects ten of the flakes and places them into the top ruffle of her skirt, folding it into her waistband. She also tucks in three pieces of usable quartz, found with the aid of accompanying children.

Returning home, Sokate is greeted by children, goats, and chickens. She picks up the iron tip of a hoe, and, sitting on a goat hide in front of her house, strikes flakes off a chert nodule she collected earlier. She then picks up a wooden bowl filled with scraper components—wooden handles, used stone scrapers, small, unused flakes—and puts the new chert and quartz flakes in it. Moving to the hearth area in front of her house, she takes a flake from the bowl. Resting the flake directly along the edge of a large basalt block that serves as a hearthstone and an anvil, she strikes the flake's edges with the hoe tip, shaping it into a scraper that will fit into the socket of the wooden handle. Although she has access to iron, Sokate tells us that she prefers using stone because it is sharper, more controllable, and easier to resharpen than iron, or even glass. But not all Konso hide workers share her opinion, and in fact, there are now only 21 of them who still use stone regularly.

She places the handle, passed down to her from her mother, into the ashes of the hearth, warming the acacia tree gum (mastic) that holds the scraper in its socket. When the mastic becomes pliable, Sokate pulls the old, used-up scraper out of the socket, then places the end of the handle back into the ashes. After a few minutes, she takes it out and removes some of the old mastic with a stick. On an earthenware sherd, she mixes fresh resin she collected earlier in the day with ashes and heats it. Winding it onto a stick, she drips it into the socket. Sokate then puts a new scraper into the socket, patting the resin down around it with her index finger, making certain that it is set at the proper 90-degree angle to the haft.

Local farmers and other artisans bring Sokate hides to scrape, paying her with grain or money. This morning she is going to scrape a cow hide, Sokate brushes it with a mixture of water and juice from the enset plant, or false banana. If the hide is too dry, removing the fat from its inner side is difficult. After the hide is saturated, she latches one end of it to a tree or post so the hide is slightly above the ground. Squatting or kneeling, she holds the hide taut with her feet to facilitate scraping it. Then with both hands holding the wooden handle, she scrapes the cow hide in long strokes, using a "pull" motion. Goat hides are laid flat on the ground with Sokate sitting with one leg on top of the hide and the other underneath to keep it taut. She scrapes a goat hide with short strokes and a "push" motion away from her body, giving better control of the scraper with the thin goat skin.

Sokate removes the fatty inner layer, shaving off long strips in a rhythmic motion. When the edge of her tool becomes dull, usually after about 60 strokes, she resharpens it. Most of the small chips she removes from the scraper to resharpen it fall into a wooden bowl or gourd. Her barefoot grandchildren periodically dump the sharp chips onto the communal trash pile just outside the village. Sokate uses the scraper until it becomes too dull for scraping and too small to resharpen further. She'll wear out two or three scraping a single cattle hide, one or two for a goat hide.

Many hide-working activities take place in Konso compounds, which are often surrounded by stone walls. A broken pot on the roof indicates the father of a household is a first-born son, a person of higher status.

After Sokate scrapes the hide, she spreads a reddish, oily paste of ground castor beans and pieces of red ocher over it. She then folds the hide over and works the mixture into it. After a few days, the skin is soft. Cow hides are then made into bedding, sandals, straps, belts, and musical instruments, while goat hides are made into bags and (now much more rarely) clothing. During harvest time, the demand for goat hides increases because more bags are needed to carry agricultural goods. Sokate then sends her granddaughter to tell the hide's owner that it is ready.

Sokate and the other Ethiopian hide workers say they are proud of their profession, as they play important economic and social roles within their villages. In addition to hide working, they may also be responsible for announcing births, deaths, and meetings, and for performing puberty initiation ceremonies and other ritual activities. Despite the usefulness of their craft and other duties in the community, Konso hide workers and other artisans, such as ironsmiths and potters, have low social status. Farmers hold them in low esteem and consider them polluted, probably because their crafts involve contact with items that are thought to be impure, like the skins of dead animals. They cannot marry outside of their artisan group, usually cannot own land, and are often excluded from political and judicial life.

Clearly, the Konso hide workers are a rich source of information from which we can address a range of questions: Can excavations of abandoned hide worker compounds provide insights into the identification of social inequality and ranking? How and in what social contexts is stone toolmaking learned? Can we differentiate women's activities from men's on the basis of stone tools?

There is a sense of urgency in our work. Many of the hide workers are elderly and have not taught their children their craft; the influx of plastic bags and Western furnishings have greatly reduced demand for their products. And many of the hide workers have abandoned the use of stone in favor of bottle glass: why hike two hours for chert when you can just walk down the road and pick up pieces of glass? We want to complete our study of the Konso hide workers as soon as possible and begin studying other groups in southern Ethiopia whose hide workers are still using flaked stone, for after 2.5 million years of stone tool use and probably more than 100,000 years of scraping hides with stone, humanity's first and longest-lasting cultural tradition is rapidly being lost.

Critical Thinking

1. How extensive is stone toolmaking today in Ethiopia?
2. In what way are the Konso hide workers unique? Have there been other such cases?
3. Why does Sokate prefer tools made of stone rather than iron?
4. For what purposes does Sokate scrape hides?
5. What social and economic roles do the hide scrapers play? What is their social standing in the community and why? What restrictions have been placed upon them?
6. Why does the author say "there is a sense of urgency about our work"?

Steven A. Brandt and **Kathryn Weedman** are in the department of anthropology at the University of Florida, Gainesville. Their work is supported by funds from the National Science Foundation.

Article 14

Yes, Wonderful Things

WILLIAM RATHJE AND CULLEN MURPHY

On a crisp October morning not long ago the sun ascended above the Atlantic Ocean and turned its gaze on a team of young researchers as they swarmed over what may be the largest archaeological site in the world. The mound they occupied covers three thousand acres and in places rises more than 155 feet above a low-lying island. Its mass, estimated at 100 million tons, and its volume, estimated at 2.9 billion cubic feet, make it one of the largest man-made structures in North America. And it is known to be a treasure trove—a Pompeii, a Tikal, a Valley of the Kings—of artifacts from the most advanced civilization the planet has ever seen. Overhead sea gulls cackled and cawed, alighting now and then to peck at an artifact or skeptically observe an archaeologist at work. The surrounding landscape still supported quail and duck, but far more noticeable were the dusty, rumbling wagons and tractors of the New York City Department of Sanitation.

The site was the Fresh Kills landfill, on Staten Island, in New York City, a repository of garbage that, when shut down, in the year 2005, will have reached a height of 505 feet above sea level, making it the highest geographic feature along a fifteen-hundred-mile stretch of the Atlantic seaboard running north from Florida all the way to Maine. One sometimes hears that Fresh Kills will have to be closed when it reaches 505 feet so as not to interfere with the approach of aircraft to Newark Airport, in New Jersey, which lies just across the waterway called Arthur Kill. In reality, though, the 505-foot elevation is the result of a series of calculations designed to maximize the landfill's size while avoiding the creation of grades so steep that roads built upon the landfill can't safely be used.

Fresh Kills was originally a vast marshland, a tidal swamp. Robert Moses's plan for the area, in 1948, was to dump enough garbage there to fill the marshland up—a process that would take, according to one estimate, until 1968—and then to develop the site, building houses, attracting light industry, and setting aside open space for recreational use. ("The Fresh Kills landfill project," a 1951 report to Mayor Vincent R. Impelliteri observed, "cannot fail to affect constructively a wide area around it. It is at once practical and idealistic.") Something along these lines may yet happen when Fresh Kills is closed. Until then, however, it is the largest active landfill in the world. It is twenty-five times the size of the Great Pyramid of Khufu at Giza, forty times the size of the Temple of the Sun at Teotihuacan. The volume of Fresh Kills is approaching that of the Great Wall of China, and by one estimate will surpass it at some point in the next few years. It is the sheer physical stature of Fresh Kills in the hulking world of landfills that explains why archaeologists were drawn to the place.

To the archaeologists of the University of Arizona's Garbage Project, which is now entering its twentieth year, landfills represent valuable lodes of information that may, when mined and interpreted, produce valuable insights—insights not into the nature of some past society, of course, but into the nature of our own. Garbage is among humanity's most prodigious physical legacies to those who have yet to be born; if we can come to understand our discards, Garbage Project archaeologists argue, then we will better understand the world in which we live. It is this conviction that prompts Garbage Project researchers to look upon the steaming detritus of daily existence with the same quiet excitement displayed by Howard Carter and Lord George Edward Carnarvon at the unpillaged, unopened tomb of Tutankhamun.

"Can you see anything?" Carnarvon asked as Carter thrust a lighted candle through a hole into the gloom of the first antechamber. "Yes," Carter replied. "Wonderful things."

Garbage archaeology can be conducted in several ways. At Fresh Kills the method of excavation involved a mobile derrick and a thirteen-hundred-pound bucket auger, the latter of which would be sunk into various parts of the landfill to retrieve samples of garbage from selected strata. At 6:15 A.M. Buddy Kellett of the company Kellett's Well Boring, Inc., which had assisted with several previous Garbage Project landfill digs, drove one of the company's trucks, with derrick and auger collapsed for travel, straight up the steep slope of one of the landfill mounds. Two-thirds of the way up, the Garbage Project crew directed Kellett to a small patch of level ground. Four hydraulic posts were deployed from the stationary vehicle, extending outward to keep it safely moored. Now the derrick was raised. It supported a long metal rod that in turn housed two other metal rods; the apparatus, when pulled to its full length, like a telescope, was capable of penetrating the landfill to a depth of ninety-seven feet—enough at this particular spot to go clear through its bottom and into the original marsh that Fresh Kills had been (or into what was left of it). At the end of the rods was the auger, a large bucket made of high-tension steel: four feet high, three feet in diameter, and open at the bottom like a cookie cutter, with six graphite-and-steel teeth around the bottom's circumference. The bucket would spin at about thirty revolutions per minute and with such force that virtually nothing could impede its descent. At a Garbage Project excavation in Sunnyvale, California, in 1988, one of the first things the bucket hit in the cover dirt a few feet below the surface of the Sunnyvale Landfill was the skeleton of a car. The bucket's teeth snapped the axle, and drilled on.

The digging at Fresh Kills began. Down the whirring bucket plunged. Moments later it returned with a gasp, laden with garbage that, when released, spewed a thin vapor into the chill autumnal air. The smell was pungent, somewhere between sweet and disagreeable. Kellett's rig operator, David Spillers, did his job with the relaxation that comes of familiarity, seemingly oblivious to the harsh grindings and sharp clanks. The rest of the archaeological crew, wearing cloth aprons and heavy rubber gloves, went about their duties with practiced efficiency and considerable speed. They were veteran members of the Garbage Project's A-Team—its landfill-excavating arm—and had been through it all before.

Again a bucketful of garbage rose out of the ground. As soon as it was dumped Masakazu Tani, at the time a Japanese graduate student in anthropology at the University of Arizona (his Ph.D. thesis, recently completed, involves identifying activity areas in ancient sites on the basis of distributions of litter), plunged a thermometer into the warm mass. "Forty-three degrees centigrade," Tani called out. The temperature (equivalent to 109.4 degrees Fahrenheit) was duly logged. The garbage was then given a brusque preliminary examination to determine its generic source and, if possible, its date of origin. In this case the presence of telltale domestic items, and of legible newspapers, made both tasks easy. Gavin Archer, another anthropologist and a research associate of the Garbage Project, made a notation in the running log that he would keep all day long: "Household, circa 1977." Before the next sample was pulled up Douglas Wilson, an anthropologist who specializes in household hazardous waste, stepped up to the auger hole and played out a weighted tape measure, eventually calling out, "Thirty-five feet." As a safety precaution, Wilson, like any other crew member working close to the sunken shaft on depth-measure duty, wore a leather harness tethered to a nearby vehicle. The esophagus created by the bucket auger was just large enough to accept a human being, and anyone slipping untethered a story or two into this narrow, oxygen-starved cavity would die of asphyxiation before any rescue could be attempted.

Most of the bucketfuls of garbage received no more attention than did the load labeled "Household, circa 1977." Some basic data were recorded for tracking purposes, and the garbage was left on a quickly accumulating backdirt pile. But as each of what would finally be fourteen wells grew deeper and deeper, at regular intervals (either every five or every ten feet) samples were taken and preserved for full-dress analysis. On those occasions Wilson Hughes, the methodical and serenely ursine co-director and field supervisor of the Garbage Project, and the man responsible for day-to-day logistics at the Fresh Kills dig, would call out to the bucket operator over the noise of the engine: "We'll take the next bucket." Then Hughes and Wilson would race toward the rig in a running crouch, like medics toward a helicopter, a plywood sampling board between them. Running in behind came a team of microbiologists and civil engineers assembled from the University of Oklahoma, the University of Wisconsin, and Procter & Gamble's environmental laboratory. They brought with them a variety of containers and sealing devices to preserve samples in an oxygen-free environment—an environment that would allow colonies of the anaerobic bacteria that cause most of the biodegradation in landfills (to the extent that biodegradation occurs) to survive for later analysis. Behind the biologists and engineers came other Garbage Project personnel with an assortment of wire mesh screens and saw horses.

Within seconds of the bucket's removal from the ground, the operator maneuvered it directly over the sampling board, and released the contents. The pile was attacked first by Phillip Zack, a civil engineering student from the University of Wisconsin, who, as the temperature was being recorded, directed portions of the material into a variety of airtight conveyances. Then other members of the team moved in—the people who would shovel the steaming refuse atop the wire mesh; the people who would sort and bag whatever didn't go through the mesh; the people who would pour into bags or cannisters or jars whatever did go through the mesh; the people who would label everything for the trip either back to Tucson and the Garbage Project's holding bins or to the laboratories of the various microbiologists. (The shortest trip was to the trailer-laboratory that Procter & Gamble scientists had driven from Cincinnati and parked at the edge of the landfill.) The whole sample-collection process, from dumping to sorting to storing, took no more than twelve minutes. During the Fresh Kills dig it was repeated forty-four times at various places and various depths.

As morning edged toward afternoon the bucket auger began to near the limits of its reach in one of the wells. Down through the first thirty-five feet, a depth that in this well would date back to around 1984, the landfill had been relatively dry. Food waste and yard waste—hot dogs, bread, and grass clippings, for example—were fairly well preserved. Newspapers remained intact and easy to read, their lurid headlines ("Woman Butchered-Ex-Hubby Held") calling to mind a handful of yesterday's tragedies. Beyond thirty-five feet, however, the landfill became increasingly wet, the garbage increasingly unidentifiable. At sixty feet, a stratum in this well containing garbage from the 1940s and 1950s, the bucket grabbed a sample and pulled it toward the surface. The Garbage Project team ran forward with their equipment, positioning themselves underneath. The bucket rose majestically as the operator sat at the controls, shouting something over the noise. As near as anyone can reconstruct it now, he was saying, "You boys might want to back off some, 'cause if this wind hits that bucket. . . ." The operator broke off because the wind did hit that bucket, and the material inside—a gray slime, redolent of putrefaction—thoroughly showered the crew. It would be an exaggeration to suggest that the victims were elated by this development, but their curiosity was certainly piqued, because on only one previous excavation had slime like this turned up in a landfill. What was the stuff made of? How had it come to be? What did its existence mean? The crew members doggedly collected all the usual samples, plus a few extra bottles of slime for special study. Then they cleaned themselves off.

It would be a blessing if it were possible to study garbage in the abstract, to study garbage without having to handle it physically.[1] But that is not possible. Garbage is not mathematics. To understand garbage you have to touch it, to feel it, to sort it, to smell it. You have to pick through hundreds of tons of it, counting and weighing all the daily newspapers, the telephone books; the soiled diapers, the foam clamshells that once briefly held hamburgers, the lipstick cylinders coated with grease, the medicine vials still encasing brightly colored pills, the empty bottles of scotch, the half-full cans of paint and muddy turpentine, the forsaken toys, the cigarette butts. You have to sort and weigh and measure the volume of all the organic matter, the discards from thousands of plates: the noodles and the Cheerios and the tortillas; the pieces of pet food that have made their own gravy; the hardened jelly doughnuts, bleeding from their side wounds; the half-eaten bananas, mostly still within their peels, black and incomparably sweet in the embrace of final decay. You have to confront sticky green mountains of yard waste, and slippery brown hills of potato peels, and brittle ossuaries of chicken bones and T-bones. And then, finally, there are the "fines," the vast connecting mixture of tiny bits of paper, metal, glass, plastic, dirt, grit, and former nutrients that suffuses every landfill like a kind of grainy lymph. To understand garbage you need thick gloves and a mask and some booster shots. But the yield in knowledge—about people and their behavior as well as about garbage itself—offsets the grim working conditions.

To an archaeologist, ancient garbage pits or garbage mounds, which can usually be located within a short distance from any ruin, are always among the happiest of finds, for they contain in concentrated form the artifacts and comestibles and remnants of behavior of the people who used them. While every archaeologist dreams of discovering spectacular objects, the bread-and-butter work of archaeology involves the most common and routine kinds of discards. It is not entirely fanciful to define archaeology as the discipline that tries to understand old garbage, and to learn from that garbage something about ancient societies and ancient behaviors. The eminent archaeologist Emil Haury once wrote of the aboriginal garbage heaps of the American Southwest: "Whichever way one views the mounds—as garbage piles to avoid, or as symbols of a way of life—they nevertheless are features more productive of information than any others." When the British archaeologist Sir Leonard Woolley, in 1916, first climbed to the top of the ancient city of Carchemish, on the Euphrates River near the modern-day Turkish-Syrian border, he moistened his index finger and held it in the air. Satisfied, he scanned the region due south of the city—that is, downwind—pausing to draw on his map the location of any mounds he saw. A trench dug through the largest of these mounds revealed it to be the garbage dump Woolley was certain it was, and the exposed strata helped establish the chronological sequence for the Carchemish site as a whole. Archaeologists have been picking through ancient garbage ever since archaeology became a profession, more than a century ago, and they will no doubt go on doing so as long as garbage is produced.

Several basic points about garbage need to be emphasized at the outset. First, the creation of garbage is an unequivocal sign of a human presence. From Styrofoam cups along a roadway and urine bags on the moon there is an uninterrupted chain of garbage that reaches back more than two million years to the first "waste flake" knocked off in the knapping of the first stone tool. That the distant past often seems misty and dim is precisely because our earliest ancestors left so little garbage behind. An appreciation of the accomplishments of the first hominids became possible only after they began making stone tools, the debris from the production of which, along with the discarded tools themselves, are now probed for their secrets with electron microscopes and displayed in museums not as garbage but as "artifacts." These artifacts serve as markers—increasingly frequent and informative markers—of how our forebears coped with the evolving physical and social world. Human beings are mere placeholders in time, like zeros in a long number; their garbage seems to have more staying power, and a power to inform across the millennia that complements (and often substitutes for) that of the written word. The profligate habits of our own country and our own time—the sheer volume of the garbage that we create and must dispose of—will make our society an open book. The question is: Would we ourselves recognize our story when it is told, or will our garbage tell tales about us that we as yet do not suspect?

That brings up a second matter: If our garbage, in the eyes of the future, is destined to hold a key to the past, then surely it already holds a key to the present. This may be an obvious point, but it is one whose implications were not pursued by scholars until relatively recently. Each of us throws away dozens of items every day. All of these items are relics of specific human activities—relics no different in their inherent nature from many of those that traditional archaeologists work with (though they are, to be sure, a bit fresher). Taken as a whole the garbage of the United States, from its 93 million households and 1.5 million retail outlets and from all of its schools, hospitals, government offices, and other public facilities, is a mirror of American society. Of course, the problem with the mirror garbage offers is that, when encountered in a garbage can, dump, or landfill, it is a broken one: our civilization is reflected in billions of fragments that may reveal little in and of themselves. Fitting some of the pieces back together requires painstaking effort—effort that a small number of archaeologists and natural scientists have only just begun to apply.

A third point about garbage is that it is not an assertion but a physical fact—and thus may sometimes serve as a useful corrective. Human beings have over the centuries left many accounts describing their lives and civilizations. Many of these are little more than self-aggrandizing advertisements. The remains of the tombs, temples, and palaces of the elite are filled with personal histories as recorded by admiring relatives and fawning retainers. More such information is carved into obelisks and stelae, gouged into clay tablets, painted or printed on papyrus and paper. Historians are understandably drawn to written evidence of this kind, but garbage has often served as a kind of tattle-tale, setting the record straight.

It had long been known, for example, that French as well as Spanish forts had been erected along the coast of South Carolina during the sixteenth century, and various mounds and depressions have survived into our own time to testify to their whereabouts. Ever since the mid-nineteenth century a site on the tip of Parris Island, South Carolina, has been familiarly known as the site of a French outpost, built in 1562, that is spelled variously in old documents as Charlesfort, Charlesforte, and Charles Forte. In 1925, the Huguenot Society of South Carolina successfully lobbied Congress to erect a monument commemorating the building of Charlesfort. Subsequently, people in nearby Beaufort took up the Charlesfort theme, giving French names to streets, restaurants, and housing developments. Gift shops sold kitschy touristiana with a distinctly Gallic flavor. Those restaurants and gift shops found themselves in an awkward position when, in 1957, as a result of an analysis of discarded matter discovered at Charlesfort, a National Park Service historian, Albert Manucy, suggested that the site was of Spanish origin. Excavations begun in 1979 by the archaeologist Stanley South, which turned up such items as discarded Spanish olive jars and broken majolica pottery from Seville, confirmed Manucy's view: "Charlesfort," South established, was actually Fort San Marcos, a Spanish installation built in 1577 to protect a Spanish town named Santa Elena. (Both the fort and the town had been abandoned after only a few years.)

Garbage, then, represents physical fact, not mythology. It underscores a point that cannot be too greatly emphasized: Our private worlds consist essentially of two realities—mental reality, which encompasses beliefs, attitudes, and ideas, and material reality, which is the picture embodied in the physical record. The study of garbage reminds us that it is a rare person in whom mental and material realities completely coincide. Indeed, for the most part, the pair exist in a state of tension, if not open conflict.

Americans have always wondered, sometimes with buoyant playfulness, what their countrymen in the far future will make of Americans "now." In 1952, in a monograph he first circulated privately among colleagues and eventually published in *The Journal of Irreproducible Results,* the eminent anthropologist and linguist Joseph H. Greenberg—the man who would one day sort the roughly one thousand known Native American languages into three broad language families—imagined the unearthing of the so-called "violence texts" during an excavation of the Brooklyn Dodgers' Ebbets Field in the year A.D. 2026; what interpretation, he wondered, would be given to such newspaper reports as "Yanks Slaughter Indians" and "Reese made a sacrifice in the infield"? In 1979 the artist and writer David Macaulay published *Motel of the Mysteries,* an archaeological site-report setting forth the conclusions reached by a team of excavators in the year A.D. 4022 who have unearthed a motel dating back to 1985 (the year, Macaulay wrote, in which "an accidental reduction in postal rates on a substance called third- and fourth-class mail literally buried the North Americans under tons of brochures, fliers, and small containers called FREE"). Included in the report are illustrations of an archaeologist modeling a toilet seat, toothbrushes, and a drain stopper (or, as Macaulay describes them, "the Sacred Collar . . . the magnificent 'plasticus' ear ornaments, and the exquisite silver chain and pendant"), all assumed to be items of ritual or personal regalia. In 1982 an exhibit was mounted in New York City called "Splendors of the Sohites"—a vast display of artifacts, including "funerary vessels" (faded, dusky soda bottles) and "hermaphrodite amulets" (discarded pop-top rings), found in the SoHo section of Manhattan and dating from the Archaic Period (A.D. 1950–1961), the Classical Period (1962–1975), and the Decadent Period (1976–c.1980).

Greenberg, Macaulay, and the organizers of the Sohites exhibition all meant to have some fun, but there is an uneasy undercurrent to their work, and it is embodied in the question: What are we to make of ourselves? The Garbage Project, conceived in 1971, and officially established at the University of Arizona in 1973, was an attempt to come up with a new way of providing serious answers. It aimed to apply *real* archaeology to this very question; to see if it would be possible to investigate human behavior "from the back end," as it were. This scholarly endeavor has come to be known as garbology, and practitioners of garbology are known as garbologists. The printed citation (dated 1975) in the *Oxford English Dictionary* for the meaning of "garbology" as used here associates the term with the Garbage Project.

In the years since its founding the Garbage Project's staff members have processed more than 250,000 pounds of garbage, some of it from landfills but most of it fresh out of garbage cans in selected neighborhoods. All of this garbage has been sorted, coded, and catalogued—every piece, from bottles of furniture polish and egg-shaped pantyhose packaging to worn and shredded clothing, crumpled bubble-gum wrappers, and the full range of kitchen waste. A unique database has been built up from these cast-offs, covering virtually every aspect of American life: drinking habits, attitudes toward red meat, trends in the use of convenience foods, the strange ways in which consumers respond to shortages, the use of contraceptives, and hundreds of other matters.[2]

The antecedents of the Garbage Project in the world of scholarship and elsewhere are few but various. Some are undeniably dubious. The examination of fresh refuse is, of course, as old as the human species—just watch anyone who happens upon an old campsite, or a neighbor scavenging at a dump for spare parts or furniture. The first systematic study of the components of America's garbage dates to the early 1900s and the work of the civil engineers Rudolph Hering (in New York) and Samuel A. Greeley (in Chicago), who by 1921 had gathered enough information from enough cities to compile *Collection and Disposal of Municipal Refuse,* the first textbook on urban trash management. In academe, not much happened after that for quite some time. Out in the field, however, civil engineers and solid-waste managers did now and again sort and weigh fresh garbage as it stood in transit between its source and destination, but their categories were usually simple: paper, glass, metal. No one sorted garbage into detailed categories relating to particular consumer discard patterns. No one, for example, kept track of phenomena as specific as the number of beer cans thrown away versus the number of beer bottles, or the number of orange-juice cans thrown away versus the number of pounds of freshly squeezed oranges, or the amount of candy thrown away in the week after Halloween versus the amount thrown away in the week after Valentine's Day. And no one ever dug into the final resting places of most of America's garbage: dumps (where garbage is left in the open) and sanitary landfills (where fresh garbage is covered every night with six to eight inches of soil).

Even as America's city managers over the years oversaw—and sometimes desperately attempted to cope with—the disposal of ever-increasing amounts of garbage, the study of garbage itself took several odd detours—one into the world of the military, another into the world of celebrity-watching, and a third into the world of law enforcement.

The military's foray into garbology occurred in 1941, when two enlisted men, Horace Schwerin and Phalen Golden, were forced to discontinue a survey they were conducting among new recruits about which aspects of Army life the recruits most disliked. (Conducting polls of military personnel was, they had learned, against regulations.) Schwerin and Golden had already discovered, however, that the low quality of the food was the most frequently heard complaint, and they resolved to look into this one matter with an investigation that could not be considered a poll. What Schwerin and Golden did was to station observers in mess halls to record the types of food that were most commonly wasted and the volume of waste by type of food. The result, after 2.4 million man-meals had been observed, was a textbook example of how garbage studies can produce not only behavioral insights but also practical benefits. Schwerin and Golden discovered that 20 percent of the food prepared for Army mess halls was eventually thrown away, and that one reason for this was simply excess preparation. Here are some more of their findings, as summarized in a wartime article that appeared in the *The Saturday Evening Post:*

> Soldiers ate more if they were allowed to smoke in the mess hall. They ate more if they went promptly to table instead of waiting on line outside—perhaps because the food became cold. They ate more if they fell to on their own initiative instead of by command. They cared little for soups, and 65 percent of the kale and nearly as much of the spinach went into the garbage can. Favorite desserts were cakes and cookies, canned fruit, fruit salad, and gelatin. They ate ice cream in almost any amount that was served to them.

"That, sergeant, is an excellent piece of work," General George C. Marshall, the Army chief of staff, told Horace Schwerin after hearing a report by Schwerin on the research findings. The Army adopted many of Schwerin and Golden's recommendations, and began saving some 2.5 million pounds of food a day. It is perhaps not surprising to learn that until joining the Army Horace Schwerin had been in market research, and, among other things, had helped CBS to perfect a device for measuring audience reaction to radio shows.

The origins of an ephemeral branch of garbage studies focused on celebrities—"peeping-Tom" garbology, one might call it—seem to lie in the work of A. J. Weberman. Weberman was a gonzo journalist and yippie whose interest in the songs of Bob Dylan, and obsession with their interpretation, in 1970 prompted him to begin stealing the garbage from the cans left out in front of Dylan's Greenwich Village brownstone on MacDougal Street. Weberman didn't find much—some soiled Pampers, some old newspapers, some fast-food packaging from a nearby Blimpie Base, a shopping list with the word vanilla spelled "vanilla." He did, however, stumble into a brief but highly publicized career. This self-proclaimed "garbage guerrilla" quickly moved on to Neil Simon's garbage (it included a half-eaten bagel, scraps of lox, the Sunday Times), Muhammad Ali's (an empty can of Luck's collard greens, and empty roach bomb), and Abbie Hoffman's (a summons for hitchhiking, an unused can of deodorant, an estimate of the cost for the printing of *Steal This Book,* and the telephone numbers of Jack Anderson and Kate Millet). Weberman revealed many of his findings in an article in *Esquire* in 1971. It was antics such as his that inspired a prior meaning of the term "garbology," one very different from the definition established today.

Weberman's work inspired other garbage guerrillas. In January of 1975, the *Detroit Free Press* Sunday magazine reported on the findings from its raids on the garbage of several city notables, including the mayor, the head of the city council, the leader of a right-wing group, a food columnist, a disk jockey, and a prominent psychiatrist. Nothing much was discovered that might be deemed out of the ordinary, save for some of the contents of the garbage taken from a local Hare Krishna temple: a price tag from an Oleg Cassini garment, for example, and four ticket stubs from the Bel-Aire Drive-In Theater, which at the time was showing *Horrible House on the Hill* and *The Night God Screamed.* Six months after the *Free Press* exposé, a reporter for the *National Enquirer,* Jay Gourley, drove up to 3018 Dumbarton Avenue, N.W., in Washington, D.C., and threw the five garbage bags in front of Secretary of State Henry A. Kissinger's house into the trunk of his car. Secret Service agents swiftly blocked Gourley's departure, but after a day of questioning allowed him to proceed, the garbage still in the trunk. Among Gourley's finds: a crumpled piece of paper with a dog's teeth marks on it, upon which was written the work schedules of the Secret Service agents assigned to guard the Secretary; empty bottles of Seconal and Maalox; and a shopping list, calling for a case of Jack Daniel's, a case of Ezra Brooks bourbon, and a case of Cabin Still bourbon. Gourley later returned most of the garbage to the Kissingers—minus, he told reporters, "several dozen interesting things."

After the Kissinger episode curiosity about the garbage of celebrities seems to have abated. In 1977 the *National Enquirer* sent a reporter to poke through the garbage of President Jimmy

Carter's press secretary, Jody Powell. The reporter found so little of interest that the tabloid decided not to publish a story. In 1980 Secret Service agents apprehended A. J. Weberman as he attempted to abduct former President Richard Nixon's garbage from behind an apartment building in Manhattan. Weberman was released, without the garbage.

The third detour taken by garbage studies involves police work. Over the years, law enforcement agents looking for evidence in criminal cases have also been more-than-occasional students of garbage; the Federal Bureau of Investigation in particular has spent considerable time poring over the household trash of people in whom it maintains a professional interest. ("We take it on a case-by-case basis," an FBI spokesman says.) One of the biggest criminal cases involving garbage began in 1975 and involved Joseph "Joe Bananas" Bonanno, Sr., a resident of Tucson at the time and a man with alleged ties to organized crime that were believed to date back to the days of Al Capone. For a period of three years officers of the Arizona Drug Control District collected Bonanno's trash just before the regular pickup, replacing it with "fake" Bonanno garbage. (Local garbagemen were not employed in the operation because some of them had received anonymous threats after assisting law enforcement agencies in an earlier venture.) The haul in evidence was beyond anyone's expectations: Bonanno had apparently kept detailed records of his various transactions, mostly in Sicilian. Although Bonanno had torn up each sheet of paper into tiny pieces, forensic specialists with the Drug Control District, like archaeologists reconstructing ceramic bowls from potsherds, managed to reassemble many of the documents and with the help of the FBI got them translated. In 1980 Bonanno was found guilty of having interfered with a federal grand jury investigation into the business operations of his two sons and a nephew. He was eventually sent to jail.

Unlike law-enforcement officers or garbage guerrillas, the archaeologists of the Garbage Project are not interested in the contents of any particular individual's garbage can. Indeed, it is almost always the case that a given person's garbage is at once largely anonymous and unimaginably humdrum. Garbage most usefully comes alive when it can be viewed in the context of broad patterns, for it is mainly in patterns that the links between artifacts and behaviors can be discerned.

The seed from which the Garbage Project grew was an anthropology class conducted at the University of Arizona in 1971 that was designed to teach principles of archaeological methodology. The University of Arizona has long occupied a venerable place in the annals of American archaeology and, not surprisingly, the pursuit of archaeology there to this day is carried on in serious and innovative ways. The class in question was one in which students undertook independent projects aimed precisely at showing links between various kinds of artifacts and various kinds of behavior. For example, one student, Sharon Thomas, decided to look into the relationship between a familiar motor function ("the diffusion pattern of ketchup over hamburgers") and a person's appearance, as manifested in clothing. Thomas took up a position at "seven different hamburger dispensaries" and, as people came in to eat, labeled them "neat" or "sloppy" according to a set of criteria relating to the way they dressed. Then she recorded how each of the fifty-seven patrons she studied—the ones who ordered hamburgers—poured ketchup over their food. She discovered that sloppy people were far more likely than neat people to put ketchup on in blobs, sometimes even stirring it with their fingers. Neat people, in contrast, tended to apply the ketchup in patterns: circles, spirals, and crisscrosses. One person (a young male neatly dressed in a body shirt, flared pants, and patent-leather Oxfords) wrote with ketchup what appeared to be initials.

Two of the student investigations, conducted independently by Frank Ariza and Kelly Allen, led directly to the Garbage Project. Ariza and Allen, wanting to explore the divergence between (or correlation of) mental stereotypes and physical realities, collected garbage from two households in an affluent part of Tucson and compared it to garbage from two households in a poor and, as it happens, Mexican-American part of town. The rich and poor families, each student found, ate about the same amount of steak and hamburger, and drank about the same amount of milk. But the poor families, they learned, bought more expensive child-education items. They also bought more household cleansers. What did such findings mean? Obviously the sample—involving only four households in all—was too small for the results even to be acknowledged as representative, let alone to provide hints as to what lay behind them. However, the general nature of the research effort itself—comparing garbage samples in order to gauge behavior (and, what is more, gauging behavior unobtrusively, thereby avoiding one of the great biases inherent in much social science)—seemed to hold great promise.

A year later, in 1972, university students, under professorial direction, began borrowing samples of household garbage from different areas of Tucson, and sorting it in a lot behind a dormitory. The Garbage Project was under way. In 1973, the Garbage Project entered into an arrangement with the City of Tucson, whereby the Sanitation Division, four days a week, delivered five to eight randomly selected household pickups from designated census tracts to an analysis site that the Division set aside for the Project's sorters at a maintenance yard. (Wilson Hughes, who as mentioned earlier is the Garbage Project's co-director, was one of the first undergraduate garbage sorters.) In 1984 operations were moved to an enclosure where many of the university's dumpsters are parked, across the street from Arizona Stadium.

The excavation of landfills would come much later in the Garbage Project's history, when to its focus on issues of garbage and human behavior it added a focus on issues of garbage management. The advantage in the initial years of sorting fresh garbage over excavating landfills was a basic but important one: In landfills it is often quite difficult and in many cases impossible to get some idea, demographically speaking, of the kind of neighborhood from which any particular piece of garbage has come. The value of landfill studies is therefore limited to advancing our understanding of garbage in the aggregate. With fresh garbage, on the other hand, one can have demographic precision down to the level of a few city blocks, by directing pickups to specific census districts and cross-tabulating the findings with census data.

Needless to say, deciding just which characteristics of the collected garbage to pay attention to posed a conceptual challenge, one that was met by Wilson Hughes, who devised the "protocol" that is used by the Garbage Project to this day. Items found in garbage are sorted into one of 150 specific coded categories that can in turn be clustered into larger categories representing food (fresh food versus prepared, health food versus junk food), drugs, personal and household sanitation products, amusement-related or educational materials, communications-related materials, pet-related materials, yard-related materials, and hazardous materials. For each item the following information is recorded on a standardized form: the date on which it was collected; the census tract from which it came; the item code (for example, 001, which would be the code for "Beef"); the item's type (for example, "chuck"); its original weight or volume (in this case, derived from the packaging); its cost (also from the packaging); material composition of container; brand (if applicable); and the weight of any discarded food (if applicable). The information garnered over the years from many thousands of such forms, filled out in pursuit of a wide variety of research objectives, constitutes the Garbage Project's database. It has all been computerized and amounts to some two million lines of data drawn from some fifteen thousand household-refuse samples. The aim here has been not only to approach garbage with specific questions to answer or hypotheses to prove but also to amass sufficient quantities of information, in a systematic and open-minded way, so that with the data on hand Garbage Project researchers would be able to answer any future questions or evaluate any future hypotheses that might arise. In 1972 garbage was, after all, still terra incognita, and the first job to be done was akin to that undertaken by the explorers Lewis and Clark.

From the outset the Garbage Project has had to confront the legal and ethical issues its research involves: Was collecting and sorting someone's household garbage an unjustifiable invasion of privacy? This very question has over the years been argued repeatedly in the courts. The Fourth Amendment unequivocally guarantees Americans protection from unreasonable search and seizure. Joseph Bonanno, Sr., tried to invoke the Fourth Amendment to prevent his garbage from being used as evidence. But garbage placed in a garbage can in a public thoroughfare, where it awaits removal by impersonal refuse collectors, and where it may be picked over by scavengers looking for aluminum cans, by curious children or neighbors, and by the refuse collectors themselves (some of whom do a thriving trade in old appliances, large and small), is usually considered by the courts to have been abandoned. Therefore, the examination of the garbage by outside parties cannot be a violation of a constitutional right. In the Bonanno case, U.S. District Court Judge William Ingram ruled that investigating garbage for evidence of a crime may carry a "stench," but was not illegal. In 1988, in *California v. Greenwood,* the U.S. Supreme Court ruled by a margin of six to two that the police were entitled to conduct a warrantless search of a suspected drug dealer's garbage—a search that led to drug paraphernalia, which led in turn to warrants, arrests, and convictions. As Justice Byron White has written, "The police cannot reasonably be expected to avert their eyes from evidence of criminal activity that could have been observed by any member of the public."

Legal issues aside, the Garbage Project has taken pains to ensure that those whose garbage comes under scrutiny remain anonymous. Before obtaining garbage for study, the Project provides guarantees to communities and their garbage collectors that nothing of a personal nature will be examined and that no names or addresses or other personal information will be recorded. The Project also stipulates that all of the garbage collected (except aluminum cans, which are recycled) will be returned to the community for normal disposal.

As noted, the Garbage Project has now been sorting and evaluating garbage, with scientific rigor, for two decades. The Project has proved durable because its findings have supplied a fresh perspective on what we know—and what we think we know—about certain aspects of our lives. Medical researchers, for example, have long made it their business to question people about their eating habits in order to uncover relationships between patterns of diet and patterns of disease. These researchers have also long suspected that people—honest, well-meaning people—may often be providing information about quantities and types and even brands of food and drink consumed that is not entirely accurate. People can't readily say whether they trimmed 3.3 ounces or 5.4 ounces of fat off the last steak they ate, and they probably don't remember whether they had four, five, or seven beers in the previous week, or two eggs or three. The average person just isn't paying attention. Are there certain patterns in the way in which people wrongly "self-report" their dietary habits? Yes, there are, and Garbage Project studies have identified many of them.

Garbage archaeologists also know how much edible food is thrown away; what percentage of newspapers, cans, bottles, and other items aren't recycled; how loyal we are to brandname products and which have earned the greatest loyalty; and how much household hazardous waste is carted off to landfills and incinerators. From several truckloads of garbage and a few pieces of ancillary data—most importantly, the length of time over which the garbage was collected—the Garbage Project staff can reconstruct the community from which it came with a degree of accuracy that the Census Bureau might in some neighborhoods be unable to match.

Garbage also exposes the routine perversity of human ways. Garbage archaeologists have learned, for example, that the volume of garbage that Americans produce expands to fill the number of receptacles that are available to put it in. They have learned that we waste more of what is in short supply than of what is plentiful; that attempts by individuals to restrict consumption of certain foodstuffs are often counterbalanced by extra and inadvertent consumption of those same foodstuffs in hidden form; and that while a person's memory of what he has eaten and drunk in a given week is inevitably wide of the mark, his guess as to what a family member or even neighbor has eaten and drunk usually turns out to be more perceptive.

Some of the Garbage Project's research has prompted unusual forays into arcane aspects of popular culture. Consider the matter of those "amulets" worn by the Sohites—that is, the once-familiar detachable pop-top pull tab. Pull tabs first became important to the Garbage Project during a study of household recycling practices, conducted on behalf of the federal Environmental Protection Agency during the mid-1970s. The question arose: If a bag of household garbage contained no aluminum cans, did that mean that the household didn't dispose of any cans or that it had recycled its cans? Finding a way to answer that question was essential if a neighborhood's recycling rate was to be accurately determined. Pull tabs turned out to hold the key. A quick study revealed that most people did not drop pull tabs into the cans from which they had been wrenched; rather, the vast majority of people threw the tabs into the trash. If empty cans were stored separately for recycling, the pull tabs still went out to the curb with the rest of the garbage. A garbage sample that contained several pull tabs but no aluminum cans was a good bet to have come from a household that recycled.

All this counting of pull tabs prompted a surprising discovery one day by a student: Pull tabs were not all alike. Their configuration and even color depended on what kind of beverage they were associated with and where the beverage had been canned. Armed with this knowledge, Garbage Project researchers constructed an elaborate typology of pull tabs, enabling investigators to tease out data about beverage consumption—say, beer versus soda, Michelob versus Schlitz—even from samples of garbage that contained not a single can. Detachable pull tabs are no longer widely used in beverage cans, but the pull-tab typology remains useful even now. Among other things, in the absence of such evidence of chronology as a newspaper's dateline, pull tabs can reliably help to fix the dates of strata in a landfill. In archaeological parlance objects like these that have been widely diffused over a short period of time, and then abruptly disappear, are known as horizon markers.

The unique "punch-top" on Coors beer cans, for example, was used only between March of 1974 and June of 1977. (It was abandoned because some customers complained that they cut their thumbs pushing the holes open.) In landfills around the country, wherever Coors beer cans were discarded, punch-top cans not only identify strata associated with a narrow band of dates but also separate two epochs one from another. One might think of punch-tops playfully as the garbage equivalent of the famous iridium layer found in sediment toward the end of the Cretaceous Era, marking the moment (proponents of the theory believe) when a giant meteor crashed into the planet Earth, exterminating the dinosaurs.

All told, the Garbage Project has conducted nine full-scale excavations of municipal landfills in the United States and two smaller excavations associated with special projects. In the fall of 1991 it also excavated four sites in Canada, the data from which remains largely unanalyzed (and is not reflected in this book). The logistics of the landfill excavations are complex, and they have been overseen in all cases by Wilson Hughes. What is involved? Permission must be obtained from a raft of local officials and union leaders; indemnification notices must be provided to assure local authorities that the Garbage Project carries sufficient insurance against injury; local universities must be scoured for a supply of students to supplement the Garbage Project team; in many cases construction permits, of all things, must be obtained in advance of digging. There is also the whole matter of transportation, not only of personnel but also of large amounts of equipment. And there is the matter of personal accommodation and equipment storage. The time available for excavation is always limited, sometimes extremely so; the research program must be compressed to fit it, and the staff must be "tasked" accordingly. When the excavation has been completed the samples need to be packed and shipped—frequently on ice—back to headquarters or to specialized laboratories. All archaeologists will tell you that field work is mostly laborious, not glamorous; a landfill excavation is archaeology of the laborious kind.

For all the difficulties they present, the Garbage Project's landfill digs have acquired an increasing timeliness and relevance as concerns about solid-waste disposal have grown. Even as the Garbage Project has trained considerable attention on garbage as an analytical tool it has also taken up the problem of garbage itself—garbage as a problem, garbage as symbolized by *Mobro 4000,* the so-called "garbage barge," which sailed from Islip, Long Island, on March 22, 1987, and spent the next fifty-five days plying the seas in search of a place to deposit its 3,168 tons of cargo. Strange though it may seem, although more than 70 percent of America's household and commercial garbage ends up in landfills, very little reliable data existed until recently as to a landfill's contents and biological dynamics. Much of the conventional wisdom about garbage disposal consists of assertions that turn out, upon investigation, to be simplistic or misleading: among them, the assertion that, as trash, plastic, foam, and fast-food packaging are causes for great concern, that biodegradable items are always more desirable than nonbiodegradable ones, that on a per capita basis the nation's households are generating a lot more garbage than they used to, and that we're physically running out of places to put landfills.

This is not to say that garbage isn't a problem in need of serious attention. It is. But if they are to succeed, plans of action must be based on garbage realities. The most critical part of the garbage problem in America is that our notions about the creation and disposal of garbage are often riddled with myth. There are few other subjects of public significance on which popular and official opinion is so consistently misinformed. . . .

Gaps—large gaps—remain in our knowledge of garbage, and of how human behavior relates to it, and of how best to deal with it. But a lighted candle has at least been seized and thrust inside the antechamber.

Notes

1. A note on terminology. Several words for the things we throw away—"garbage," "trash," "refuse," "rubbish"—are used synonymously in casual speech but in fact have different meanings. *Trash* refers specifically to discards that are at least theoretically "dry"—newspapers, boxes, cans, and so on. *Garbage* refers technically to "wet" discards—food remains, yard waste, and offal. *Refuse* is an inclusive term for both the wet

discards and the dry. *Rubbish* is even more inclusive: It refers to all refuse plus construction and demolition debris. The distinction between wet and dry garbage was important in the days when cities slopped garbage to pigs, and needed to have the wet material separated from the dry; it eventually became irrelevant, but may see a revival if the idea of composting food and yard waste catches on. We will frequently use "garbage" in this book to refer to the totality of human discards because it is the word used most naturally in ordinary speech. The word is etymologically obscure, though it probably derives from Anglo-French, and its earliest associations have to do with working in the kitchen.

2. A question that always comes up is: What about garbage disposers? Garbage disposers are obviously capable of skewing the data in certain garbage categories, and Garbage Project researchers can employ a variety of techniques to compensate for the bias that garbage disposers introduce. Studies were conducted at the very outset of the Garbage Project to determine the discard differential between households with and without disposers, and one eventual result was a set of correction factors for various kinds of garbage (primarily food), broken down by subtype. As a general rule of thumb, households with disposers end up discarding in their trash about half the amount of food waste and food debris as households without disposers. It should be noted, however, that the fact that disposers have ground up some portion of a household's garbage often has little relevance to the larger issues the Garbage Project is trying to address. It means, for example, not that the Garbage Project's findings about the extent of food waste are invalid, but merely that its estimates are conservative.

Critical Thinking

1. Why does the author call the Fresh Kills landfill a "treasure trove"?
2. How is garbage archaeology conducted?
3. What are among the "happiest of finds"? Why?
4. What is the "bread and butter work" of archaeology? Why?
5. What points about archaeology does the author think need to be emphasized?
6. Why does the author emphasize the point that garbage represents a physical fact?
7. What was the goal of the Garbage Project?
8. How does the author see the systematic study of garbage conducted?
9. Why was the military foray into garbology a "textbook example" of how garbage studies can produce not only behavioral insights but also practical benefits?
10. Why were celebrities the focus of garbage studies?
11. What have been the legal arguments regarding police involvement with garbage?
12. Is the Garbage Project interested in the contents of any particular individual? Explain.
13. What is the difference between landfill studies and the study of "fresh garbage"?
14. What is the "protocol" used by the Garbage Project and what is its aim?
15. What have been the legal and ethical issues confronting the Garbage Project? How have the courts usually decided on them? How has the Garbage Project responded to the privacy issue?
16. What has the Garbage Project found with respect to patterns of diet and disease? With respect to how much edible food is thrown away?
17. What does the study of pull-tabs tell us? How are they used as horizon markers?
18. Describe the logistics of landfill excavations.

Bushmen

JOHN YELLEN

I followed Dau, kept his slim brown back directly in front of me, as we broke suddenly free from the dense Kalahari bush and crossed through the low wire fence that separated Botswana from Namibia to the West. For that moment while Dau held the smooth wires apart for me, we were out in the open, in the full hot light of the sun and then we entered the shadows, the tangled thickets of arrow grass and thorn bush and mongongo trees once again. As soon as the bush began to close in around us again, I quickly became disoriented, Dau's back my only reference point.

Even then, in that first month of 1968, while my desert boots retained their luster, I knew enough to walk behind, not next to Dau. I had expected the Kalahari Desert to be bare open sand. I had imagined myself looking out over vast stretches that swept across to the horizon. But to my surprise, I found that the dunes were covered with trees and that during the rains the grasses grew high over my head. The bare sand, where I could see it, was littered with leaves, and over these the living trees and brush threw a dappled pattern of sunlight and shade. To look in the far distance and maintain a sense of direction, to narrow my focus and pick a way between the acacia bushes and their thorns, and then to look down, just in front of my feet to search out menacing shapes, was too much for me. Already, in that first month, the Bushmen had shown me a puff adder coiled motionless by the base of an acacia tree, but not until Cumsa the Hunter came up close to it, ready to strike it with his spear, could I finally see what all those hands were pointing at.

As Dau walked, I tried to follow his lead. To my discomfort I knew that many of these bushes had thorns—the Kalahari cloaks itself in thorns—some hidden close to the ground just high enough to rake across my ankles and draw blood when I pushed through, others long and straight and white so they reflected the sun. That morning, just before the border fence, my concentration had lagged and I found myself entangled in wait-a-bit thorns that curved backwards up the branch. So I stopped and this short, brown-skinned Bushman pushed me gently backwards to release the tension, then worked the branch, thorn by thorn from my shirt and my skin.

In the mid-1960s, the South African government had decided to accurately survey the Botswana border, mark it with five-strand fence, and cut a thin firebreak on either side. At intervals they constructed survey towers, strange skeletal affairs, like oil drilling rigs, their tops poking well above the highest mongongo trees. It was to one of these that Dau led me across the border, through the midday sun. Although he would not climb it himself, since it was a white man's tower, he assumed I would. I followed his finger, his chain of logic as I started rather hesitantly up the rusted rungs. I cleared the arrow grass, the acacia bushes, finally the broad leafy crowns of the mongongo nut trees. Just short of the top I stopped and sat, hooked my feet beneath the rung below, and wrapped my arms around the metal edges of the sides.

For a month now I had copied the maps—the lines and the circles the !Kung tribesmen had drawn with their fingers in the sand. I had listened and tried to transcribe names of those places, so unintelligible with their clicks, their rising and falling tones. I had walked with Dau and the others to some of those places, to small camps near ephemeral water holes, but on the ground it was too confusing, the changes in altitude and vegetation too subtle, the sun too nearly overhead to provide any sense of where I was or from where I had come.

For the first time from the tower, I could see an order to the landscape. From up there on the tower, I could see that long thin border scar, could trace it off to the horizon to both the north and south. But beyond that, no evidence, not the slightest sign of a human hand. The Bushmen camps were too few in number, too small and well-hidden in the grass and bush to be visible from here. Likewise, the camp where we anthropologists lived, off to the east at the Dobe waterhole, that also was too small to see.

As Dau had intended, from my perch on that tower I learned a lot. At least now I could use the dunes, the shallow valleys, to know whether I was walking east and west or north and south.

In those first years with the Dobe Bushmen, I did gain at least a partial understanding of that land. And I learned to recognize many of those places, the ones that rate no name at all but are marked only by events—brief, ephemeral happenings that leave no mark on the land. I learned to walk with the Bushmen back from a hunt or a trip for honey or spear-shaft wood and listen. They talked, chattered almost constantly, decorating the bus, these no-name places as they went, putting ornaments of experience on them: "See that tree there, John? That's where we stopped, my brother and I, long before he was married, when he killed a kudu, a big female. We stopped under that tree, hung the meat up there and rested in the shade. But the flies were so bad, the biting flies, that we couldn't stay for long."

It took me a long time to realize that this chatter was not chatter at all, to understand that those remarks were gifts, a private map shared only among a few, an overlay crammed with fine, spidery writing on top of the base map with its named waterholes and large valleys, a map for friends to read. Dau would see a porcupine burrow, tiny, hidden in the vastness of the bush. And at night he could sit by the fire and move the others from point to point across the landscape to that small opening in the ground.

But as an archeologist, I had a task to do—to name those places and to discover what life had been like there in the past. "This place has a name now," I told Dau when I went back in 1976. Not

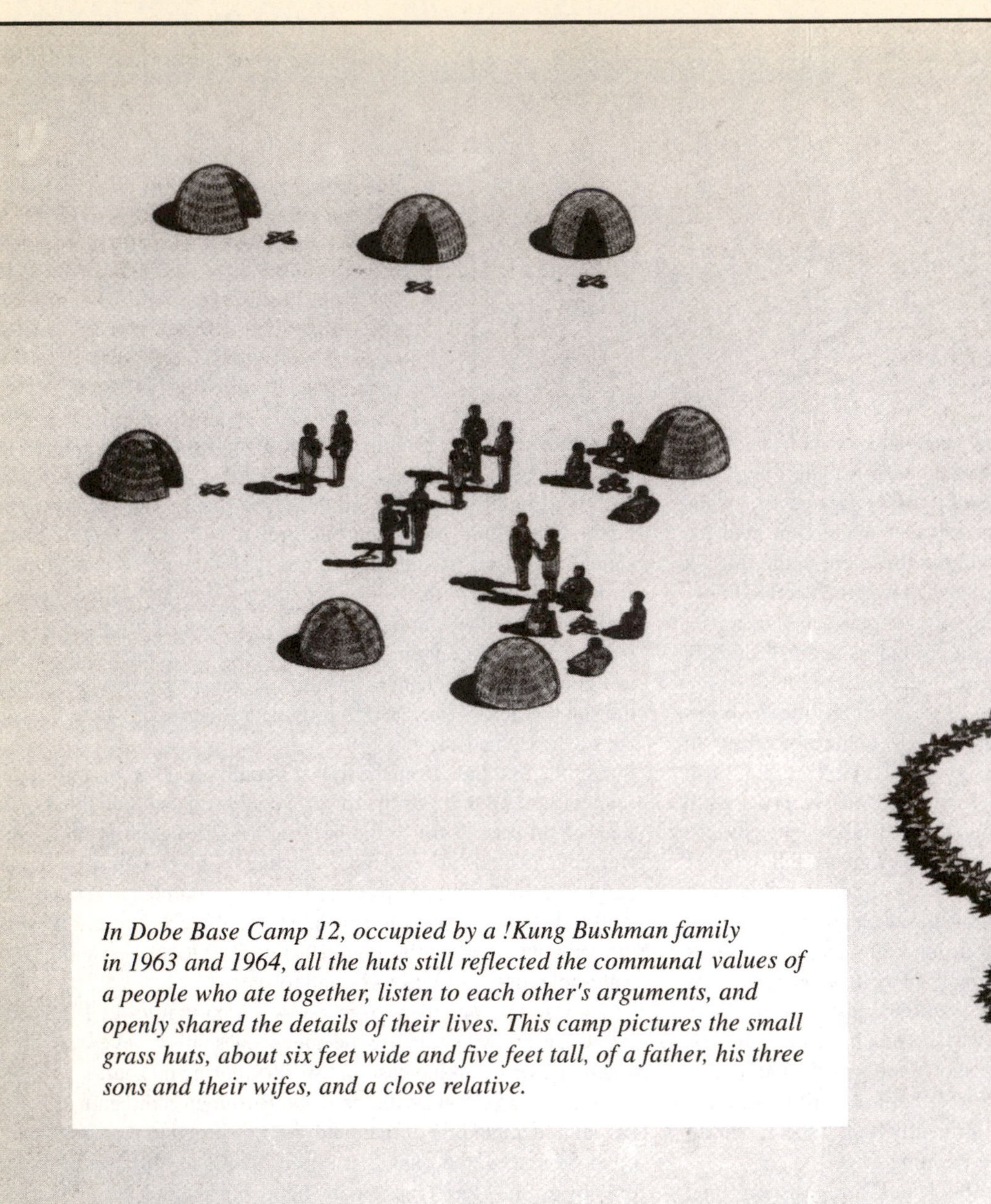

In Dobe Base Camp 12, occupied by a !Kung Bushman family in 1963 and 1964, all the huts still reflected the communal values of a people who ate together, listen to each other's arguments, and openly shared the details of their lives. This camp pictures the small grass huts, about six feet wide and five feet tall, of a father, his three sons and their wifes, and a close relative.

the chicken camp, because when I was there I kept 15 chickens, or the cobra camp, for the cobra we killed one morning among the nesting hens, but Dobe Base Camp 18. Eighteen because it's the eighteenth of these old abandoned camps I've followed you to in the last three days. See? That's what goes into this ledger, this fat bound book in waterproof ballpoint ink. We could get a reflector in here—a big piece of tin like some metal off a roof and get some satellite or a plane to photograph it. We could tell just where it is then, could mark it on one of those large aerial maps down to the nearest meter if we wanted.

We came back to these camps, these abandoned places on the ground, not once but month after month for the better part of a year. Not just Dau and myself but a whole crew of us, eight Bushmen and I, to dig, to look down into the ground. We started before the sun was too high up in the sky, and later Dau and I sat in the shade sipping thick, rich tea. I asked questions and he talked.

"One day when I was living here, I shot a kudu: an adult female. Hit it with one arrow in the flank. But it went too far and we never found it. Then another day my brother hit a wildebeest, another adult female and that one we got. We carried it back to camp here and ate it."

"What other meat did you eat here, Dau?"

"One, no two, steenbok, it was."

1948: 28 years ago by my counting was when Dau, his brothers, his family were here. How could he remember the detail? This man sat in the shade and recalled trivial events that have repeated themselves in more or less the same way at so many places over the last three decades.

We dug day after day in the old camps—and found what Dau said we should. Bones, decomposing, but still identifiable: bones of wildebeest and steenbok among the charcoal and mongongo nut shells.

We dug our squares, sifting through the sand for bones. And when I dumped the bones, the odd ostrich eggshell bead, the other bits and pieces out onto the bridge table to sort, so much of what my eyes and ears told me was confirmed in this most tangible form. If excavation in one square revealed the bones of a wildebeest or kudi or other large antelope, then the others would contain them as

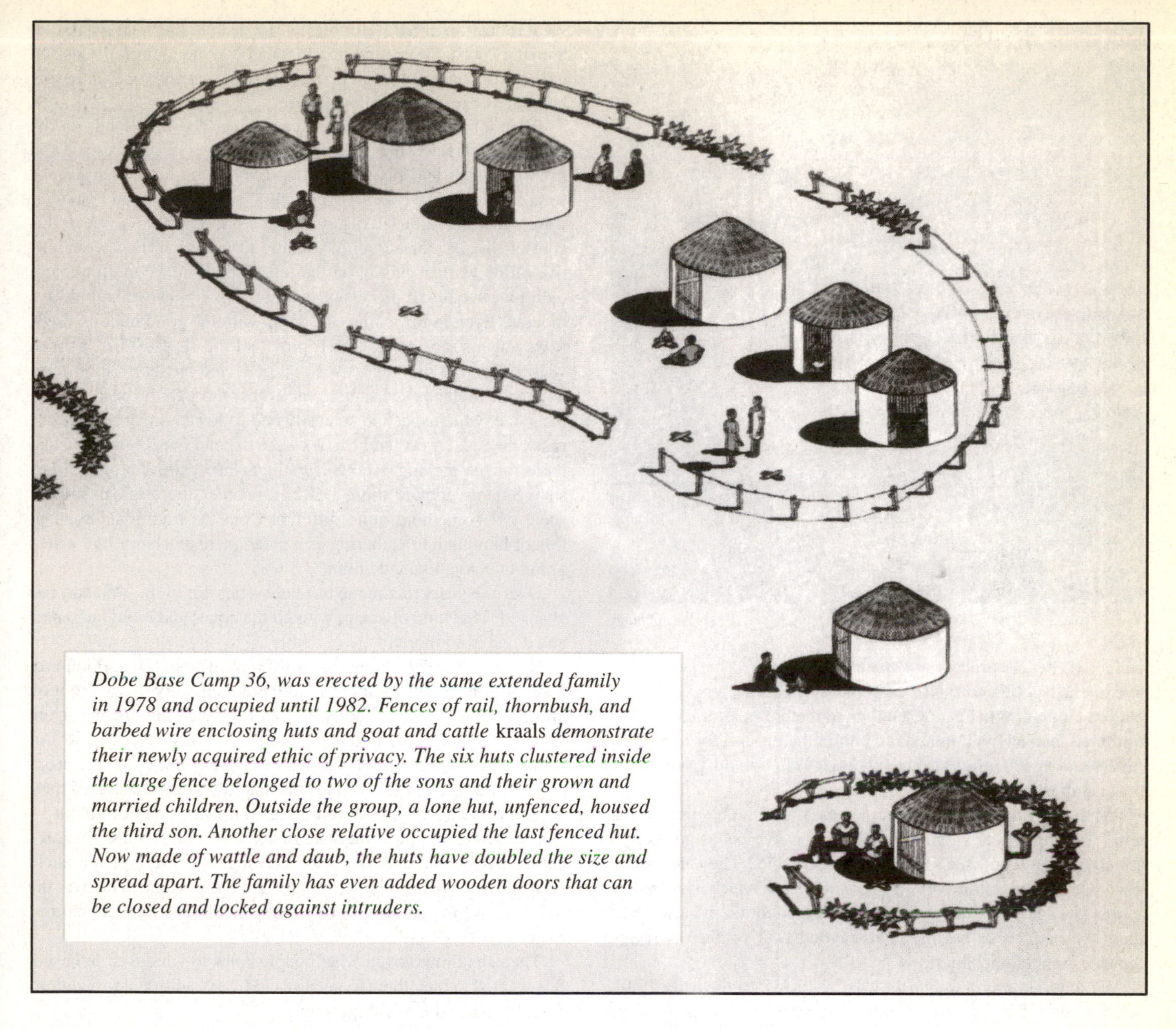

Dobe Base Camp 36, was erected by the same extended family in 1978 and occupied until 1982. Fences of rail, thornbush, and barbed wire enclosing huts and goat and cattle kraals *demonstrate their newly acquired ethic of privacy. The six huts clustered inside the large fence belonged to two of the sons and their grown and married children. Outside the group, a lone hut, unfenced, housed the third son. Another close relative occupied the last fenced hut. Now made of wattle and daub, the huts have doubled the size and spread apart. The family has even added wooden doors that can be closed and locked against intruders.*

well. In an environment as unpredictable as the Kalahari, where the game was hard to find and the probability of failure high, survival depended on sharing, on spreading the risk. And the bones, distributed almost evenly around the individual family hearths confirmed that. What also impressed me was how little else other than the bones there was. Most archeological sites contain a broad range of debris. But in those years the Bushmen owned so little. Two spears or wooden digging sticks or strings of ostrich eggshell beads were of no more use than one. Better to share, to give away meat or extra belongings and through such gifts create a web of debts, of obligations that some day would be repaid. In 1948, even in 1965, to accumulate material goods made no sense.

When it was hot, which was most of the year, I arranged the bridge table and two chairs in a patch of nearby shade. We sat there with the bound black and red ledger and dumped the bones in a heap in the center of the table, then sorted them out. I did the easy stuff, separated out the turtle shells, the bird bones, set each in a small pile around the table's edge. Dau did the harder part, separated the steenbok from the duiker, the wildebeest from kudu, held small splintered bone fragments and turned them over and over in his hands. We went through the piles then, one by one, moved each in its turn to the center of the table, sorted them into finer categories, body part by body part, bone by bone. Cryptic notes, bits of data that accumulated page by page. The bones with their sand and grit were transformed into numbers in rows and columns, classes and subclasses which would, I hoped, emerge from some computer to reveal a grander order, a design, an underlying truth.

Taphonomy: That's the proper term for it. The study of burial and preservation. Archeologists dig lots of bones out of the ground, not just from recent places such as these but from sites that span the millions of years of mankind's existence. On the basis of the bones, we try to learn about those ancient people. We try to reconstruct their diet, figure out how the animals were hunted, how they were killed, butchered, and shared.

What appealed to me about the Dobe situation, why I followed Dau, walked out his youth and his early manhood back and forth around the waterhole was the neat, almost laboratory situation Dobe offered. A natural experiment. I could go to a modern camp,

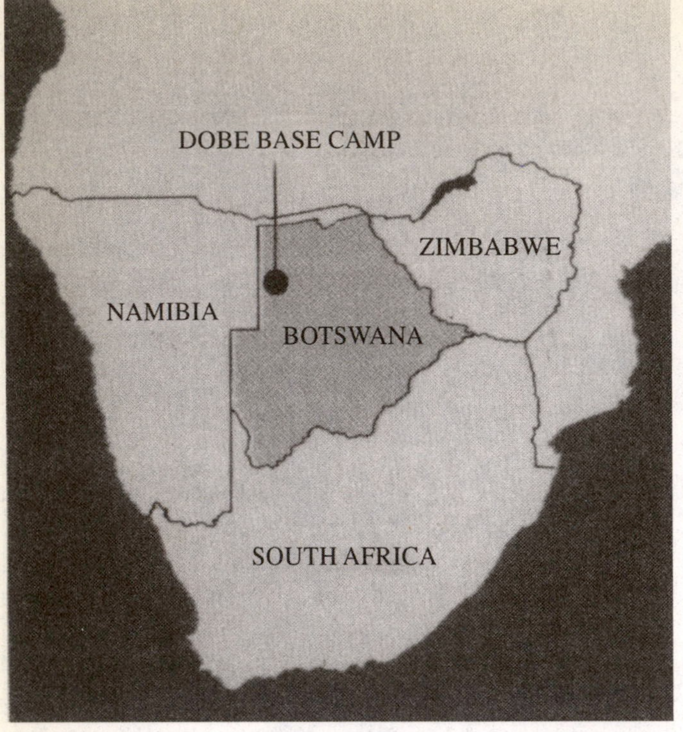

© J. Wisenbaugh

collect those discarded food bones even before the jackals and hyenas had gotten to them, examine and count them, watch the pattern emerge. What happened then to the bones after they'd been trampled, picked over, rained on, lain in the ground for five years? Five years ago? Dobe Base Camp 21, 1971. I could go there, dig up a sample and find out.

What went on farther and farther back in time? Is there a pattern? Try eight years ago. 1968, DBC 18. We could go there to the cobra camp and see. Thirty-four years ago? The camp where Tsaa with the beautiful wife was born. One can watch, can see how things fall apart, can make graphs, curves, shoot them back, watch them arc backwards beyond Dau, beyond Dau's father, back into the true archeological past.

We dug our way through the DBCs, back into the early 1940s, listening day after day to the South African soap operas on the short-wave radio, and our consumption of plastic bags went down and down. Slim pickings in the bone department. And the bones we did find tended to be rotten: They fragmented, fell apart in the sieve.

So we left the 1940s, collapsed the bridge table and the folding chairs and went to that site that played such a crucial role for anthropologists: DBC 12, the 1963 camp where those old myths about hunters and gatherers came up against the hard rock of truth.

They built this camp just after Richard Lee, the pioneer, arrived. They lived there through the winter and hunted warthog with spears and a pack of dogs so good they remember each by name to this day. Richard lived there with them. He watched them—what they did, what they ate, weighed food on his small scale slung with a rope from an acacia tree. He weighed people, sat in camp day after day with his notebook and his wristwatch and scale. He recorded times: when each person left camp in the morning, when each returned for the day.

In this small remnant group, one of the last in the world still living by hunting and gathering, it should be possible, he believed, to see a reflection, a faint glimmer of the distant universal past of all humanity, a common condition that had continued for millions and millions of years. He went there because of that and for that reason, later on, the rest of us followed him.

What he found in that desert camp, that dry, hard land, set the anthropological world back on its collective ear. What his scale and his wristwatch and his systematic scribbles showed was that we were fooled, that we had it all wrong. To be a hunter and gatherer wasn't that bad after all. They didn't work that hard, even in this land of thorns: For an adult, it came to less time than a nine-to-five office worker puts in on the job. They lived a long time, too, didn't wear out and die young but old-looking, as we had always thought. Even in this camp, the camp with the good hunting dogs, it was plants, not meat, which provided the staff of life. Women walked through the nut groves and collected nuts with their toes, dug in the molapos and sang to each other through the bush. Unlike the game, which spooked so easily and followed the unpredictable rains, the nuts, roots, and berries were dependable, there in plenty, there for the picking. Another distinguished anthropologist, Marshall Sahlins, termed those DBC 12 people "the original affluent society"—something quite different from the traditional conception of hunting and gathering as a mean, hard existence half a step ahead of starvation and doom.

Over the years that name has held—but life in the Kalahari has changed. That kind of camp, with all the bones and mongongo nuts and dogs, is no more.

By the mid-1970s, things were different at Dobe. Diane Gelburd, another of the anthropologists out there then, only needed to look around her to see how the Bushman lifestyle had changed from the way Richard recorded it, from how Sahlins described it. But what had changed the people at DBC 12 who believed that property should be commonly held and shared? What had altered their system of values? That same winter Diane decided to find out.

She devised a simple measure of acculturation that used pictures cut from magazines: an airplane, a sewing machine, a gold mine in South Africa. (Almost no one got the gold mine right.) That was the most enjoyable part of the study. They all liked to look at pictures, to guess.

Then she turned from what people knew to what they believed. She wanted to rank them along a scale, from traditional to acculturated. So again she asked questions:

"Will your children be tattooed?"

To women: "If you were having a difficult childbirth and a white doctor were there, would you ask for assistance?"

To men: "If someone asked you for permission to marry your daughter would you demand (the traditional) bride service?"

Another question so stereotyped that in our own society one would be too embarrassed to ask it: "Would you let your child marry someone from another tribe—a Tswana or a Herero—a white person?"

First knowledge, then belief, and finally material culture. She did the less sensitive questions first. "Do you have a field? What do you grow? What kind of animals do you have? How many of what?" Then came the hard part: She needed to see what people actually owned. I tagged along with her one day and remember the whispers inside one dark mud hut. Trunks were unlocked and hurriedly unpacked away from the entrance to shield them from sight. A blanket spread out on a trunk revealed the secret wealth that belied their statements: "Me? I have nothing." In the semidarkness she made her inventory. Then the trunks were hastily repacked and relocked with relief.

She went through the data, looked at those lists of belongings, itemized them in computer printouts. Here's a man who still hunts. The printout shows it. He has a bow and quiver and arrows on which the poison is kept fresh. He has a spear and snares for birds. He has a small steenbok skin bag, a traditional carryall that rests neatly under his arm.

He also has 19 goats and two donkeys, bought from the Herero or Tswana, who now get Dobe Bushmen to help plant their fields and herd their cows. They pay in livestock, hand-me-down clothing, blankets, and sometimes cash. He has three large metal trunks crammed full: One is packed to the top with shoes, shirts, and pants, most well-worn. He has two large linen mosquito nets, 10 tin cups, and a metal file. He has ropes of beads: strand upon strand—over 200 in all, pounds of small colored glass beads made in Czechoslovakia that I had bought in Johannesburg years earlier. He has four large iron pots and a five-gallon plastic jerry can. He has a plow, a gift from the anthropologists. He has a bridle and bit, light blankets, a large tin basin. He has six pieces of silverware, a mirror and hairbrush, two billycans. His wife and his children together couldn't carry all that. The trunks are too heavy and too large for one person to carry so you would have to have two people for each. What about the plow, those heavy iron pots? Quite a job to carry those through bush, through the thick thorns.

But here is the surprising part. Talk to that man. Read the printout. See what he knows, what he believes. It isn't surprising that he speaks the Herero language and Setswana fluently or that he has worked for the Herero, the anthropologists. Nothing startling there. A budding Dobe capitalist. But then comes the shock: He espouses the traditional values.

"Bushmen share things, John. We share things and depend on each other, help each other out. That's what makes us different from the black people."

But the same person, his back to the door, opens his trunks, unlocks them one by one, lays out the blankets, the beads, then quickly closes each before he opens the next.

Multiply that. Make a whole village of people like that, and you can see the cumulative effect: You can actually measure it. As time goes on, as people come to own more possessions; the huts move farther and farther apart.

In the old days a camp was cosy, intimate and close. You could sit there by one fire and look into the other grass huts, see what the other people were doing, what they were making or eating. You heard the conversations, the arguments and banter.

We ask them why the new pattern?

Says Dau: "It's because of the livestock that we put our huts this way. They can eat the grass from the roofs and the sides of our houses. So we have to build fences to keep them away and to do that, you must have room between the huts."

I look up from the fire, glance around the camp, say nothing. No fences there. Not a single one around any of the huts, although I concede that one day they probably will build them. But why construct a lot of separate small fences, one around each hut? Why not clump the huts together the way they did in the old days and make a single large fence around the lot? Certainly a more efficient approach. Why worry about fences now in any case? The only exposed grass is on the roofs, protected by straight mud walls and nothing short of an elephant or giraffe could eat it.

Xashe's answer is different. Another brief reply. An attempt to dispose of the subject politely but quickly. "It's fire, John. That's what we're worried about. If we put our houses too close together, if one catches fire, the others will burn as well. We don't want one fire to burn all our houses down. That's why we build them so far apart."

But why worry about fire now? What about in the old days when the huts were so close, cheek by jowl? Why is it that when the huts were really vulnerable, when they were built entirely of dried grass, you didn't worry about fires then?

You read Diane's interviews and look at those lists of how much people own. You see those shielded mud huts with doors spaced, so far apart. You also listen to the people you like and trust. People who always have been honest with you. You hear their explanations and realize the evasions are not for you but for themselves. You see things they can't. But nothing can be done. It would be ludicrous to tell these brothers: "Don't you see, my friends, the lack of concordance between your values and the changing reality of your world?"

Now, years after the DBC study, I sit with data spread out before me and it is so clear. Richard's camp in 1963: just grass huts, a hearth in front of each. Huts and hearths in a circle, nothing more. 1968: more of the same. The following year though the first *kraal* appears, just a small thorn enclosure, some acacia bushes cut and dragged haphazardly together for their first few goats. It's set apart way out behind the circle of huts. On one goes, from plot to plot, following the pattern from year to year. The huts change from grass to mud. They become larger, more solidly built. Goats, a few at first, then more of them. So you build a fence around your house to keep them away from the grass roofs. The *kraals* grow larger, move in closer to be incorporated finally into the circle of huts itself. The huts become spaced farther and farther apart, seemingly repelled over time, one from the next. People, families move farther apart.

The bones tell the same story. 1947: All the bones from wild animals, game caught in snares or shot with poisoned arrows—game taken from the bush. By 1964 a few goat bones, a cow bone or two, but not many. Less than 20 percent of the total. Look then at the early 1970s and watch the line on the graph climb slowly upwards—by 1976 over 80 percent from domesticated stock.

But what explains the shattering of this society? Why is this hunting and gathering way of life, so resilient in the face of uncertainty, falling apart? It hasn't been a direct force—a war, the ravages of disease. It is the internal conflicts, the tensions, the inconsistencies, the impossibility of reconciling such different views of the world.

At Dobe it is happening to them all together. All of the huts have moved farther apart in lockstep, which makes it harder for them to see how incompatible the old system is with the new. But Rakudu, a Bushman who lived at the Mahopa waterhole eight miles down the valley from Dobe, was a step ahead of the rest. He experienced, before the rest of them, their collective fate.

When I was at the Cobra Camp in 1969, Rakudu lived down near Mahopa, off on his own, a mile or so away from the pastoral Herero villages. He had two hats and a very deep bass voice, both so strange, so out of place in a Bushman. He was a comical sort of man with the hats and that voice and a large Adam's apple that bobbed up and down.

The one hat must have been a leftover from the German-Herero wars because no one in Botswana wore a hat like that—a real pith helmet with a solid top and rounded brim. It had been cared for over the years because, although soiled and faded, it still retained the original strap that tucks beneath the chin. The second hat was also unique—a World War I aviator's hat, one of those leather sacks that fits tightly over the head and buckles under the chin. Only the goggles were missing.

I should have seen then how out of place the ownership of two hats was in that hunter-gatherer world. Give two hats like that to any of the others and one would have been given away on the spot. A month or two later, the other would become a gift as well. Moving goods as gifts and favors along that chain of human ties. That was the way to maintain those links, to keep them strong.

When I went to Rakudu's village and realized what he was up to, I could see that he was one of a kind. The mud-walled huts in his village made it look like a Herero village—not a grass hut in sight. And when I came, Rakudu pulled out a hand-carved wood and leather chair and set it in the shade. This village was different from any of the Bushman camps I had seen. Mud huts set out in a circle, real clay storage bins to hold the corn—not platforms in a tree—and *kraals* for lots of goats and donkeys. He had a large field, too, several years before the first one appeared at Dobe.

Why shouldn't Bushmen do it—build their own villages, model their subsistence after the Herero? To plant a field, to tend goats, to build mud-walled houses like that was not hard to do. Work for the Herero a while and get an axe, accumulate the nucleus of a herd, buy or borrow the seeds. That year the rains were long and heavy. The sand held the water and the crickets and the birds didn't come. So the harvest was good, and I could sit there in the carved chair and look at Rakudu's herd of goats and their young ones and admire him for his industry, for what he had done.

Only a year later I saw him and his eldest son just outside the Cobra Camp. I went over and sat in the sand and listened to the negotiations for the marriage Rakudu was trying to arrange. His son's most recent wife had run away, and Rakudu was discussing a union between his son and Dau the Elder's oldest daughter who was just approaching marriageable age. They talked about names and Dau the Elder explained why the marriage couldn't take place. It was clear that the objection was trivial, that he was making an excuse. Even I could see that his explanation was a face-saving gesture to make the refusal easier for all of them.

Later I asked Dau the Elder why he did it. It seemed like a good deal to me. "Rakudu has all that wealth, those goats and field. I'd think that you would be anxious to be linked with a family like that. Look at all you have to gain. Is the son difficult? Did he beat his last wife?"

"She left because she was embarrassed. The wife before her ran away for the same reason and so did the younger brother's wife," he said. "Both brothers treated their wives well. The problem wasn't that. It was when the wives' relatives came. That's when it became so hard for the women because Rakudu and his sons are such stingy men. They wouldn't give anything away, wouldn't share anything with them. Rakudu has a big herd just like the Herero, and he wouldn't kill goats for them to eat."

Not the way Bushmen should act toward relatives, not by the traditional value system at least. Sharing, the most deeply held Bushman belief, and that man with the two hats wouldn't go along. Herero are different. You can't expect them to act properly, to show what is only common decency; you must take them as they are. But someone like Rakudu, a Bushman, should know better than that. So the wives walked out and left for good.

But Rakudu understood what was happening, how he was trapped—and he tried to respond. If you can't kill too many goats from the herd that has become essential to you, perhaps you can find something else of value to give away. Rakudu thought he had an answer.

He raised tobacco in one section of his field. Tobacco, a plant not really adapted to a place like the northern Kalahari, has to be weeded, watered by hand, and paid special care. Rakudu did that and for one year at least harvested a tobacco crop.

Bushmen crave tobacco and Rakudu hoped he had found a solution—that they would accept tobacco in place of goats, in place of mealie meal. A good try. Perhaps the only one open to him. But, as it turned out, not good enough. Rakudu's son could not find a wife.

Ironic that a culture can die yet not a single person perish. A sense of identity, of a shared set of rules, of participation in a single destiny binds individuals together into a tribe or cultural group. Let that survive long enough, let the participants pass this sense through enough generations, one to the next, create enough debris, and they will find their way into the archeological record, into the study of cultures remembered only by their traces left on the land.

Rakudu bought out. He, his wife, and his two sons sold their goats for cash, took the money and walked west, across the border scar that the South Africans had cut, through the smooth fence wire and down the hard calcrete road beyond. They became wards of the Afrikaaners, were lost to their own culture, let their fate pass into hands other than their own. At Chum kwe, the mission station across the border 34 miles to the west, they were given numbers and the right to stand in line with the others and have mealie meal and other of life's physical essentials handed out to them. As wards of the state, that became their right. When the problems, the contradictions of your life are insoluble, a paternalistic hand provides one easy out.

Dau stayed at Dobe. Drive there today and you can find his mud-walled hut just by the waterhole. But he understands: He has married off his daughter, his first-born girl to a wealthy Chum kwe man who drives a tractor—an old man, more than twice her age, and by traditional Bushmen standards not an appropriate match. Given the chance, one by one, the others will do the same.

Critical Thinking

1. Describe the nature of the Bushmen's map of their territory and how the author came to learn it.
2. What did the author learn at the 1948 camp site?
3. What is "taphonomy" and what can be learned from it?
4. In what sense were the Dobe offering a "natural experiment"?
5. In what respects did we "have it all wrong" about hunters and gatherers?
6. How does the author describe the changes in Bushmen lifestyle over time? How does the author explain them and with what evidence?

John Yellen, director of the anthropology program at the National Science Foundation, has returned to the Kalahari four times since 1968.

Article 16

The Maya Collapses

JARED DIAMOND

By now, millions of modern tourists have visited ruins of the ancient Maya civilization that collapsed over a thousand years ago in Mexico's Yucatán Peninsula and adjacent parts of Central America. All of us love a romantic mystery, and the Maya offer us one at our doorstep, almost as close for Americans as the Anasazi ruins. To visit a former Maya city, we need only board a direct flight from the U.S. to the modern Mexican state capital city of Mérida, jump into a rental car or minibus, and drive an hour on a paved highway [map, p. 161, omitted].

Today, many Maya ruins, with their great temples and monuments, still lie surrounded by jungle, far from current human settlement [Plate 12, omitted]. Yet they were once the sites of the New World's most advanced Native American civilization before European arrival, and the only one with extensive deciphered written texts. How could ancient peoples have supported urban societies in areas where few farmers eke out a living today? The Maya cities impress us not only with that mystery and with their beauty, but also because they are "pure" archaeological sites. That is, their locations became depopulated, so they were not covered up by later buildings as were so many other ancient cities, like the Aztec capital of Tenochtitlan (now buried under modern Mexico City) and Rome.

Maya cities remained deserted, hidden by trees, and virtually unknown to the outside world until rediscovered in 1839 by a rich American lawyer named John Stephens, together with the English draftsman Frederick Catherwood. Having heard rumors of ruins in the jungle, Stephens got President Martin Van Buren to appoint him ambassador to the Confederation of Central American Republics, an amorphous political entity then extending from modern Guatemala to Nicaragua, as a front for his archaeological explorations. Stephens and Catherwood ended up exploring 44 sites and cities. From the extraordinary quality of the buildings and the art, they realized that these were not the work of savages (in their words) but of a vanished high civilization. They recognized that some of the carvings on the stone monuments constituted writing, and they correctly guessed that it related historical events and the names of people. On his return, Stephens wrote two travel books, illustrated by Catherwood and describing the ruins, that became best sellers.

A few quotes from Stephens's writings will give a sense of the romantic appeal of the Maya: "The city was desolate. No remnant of this race hangs round the ruins, with traditions handed down from father to son and from generation to generation. It lay before us like a shattered bark in the midst of the ocean, her mast gone, her name effaced, her crew perished, and none to tell whence she came, to whom she belonged, how long on her journey, or what caused her destruction. . . . Architecture, sculpture, and painting, all the arts which embellish life, had flourished in this overgrown forest; orators, warriors, and statesmen, beauty, ambition, and glory had lived and passed away, and none knew that such things had been, or could tell of their past existence. . . . Here were the remains of a cultivated, polished, and peculiar people, who had passed through all the stages incident to the rise and fall of nations; reached their golden age, and perished. . . . We went up to their desolate temples and fallen altars; and wherever we moved we saw the evidence of their taste, their skill in arts. . . . We called back into life the strange people who gazed in sadness from the wall; pictured them, in fanciful costumes and adorned with plumes of feather, ascending the terraces of the palace and the steps leading to the temples. . . . In the romance of the world's history nothing ever impressed me more forcibly than the spectacle of this once great and lovely city, overturned, desolate, and lost, . . . overgrown with trees for miles around, and without even a name to distinguish it." Those sensations are what tourists drawn to Maya ruins still feel today, and why we find the Maya collapse so fascinating.

The Maya story has several advantages for all of us interested in prehistoric collapses. First, the Maya written records that have survived, although frustratingly incomplete, are still useful for reconstructing Maya history in much greater detail than we can reconstruct Easter Island, or even Anasazi history with its tree rings and packrat middens. The great art and architecture of Maya cities have resulted in far more archaeologists studying the Maya than would have been the case if they had just been illiterate hunter-gatherers living in archaeologically invisible hovels. Climatologists and paleoecologists have recently been able to recognize several signals of ancient climate and environmental changes that contributed to the Maya collapse.

Finally, today there are still Maya people living in their ancient homeland and speaking Maya languages. Because much ancient Maya culture survived the collapse, early European visitors to the homeland recorded information about contemporary Maya society that played a vital role in our understanding ancient Maya society. The first Maya contact with Europeans came already in 1502, just 10 years after Christopher Columbus's "discovery" of the New World, when Columbus on the last of his four voyages captured a trading canoe that may have been Maya. In 1527 the Spanish began in earnest to conquer the Maya, but it was not until 1697 that they subdued the last principality. Thus, the Spanish had opportunities to observe independent Maya societies for a period of nearly two centuries. Especially important, both for bad and for good, was the bishop Diego de Landa, who resided in the Yucatán Peninsula for most of the years from 1549 to 1578. On the one hand, in one of history's worst acts of cultural vandalism, he burned all Maya manuscripts that he could locate in his effort to eliminate "paganism," so that only four survive today. On the other hand, he wrote a detailed account of Maya society, and he obtained from an informant a garbled explanation of Maya writing that eventually, nearly four centuries later, turned out to offer clues to its decipherment.

A further reason for our devoting a chapter to the Maya is to provide an antidote to our other chapters on past societies, which consist disproportionately of small societies in somewhat fragile and geographically isolated environments, and behind the cutting edge of contemporary technology and culture. The Maya were none of those things. Instead, they were culturally the most advanced society (or among the most advanced ones) in the pre-Columbian New World, the only one with extensive preserved writing, and located within one of the two heartlands of New World civilization (Mesoamerica). While their environment did present some problems associated with its karst terrain and unpredictably fluctuating rainfall, it does not rank as notably fragile by world standards, and it was certainly less fragile than the environments of ancient Easter Island, the Anasazi area, Greenland, or modern Australia. Lest one be misled into thinking that crashes are a risk only for small peripheral societies in fragile areas, the Maya warn us that crashes can also befall the most advanced and creative societies.

From the perspective of our five-point framework for understanding societal collapses, the Maya illustrate four of our points. They did damage their environment, especially by deforestation and erosion. Climate changes (droughts) did contribute to the Maya collapse, probably repeatedly. Hostilities among the Maya themselves did play a large role. Finally, political/cultural factors, especially the competition among kings and nobles that led to a chronic emphasis on war and erecting monuments rather than on solving underlying problems, also contributed. The remaining item on our five-point list, trade or cessation of trade with external friendly societies, does not appear to have been essential in sustaining the Maya or in causing their downfall. While obsidian (their preferred raw material for making into stone tools), jade, gold, and shells were imported into the Maya area, the latter three items were non-essential luxuries. Obsidian tools remained widely distributed in the Maya area long after the political collapse, so obsidian was evidently never in short supply.

To understand the Maya, let's begin by considering their environment, which we think of as "jungle" or "tropical rainforest." That's not true, and the reason why not proves to be important. Properly speaking, tropical rainforests grow in high-rainfall equatorial areas that remain wet or humid all year round. But the Maya homeland lies more than a thousand miles from the equator, at latitudes 17° to 22°N, in a habitat termed a "seasonal tropical forest." That is, while there does tend to be a rainy season from May to October, there is also a dry season from January through April. If one focuses on the wet months, one calls the Maya homeland a "seasonal tropical forest"; if one focuses on the dry months, one could instead describe it as a "seasonal desert."

From north to south in the Yucatán Peninsula, rainfall increases from 18 to 100 inches per year, and the soils become thicker, so that the southern peninsula was agriculturally more productive and supported denser populations. But rainfall in the Maya homeland is unpredictably variable between years; some recent years have had three or four times more rain than other years. Also, the timing of rainfall within the year is somewhat unpredictable, so it can easily happen that farmers plant their crops in anticipation of rain and then the rains do not come when expected. As a result, modern farmers attempting to grow corn in the ancient Maya homelands have faced frequent crop failures, especially in the north. The ancient Maya were presumably more experienced and did better, but nevertheless they too must have faced risks of crop failures from droughts and hurricanes.

Although southern Maya areas received more rainfall than northern areas, problems of water were paradoxically more severe in the wet south. While that made things hard for ancient Maya living in the south, it has also made things hard for modern archaeologists who have difficulty understanding why ancient droughts would have caused bigger problems in the wet south than in the dry north. The likely explanation is that a lens of freshwater underlies the Yucatán Peninsula, but surface elevation increases from north to south, so that as one moves south the land surface lies increasingly higher above the water table. In the northern peninsula the elevation is sufficiently low that the ancient Maya were able to reach the water table at deep sinkholes called cenotes, or at deep caves; all tourists who have visited the Maya city of Chichén Itzá will remember the great cenotes there. In low-elevation north coastal areas without sinkholes, the Maya may have been able to get down to the water table by digging wells up to 75 feet deep. Water is readily available in many parts of Belize that have rivers, along the Usumacinta River in the west, and around a few lakes in the Petén area of the south. But much of the south lies too high above the water table for cenotes or wells to reach down to it. Making matters worse, most of the Yucatán Peninsula consists of karst, a porous sponge-like limestone terrain where rain runs straight into the ground and where little or no surface water remains available.

How did those dense southern Maya populations deal with their resulting water problem? It initially surprises us that many of their cities were not built next to the few rivers but instead on promontories in rolling uplands. The explanation is that the Maya excavated depressions, modified natural depressions, and then plugged up leaks in the karst by plastering the bottoms of the depressions in order to create cisterns and reservoirs, which collected rain from large plastered catchment basins and stored it for use in the dry season. For example, reservoirs at the Maya city of Tikal held enough water to meet the drinking water needs of about 10,000 people for a period of 18 months. At the city of Coba the Maya built dikes around a lake in order to raise its level and make their water supply more reliable. But the inhabitants of Tikal and other cities dependent on reservoirs for drinking water would still have been in deep trouble if 18 months passed without rain in a prolonged drought. A shorter drought in which they exhausted their stored food supplies might already have gotten them in deep trouble through starvation, because growing crops required rain rather than reservoirs.

Of particular importance for our purposes are the details of Maya agriculture, which was based on crops domesticated in Mexico—especially corn with beans being second in importance. For the elite as well as commoners, corn constituted at least 70% of the Maya diet, as deduced from isotope analyses of ancient Maya skeletons. Their sole domestic animals were the dog, turkey, Muscovy duck, and a stingless bee yielding honey, while their most important wild meat source was deer that they hunted, plus fish at some sites. However, the few animal bones at Maya archaeological sites suggest that the quantity of meat available to the Maya was low. Venison was mainly a luxury food for the elite.

It was formerly believed that Maya farming was based on slash-and-burn agriculture (so-called swidden agriculture) in which forest is cleared and burned, crops are grown in the resulting field for a year or a few years until the soil is exhausted, and then the field is abandoned for a long fallow period of 15 or 20 years until regrowth of wild vegetation restores fertility to the soil. Because most of the landscape under a swidden agricultural system is fallow at any given time, it can support only modest population densities. Thus, it was a surprise for archaeologists to discover that ancient Maya population densities, estimated from numbers of stone foundations of farmhouses, were often far higher than what swidden agriculture could support. The actual values are the subject of much dispute and evidently varied among areas, but frequently cited estimates reach 250 to 750, possibly even 1,500, people per square mile. (For comparison, even today the two most densely populated countries in Africa, Rwanda and Burundi, have population densities of only about 750 and 540 people per square mile, respectively.) Hence the ancient Maya must have had some means of increasing agricultural production beyond what was possible through swidden alone.

Many Maya areas do show remains of agricultural structures designed to increase production, such as terracing of hill slopes to retain soil and moisture, irrigation systems, and arrays of canals and drained or raised fields. The latter systems, which are well attested elsewhere in the world and which require a lot of labor to construct, but which reward the labor with increased food production, involve digging canals to drain a waterlogged area, fertilizing and raising the level of the fields between the canals by dumping muck and water hyacinths dredged out of canals onto the fields, and thereby keeping the fields themselves from being inundated. Besides harvesting crops grown over the fields, farmers with raised fields also "grow" wild fish and turtles in the canals (actually, let them grow themselves) as an additional food source. However, other Maya areas, such as the well-studied cities of Copán and Tikal, show little archaeological evidence of terracing, irrigation, or raised- or drained-field systems. Instead, their inhabitants must have used archaeologically invisible means to increase food production, by mulching, floodwater farming, shortening the time that a field is left fallow, and tilling the soil to restore soil fertility, or in the extreme omitting the fallow period entirely and growing crops every year, or in especially moist areas growing two crops per year.

Socially stratified societies, including modern American and European society, consist of farmers who produce food, plus non-farmers such as bureaucrats and soldiers who do not produce food but merely consume the food grown by the farmers and are in effect parasites on farmers. Hence in any stratified society the farmers must grow enough surplus food to meet not only their own needs but also those of the other consumers. The number of non-producing consumers that can be supported depends on the society's agricultural productivity. In the United States today, with its highly efficient agriculture, farmers make up only 2% of our population, and each farmer can feed on the average 125 other people (American non-farmers plus people in export markets overseas). Ancient Egyptian agriculture, although much less efficient than modern mechanized agriculture, was still efficient enough for an Egyptian peasant to produce five times the food required for himself and his family. But a Maya peasant could produce only twice the needs of himself and his family. At least 70% of Maya society consisted of peasants. That's because Maya agriculture suffered from several limitations.

First, it yielded little protein. Corn, by far the dominant crop, has a lower protein content than the Old World staples of wheat and barley. The few edible domestic animals already mentioned included no large ones and yielded much less meat than did Old World cows, sheep, pigs, and goats. The Maya depended on a narrower range of crops than did Andean farmers (who in addition to corn also had potatoes, high-protein quinoa, and many other plants, plus llamas for meat), and much narrower again than the variety of crops in China and in western Eurasia.

Another limitation was that Maya corn agriculture was less intensive and productive than the Aztecs' *chinampas* (a very productive type of raised-field agriculture), the raised fields of the Tiwanaku civilization of the Andes, Moche irrigation on the coast of Peru, or fields tilled by animal-drawn plows over much of Eurasia.

Still a further limitation arose from the humid climate of the Maya area, which made it difficult to store corn beyond a year, whereas the Anasazi living in the dry climate of the U.S. Southwest could store it for three years.

Finally, unlike Andean Indians with their llamas, and unlike Old World peoples with their horses, oxen, donkeys, and camels, the Maya had no animal-powered transport or plows. All overland transport for the Maya went on the backs of human porters. But if you send out a porter carrying a load of corn to accompany an army into the field, some of that load of corn is required to feed the porter himself on the trip out, and some more to feed him on the trip back, leaving only a fraction of the load available to feed the army. The longer the trip, the less of the load is left over from the porter's own requirements. Beyond a march of a few days to a week, it becomes uneconomical to send porters carrying corn to provision armies or markets. Thus, the modest productivity of Maya agriculture, and their lack of draft animals, severely limited the duration and distance possible for their military campaigns.

We are accustomed to thinking of military success as determined by quality of weaponry, rather than by food supply. But a clear example of how improvements in food supply may decisively increase military success comes from the history of Maori New Zealand. The Maori are the Polynesian people who were the first to settle New Zealand. Traditionally, they fought frequent fierce wars against each other, but only against closely neighboring tribes. Those wars were limited by the modest productivity of their agriculture, whose staple crop was sweet potatoes. It was not possible to grow enough sweet potatoes to feed an army in the field for a long time or on distant marches. When Europeans arrived in New Zealand, they brought potatoes, which beginning around 1815 considerably increased Maori crop yields. Maori could now grow enough food to supply armies in the field for many weeks. The result was a 15-year period in Maori history, from 1818 until 1833, when Maori tribes that had acquired potatoes and guns from the English sent armies out on raids to attack tribes hundreds of miles away that had not yet acquired potatoes and guns. Thus, the potato's productivity relieved previous limitations on Maori warfare, similar to the limitations that low-productivity corn agriculture imposed on Maya warfare.

Those food supply considerations may contribute to explaining why Maya society remained politically divided among small kingdoms that were perpetually at war with each other, and that never became unified into large empires like the Aztec Empire of the Valley of Mexico (fed with the help of their *chinampa* agriculture and other forms of intensification) or the Inca Empire of the Andes (fed by more diverse crops carried by llamas over well-built roads). Maya armies and bureaucracies remained small and unable to mount lengthy campaigns over long distances. (Even much later, in 1848, when the Maya revolted against their Mexican overlords and a Maya army seemed to be on the verge of victory, the army had to break off fighting and go home to harvest another crop of corn.) Many Maya kingdoms held populations of only up to 25,000 to 50,000 people, none over half a million, within a radius of two or three days' walk from the king's palace. (The actual numbers are again highly controversial among archaeologists.) From the tops of the temples of some Maya kingdoms, it was possible to see the temples of the nearest kingdom. Maya cities remained small (mostly less than one square mile in area), without the large populations and big markets of Teotihuacán and Tenochtitlán in the Valley of Mexico, or of Chan-Chan and Cuzco in Peru, and without archaeological evidence of the royally managed food storage and trade that characterized ancient Greece and Mesopotamia.

Now for a quick crash-course in Maya history. The Maya area is part of the larger ancient Native American cultural region known as Mesoamerica, which extended approximately from Central Mexico to Honduras and constituted (along with the Andes of South America) one of the two New World centers of innovation before European arrival. The Maya shared much in common with other Mesoamerican societies not only in what they possessed, but also in what they lacked. For example, surprisingly to modern Westerners with expectations based on Old World civilizations, Mesoamerican societies lacked metal tools, pulleys and other machines, wheels (except locally as toys), boats with sails, and domestic animals large enough to carry loads or pull a plow. All of those great Maya temples were constructed by stone and wooden tools and by human muscle power alone.

Of the ingredients of Maya civilization, many were acquired by the Maya from elsewhere in Mesoamerica. For instance, Mesoamerican agriculture, cities, and writing first arose outside the Maya area itself, in valleys and coastal lowlands to the west and southwest, where corn and beans and squash were domesticated and became important dietary components by 3000 B.C., pottery arose around 2500 B.C., villages by 1500 B.C., cities among the Olmecs by 1200 B.C., writing appeared among the Zapotecs in Oaxaca around or after 600 B.C., and the first states arose around 300 B.C. Two complementary calendars, a solar calendar of 365 days and a ritual calendar of 260 days, also arose outside the Maya area. Other elements of Maya civilization were either invented, perfected, or modified by the Maya themselves.

Within the Maya area, villages and pottery appeared around or after 1000 B.C., substantial buildings around 500 B.C., and writing around 400 B.C. All preserved ancient Maya writing, constituting a total of about 15,000 inscriptions, is on stone and pottery and deals only with kings, nobles, and their conquests [Plate 13, omitted]. There is not a single mention of commoners. When Spaniards arrived, the Maya were still using bark paper coated with plaster to write books, of which the sole four that escaped Bishop Landa's fires turned out to be treatises on astronomy and the calendar. The ancient Maya also had had such bark-paper books, often depicted on their pottery, but only decayed remains of them have survived in tombs.

The famous Maya Long Count calendar begins on August 11, 3114 B.C.—just as our own calendar begins on January 1 of the first year of the Christian era. We know the significance to us of that day-zero of our calendar: it's the supposed beginning of the year in which Christ was born. Presumably the Maya also attached some significance to their own day zero, but we don't know what it was. The first preserved Long Count date is only A.D. 197 for a monument in the Maya area and 36 B.C. outside the Maya area, indicating that the Long Count calendar's day-zero was backdated to August 11, 3114 B.C. long after the facts; there was no writing anywhere in the New World then, nor would there be for 2,500 years after that date.

Our calendar is divided into units of days, weeks, months, years, decades, centuries, and millennia: for example, the date of February 19, 2003, on which I wrote the first draft of this paragraph, means the 19th day of the second month in the third year of the first decade of the first century of the third millennium beginning with the birth of Christ. Similarly, the Maya Long Count calendar named dates in units of days (*kin*), 20 days (*uinal*), 360 days (*tun*), 7,200 days or approximately 20 years (*katunn*), and 144,000 days or approximately 400 years (*baktun*). All of Maya history falls into baktuns 8, 9, and 10.

The so-called Classic period of Maya civilization begins in baktun 8, around A.D. 250, when evidence for the first kings and dynasties appears. Among the glyphs (written signs) on Maya monuments, students of Maya writing recognized a few dozen, each of which was concentrated in its own geographic area, and which are now considered to have had the approximate meaning of dynasties or kingdoms. In addition to Maya kings having their own name glyphs and palaces, many nobles also had their own inscriptions and palaces. In Maya society the king also functioned as high priest carrying the responsibility to attend to astronomical and calendrical rituals, and thereby to bring rain and prosperity, which the king claimed to have the supernatural power to deliver because of his asserted family relationship to the gods. That is, there was a tacitly understood quid pro quo: the reason why the peasants supported the luxurious lifestyle of the king and his court, fed him corn and venison, and built his palaces was because he had made implicit big promises to the peasants. As we shall see, kings got into trouble with their peasants if a drought came, because that was tantamount to the breaking of a royal promise.

From A.D. 250 onwards, the Maya population (as judged from the number of archaeologically attested house sites), the number of monuments and buildings, and the number of Long Count dates on monuments and pottery increased almost exponentially, to reach peak numbers in the 8th century A.D. The largest monuments were erected towards the end of that Classic period. Numbers of all three of those indicators of a complex society declined throughout the 9th century, until the last known Long Count date on any monument fell in baktun 10, in the year A.D. 909. That decline of Maya population, architecture, and the Long Count calendar constitutes what is known as the Classic Maya collapse.

As an example of the collapse, let's consider in more detail a small but densely built city whose ruins now lie in western Honduras at a site known as Copán, and described in two recent books by archaeologist David Webster. For agricultural purposes the best land in the Copán area consists of five pockets of flat land with fertile alluvial soil along a river valley, with a tiny total area of only 10 square miles; the largest of those five pockets, known as the Copán pocket, has an area of only 5 square miles. Much of the land around Copán consists of steep hills, and nearly half of the hill area has a slope above 16% (approximately double the slope of the steepest grade that you are likely to encounter on an American highway). Soil in the hills is less fertile, more acidic, and poorer in phosphate than valley soil. Today, corn yields from valley-bottom fields are two or three times those of fields on hill slopes, which suffer rapid erosion and lose three-quarters of their productivity within a decade of farming.

As judged by numbers of house sites, population growth in the Copán Valley rose steeply from the 5th century up to a peak estimated at around 27,000 people at A.D. 750–900. Maya written history at Copán begins in the year with a Long Count date corresponding to A.D. 426, when later monuments record retrospectively that some person related to nobles at Tikal and Teotihuacán arrived. Construction of royal monuments glorifying kings was especially massive between A.D. 650 and 750. After A.D. 700, nobles other than kings also got into the act and began erecting their own palaces, of which there were about twenty by the year A.D. 800, when one of those palaces is known to have consisted of 50 buildings with room for about 250 people. All of those nobles and their courts would have increased the burden that the king and his own court imposed on the peasants. The last big buildings at Copán were put up around A.D. 800, and the last Long Count date on an incomplete altar possibly bearing a king's name has the date of A.D. 822.

Archaeological surveys of different types of habitats in the Copán Valley show that they were occupied in a regular sequence. The first area farmed was the large Copán pocket of valley bottomland, followed by occupation of the other four bottomland pockets. During that time the human population was growing, but there was not yet occupation of the hills. Hence that increased population must have been accommodated by intensifying production in the bottomland pockets by some combination of shorter fallow periods, double-cropping, and possibly some irrigation.

By the year A.D. 650, people started to occupy the hill slopes, but those hill sites were cultivated only for about a century. The percentage of Copán's total population that was in the hills, rather than in the valleys, reached a maximum of 41%, then declined until the population again became concentrated in the valley pockets. What caused that pullback of population from the hills? Excavation of the foundations of buildings in the valley floor showed that they became covered with sediment during the 8th century, meaning that the hill slopes were getting eroded and probably also leached of nutrients. Those acidic infertile hill soils were being carried down into the valley and blanketing the more fertile valley soils, where they would have reduced agricultural yields. This ancient quick abandonment of hillsides coincides with modern Maya experience that fields in the hills have low fertility and that their soils become rapidly exhausted.

The reason for that erosion of the hillsides is clear: the forests that formerly covered them and protected their soils were being cut down. Dated pollen samples show that the pine forests originally covering the upper elevations of the hill slopes were eventually all cleared. Calculation suggests that most of those felled pine trees were being burned for fuel, while the rest were used for construction or for making plaster. At other Maya sites from the pre-Classic era, where the Maya went overboard in lavish use of thick plaster on buildings, plaster production may have been a major cause of deforestation. Besides causing sediment accumulation in the valleys and depriving valley inhabitants of wood supplies, that deforestation may have begun to cause a "man-made drought" in the valley bottom because forests play a major role in water cycling, such that massive deforestation tends to result in lowered rainfall.

Hundreds of skeletons recovered from Copán archaeological sites have been studied for signs of disease and malnutrition, such as porous bones and stress lines in the teeth. These skeletal signs show that the health of Copán's inhabitants deteriorated from A.D. 650 to 850, both among the elite and among the commoners, although the health of commoners was worse.

Recall that Copán's population was increasing steeply while the hills were being occupied. The subsequent abandonment of all of those fields in the hills meant that the burden of feeding the extra population formerly dependent on the hills now fell increasingly on the valley floor, and that more and more people were competing for the food grown on those 10 square miles of valley bottomland. That would have led to fighting among the farmers themselves for the best land, or for any land, just as in modern Rwanda. Because Copán's king was failing to deliver on his promises of rain and prosperity in return for the power and luxuries that he claimed, he would have been the scapegoat for this agricultural failure. That may explain why the last that we hear from any Copán king is A.D. 822 (that last Long Count date at Copán), and why the royal palace was burned around A.D. 850. However, the continued production of some luxury goods suggest that some nobles managed to carry on with their lifestyle after the king's downfall, until around A.D. 975.

To judge from datable pieces of obsidian, Copán's total population decreased more gradually than did its signs of kings and nobles. The estimated population in the year A.D. 950 was still around 15,000, or 54% of the peak population of 27,000. That population continued to dwindle, until there are no more signs of anyone in the Copán Valley by around A.D. 1250. The reappearance of pollen from forest trees thereafter provides independent evidence that the valley became virtually empty of people, and that the forests could at last begin to recover.

The general outline of Maya history that I have just related, and the example of Copán's history in particular, illustrates why we talk about "the Maya collapse." But the story grows more complicated, for at least five reasons.

First, there was not only that enormous Classic collapse, but at least two previous smaller collapses at some sites, one around the year A.D. 150 when El Mirador and some other Maya cities collapsed (the so-called pre-Classic collapse), the other (the so-called Maya hiatus) in the late 6th century and early 7th century, a period when no monuments were erected at the well-studied site of Tikal. There were also some post-Classic collapses in areas whose populations survived the Classic collapse or increased after it—such as the fall of Chichén Itzá around 1250 and of Mayapán around 1450.

Second, the Classic collapse was obviously not complete, because there were hundreds of thousands of Maya who met and fought the Spaniards—far fewer Maya than during the Classic peak, but still far more people than in the other ancient societies discussed in detail in this book. Those survivors were concentrated in areas with stable water supplies, especially in the north with its cenotes, the coastal lowlands with their wells, near a southern lake, and along rivers and lagoons at lower elevations. However, population otherwise disappeared almost completely in what previously had been the Maya heartland in the south.

Third, the collapse of population (as gauged by numbers of house sites and of obsidian tools) was in some cases much slower than the decline in numbers of Long Count dates, as I already mentioned for Copán. What collapsed quickly during the Classic collapse was the institution of kingship and the Long Count calendar.

Fourth, many apparent collapses of cities were really nothing more than "power cycling": i.e., particular cities becoming more powerful, then declining or getting conquered, and then rising again and conquering their neighbors, without changes in the whole population. For example, in the year 562 Tikal was defeated by its rivals Caracol and Calakmul, and its king was captured and killed. However, Tikal then gradually gained strength again and finally conquered its rivals in 695, long before Tikal joined many other Maya cities in the Classic collapse (last dated Tikal monuments A.D. 869). Similarly, Copán grew in power until the year 738, when its king Waxaklahuun Ub'aah K'awil (a name better known to Maya enthusiasts today by its unforgettable translation of "18 Rabbit") was captured and put to death by the rival city of Quirigua, but then Copán thrived during the following half-century under more fortunate kings.

Finally, cities in different parts of the Maya area rose and fell on different trajectories. For example, the Puuc region in the northwest Yucatán Peninsula, after being almost empty of people in the year 700, exploded in population after 750 while the southern cities were collapsing, peaked in population between 900 and 925, and then collapsed in turn between 950 and 1000. El Mirador, a huge site in the center of the Maya area with one of the world's largest pyramids, was settled in 200 B.C. and abandoned around A.D. 150, long before the rise of Copán. Chichén Itzá in the northern peninsula grew after A.D. 850 and was the main northern center around 1000, only to be destroyed in a civil war around 1250.

Some archaeologists focus on these five types of complications and don't want to recognize a Classic Maya collapse at all. But this overlooks the obvious facts that cry out for explanation: the disappearance of between 90 and 99% of the Maya population after A.D. 800, especially in the formerly most densely populated area of the southern lowlands, and the disappearance of kings, Long Count calendars, and other complex political and cultural institutions. That's why we talk about a Classic Maya collapse, a collapse both of population and of culture that needs explaining.

Two other phenomena that I have mentioned briefly as contributing to Maya collapses require more discussion: the roles of warfare and of drought.

Archaeologists for a long time believed the ancient Maya to be gentle and peaceful people. We now know that Maya warfare was intense, chronic, and unresolvable, because limitations of food supply and transportation made it impossible for any Maya principality to unite the whole region in an empire, in the way that the Aztecs and Incas united Central Mexico and the Andes, respectively. The archaeological record shows that wars became more intense and frequent towards the time of the Classic collapse. That evidence comes from discoveries of several types over the last 55 years: archaeological excavations of massive fortifications surrounding many Maya sites; vivid depictions of warfare and captives on stone monuments, vases [Plate 14, omitted], and on the famous painted murals discovered in 1946 at Bonampak; and the decipherment of Maya writing, much of which proved to consist of royal inscriptions boasting of conquests. Maya kings fought to take one another captive, one of the unfortunate losers being Copán's King 18 Rabbit. Captives were tortured in unpleasant ways depicted dearly on the monuments and murals (such as yanking fingers out of sockets, pulling out teeth, cutting off the lower jaw, trimming off the lips and fingertips, pulling out the fingernails, and driving a pin through the lips), culminating (sometimes several years later) in the sacrifice of the captive in other equally unpleasant ways (such as tying the captive up into a ball by binding the arms and legs together, then rolling the balled-up captive down the steep stone staircase of a temple).

Maya warfare involved several well-documented types of violence: wars between separate kingdoms; attempts of cities within a kingdom to secede by revolting against the capital; and civil wars resulting from frequent violent attempts by would-be kings to usurp the throne. All of these types were described or depicted on monuments, because they involved kings and nobles. Not considered worthy of description, but probably even more frequent, were fights between commoners over land, as overpopulation became excessive and as land became scarce.

The other phenomenon important to understanding Maya collapses is the repeated occurrence of droughts, studied especially by Mark Brenner, David Hodell, the late Edward Deevey, and their colleagues at the University of Florida, and discussed in a recent book by Richardson Gill. Cores bored into layers of sediments at the bottoms of Maya lakes yield many measurements that let us infer droughts and environmental changes. For example, gypsum (a.k.a. calcium sulfate) precipitates out of solution in a lake into sediments when lake water becomes concentrated by evaporation during a drought. Water containing the heavy form of oxygen known as the isotope oxygen-18 also becomes concentrated during droughts, while water containing the lighter isotope oxygen-16 evaporates away. Molluscs and crustacea living in the lake take up oxygen to lay down in their shells, which remain preserved in the lake sediments, waiting for climatologists to analyze for those oxygen isotopes long after the little animals have died. Radiocarbon dating of a sediment layer identifies the approximate year when the drought or rainfall conditions inferred from those gypsum and oxygen isotope measurements were prevailing. The same lake sediment cores provide palynologists with information about deforestation (which shows up as a decrease in pollen from forest trees at the expense of an increase in grass pollen), and also soil erosion (which shows up as a thick clay deposit and minerals from the washed-down soil).

Based on these studies of radiocarbon-dated layers from lake sediment cores, climatologists and paleoecologists conclude that the Maya area was relatively wet from about 5500 B.C. until 500 B.C. The following period from 475 to 250 B.C., just before the rise of pre-Classic Maya civilization, was dry. The pre-Classic rise may have been facilitated by the return of wetter conditions after 250 B.C., but then a drought from A.D. 125 until A.D. 250 was associated with the pre-Classic collapse at ELL Mirador and other sites. That collapse was followed by the resumption of wetter conditions and of the buildup of Classic Maya cities, temporarily interrupted by a drought around A.D. 600 corresponding to a decline at Tikal and some other sites. Finally, around A.D. 760 there began the worst drought in the last 7,000 years, peaking around the year A.D. 800, and suspiciously associated with the Classic collapse.

Careful analysis of the frequency of droughts in the Maya area shows a tendency for them to recur at intervals of about 208 years. Those drought cycles may result from small variations in the sun's radiation, possibly made more severe in the Maya area as a result of the rainfall gradient in the Yucatán (drier in the north, wetter in the south) shifting southwards. One might expect those changes in the sun's radiation to affect not just the Maya region but, to varying degrees, the whole world. In fact, climatologists have noted that some other famous collapses of prehistoric civilizations far from the Maya realm appear to coincide with the peaks of those drought cycles, such as the collapse of the world's first empire (the Akkadian Empire of Mesopotamia) around 2170 B.C., the collapse of Moche IV civilization on the Peruvian coast around A.D. 600, and the collapse of Tiwanaku civilization in the Andes around A.D. 1100.

In the most naïve form of the hypothesis that drought contributed to causing the Classic collapse, one could imagine a single drought around A.D. 800 uniformly affecting the whole realm and triggering the fall of all Maya centers simultaneously. Actually, as we have seen, the Classic collapse hit different centers at slightly different times in the period A.D. 760–910, while sparing other centers. That fact makes many Maya specialists skeptical of a role of drought.

But a properly cautious climatologist would not state the drought hypothesis in that implausibly oversimplied form. Finer-resolution variation in rainfall from one year to the next can be calculated from annually banded sediments that rivers wash into ocean basins near the coast. These yield the conclusion that "The Drought" around A.D. 800 actually had four peaks, the first of them less severe: two dry years around A.D. 760, then an even drier decade around A.D. 810–820, three drier years around A.D. 860, and six drier years around A.D. 910. Interestingly, Richardson Gill concluded, from the latest dates on stone monuments at various large Maya centers, that collapse dates vary among sites and fall into three clusters: around A.D. 810, 860, and 910, in agreement with the dates for the three most severe droughts. It would not be at all surprising if a drought in any given year varied locally in its severity, hence if a series of droughts caused different Maya centers to collapse in different years, while sparing centers with reliable water supplies such as cenotes, wells, and lakes.

The area most affected by the Classic collapse was the southern lowlands, probably for the two reasons already mentioned: it was the area with the densest population, and it may also have had the most severe water problems because it lay too high above the water table for water to be obtained from cenotes or wells when the rains failed. The southern lowlands lost more than 99% of their population in the course of the Classic collapse. For example, the population of the Central Petén at the peak of the Classic Maya period is variously estimated at between 3,000,000 and 14,000,000 people, but there were only about 30,000 people there at the time that the Spanish arrived. When Cortés and his Spanish army passed through the Central Petén in 1524 and 1525, they nearly starved because they encountered so few villages from which to acquire corn. Cortés passed within a few miles of the ruins of the great Classic cities of Tikal and Palenque, but he heard or saw nothing of them because they were covered by jungle and almost nobody was living in the vicinity.

How did such a huge population of millions of people disappear? By analogy with the cases of the Anasazi and of subsequent Pueblo Indian societies during droughts in the U.S. Southwest, we infer that some people from the southern Maya lowlands survived by fleeing to areas of the northern Yucatán endowed with cenotes or wells, where a rapid population increase took place around the time of the Maya collapse. But there is no sign of all those millions of southern lowland inhabitants surviving to be accommodated as immigrants in the north, just as there is no sign of thousands of Anasazi refugees being received as immigrants into surviving pueblos. As in the U.S. Southwest during droughts, some of that Maya population decrease surely involved people dying of starvation or thirst, or killing each other in struggles over increasingly scarce resources. The other part of the decrease may reflect a slower decrease in the birthrate or child survival rate over the course of many decades. That is, depopulation probably involved both a higher death rate and a lower birth rate.

In the Maya area as elsewhere, the past is a lesson for the present. From the time of Spanish arrival, the Central Petén's population declined further to about 3,000 in A.D. 1714, as a result of deaths from diseases and other causes associated with Spanish occupation. By the 1960s, the Central Petén's population had risen back only to 25,000, still less than 1% of what it had been at the Classic Maya peak. Thereafter, however, immigrants flooded into the Central Petén, building up its population to about 300,000 in the 1980s, and ushering in a new era of deforestation and erosion. Today, half of the Petén is once again deforested and ecologically degraded. One-quarter of all the forests of Honduras were destroyed between 1964 and 1989.

To summarize the Classic Maya collapse, we can tentatively identify five strands. I acknowledge, however, that Maya archaeologists still disagree vigorously among themselves—in part, because the different strands evidently varied in importance among different parts of the Maya realm; because detailed archaeological studies are available for only some Maya sites; and because it remains puzzling why most of the Maya heartland remained nearly empty of population and failed to recover after the collapse and after regrowth of forests.

With those caveats, it appears to me that one strand consisted of population growth outstripping available resources. As the archaeologist David Webster succinctly puts it, "Too many farmers grew too many crops on too much of the landscape." Compounding that mismatch between population and resources was the second strand: the effects of deforestation and hillside erosion, which caused a decrease in the amount of useable farmland at a time when more rather than less farmland was needed, and possibly exacerbated by an anthropogenic drought resulting from deforestation, by soil nutrient depletion and other soil problems, and by the struggle to prevent bracken ferns from overrunning the fields.

The third strand consisted of increased fighting, as more and more people fought over fewer resources. Maya warfare, already endemic, peaked just before the collapse. That is not surprising when one reflects that at least 5,000,000 people, perhaps many more, were crammed into an area smaller than the state of Colorado (104,000 square miles). That warfare would have decreased further the amount of land available for agriculture, by creating no-man's lands between principalities where it was now unsafe to farm. Bringing matters to a head was the strand of climate change. The drought at the time of the Classic collapse was not the first drought that the Maya had lived through, but it was the most severe. At the time of previous droughts, there were still uninhabited parts of the Maya landscape, and people at a site affected by drought could save themselves by moving to another site. However, by the time of the Classic collapse the landscape was now full, there was no useful unoccupied land in the vicinity on which to begin anew, and the whole population could not be accommodated in the few areas that continued to have reliable water supplies.

As our fifth strand, we have to wonder why the kings and nobles failed to recognize and solve these seemingly obvious problems undermining their society. Their attention was evidently focused on their short-term concerns of enriching themselves, waging wars, erecting monuments, competing with each other, and extracting enough food from the peasants to support all those activities. Like most leaders throughout human history, the Maya kings and nobles did not heed long-term problems, insofar as they perceived them.

Finally, while we still have some other past societies to consider in this book before we switch our attention to the modern world, we must already be struck by some parallels between the Maya and the past societies discussed in Chapters 2–4. As on Easter Island, Mangareva, and among the Anasazi, Maya environmental and population problems led to increasing warfare and civil strife. As on Easter Island and at Chaco Canyon, Maya peak population numbers were followed swiftly by political and social collapse. Paralleling the eventual extension of agriculture from Easter Island's coastal lowlands to its uplands, and from the Mimbres floodplain to the hills, Copán's inhabitants also expanded from the floodplain to the more fragile hill slopes, leaving them with a larger population to feed when the agricultural boom in the hills went bust. Like Easter Island chiefs erecting ever larger statues, eventually crowned by pukao, and like Anasazi elite treating themselves to necklaces of 2,000 turquoise beads, Maya kings sought to outdo each other with more and more impressive temples, covered with thicker and thicker plaster—reminiscent in turn of the extravagant conspicuous consumption by modern American CEOs. The passivity of Easter chiefs and Maya kings in the face of the real big threats to their societies completes our list of disquieting parallels.

Critical Thinking

1. Why is it comparatively easy to tell the story of the Maya collapses?
2. What four points help to understand the Maya collapses? Which of the five points does not seem to apply?
3. How does the author describe the variable environmental factors affecting the Maya and how they coped with them?
4. How did the Maya compare with some other stratified societies with respect to their productive ability, including its limitations and deficiencies?
5. Why do we know so little about Maya commoners?
6. What were the responsibilities of the kings? How could this get them into trouble?
7. How does the site of Copán serve as an example of a Maya collapse?
8. Why is the story of the Maya collapses more complicated than it would at first seem?
9. Discuss in detail the contributions of warfare and drought to the Maya collapses.
10. Why were the southern lowlands most affected by the Classic collapse? What probably happened to the people?
11. How does the author describe the five strands contributing to the Classic Maya collapse?

UNIT 3

Techniques in Archaeology

Unit Selections

Learning Outcomes

After reading this Unit, you will be able to:

- Summarize the advances made in techniques to date archaeological sites in the last 50 years.
- Discuss the use of laser technology in identifying Mayan archaeological sites in the rainforest.
- Discuss the vulcanization process used by the ancient Mayans in making rubber products.
- List the uses to which the Maya were able to put rubber and explain how they were able to make such a variety of products.
- Discuss the role of climate change in Viking migrations.
- Explain how tree rings and history combine to tell us about the fate of Angkor in present-day Cambodia.
- Discuss the importance of forensics to archaeology.
- Using examples, show how forensic anthropology can contribute to airline safety and human rights work.

Student Website

www.mhhe.com/cls

Internet References

American Anthropologist
www.aaanet.org

GIS and Remote Sensing for Archaeology: Burgundy, France
www.informatics.org/france/france.html

Radiocarbon Dating for Archaeology
www.rlaha.ox.ac.uk/orau/index.html

Zeno's Forensic Page
http://forensic.to/forensic.html

Archaeology has evolved significantly from being an exercise in separating the remains of past human behavior from the "dirt." And as such, archaeology in turn employs a diversified group of highly sophisticated techniques. Digging in itself has gone through its own evolution of techniques, ranging from the wild thrashings of Heinrich Schielmann to the obsessive, military-like precise technique of Sir Mortimer Wheeler. Archaeology continues to expand the use of a multidisciplinary approach, and is therefore incorporating more techniques that will prove to enlighten us about our human past.

The most well known technique to be developed in archaeology was radiocarbon dating. This provides archaeologists with one of their most valuable means of establishing the age of archaeological materials. This technique was a major revolution in archaeology, and was developed by W. F. Libby at UCLA in 1949. It has enabled archaeologists, for the first time (in all of history and prehistory) to have an empirical means of determining the age of archaeological sites in terms of absolute years. This dating technique is based on the principle of radioactive decay in which unstable radioactive isotopes transform into stable elements at a constant rate. In order to qualify their accuracy, dates are presented with a standard statistical margin of error. Great care is taken with respect to any factors that may skew the results of materials being dated. It can date materials as far back as 45,000 B.P. (before present). The word "present" was designated to be 1950 C.E. As the technique is perfected, it may be able to date organic matter of even earlier times. Radiocarbon dating is limited to the dating of organic materials. It cannot directly date such things as stone tools, but it may do so indirectly by dating the layer in which the tools were deposited. Other new, cleverly devised radiometric techniques are being developed to suit specific conditions to date archaeological remains by association.

The preservation of archaeological materials is dependent upon many variables. These include the original material of the artifact and the conditions of the site in which it is preserved. For example, a nineteenth-century adobe mission on the Mojave Desert in California may be so weathered as to be unrecognizable. This is due to the fact that extreme temperatures, varying from very hot to very cold, typical of a low-desert region, tend to rapidly destroy any kind of organic matter. On the other hand, consistently wet or consistently dry conditions tend to preserve organic matter in a relatively pristine state for a long period of time. Thus, human remains tend to be well preserved in bogs—as in Denmark and in the arid coastal deserts of Peru. In Denmark, the conditions are constantly moist. In the coastal deserts of Peru, the conditions remain dry. Therefore, archaeological material may be preserved for many thousands of years.

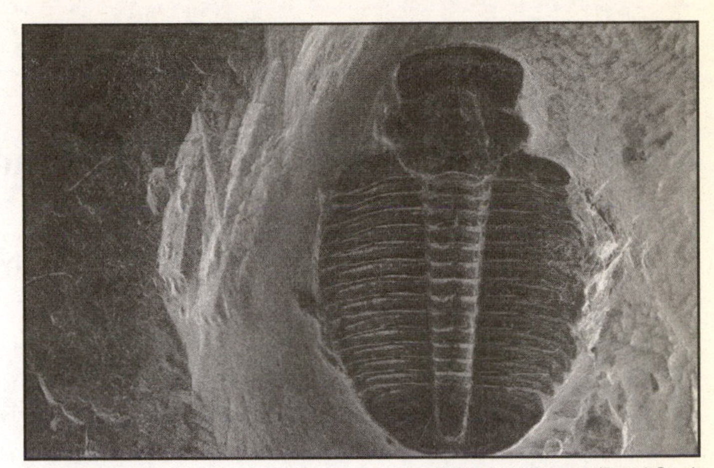

Since the discovery of radiocarbon dating, numerous other techniques have been invented that have their applications to archaeology to further clarify dates, preserve, and in general, add to the ability of archaeologists to do cultural historical reconstruction. Discussed in this section are some of the extraordinary applications of such varied hard sciences as nuclear physics, laser technology, and computers. We can now describe sites in terms of time-space systemics and virtual reality in a way that exceeds recent science fiction. Remote sensing devices from outer space allow sites to be reconstructed without invasive excavation. There are even sensing devices that can, from an airplane, "see" through the rainforest canopy to find previously hidden Mayan settlements. It seems that nothing will escape detection by future archaeologists.

Archaeologists sometimes rely on the use of forensic specialists to present images of the past that we could never before see. Used in conjunction with the exponential knowledge from DNA analysis, our images of the past became as detailed as that captured on a digital camera. Unglazed cooking pots have been tested to yield information on prehistoric diets through molecular analysis. Because clams add a tiny layer of carbonate each day and each layer reflects the weather conditions at the time, we can now tell what kind of day a clam had 350 million years ago. By inference, of course, we can also tell what was happening to the human environments in more recent times.

In spite of the ever-increasing sophistication of tools available to the archaeologist, the simple time-tested technique of archaeological surveying still helps reconstruct sites, again without invasive excavation. The future of archaeology will increasingly depend on techniques to maximize preservation of sites and minimize archaeological excavation.

Article 17

Lasers in the Jungle

Airborne sensors reveal a vast Maya landscape.

ARLEN F. CHASE, DIANE Z. CHASE, AND JOHN F. WEISHAMPEL

Even when one is almost directly on top of them, many Maya sites are impossible to see. In the jungle, small palms and brush can spring to 14 feet high in a year, filling the space between towering cedar, mahogany, ramon, and ceiba trees. When we *can* find large Maya sites, we cannot easily map them because it is expensive and labor-intensive. Even modern electronic distance meters have limited functionality; if we can't see through the trees, neither can they. So we cut paths with machetes, scramble through thick underbrush, and wonder what we might be missing. The ability to see through this dense, steamy jungle has long been the dream of Maya archaeologists.

These difficulties have led us to underestimate the accomplishments and ingenuity of the ancient Maya. There is little agreement among archaeologists over just how big some Maya cities were, how many people lived in them, or how intensively their residents modified the landscape. It often appears that sites in more easily studied areas of the world—plains, sparse forests, or areas cleared in modern times—are larger and more complex than their tropical forest counterparts. Does this impression reflect the inability of ancient humans to create large, sustainable settlements in the tropics, or is it the result of incomplete investigations, hampered by the complications of working in a rainforest?

For more than 25 years, we—a multidisciplinary team from the University of Central Florida—have struggled to document the jungle-covered archaeological remains at Caracol in western Belize. Caracol was occupied from 600 B.C. to A.D 900 by a population that we believe peaked with at least 115,000 inhabitants. A system of radial roads, or causeways, links different parts of the site across most of Belize's lush Vaca Plateau. We have mapped, using traditional on-the-ground techniques, approximately 9 square miles of settlement, 1.3 square miles of terracing, and 25 miles of causeways. We have also studied the buildings and pyramids of the site's center, as well as 118 residential groups that consist of rubble foundations and stone buildings arranged around a central plaza. Our work so far clearly establishes Caracol as the largest known archaeological site in the southern Maya lowlands, but reconnaissance and scouting suggest that the city was even larger than was previously thought. Despite the quantity of data we have, there are still lingering questions about the site's true size and population, and about the density of the terrace systems that the ancient Maya constructed for agriculture. To answer these difficult questions without spending another 25 years in the field, we clearly needed a new strategy—a way to "see" through the dense forest covering the archaeological remains.

For the last three decades archaeologists all over the world have been using space-based imaging tools to better understand ancient landscape and settlement patterns. Like their colleagues, Maya archaeologists have turned to these techniques to overcome the complications of working beneath a forest canopy—but often with little success. Generally, we have only been able to see archaeological features that extend above the canopy, are in areas devoid of vegetation, or disrupt the forest in a bold way. Even large pyramids can escape the eye in the sky. A newer remote-sensing technology called LiDAR (Light Detection and Ranging), operated from a plane rather than a satellite, has helped us penetrate the jungle of Caracol and promises to revolutionize our understanding of Maya civilization. (Laser-based on-the-ground scanning, featured in "The Past in High-Def," May/June 2009, is also gaining traction in the archaeological world.)

In addition to a detailed study of existing satellite imagery, the Caracol remote-sensing project, funded by NASA, was designed to determine if LiDAR can be used to see below the forest canopy to provide images of a complete ancient Maya landscape. It was even more successful than we had hoped. Just a few days of flyovers and three weeks of processing yielded a far superior picture of Caracol than on-the-ground mapping ever had.

Airborne LiDAR works by sending out billions of laser pulses from a plane—in this case one operated by the National Science Foundation-supported National Center for Airborne Laser Mapping—half a mile above the canopy. Carefully calibrated sensors measure the pulses that bounce back. Initially, the lasers are refracted by the tops of trees, producing a detailed record of the forest cover. But treetops are porous, so some photons penetrate deeper, while others reach all the way to the ground and reflect back from the underlying surface terrain—and any buildings or ancient structures on it. The result is an accurate, three-dimensional map of both the forest canopy and the ground elevation beneath it. For looking at Maya sites, it was important to take the measurements at the end of the dry season, when the forest is the most depleted. This laser-sensing technology is not by itself new, but has been refined—we used a significantly advanced airborne laser swath mapping (ALSM) system that swept across a 1,500-foot-wide area with each pass of the plane. The Caracol data represent the first time that the ALSM technology has been applied across an extensive region in the Maya area, and the results were stunning.

Seemingly without effort, the system produced a detailed view of nearly 80 square miles—only 13 percent of which had previously been mapped—revealing topography, ancient structures, causeways, and agricultural terraces. The data show the full extent of Caracol, how the settlement was structured, and how the ancient Maya radically modified their landscape to create a sustainable urban environment, challenging long-held assumptions about the development of civilization in the tropics.

The LiDAR data confirm that Caracol was a low-density agricultural city encompassing some 70 square miles. Our previous on-the-ground work had documented multiple causeways, but the LiDAR images revealed 11 new ones and 5 new causeway termini (concentrations of buildings at the ends of roads), revealing the site's entire communication and transportation infrastructure at its height during the Late Classic Period (A.D 550–900). Equally important, the LiDAR images clearly show unmodified hills and valleys at the edges of the surveyed area, indicating the limits of the site and providing hints about why the Maya of Caracol settled where they did and how the city expanded over time.

The study clearly confirms our earlier population estimates for Caracol, and also documents the extent to which the people of the city modified the land to feed themselves. We were particularly impressed with LiDAR's ability to reveal Caracol's agricultural terraces. We had documented these structures in on-the-ground surveys, but it was near-impossible to imagine the extent of the modified landscape. The remote-sensing data show that almost all of the Caracol landscape had been altered; soil- and water-conserving terraces cover entire valleys and hills, making it clear that agricultural production and sustainability were critical to the ancient Maya. Airborne LiDAR is clearly the tool that Maya archaeologists have been waiting for.

LiDAR results dwarf what was possible before, even through long-term archaeological projects, such as those at Tikal in Guatemala and Calakmul in Mexico, but the technology has drawbacks. It may not record the remains of completely perishable structures, which may leave only a few lines of stone, though our results suggest it can distinguish features less than a foot high. On-the-ground confirmation, traditional mapping, and excavation are still necessary to add information about how buildings were used, details, and dating. But because LiDAR covers large areas so efficiently, it could ultimately replace traditional mapping in tropical rainforests, and drive new archaeological research by revealing unusual settlement patterns and identifying new locales for on-the-ground work. At Caracol, for example, we found previously unknown clusters of complex architecture that are not directly tied to the Late Classic causeway system. Possibly areas of craft or pottery production or the remains of earlier settlements, these are prime targets for future archaeological investigation.

Understanding the scale of a modified Maya landscape will also help us compare the Maya with other ancient civilizations more effectively. Remote-sensing techniques used in the Amazon Basin and Southeast Asia have revolutionized our thinking about ancient cultures there. Satellite imaging, combined with on-the-ground GPS mapping, for example, demonstrated that complex and populous societies occupied the Amazonian rainforest before European contact. And at Angkor in Cambodia, remote sensing helped delineate a metropolitan area that covers nearly 400 square miles and led to new interpretations of the site's complex water systems and eventual abandonment. At Caracol, we see a large, low-density, agricultural city that thrived in a tropical environment. But where the people of Angkor made extensive and difficult-to-maintain hydrological changes to grow enough food to feed themselves, Caracol's inhabitants focused on the intensive creation of sustainable terraced fields. These terraces not only controlled water flow during the rainy season, which reduced erosion, but also retained water longer. Using the terraces, the ancient Maya could produce multiple harvests of maize, beans, squash, and other crops in a single year, and nutrients could be replenished by fertilizing the earth with night soil and compost. Combined with the appropriate spacing of settlements and reservoirs, the recycling of garbage, and a causeway system to communicate and distribute resources, the agricultural terrace system was designed to work with its environment—and support the daily needs of more than 100,000 city dwellers.

For too long, Maya archaeologists have been blinded by the jungle, able only to sample once-wondrous cities and speculate about vanished people. The airborne LiDAR data will help us finally dispel preconceived notions about ancient tropical civilizations—that they were limited in size and sophistication—by letting us peer through the trees. In a broader sense, we will even be able to connect sites with one another and detect political boundaries to reconstruct ancient tropical polities in full. Imagine being able to see and map the entire Maya world—its fields and pyramids, its houses and trade routes, its interactions and conflicts. But that is in the future. For now, it is enough to be able to see the entire urban landscape of one ancient Maya city, and know that palm fronds and tangled forest will no longer obscure our view of the past.

Critical Thinking

1. What have been some of the difficulties in finding and mapping Maya sites? What have been the consequences of such difficulties for archaeologists?
2. What has the multidisciplinary team been able to accomplish over the past 25 years at Caracol and how?
3. What have been some of the "lingering questions" and what has been needed to answer them?
4. Why have space-based imaging tools been of limited use?
5. How do the laser-sensing systems work and how have they improved upon the archaeological findings at Caracol?
6. What are the drawbacks of the new technology? What are some of its potential benefits?
7. How have remote-sensing techniques revolutionized our thinking about ancient cultures in the Amazon Basin and in Southeast Asia?
8. How does the author contrast the agriculture of Caracol with that of Angkor? What were some of the benefits of the Caracol system?
9. What does the author see as the future for Maya archaeologists?

Mayas Mastered Rubber Long before Goodyear

They used various formulas to make bouncy balls, glue and even resilient rubber sandals, a study finds.

THOMAS H. MAUGH II

Hundreds and perhaps even thousands of years before Charles Goodyear discovered the vulcanization process that made commercial rubber viable, Mesoamerican peoples were carrying out a similar process to produce rubber artifacts for a broad variety of uses, two MIT researchers have found.

By varying the amount of materials they added to raw rubber, Mesoamericans were able to produce bouncy rubber balls for the Mayas' ceremonial games, resilient rubber sandals and sticky material used to glue implements to handles, the research shows.

The researchers "have compiled a compelling case that ancient Mesoamerican peoples were the first polymer scientists, exerting substantial control over the mechanical properties of rubber for various applications," said materials scientist John McCloy of the Pacific Northwest National Laboratory, who was not involved in the research.

Ancient rubber footwear has not been found at archaeological sites, but written records of the Spanish conquistadores indicate that the indigenous peoples wore them. Archaeologists have found rubber balls, bands, statues and adhesives.

Rubber is a latex material produced from the sap of a variety of trees. Mesoamericans got it from what is now known as the Panama rubber tree, *Castilla elastica.* But the rubber produced as the sap dries is sticky and, ultimately, brittle.

The current research derives from a simple question asked by then-MIT-undergraduate Michael J. Tarkanian in a freshman archaeology class in 1996: How did the Maya produce bouncy rubber balls from this material?

Intrigued, the course's teacher, materials scientist Dorothy Hosler, did some quick research and "a few days later, she e-mailed me and said no one has ever answered the question," Tarkanian said in a telephone interview.

That kicked off what has so far been a 14-year collaboration between the two scientists.

Thorough study of written records of the Spanish conquerors indicated that the Maya made their balls by mixing the latex with juice from the morning glory, *Ipomoea alba,* a vine that grows throughout the region. In 1999, Hosler and Tarkanian reported that they could make bouncy rubber balls by mixing equal amounts of latex and morning glory juice and heating them.

"But doing the work, I noticed that different ratios [of the two ingredients] produced different properties," Tarkanian said.

Ultimately, as they will report in a forthcoming issue of the journal *Latin American Antiquity,* they found different formulas that provided different characteristics. A 50-50 mixture produced a bouncy rubber ball, for example, while adding one part morning glory to three parts latex produced a strong, durable material suitable for sandals.

Adding no morning glory produces a material that is a good adhesive. In the paper, they characterize for the first time the physical and chemical properties of each form.

The oldest known rubber balls from the region date to 1600 B.C., suggesting that the indigenous peoples possessed this knowledge at least that far back. By the time the Spaniards arrived in the 16th century, Tarkanian said, "there was a large rubber industry in the region," producing 16,000 rubber balls each year and large numbers of rubber statues, sandals, bands and other products.

Most of these were produced in outlying areas and shipped to Tikal, the Maya capital, as tax payments.

Around 1839, American inventor Charles Goodyear came up with the vulcanization process, in which latex from the Brazilian rubber tree is heated with sulfur. The sulfur causes the polymer chains of the latex to become cross-linked, making them stronger, more durable and more elastic.

The morning glory juice has sulfur-containing amino acids that apparently do much the same thing, Tarkanian said. The density of cross-links is much greater in the vulcanized rubber, however.

Tarkanian and Hosler have not yet identified a unique chemical signature of their lab-produced material that can be compared directly to archaeological samples—a process that is complicated by the tendency of rubbers to deteriorate over long periods. But they have noted that certain proteins in the raw latex are removed during their manufacturing process. Analysis of some ancient artifacts indicates the same proteins are missing there as well.

Archaeologist Frances Berdan of CSU San Bernardino said in a statement that the work has implications well beyond rubber. "There are other areas of production where the pre-Hispanic peoples cleverly combined materials to achieve enhanced products," she said.

The MIT work should encourage researchers to investigate these other areas as well, she said.

Critical Thinking

1. What was the process used by Mesoamericans to produce rubber and to what uses did they put it?
2. What is the archaeological and historical evidence for such uses?
3. Be familiar with the various materials and processes that were probably used to fashion the various products and their uses.
4. When were the first rubber balls produced?
5. Be familiar with the vulcanization process developed by Charles Goodyear and its similarity to the ancient Mesoamerican process.

How Climate Shaped Humanity

Could the study of hard times in the past teach us how to face the future?

ANDREW GRANT

While climate researchers struggle to refine their projections of the changing global climate and to anticipate the social impact of those shifts, a growing number of scientists are realizing that the past may contain valuable lessons about our future.

Humans have faced environmental changes before. In fact, those changes molded every facet of life—what food could be cultivated, what kind of clothing and shelters were required, what goods were produced—and most likely played a role in determining which civilizations thrived and which perished. In the distant past, climate variations may have shaped the very nature of our species. Earth scientists and climatologists are joining forces with archaeologists and anthropologists to build a comprehensive understanding of the climate record that is written into our own past. "Climate change is one of the most neglected aspects of human history," says Brian Fagan, an anthropologist who has written multiple books on the topic. "Now we are acquiring tools to look at its effects on human society."

This work builds on studies of paleontological climate clues—tree rings, ice cores, clamshells, even the inner ears of fish—that have been used to reconstruct ancient temperatures and humidities, providing a broad look at past conditions on earth. Better instruments and techniques have brought an unprecedented level of precision to these analyses, allowing researchers to zoom in on ever narrower timescales relevant for understanding climatic effects on human populations.

Clams, for example, add a tiny layer of carbonate to their shells virtually every day of their lives, which typically span two to nine years. Using a new micromilling technique that harvests thin samples from the shells, scientists can probe each layer for a particular isotope of oxygen that varies in step with temperature, essentially providing a daily weather report over the life of the clam. "We are getting to the point where we can look at paleoweather—how hot it got in the summer, individual major storms—rather than just paleoclimate," says William Patterson, a geologist at the University of Saskatchewan in Canada, who developed the technique. By analyzing clamshells unearthed on Canada's Melville Island, he can pinpoint individual summers in the region dating back 370 million years.

Patterson's latest study looks at a far more recent era. He has analyzed clamshells to gain perspective on the Vikings, who migrated from Europe's mainland to Iceland, Greenland, and northeastern stretches of North America hundreds of years before Columbus. Patterson's findings, published in March, suggest that Viking settlers in Iceland ran into trouble when a cool period hit around A.D. 970, just a few decades after they arrived. Summer temperatures there dropped 9 degrees Fahrenheit.

Writings confirm that this period was a difficult one for Norse settlements in the area, marked by devastating crop failures. "Men ate foxes and ravens. . . .The old and helpless were killed and thrown over cliffs," reads one contemporary account. "We have written records that we can evaluate by looking at the cold, hard facts" from physical evidence, Patterson says, allowing scientists to quantify the cold spell for the first time. The Vikings' experience indicates that "when the climate changes, the most vulnerable, marginal environments fail first," Patterson says.

His study joins a burgeoning collection of research documenting climate's role in the rise and fall of ancient civilizations. In another March study, dendroclimatologist Brendan Buckley of Columbia University examined tree rings that yielded clues to the fate of Angkor, a once-bustling city in what is now Cambodia that thrived for five centuries before mysteriously collapsing in the 1400s. Buckley's analysis of tree rings from a species of cypress in the region revealed that 13 of the 40 driest years in the 760-year record were clustered close together in the late 14th and early 15th centuries. These droughts, he realized, corresponded to the time of Angkor's fall.

Historians have pegged the city's demise on war and social conflict. Climate was probably just one of many factors that brought it down, but prolonged drought probably exacerbated the political and societal problems. And while Angkor was overwhelmed by climate change at the scale of a few decades, Buckley says, "a more nimble society might be able to adapt in response."

Pushing this theme further, Ezra Zubrow of the University of Buffalo is launching a gargantuan undertaking in areas of

Russia, Finland, and Canada aimed at understanding how the people there adapted to a rapid temperature rise that occurred about 5,000 years ago. "This can give us some perspective on how people respond to a warming world with more drought," Fagan says. "You can't understand the present and future without looking at the past."

Other researchers are exploring deep timescales to look for climate's influence on our evolutionary origins. In March the National Research Council (NRC) published a report urging more research into whether "critical junctures in human evolution and behavioral development may have been affected by the environmental characteristics of the areas where hominids evolved." The report highlights evidence of a dramatic shift toward drier conditions in Africa about 2.8 million years ago. Soon afterward, members of our genus, *Homo,* started using stone tools.

Various human species, including our own *Homo sapiens,* have endured ice ages and warming periods as well as floods and droughts. These ups and downs might have forced our ancestors to adapt quickly; big-brained humans may have had a survival edge in an unstable environment. Peter deMenocal, a Columbia University paleoceanographer who coauthored the NRC report, says "our study of human evolution in the context of major changes in African climate indicates that our species was honed by climate."

Critical Thinking

1. In what respects have environmental changes "molded every facet" of human life in the past?
2. What can we learn from the life of a clam?
3. How has the study of clams supplemented historical records in our understanding of Viking migrations?
4. What does the Viking experience teach us in general?
5. What have tree rings, combined with history, taught us about the fate of Angkor?
6. What evidence is there that "our species was honed by climate"?

Article 20

Profile of an Anthropologist: No Bone Unturned

PATRICK HUYGHE

The research of some physical anthropologists and archaeologists involves the discovery and analysis of old bones (as well as artifacts and other remains). Most often these bones represent only part of a skeleton or maybe the mixture of parts of several skeletons. Often these remains are smashed, burned, or partially destroyed. Over the years, physical anthropologists have developed a remarkable repertoire of skills and techniques for teasing the greatest possible amount of information out of sparse material remains.

Although originally developed for basic research, the methods of physical anthropology can be directly applied to contemporary human problems. . . . In this profile, we look briefly at the career of Clyde C. Snow, a physical anthropologist who has put these skills to work in a number of different settings. . . .

As you read this selection, ask yourself the following questions:

- Given what you know of physical anthropology, what sort of work would a physical anthropologist do for the Federal Aviation Administration?
- What is anthropometry? *How might anthropometric surveys of pilots and passengers help in the design of aircraft equipment?*
- What is forensic anthropology? *How can a biological anthropologist be an expert witness in legal proceedings?*

Clyde Snow is never in a hurry. He knows he's late. He's always late. For Snow, being late is part of the job. In fact, he doesn't usually begin to work until death has stripped some poor individual to the bone, and no one—neither the local homicide detectives nor the pathologists—can figure out who once gave identity to the skeletonized remains. No one, that is, except a shrewd, laconic, 60-year-old forensic anthropologist.

Snow strolls into the Cook County Medical Examiner's Office in Chicago on this brisk October morning wearing a pair of Lucchese cowboy boots and a three-piece pin-striped suit. Waiting for him in autopsy room 160 are a bunch of naked skeletons found in Illinois, Wisconsin, and Minnesota since his last visit. Snow, a native Texan who now lives in rural Oklahoma, makes the trip up to Chicago some six times a year. The first case on his agenda is a pale brown skull found in the garbage of an abandoned building once occupied by a Chicago cosmetics company.

Snow turns the skull over slowly in his hands, a cigarette dangling from his fingers. One often does. Snow does not seem overly concerned about mortality, though its tragedy surrounds him daily.

"There's some trauma here," he says, examining a rough edge at the lower back of the skull. He points out the area to Jim Elliott, a homicide detective with the Chicago police. "This looks like a chopping blow by a heavy bladed instrument. Almost like a decapitation." In a place where the whining of bone saws drifts through hallways and the sweet-sour smell of death hangs in the air, the word surprises no one.

Snow begins thinking aloud. "I think what we're looking at here is a female, or maybe a small male, about thirty to forty years old. Probably Asian." He turns the skull upside down, pointing out the degree of wear on the teeth. "This was somebody who lived on a really rough diet. We don't normally find this kind of dental wear in a modern Western population."

"How long has it been around?" Elliott asks.

Snow raises the skull up to his nose. "It doesn't have any decompositional odors," he says. He pokes a finger in the skull's nooks and crannies. "There's no soft tissue left. It's good and dry. And it doesn't show signs of having been buried. I would say that this has been lying around in an attic or a box for years. It feels like a souvenir skull," says Snow.

Souvenir skulls, usually those of Japanese soldiers, were popular with U.S. troops serving in the Pacific during World War II; there was also a trade in skulls during the Vietnam War years. On closer inspection, though, Snow begins to wonder about the skull's Asian origins—the broad nasal aperture and the jutting forth of the upper-tooth-bearing part of the face suggest Melanesian features. Sifting through the objects found in the abandoned building with the skull, he finds several loose-leaf albums of 35-millimeter transparencies documenting life among the highland tribes of New Guinea. The slides, shot by an anthropologist, include graphic scenes of ritual warfare. The skull, Snow concludes, is more likely to be a trophy from one of these tribal battles than the result of a local Chicago homicide.

"So you'd treat it like found property?" Elliott asks finally. "Like somebody's garage-sale property?"

"Exactly," says Snow.

Clyde Snow is perhaps the world's most sought-after forensic anthropologist. People have been calling upon him to identify skeletons for more than a quarter of a century. Every year he's involved in some 75 cases of identification, most of them without fanfare. "He's an old scudder who doesn't have to blow his own whistle," says Walter Birkby, a forensic anthropologist at the University of Arizona. "He know's he's good."

Yet over the years Snow's work has turned him into something of an unlikely celebrity. He has been called upon to identify the remains of the Nazi war criminal Josef Mengele, reconstruct the face of the Egyptian boy-king Tutankhamen, confirm the authenticity of the body autopsied as that of President John F. Kennedy, and examine the skeletal remains of General Custer's men at the battlefield of the Little Bighorn. He has also been involved in the grim task of identifying the bodies in some of the United States' worst airline accidents.

Such is his legend that cases are sometimes attributed to him in which he played no part. He did not, as *The New York Times* reported, identify the remains of the crew of the *Challenger* disaster. But the man is often the equal of his myth. For the past four years, setting his personal safety aside, Snow has spent much of his time in Argentina, searching for the graves and identities of some of the thousands who "disappeared" between 1976 and 1983, during Argentina's military regime.

Snow did not set out to rescue the dead from oblivion. For almost two decades, until 1979, he was a physical anthropologist at the Civil Aeromedical Institute, part of the Federal Aviation Administration in Oklahoma City. Snow's job was to help engineers improve aircraft design and safety features by providing them with data on the human frame.

One study, he recalls, was initiated in response to complaints from a flight attendants' organization. An analysis of accident patterns had revealed that inadequate restraints on flight attendants' jump seats were leading to deaths and injuries and that aircraft doors weighing several hundred pounds were impeding evacuation efforts. Snow points out that ensuring the survival of passengers in emergencies is largely the flight attendants' responsibility. "If they are injured or killed in a crash, you're going to find a lot of dead passengers."

Reasoning that equipment might be improved if engineers had more data on the size and strength of those who use it, Snow undertook a study that required meticulous measurement. When his report was issued in 1975, Senator William Proxmire was outraged that $57,800 of the taxpayers' money had been spent to caliper 423 airline stewardesses from head to toe. Yet the study, which received one of the senator's dubious Golden Fleece Awards, was firmly supported by both the FAA and the Association of Flight Attendants. "I can't imagine," says Snow with obvious delight, "how much coffee Proxmire got spilled on him in the next few months."

It was during his tenure at the FAA that he developed an interest in forensic work. Over the years the Oklahoma police frequently consulted the physical anthropologist for help in identifying crime victims. "The FAA figured it was a kind of community service to let me work on these cases," he says.

The experience also helped to prepare him for the grim task of identifying the victims of air disasters. In December 1972, when a United Airlines plane crashed outside Chicago, killing 43 of the 61 people aboard (including the wife of Watergate conspirator Howard Hunt, who was found with $10,000 in her purse), Snow was brought in to help examine the bodies. That same year, with Snow's help, forensic anthropology was recognized as a specialty by the American Academy of Forensic Sciences. "It got a lot of anthropologists interested in forensics," he says, "and it made a lot of pathologists out there aware that there were anthropologists who could help them."

Each nameless skeleton poses a unique mystery for Snow. But some, like the second case awaiting him back in the autopsy room at the Cook County morgue, are more challenging than others. This one is a real chiller. In a large cardboard box lies a jumble of bones along with a tattered leg from a pair of blue jeans, a sock shrunk tightly around the bones of a foot, a pair of Nike running shoes without shoelaces, and, inside the hood of a blue windbreaker, a mass of stringy, blood-caked hair. The remains were discovered frozen in ice about 20 miles outside Milwaukee. A rusted bicycle was found lying close by. Paul Hibbard, chief deputy medical examiner for Waukesha County, who brought the skeleton to Chicago, says no one has been reported missing.

Snow lifts the bones out of the box and begins reconstructing the skeleton on an autopsy table. "There are two hundred six bones and thirty-two teeth in the human body," he says, "and each has a story to tell." Because bone is dynamic, living tissue, many of life's significant events—injuries, illness, childbearing—leave their mark on the body's internal framework. Put together the stories told by these bones, he says, and what you have is a person's "osteobiography."

Snow begins by determining the sex of the skeleton, which is not always obvious. He tells the story of a skeleton that was brought to his FAA office in the late 1970s. It had been found along with some women's clothes and a purse in a local back lot, and the police had assumed that it was female. But when Snow examined the bones, he realized that "at six foot three, she would have probably have been the tallest female in Oklahoma."

Then Snow recalled that six months earlier the custodian in his building had suddenly not shown up for work. The man's supervisor later mentioned to Snow, "You know, one of these days when they find Ronnie, he's going to be dressed as a woman." Ronnie, it turned out, was a weekend transvestite. A copy of his dental records later confirmed that the skeleton in women's clothing was indeed Snow's janitor.

The Wisconsin bike rider is also male. Snow picks out two large bones that look something like twisted oysters—the innominates, or hipbones, which along with the sacrum, or lower backbone, form the pelvis. This pelvis is narrow and steep-walled like a male's, not broad and shallow like a female's. And the sciatic notch (the V-shaped space where the sciatic nerve passes through the hipbone) is narrow, as is normal in a male. Snow can also determine a skeleton's sex by checking the size of the mastoid processes (the bony knobs at the base of the skull) and the prominence of the brow ridge, or by measuring the head of an available limb bone, which is typically broader in males.

From an examination of the skull he concludes that the bike rider is "predominantly Caucasoid." A score of bony traits help the forensic anthropologist assign a skeleton to one of the three major racial groups: Negroid, Caucasoid, or Mongoloid. Snow notes that the ridge of the boy's nose is high and salient, as it is in whites. In Negroids and Mongoloids (which include American Indians as well as most Asians) the nose tends to be broad in relation to its height. However, the boy's nasal margins are somewhat smoothed down, usually a Mongoloid feature. "Possibly a bit of American Indian admixture," says Snow. "Do you have Indians in your area?" Hibbard nods.

Age is next. Snow takes the skull and turns it upside down, pointing out the basilar joint, the junction between the two major bones that form the underside of the skull. In a child the joint would still be open to allow room for growth, but here the joint has fused—something that usually happens in the late teen years. On the other hand, he says, pointing to the zigzagging lines on the dome of the skull, the cranial sutures are open. The cranial sutures, which join the bones of the braincase, begin to fuse and disappear in the mid-twenties.

Next Snow picks up a femur and looks for signs of growth at the point where the shaft meets the knobbed end. The thin plates of cartilage—areas of incomplete calcification—that are visible at this point suggest that the boy hadn't yet attained his full height. Snow double-checks with an examination of the pubic symphysis, the joint where the two hipbones meet. The ridges in this area, which fill in and smooth over in adulthood, are still clearly marked. He concludes that the skeleton is that of a boy between 15 and 20 years old.

"One of the things you learn is to be pretty conservative," says Snow. "It's very impressive when you tell the police, 'This person is eighteen years old,' and he turns out to be eighteen. The problem is, if the person is fifteen you've blown it—you probably won't find him. Looking for a missing person is like trying to catch fish. Better get a big net and do your own sorting."

Snow then picks up a leg bone, measures it with a set of calipers, and enters the data into a portable computer. Using the known correlation between the height and length of the long limb bones, he quickly estimates the boy's height. "He's five foot six and a half to five foot eleven," says Snow. "Medium build, not excessively muscular, judging from the muscle attachments that we see." He points to the grainy ridges that appear where muscle attaches itself to the bone. The most prominent attachments show up on the teenager's right arm bone, indicating right-handedness.

Then Snow examines the ribs one by one for signs of injury. He finds no stab wounds, cuts, or bullet holes, here or elsewhere on the skeleton. He picks up the hyoid bone from the boy's throat and looks for the tell-tale fracture signs that would suggest the boy was strangled. But, to Snow's frustration, he can find no obvious cause of death. In hopes of identifying the missing teenager, he suggests sending the skull, hair, and boy's description to Betty Pat Gatliff, a medical illustrator and sculptor in Oklahoma who does facial reconstructions.

Six weeks later photographs of the boy's likeness appear in the *Milwaukee Sentinel*. "If you persist long enough," says Snow, "eighty-five to ninety percent of the cases eventually get positively identified, but it can take anywhere from a few weeks to a few years."

Snow and Gatliff have collaborated many times, but never with more glitz than in 1983, when Snow was commissioned by Patrick Barry, a Miami orthopedic surgeon and amateur Egyptologist, to reconstruct the face of the Egyptian boy-king Tutankhamen. Normally a facial reconstruction begins with a skull, but since Tutankhamen's 3,000-year-old remains were in Egypt, Snow had to make do with the skull measurements from a 1925 postmortem and X-rays taken in 1975. A plaster model of the skull was made, and on the basis on Snow's report—"his skull is Caucasoid with some Negroid admixtures"—Gatliff put a face on it. What did Tutankhamen look like? Very much like the gold mask on his sarcophagus, says Snow, confirming that it was, indeed, his portrait.

Many cite Snow's use of facial reconstructions as one of his most important contributions to the field. Snow, typically self-effacing, says that Gatliff "does all the work." The identification of skeletal remains, he stresses, is often a collaboration between pathologists, odontologists, radiologists, and medical artists using a variety of forensic techniques.

One of Snow's last tasks at the FAA was to help identify the dead from the worst airline accident in U.S. history. On May 25, 1979, a DC-10 crashed shortly after takeoff from Chicago's O'Hare Airport, killing 273 people. The task facing Snow and more than a dozen forensic specialists was horrific. "No one ever sat down and counted," says Snow, "but we estimated ten thousand to twelve thousand pieces or parts of bodies." Nearly 80 percent of the victims were identified on the basis of dental evidence and fingerprints. Snow and forensic radiologist John Fitzpatrick later managed to identify two dozen others by comparing postmortem X-rays with X-rays taken during the victim's lifetime.

Next to dental records, such X-ray comparisons are the most common way of obtaining positive identifications. In 1978, when a congressional committee reviewed the evidence on John F. Kennedy's assassination, Snow used X-rays to show that the body autopsied at Bethesda Naval Hospital was indeed that of the late president and had not—as some conspiracy theorists believed—been switched.

The issue was resolved on the evidence of Kennedy's "sinus print," the scalloplike pattern on the upper margins of the sinuses that is visible in X-rays of the forehead. So characteristic is a person's sinus print that courts throughout the world accept the matching of antemortem and postmortem X-rays of the sinuses as positive identification.

Yet another technique in the forensic specialist's repertoire is photo superposition. Snow used it in 1977 to help identify the mummy of a famous Oklahoma outlaw named Elmer J. McCurdy, who was killed by a posse after holding up a train in 1911. For years the mummy had been exhibited as a "dummy" in a California funhouse—until it was found to have a real human skeleton inside it. Ownership of the mummy was eventually traced back to a funeral parlor in Oklahoma, where McCurdy had been embalmed and exhibited as "the bandit who wouldn't give up."

Using two video cameras and an image processor, Snow superposed the mummy's profile on a photograph of McCurdy that was taken shortly after his death. When displayed on a single monitor, the two coincided to a remarkable degree. Convinced by the evidence, Thomas Noguchi, then Los Angeles County corner, signed McCurdy's death certificate ("Last known occupation: Train robber") and allowed the outlaw's bones to be returned to Oklahoma for a decent burial.

It was this technique that also allowed forensic scientists to identify the remains of the Nazi "Angel of Death," Josef Mengele, in the summer of 1985. A team of investigators, including Snow and West German forensic anthropologist Richard Helmer, flew to Brazil after an Austrian couple claimed that Mengele lay buried in a grave on a São Paulo hillside. Tests revealed that the stature, age, and hair color of the unearthed skeleton were consistent with information in Mengele's SS files; yet without X-rays or dental records, the scientists still lacked conclusive evidence. When an image of the reconstructed skull was superposed on 1930s photographs of Mengele, however, the match was eerily compelling. All doubts were removed a few months later when Mengele's dental X-rays were tracked down.

In 1979 Snow retired from the FAA to the rolling hills of Norman, Oklahoma, where he and his wife, Jerry, live in a sprawling, early-1960s ranch house. Unlike his 50 or so fellow forensic anthropologists, most of whom are tied to academic positions, Snow is free to pursue his consultancy work full-time. Judging from the number of miles that he logs in the average month, Snow is clearly not ready to retire for good.

His recent projects include a reexamination of the skeletal remains found at the site of the Battle of the Little Bighorn, where more than a century ago Custer and his 210 men were killed by Sioux and Cheyenne warriors. Although most of the enlisted men's remains were moved to a mass grave in 1881, an excavation of the battlefield in the past few years uncovered an additional 375 bones and 36 teeth. Snow, teaming up again with Fitzpatrick, determined that these remains belonged to 34 individuals.

The historical accounts of Custer's desperate last stand are vividly confirmed by their findings. Snow identified one skeleton as that of a soldier between the ages of 19 and 23 who weighed around 150 pounds and stood about five foot eight. He'd sustained gunshot wounds to his chest and left forearm. Heavy blows to his head had fractured his skull and sheared off his teeth. Gashed thigh bones indicated that his body was later dismembered with an ax or hatchet.

Given the condition and number of the bodies, Snow seriously questions the accuracy of the identifications made by the original nineteenth-century burial crews. He doubts, for example, that the skeleton buried at West Point is General Custer's.

For the last four years Snow has devoted much of his time to helping two countries come to terms with the horrors of a much more recent past. As part of a group sponsored by the American Association for the Advancement of Science, he has been helping the Argentinian National Commission on Disappeared Persons to determine the fate of some of those who vanished during their country's harsh military rule: between 1976 and 1983 at least 10,000 people were systematically swept off the streets by roving death squads to be tortured, killed, and buried in unmarked graves. In December 1986, at the invitation of the Aquino government's Human Rights Commission, Snow also spent several weeks training Philippine scientists to investigate the disappearances that occurred under the Marcos regime.

But it is in Argentina where Snow has done the bulk of his human-rights work. He has spent more than 27 months in and around Buenos Aires, first training a small group of local medical and anthropology students in the techniques of forensic investigation, and later helping them carefully exhume and examine scores of the *desaparecidos,* or disappeared ones.

Only 25 victims have so far been positively identified. But the evidence has helped convict seven junta members and other high-ranking military and police officers. The idea is not necessarily to identify all 10,000 of the missing, says Snow. "If you have a colonel who ran a detention center where maybe five hundred people were killed, you don't have to nail them with five hundred deaths. Just one or two should be sufficient to get him convicted." Forensic evidence from Snow's team may be used to prosecute several other military officers, including General Suarez Mason. Mason is the former commander of the I Army Corps in Buenos Aires and is believed to be responsible for thousands of disappearances. He was recently extradited from San Francisco back to Argentina, where he is expected to stand trial this winter [1988].

The investigations have been hampered by a frustrating lack of antemortem information. In 1984, when commission lawyers took depositions from relatives and friends of the disappeared, they often failed to obtain such basic information as the victim's height, weight, or hair color. Nor did they ask for the missing person's X-rays (which in Argentina are given to the patient) or the address of the victim's dentist. The problem was compounded by the inexperience of those who carried out the first mass exhumations prior to Snow's arrival. Many of the skeletons were inadvertently destroyed by bulldozers as they were brought up.

Every unearthed skeleton that shows signs of gunfire, however, helps to erode the claim once made by many in the Argentinian military that most of the *desaparecidos* are alive and well and living in Mexico City, Madrid, or Paris. Snow recalls the case of a 17-year-old boy named Gabriel Dunayavich, who disappeared in the summer of 1976. He was walking home from a movie with his girlfriend when a Ford Falcon with no license plates snatched him off the street. The police later found his body and that of another boy and girl dumped by the roadside on the outskirts of Buenos Aires. The police went through the motions of an investigation, taking photographs and doing an autopsy, then buried the three teenagers in an unmarked grave.

A decade later Snow, with the help of the boy's family, traced the autopsy reports, the police photographs, and the grave of the three youngsters. Each of them had four or five closely spaced bullet wounds in the upper chest—the signature, says Snow, of an automatic weapon. Two also had wounds on their arms from bullets that had entered behind the elbow and exited from the forearm.

"That means they were conscious when they were shot," says Snow. "When a gun was pointed at them, they naturally raised their arm." It's details like these that help to authenticate the last moments of the victims and bring a dimension of reality to the judges and jury.

Each time Snow returns from Argentina he says that this will be the last time. A few months later he is back in Buenos Aires. "There's always more work to do," he says. It is, he admits quietly, "terrible work."

"These were such brutal, cold-blooded crimes," he says. "The people who committed them not only murdered; they had a system to eliminate all trace that their victims even existed."

Snow will not let them obliterate their crimes so conveniently. "There are human-rights violations going on all around the world," he says. "But to me murder is murder, regardless of the motive. I hope that we are sending a message to governments who murder in the name of politics that they can be held to account."

Critical Thinking

1. Using Clyde Snow as an example, what does a forensic anthropologist do? How was he instrumental in improving aircraft design and safety?
2. What is "osteobiography"?
3. How does Snow determine the various characteristics of an individual from the skeleton?
4. What conclusions did Clyde Snow draw from his reexamination of the skeletal remains at the Battle of the Little Bighorn?
5. What kind of human rights work has Snow done? How have the investigations been hampered? What findings did he come to?

UNIT 4

Pre-Historic Archaeology

Unit Selections

Learning Outcomes

After reading this Unit, you will be able to:

- Describe what happened to the Neandertals.
- Discuss the extent to which the Neandertals are part of our ancestry.
- Discuss when, where, and how modern humans evolved.
- Discuss whether the modern humans that came out of Africa replaced archaic *Homo sapiens* or mated with them.
- Describe and explain the "Upper Paleolithic Revolution."
- Explain the cave art of Upper Paleolithic France as an outgrowth of shamanic religion.
- Discuss the extent to which children may have participated in the creation of the cave art of the Paleolithic period.
- Discuss the potential symbolism of the abstract markings on the walls of the painted caves in southern France.
- Explain how the symbolism in the cave paintings may be the first evidence of a rudimentary written language system.

Student Website

www.mhhe.com/cls

Internet References

Bradshaw Foundation
www.bradshawfoundation.com/clottes/index.php

Department of Human Evolution/Max Planck Institute
www.eva.mpg.de/evolution

Turkana Basin Institute
www.turkanabasin.org

One of the most intriguing aspects of archaeology has to do with human beginnings. As Chris Stringer observes (in "Human Evolution: The Long, Winding Road to Modern Man"), "our species' origins have been a source of fascination for millennia and account for the huge range of creation myths that are recorded in different cultures." The search for clues as to where we come from and how we came to be as we are goes to the heart of what archaeology in particular and anthropology in general are all about. Just as cultural anthropologists seek to understand contemporary cultures as a means for gaining insights into our own way of life and biological anthropologists probe into our evolutionary past in order to comprehend our biological present, so archaeologists seek to understand the material remains of past cultures in order to reconstruct the pathways to the here and now. (See "Twilight of the Neandertals" and "Refuting a Myth about Human Origins.")

There is much in this section that deals with the biological, anatomical, and genetic aspects of our evolutionary development, but don't be misled into thinking that archaeologists are not just as involved as paleoanthropologists in seeking to understand who we are in terms of what we once were. Yes, there are the bones to be studied as a way of reconstructing our anatomical and biological evolutionary past (which require archaeological techniques to recover by the way), but alongside them are often the remains of artifacts, ranging from crude stone tools of 2 million years ago to some of the most incredibly beautiful artwork in the painted caves of southern France, much of which would be worthy of inclusion in the Louvre. (See "Paleolithic Cave Art in France" by Jean Clottes and be sure to take in the color graphics and video at the accompanying website, www.bradshawfoundation.com/clottes/index.php.) After all, it is the archaeological evidence that provides us with the all-important cultural context, which has enabled our species to survive and develop to the point where we are today.

Unfortunately, nothing about our past is as simple, tangible, and straightforward as the purveyors of "bones and stones" would like to have it. There are interpretations to be made, biases to overcome and differences in perspectives to be resolved. This section is appropriately rife with controversy, conflict, and calumny. (For an example of the latter, read Stringer's charge of racism against Carleton Coon.) But archaeology, after all, is a science and in all of the sciences, new evidence raises new questions (see "Children of Prehistory" and "The Writing on the Cave Wall"), resolves old ones amicably (as in "A New View of the Birth of *Homo sapiens*") or shakes things up even more (see "Rethinking the Hobbits of Indonesia"). And so we learn that 2–5-year-old kids may have generated the bulk of Rouffignac's ancient ceiling designs and that much of the prehistoric cave art in general may have been the product of "playful youngsters and graffiti-minded teenagers." And who would have thought that Chris Stringer and Milford Wolpoff, long-time adversaries in the human origins debate, would find their views converging and could sit down and have a beer together (each one thinking he had won the debate)? Finally, how could we possibly entertain the notion that a branch of small-brained, early hominins, hardly more than three feet tall and wielding some of the crudest stone tools ever made, could make the journey from Africa all the way to a tiny island in Indonesia as early as two million years ago?

© Melba Photo Agency/PunchStock

So, what are we to make of all these claims? To those sitting on the sidelines, the controversies can be exciting, confusing, exasperating or a combination of all three. To those scientists working in the thick of it, that's archaeology!

Twilight of the Neandertals

Paleoanthropologists know more about Neandertals than any other extinct human. But their demise remains a mystery, one that gets curiouser and curiouser.

KATE WONG

Some 28,000 years ago in what is now the British territory of Gibraltar, a group of Neandertals eked out a living along the rocky Mediterranean coast. They were quite possibly the last of their kind. Elsewhere in Europe and western Asia, Neandertals had disappeared thousands of years earlier, after having ruled for more than 200,000 years. The Iberian Peninsula, with its comparatively mild climate and rich array of animals and plants, seems to have been the final stronghold. Soon, however, the Gibraltar population, too, would die out, leaving behind only a smattering of their stone tools and the charred remnants of their campfires.

Ever since the discovery of the first Neandertal fossil in 1856, scientists have debated the place of these bygone humans on the family tree and what became of them. For decades two competing theories have dominated the discourse. One holds that Neandertals were an archaic variant of our own species, *Homo sapiens,* that evolved into or was assimilated by the anatomically modern European population. The other posits that the Neandertals were a separate species, *H. neanderthalensis,* that modern humans swiftly extirpated on entering the archaic hominid's territory.

Over the past decade, however, two key findings have shifted the fulcrum of the debate away from the question of whether Neandertals and moderns made love or war. One is that analyses of Neandertal DNA have yet to yield the signs of interbreeding with modern humans that many researchers expected to see if the two groups mingled significantly. The other is that improvements in dating methods show that rather than disappearing immediately after the moderns invaded Europe, starting a little more than 40,000 years ago, the Neandertals survived for nearly 15,000 years after moderns moved in—hardly the rapid replacement adherents to the blitzkrieg theory envisioned.

These revelations have prompted a number of researchers to look more carefully at other factors that might have led to Neandertal extinction. What they are finding suggests that the answer involves a complicated interplay of stresses.

Hypothesis 1
Did Climate Change Doom the Neandertals?

Starting perhaps around 55,000 years ago, climate in Eurasia began to swing wildly from frigid to mild and back again in the span of decades. During the cold snaps, ice sheets advanced and treeless tundra replaced wooded environments across much of the Neandertals' range. Shifts in the available prey animals accompanied these changes. Wide spacing between past climate fluctuations allowed diminished Neandertal populations sufficient time to bounce back and adapt to the new conditions.

This time, however, the rapidity of the changes may have made recovery impossible. By 30,000 years ago only a few pockets of Neandertals survived, hanging on in the Iberian Peninsula, with its comparatively mild climate and rich resources. These groups were too small and fragmented to sustain themselves, however, and eventually they disappeared.

Key Concepts

- Neandertals, our closest relatives, ruled Europe and western Asia for more than 200,000 years. But sometime after 28,000 years ago, they vanished.
- Scientists have long debated what led to their disappearance. The latest extinction theories focus on climate change and subtle differences in behavior and biology that might have given modern humans an advantage over the Neandertals.

—The Editors

A World in Flux

One of the most informative new lines of evidence bearing on why the Neandertals died out is paleoclimate data. Scholars have known for some time that Neandertals experienced both glacial conditions and milder interglacial conditions during their long reign. In recent years, however, analyses of isotopes trapped in primeval ice, ocean sediments and pollen retrieved from such locales as Greenland, Venezuela and Italy have enabled investigators to reconstruct a far finer-grained picture of the climate shifts that occurred during a period known as oxygen isotope stage 3 (OIS-3). Spanning the time between roughly 65,000 and 25,000 years ago, OIS-3 began with moderate conditions and culminated with the ice sheets blanketing northern Europe.

Considering that Neandertals were the only hominids in Europe at the beginning of OIS-3 and moderns were the only ones there by the end of it, experts have wondered whether the plummeting temperatures might have caused the Neandertals to perish, perhaps because they could not find enough food or keep sufficiently warm. Yet arguing for that scenario has proved tricky for one essential reason: Neandertals had faced glacial conditions before and persevered.

In fact, numerous aspects of Neandertal biology and behavior indicate that they were well suited to the cold. Their barrel chests and stocky limbs would have conserved body heat, although they would have additionally needed clothing fashioned from animal pelts to stave off the chill. And their brawny build seems to have been adapted to their ambush-style hunting of large, relatively solitary mammals—such as woolly rhinoceroses—that roamed northern and central Europe during the cold snaps. (Other distinctive Neandertal features, such as the form of the prominent brow, may have been adaptively neutral traits that became established through genetic drift, rather than selection.)

But the isotope data reveal that far from progressing steadily from mild to frigid, the climate became increasingly unstable heading into the last glacial maximum, swinging severely and abruptly. With that flux came profound ecological change: forests gave way to treeless grassland; reindeer replaced certain kinds of rhinoceroses. So rapid were these oscillations that over the course of an individual's lifetime, all the plants and animals that a person had grown up with could vanish and be replaced with unfamiliar flora and fauna. And then, just as quickly, the environment could change back again.

It is this seesawing of environmental conditions—not necessarily the cold, per se—that gradually pushed Neandertal populations to the point of no return, according to scenarios posited by such experts as evolutionary ecologist Clive Finlayson of the Gibraltar Museum, who directs the excavations at several cave sites in Gibraltar. These shifts would have demanded that Neandertals adopt a new way of life in very short order. For example, the replacement of wooded areas with open grassland would have left ambush hunters without any trees to hide behind, he says. To survive, the Neandertals would have had to alter the way they hunted.

Some Neandertals did adapt to their changing world, as evidenced by shifts in their tool types and prey. But many probably died out during these fluctuations, leaving behind ever more fragmented populations. Under normal circumstances, these archaic humans might have been able to bounce back, as they had previously, when the fluctuations were fewer and farther between. This time, however, the rapidity of the environmental change left insufficient time for recovery. Eventually, Finlayson argues, the repeated climatic insults left the Neandertal populations so diminished that they could no longer sustain themselves.

The results of a genetic study published this past April in *PLoS One* by Virginie Fabre and her colleagues at the University of the Mediterranean in Marseille support the notion that Neandertal populations were fragmented, Finlayson says. That analysis of Neandertal mitochondrial DNA found that the Neandertals could be divided into three subgroups—one in western Europe, another in southern Europe and a third in western Asia—and that population size ebbed and flowed.

Invasive Species

For other researchers, however, the fact that the Neandertals entirely disappeared only after moderns entered Europe clearly indicates that the invaders had a hand in the extinction, even if the newcomers did not kill the earlier settlers outright. Probably, say those who hold this view, the Neandertals ended up competing with the incoming moderns for food and gradually lost ground. Exactly what ultimately gave moderns their winning edge remains a matter of considerable disagreement, though.

One possibility is that modern humans were less picky about what they ate. Analyses of Neandertal bone chemistry conducted

Resurrecting the Neandertal

Later this year researchers led by Svante Pääbo of the Max Planck Institute for Evolutionary Anthropology in Leipzig, Germany, are expected to publish a rough draft of the Neandertal genome. The work has prompted speculation that scientists might one day be able to bring back this extinct human. Such a feat, if it were technically possible, would raise all sorts of ethical quandaries: What rights would a Neandertal have? Would this individual live in a lab, or a zoo, or a household?

Moral concerns aside, what could researchers actually learn from a resurrected Neandertal? The answer is: less than you might think. A Neandertal born and raised in a modern setting would not have built-in Ice Age wisdom to impart to us, such as how to make a Mousterian stone tool or bring down a woolly rhinoceros. Indeed, he would not be able to tell scholars anything about the culture of his people. It is possible, however, that studying Neandertal biology and cognition could reveal as yet unknown differences between these archaic hominids and modern ones that might have given moderns a survival advantage.

Hypothesis 2
Were the Neandertals Outsmarted by Modern Humans?

A long-standing theory of Neandertal extinction holds that modern humans outcompeted Neandertals with their superior smarts. But mounting evidence indicates that Neandertals engaged in many of the same sophisticated behaviors once attributed to moderns alone (*table*). The findings reveal that at least some Neandertals were capable of symbolic thought—and therefore probably language—and that they had the tools and the know-how to pursue a wide range of foods. Still, these practices seem to have been more entrenched in modern human culture than in that of Neandertals, which may have given moderns the upper hand.

Table Evidence of Modern Behavior among Neandertals

Trait	Common	Occasional	Absent	Uncertain
Art				√
Pigment use	√			
Jewelry		√		
Symbolic burial of dead				√
Long-distance exchange				√
Microliths		√		
Barbed points			√	
Bone tools		√		
Blades		√		
Needles			√	
Exploitation of marine resources		√		
Bird hunting		√		
Division of labor			√	

by Hervé Bocherens of the University of Tubingen in Germany suggest that at least some of these hominids specialized in large mammals, such as woolly rhinoceroses, which were relatively rare. Early modern humans, on the other hand, ate all manner of animals and plants. Thus, when moderns moved into Neandertal territory and started taking some of these large animals for themselves, so the argument goes, the Neandertals would have been in trouble. Moderns, meanwhile, could supplement the big kills with smaller animals and plant foods.

"Neandertals had a Neandertal way of doing things, and it was great as long as they weren't competing with moderns," observes archaeologist Curtis W. Marean of Arizona State University. In contrast, Marean says, the moderns, who evolved under tropical conditions in Africa, were able to enter entirely different environments and very quickly come up with creative ways to deal with the novel circumstances they encountered. "The key difference is that Neandertals were just not as advanced cognitively as modern humans," he asserts.

Marean is not alone in thinking that Neandertals were one-trick ponies. A long-standing view holds that moderns outsmarted the Neandertals with not only their superior tool technology and survival tactics but also their gift of gab, which might have helped them form stronger social networks. The Neandertal dullards, in this view, did not stand a chance against the newcomers.

But a growing body of evidence indicates that Neandertals were savvier than they have been given credit for. In fact, they apparently engaged in many of the behaviors once believed to be strictly the purview of modern humans. As paleoanthropologist Christopher B. Stringer of London's Natural History Museum puts it, "the boundary between Neandertals and moderns has gotten fuzzier."

Sites in Gibraltar have yielded some of the most recent findings blurring the line between the two human groups. In September 2008 Stringer and his colleagues reported on evidence that Neandertals at Gorham's Cave and next-door Vanguard Cave hunted dolphins and seals as well as gathered shellfish. An as yet unpublished work shows that they were eating birds and rabbits, too. The discoveries in Gilbraltar, along with finds from a handful of other sites, upend the received wisdom that moderns alone exploited marine resources and small game.

More evidence blurring the line between Neandertal and modern human behavior has come from the site of Hohle Fels in southwestern Germany. There paleoanthropologist Bruce Hardy of Kenyon College was able to compare artifacts made by Neandertals who inhabited the cave between 36,000 and 40,000 years ago with artifacts from modern humans who resided there between 33,000 and 36,000 years ago under similar climate and environmental conditions. In a presentation given this past April to the Paleoanthropology Society in Chicago, Hardy reported that his analysis of the wear patterns on the tools and the residues from substances with which the tools came into contact revealed that although the modern humans created a larger variety of tools than did the Neandertals, the groups engaged in mostly the same activities at Hohle Fels.

These activities include such sophisticated practices as using tree resin to bind stone points to wooden handles, employing stone points as thrusting or projectile weapons, and crafting implements from bone and wood. As to why the Hohle Fels Neandertals made fewer types of tools than did the moderns who lived there afterward, Hardy surmises that they were able to get the job done without them. "You don't need a grapefruit spoon to eat a grapefruit," he says.

The claim that Neandertals lacked language, too, seems unlikely in light of recent discoveries. Researchers now know that at least some of them decorated their bodies with jewelry and probably pigment. Such physical manifestations of symbolic behavior are often used as a proxy for language when reconstructing behavior from the archaeological record. And in 2007 researchers led by Johannes Krause of the Max Planck Institute for Evolutionary Anthropology in Leipzig, Germany, reported that analyses of Neandertal DNA have shown that these hominids had the same version of the speech-enabling gene *FOXP2* that modern humans carry.

Tiebreakers

With the gap between Neandertal and modern human behavior narrowing, many researchers are now looking to subtle differences in culture and biology to explain why the Neandertals lost out. "Worsening and highly unstable climatic conditions would have made competition among human groups all the more fierce," reflects paleoanthropologist Katerina Harvati, also at Max Planck. "In this context, even small advantages would become extremely important and might spell the difference between survival and death."

Stringer, for his part, theorizes that the moderns' somewhat wider range of cultural adaptations provided a slightly superior buffer against hard times. For example, needles left behind by modern humans hint that they had tailored clothing and tents, all the better for keeping the cold at bay. Neandertals, meanwhile, left behind no such signs of sewing and are believed by some to have had more crudely assembled apparel and shelters as a result.

Neandertals and moderns may have also differed in the way they divvied up the chores among group members. In a paper published in *Current Anthropology* in 2006, archaeologists Steven L. Kuhn and Mary C. Stiner, both at the University of Arizona, hypothesized that the varied diet of early modern Europeans would have favored a division of labor in which men hunted the larger game and women collected and prepared nuts, seeds and berries. In contrast, the Neandertal focus on large game probably meant that their women and children joined in the hunt, possibly helping to drive animals toward the waiting men. By creating both a more reliable food supply and a safer environment for rearing children, division of labor could have enabled modern human populations to expand at the expense of the Neandertals.

However the Neandertals obtained their food, they needed lots of it. "Neandertals were the SUVs of the hominid world," says paleoanthropologist Leslie Aiello of the Wenner-Gren Foundation in New York City. A number of studies aimed at estimating Neandertal metabolic rates have concluded that these archaic hominids required significantly more calories to survive than the rival moderns did.

Hominid energetics expert Karen Steudel-Numbers of the University of Wisconsin–Madison has determined, for example, that the energetic cost of locomotion was 32 percent higher in Neandertals than in anatomically modern humans, thanks to the archaic hominids' burly build and short shinbones, which would have shortened their stride. In terms of daily energy needs, the Neandertals would have required somewhere between 100 and 350 calories more than moderns living in the same climates, according to a model developed by Andrew W. Froehle of the University of California, San Diego, and Steven E. Churchill of Duke University. Modern humans, then, might have outcompeted Neandertals simply by virtue of being more fuel-efficient: using less energy for baseline functions meant that moderns could devote more energy to reproducing and ensuring the survival of their young.

One more distinction between Neandertals and moderns deserves mention, one that could have enhanced modern survival in important ways. Research led by Rachel Caspari of Central Michigan University has shown that around 30,000 years ago, the number of modern humans who lived to be old enough to be grandparents began to skyrocket. Exactly what spurred this increase in longevity is uncertain, but the change had two key consequences. First, people had more reproductive years, thus increasing their fertility potential. Second, they had more time over which to acquire specialized knowledge and pass it on to the next generation—where to find drinking water in times of drought, for instance. "Long-term survivorship gives the potential for bigger social networks and greater knowledge stores," Stringer comments. Among the shorter-lived Neandertals, in contrast, knowledge was more likely to disappear, he surmises.

More clues to why the Neandertals faded away may come from analysis of the Neandertal genome, the full sequence of which is due out this year. But answers are likely to be slow to surface, because scientists know so little about the functional significance of most regions of the modern genome, never mind the Neandertal one. "We're a long way from being able to read what the [Neandertal] genome is telling us," Stringer says. Still, future analyses could conceivably pinpoint cognitive or metabolic differences between the two groups, for example, and provide a more definitive answer to the question of whether Neandertals and moderns interbred.

The Stone Age whodunit is far from solved. But researchers are converging on one conclusion: regardless of whether climate or competition with moderns, or some combination thereof, was the prime mover in the decline of the Neandertals, the precise factors governing the extinction of individual populations of these archaic hominids almost certainly varied from group to group. Some may have perished from disease, others from inbreeding. "Each valley may tell its own story," Finlayson remarks.

As for the last known Neandertals, the ones who lived in Gibraltar's seaside caves some 28,000 years ago, Finlayson is certain that they did not spend their days competing with moderns, because moderns seem not to have settled there until thousands of years after the Neandertals were gone. The rest of their story, however, remains to be discovered.

More to Explore

Older Age Becomes Common Late in Human Evolution. Rachel Caspari and Sang-Hee Lee in *Proceedings of the National Academy of Sciences USA,* Vol. 101, No. 30, pages 10895–10900; July 27, 2004.

Rapid Ecological Turnover and Its Impact on Neanderthal and Other Human Populations. Clive Finlayson and José S. Carrión in *Trends in Ecology and Evolution,* Vol. 22, No. 4, pages 213–222; 2007.

Heading North: An Africanist Perspective on the Replacement of Neanderthals by Modern Humans. Curtis W. Marean in *Rethinking the Human Revolution.* Edited by Paul Mellars et al. McDonald Institute for Archaeological Research, Cambridge, 2007.

Neanderthal Exploitation of Marine Mammals in Gibraltar. C. B. Stringer et al. in *Proceedings of the National Academy of Sciences USA,* Vol. 105, No. 38, pages 14319–14324; September 23, 2008.

Critical Thinking

1. What have been the two competing theories regarding the relationship between Neanderthals and ourselves? What two key findings have shifted the fulcrum of the debate?
2. Why would the "seesawing" of environmental conditions contribute to Neanderthal extinction in spite of their biological adaptations to the cold?
3. What evidence is there that Neanderthal populations were fragmented?
4. What have been the claims that modern humans had something to do with Neanderthals' extinction? What is the counter-evidence?
5. What may have been the "tiebreakers" that caused the Neanderthals to lose out, and why?

Article 22

Human Evolution: The Long, Winding Road to Modern Man

CHRIS STRINGER

Our species' origins have been a source of fascination for millennia and account for the huge range of creation myths that are recorded in different cultures. Linnaeus, that great classifier of living things, gave us our biological name *Homo sapiens* (meaning "wise man") and our high rounded skulls certainly make us distinctive, as do our small brow ridges and chins. However, we are also remarkable for our language, art and complex technology.

The question is: where did these features evolve? Where can humanity place its homeland? In terms of our earliest ancestors, the answer is generally agreed to be Africa. It was here that our first ape-like ancestors began to make their homes on the savannah. However, a fierce debate has continued about whether it was also the ultimate birthplace of our own species.

Forty years ago, no one believed that modern humans could have originated in Africa. In some cases this idea was based on fading racist agendas. For example, in 1962, the American anthropologist Carleton Coon claimed that "If Africa was the cradle of mankind, it was only an indifferent kindergarten. Europe and Asia were our principal schools."

Part of the confusion was due to the lack of well-dated fossil and archaeological evidence. In the intervening years, however, I have been privileged to be involved in helping to accumulate data—fossil, chronological, archaeological and genetic—that show our species did have a recent African origin. But as the latest evidence shows, this origin was complex and in my new book, *The Origin of Our Species,* I try to make it clear what it means to be human and change perceptions about our origins.

I had been fascinated by ancient humans called Neanderthals even as a 10-year-old, and in 1971, as a 23-year-old student, I left London on a four-month research trip to museums and institutes in 10 European countries to gather data on the shapes of skulls of Neanderthals and of their modern-looking successors in Europe, the Cro-Magnons. My purpose was to test the then popular theory which held that Neanderthals and people like them in each region of the ancient world were the ancestors of people in those same regions today. I had only a modest grant, and so I drove my old car, sleeping in it, camping or staying in youth hostels—in Belgium I even spent one night in a shelter for the homeless. I survived border confrontations and two robberies, but by the end of my 5,000-mile trip I had collected one of the largest data sets of Neanderthal and early modern skull measurements assembled up to that time.

Over the next three years I added data on other ancient and modern samples, and the results were clear: Neanderthals had evolved their own special characteristics, and did not look like ancestors for the Cro-Magnons or for any modern people. The issue was: where had our species evolved? In 1974 I was unable to say, but taking up a research post at the Natural History Museum meant I could continue the quest.

My research uncovered clues, however, and over the next decade my work—along with that of a few others—focused on Africa as the most likely homeland of our species. We remained an isolated minority until 1987, when the paper "Mitochondrial DNA and Human Evolution," was published by Rebecca Cann, Mark Stoneking and Allan Wilson. It put modern human origins on the front pages of newspapers all over the world for the first time for it showed that a tiny and peculiar part of our genome, inherited only through mothers and daughters, derived from an African ancestor about 200,000 years ago. This woman became known as Mitochondrial Eve. A furor followed, as anthropologists rowed over the implications for human evolution.

After that, the "out of Africa" theory—or as I prefer to call it "the recent African origin" model for our origins—really took off. My version depicted the following background. The ancient species *Homo erectus* survived in East Asia and Indonesia but evolved into *Homo heidelbergensis* in Europe and Africa. (This last species had been named from a 600,000-year-old jawbone found in Germany in 1907.) Then, about 400,000 years ago, *H. heidelbergensis* underwent an evolutionary split: north of the Mediterranean it developed into the Neanderthals, while to the south, in Africa, it became us, modern humans. Finally, about 60,000 years ago *Homo sapiens* began to leave Africa and by 40,000 years ago, with the advantages of more complex tools and behaviours, spread into Asia and Europe, where we replaced the Neanderthals and all the other archaic people outside of Africa. In other words, under our skins, we are all Africans.

Not every scientist agreed, however. One group continued to support the idea of multiregional evolution, an updated version of ideas from the 1930s. It envisaged deep parallel lines of evolution in each inhabited region of Africa, Europe, Asia and Australasia, stretching from local variants of *H. erectus* right through to living people in the same areas today. These lines did not diverge through time, since they were glued together by interbreeding across the ancient world, so modern features could gradually evolve, spread and accumulate, alongside long-term regional differences in things like the shape of the face and the size of the nose.

A different model, known as the assimilation model, took the new fossil and genetic data on board and gave Africa a key role in the evolution of modern features. However, this model envisaged a much more gradual spread of those features from Africa than did mine. Neanderthals and archaic people like them were assimilated through widespread interbreeding. Thus the evolutionary establishment of modern features was a blending process rather than a rapid replacement.

So who was right? Genetic data continued to accumulate through the 1990s in support of the recent African origin model, both from recent human populations and Neanderthal fossils. Recent massive improvements in recovery and analysis of ancient DNA have produced even more information, some of it very surprising. Fossil fragments from Croatia have yielded up a nearly entire Neanderthal genome, providing rich data that promise insights into their biology—from eye colour and hair type through to skull shape and brain functions. These latest results have largely confirmed a separation from our lineage about 350,000 years ago. But when the new Neanderthal genome was compared in detail with modern humans from different continents, the results produced an intriguing twist to our evolutionary story: the genomes of people from Europe, China and New Guinea lay slightly closer to the Neanderthal sequence than did those of Africans. Thus if you are European, Asian or New Guinean, you could have 2.5% of Neanderthal DNA in your genetic make-up.

The most likely explanation for this discovery is that the ancestors of today's Europeans, Asians and New Guineans interbred with Neanderthals (or at least with a population that had a component of Neanderthal genes) in North Africa, Arabia or the Middle East, as they exited Africa about 60,000 years ago. That ancient human exodus may have involved only a few thousand people, so it would have taken the absorption of only a few Neanderthals into a group of *H. sapiens* for the genetic effect—greatly magnified as modern human numbers exploded—to be felt tens of thousands of years later.

The breakthrough in reconstructing a Neanderthal genome has been mirrored across Asia in equally remarkable work on the human group that has become known as the "Denisovans." A fossil finger bone, about 40,000 years old, found in Denisova Cave, Siberia, together with a huge molar tooth, could not be assigned to a particular human species, though it has also had much of its genome reconstructed. This has revealed a previously unrecognised Asian offshoot of the Neanderthal line, but again with a twist. These Denisovans are also related to one group of living humans—the Melanesians of southeast Asia (and probably their Australian neighbours too). These groups also carry about 5% of Denisovan DNA from another interbreeding event that must have happened as their ancestors passed through southern Asia over 40,000 years ago.

So where does this added complexity and evidence of interbreeding with Neanderthals and Denisovans leave my favoured Recent African Origins model? Has it been disproved in favour of the multiregional model, as some have claimed? I don't think so. As we have seen, back in 1970, no scientists held the view that Africa was the evolutionary home of modern humans; the region was considered backward and largely irrelevant, with the pendulum of scientific opinion strongly swinging towards non-African and Neanderthal ancestry models. Twenty years later, the pendulum was starting to move in favour of our African origins, as fossil evidence began to be reinforced by the clear signals of mitochondrial DNA. The pendulum swung even further with growing fossil, archaeological and genetic data in the 1990s.

Now, the advent of huge amounts of DNA data, including the Neanderthal and Denisovan genomes, has halted and even reversed that pendulum swing, away from absolute replacement. Instead we are looking at a mixed replacement-hybridisation or "leaky replacement" model. This dynamism is what makes studying human evolution so fascinating. Science is not about being right or wrong, but about gradually approaching truth about the natural world.

The big picture is that we are still predominantly of recent African origin (more than 90% of our genetic ancestry). But is there a special reason for this observation? Overall, the pre-eminence of Africa in the story of our origins does not involve a special evolutionary pathway but is a question of the continent's consistently large habitable areas which gave greater opportunities for morphological and behavioural variations, and for genetic and behavioural innovations to develop and be conserved. "Modernity" was not a package that had an origin in one African time, place and population, but was a composite whose elements appeared at different times and places, and then gradually coalesced to assume the form we recognise today.

My studies have led me to a greater recognition in recent human evolution of the forces of demography (the need for large populations and social networks to make progress), drift and contingency (chance events), and cultural rather than natural selection than I had considered before. It seems that cultural "progress" was a stop-start affair for much of our evolution, until human groups were large, had long-lived individuals, and wide social networks, all helping to maximise the chances that innovations would survive and accumulate.

Linnaeus said of *Homo sapiens* "know thyself." Knowing ourselves means a recognition that becoming modern is the path we perceive when looking back on our own evolutionary history. That history seems special to us, of course, because we owe our very existence to it. Those figures of human species (usually males, who become increasingly hairless and light-skinned) marching boldly across the page have illustrated our evolution in many popular articles, but they have wrongly enshrined the view that evolution was simply a progression leading to us, its pinnacle and final achievement.

Nothing could be further from the truth. There were plenty of other paths that could have been taken; many would have led to no humans at all, others to extinction, and yet others to a different version of "modernity." We can inhabit only one version of being human—the only version that survives today—but what is fascinating is that palaeoanthropology shows us those other paths to becoming human, their successes and their eventual demise, whether through failure or just sheer bad luck.

Sometimes the difference between failure and success in evolution is a narrow one. We are certainly on a knife-edge now, as we confront an overpopulated planet and the prospect of global climate change on a scale that humans have never faced before. Let's hope our species is up to the challenge.

Critical Thinking

1. What are the features of our species that make us distinctive and remarkable?
2. Where did our species evolve? What has the "fierce debate" been about?
3. What was the belief forty years ago and why?
4. As a student, what theory did the author test and how? What were his results? How did mitochondrial DNA confirm this?
5. What was the author's version of the "out of Africa" theory?
6. What was the "multiregional view"? The "assimilation model"?
7. What has recent genetic data shown about the separation of our species from Neanderthals? What is the "intriguing twist"?
8. What is the most likely explanation for this discovery, according to the author?
9. How has the breakthrough in reconstructing a Neanderthal genome been mirrored across Asia and what have been the results?
10. What is the "leaky replacement" model?
11. What is the "big picture," according to the author?
12. How and why was Africa conducive to the development of our "modernity"?
13. When and why did cultural "progress" cease to be a stop-start affair for our species?
14. Why does the author take issue with the view that evolution was simply a progression leading to us?

Professor Chris Stringer is the research leader in human origins at the Natural History Museum, London.

Article 23

A New View of the Birth of *Homo sapiens*

New genomic data are settling an old argument about how our species evolved.

ANN GIBBONS

For 27 years, Chris Stringer and Milford Wolpoff have been at odds about where and how our species was born. Stringer, a paleoanthropologist at the Natural History Museum in London, held that modern humans came out of Africa, spread around the world, and replaced, rather than mated with, the archaic humans they met. But Wolpoff, of the University of Michigan, Ann Arbor, argued that a single, worldwide species of human, including archaic forms outside of Africa, met, mingled and had offspring, and so produced *Homo sapiens.* The battle has been long and bitter: When reviewing a manuscript in the 1980s, Wolpoff scribbled "Stringer's desperate argument" under a chart; in a 1996 book, Stringer wrote that "attention to inconvenient details has never been part of the Wolpoff style." At one tense meeting, the pair presented opposing views in rival sessions on the same day—and Wolpoff didn't invite Stringer to the meeting's press conference. "It was difficult for a long time," recalls Stringer.

Then, in the past year, geneticists announced the nearly complete nuclear genomes of two different archaic humans: Neandertals, and their enigmatic eastern cousins from southern Siberia. These data provide a much higher resolution view of our past, much as a new telescope allows astronomers to see farther back in time in the universe. When compared with the genomes of living people, the ancient genomes allow anthropologists to thoroughly test the competing models of human origins for the first time.

The DNA data suggest not one but at least two instances of interbreeding between archaic and modern humans, raising the question of whether *H. sapiens* at that point was a distinct species (see box, The Species Problem). And so they appear to refute the complete replacement aspect of the Out of Africa model. "[Modern humans] are certainly coming out of Africa, but we're finding evidence of low levels of admixture wherever you look," says evolutionary geneticist Michael Hammer of the University of Arizona in Tucson. Stringer admits: "The story has undoubtedly got a whole lot more complicated."

But the genomic data don't prove the classic multiregionalism model correct either. They suggest only a small amount of interbreeding, presumably at the margins where invading moderns met archaic groups that were the worldwide descendants of *H. erectus,* the human ancestor that left Africa 1.8 million years ago. "I have lately taken to talking about the best model as replacement with hybridization, . . . [or] 'leaky replacement,'" says paleogeneticist Svante Pääbo of the Max Planck Institute for Evolutionary Anthropology in Leipzig, lead author of the two nuclear genome studies.

The new picture most resembles so-called assimilation models, which got relatively little attention over the years. "This means so much," says Fred Smith of Illinois State University in Normal, who proposed such a model. "I just thought 'Hallelujah! No matter what anybody else says, I was as close to correct as anybody.'"

Evolving Models

Stringer and others first proposed Africa as the birthplace of modern humans back in the mid-1980s. The same year, researchers published a landmark study that traced the maternally inherited mitochondrial DNA (mtDNA) of all living people to a female ancestor that lived in Africa about 200,000 years ago, dubbed mitochondrial Eve. She caught the attention of the popular press, landing on the cover of *Newsweek* and *Time.*

Additional studies of living people—from Y chromosomes to snippets of nuclear DNA to the entire mtDNA genome—consistently found that Africans were the most diverse genetically. This suggests that modern humans arose in Africa, where they had more time to accumulate mutations than on other continents (*Science,* 17 November 2006, p. 1068). Meanwhile, ancient DNA technology also took off. Pääbo's group sequenced first a few bits of Neandertal mitochondrial DNA in 1997, then the entire mitochondrial genomes of several Neandertals—and found them to be distinct from those of living people. So ancient DNA, too, argued against the idea of mixing between Neandertals and moderns. Over the years the replacement model became the leading theory, with only a stubborn few, including Wolpoff, holding to multiregionalism.

The Species Problem

Our ancestors had sex with at least two kinds of archaic humans at two different times and places—and those liaisons produced surviving children, according to the latest ancient DNA research (see main text). But were the participants in these prehistoric encounters members of separate species? Doesn't a species, by definition, breed only with others of that species?

These are the questions paleogeneticist Svante Pääbo dodged twice last year. His team published two papers proposing that both Neandertals and mysterious humans from Denisova Cave in Siberia interbred with ancient modern humans. But the researchers avoided the thorny question of species designation and simply referred to Neandertals, Denisovans, and modern humans as "populations." "I think discussion of what is a species and what is a subspecies is a sterile academic endeavor," says Pääbo, who works at the Max Planck Institute for Evolutionary Anthropology in Leipzig, Germany.

The question of how to define a species has divided researchers for centuries. Darwin's words in *On the Origin of Species* still hold: "No one definition has satisfied all naturalists." However, many scientists use the biological species concept proposed by Ernst Mayr: "groups of actually or potentially interbreeding natural populations, which are reproductively isolated from other such groups."

The draft versions of the Neandertal and Denisovan nuclear genomes show low levels of interbreeding between each of them and modern humans. Apply Mayr's definition strictly, and all three must be considered *Homo sapiens*. "They mated with each other. We'll call them the same species," says molecular anthropologist John Hawks of the University of Wisconsin, Madison.

But that's a minority view among paleoanthropologists. Many consider Neandertals a species separate from modern humans because the anatomical and developmental differences are "an order of magnitude higher than anything we can observe between extant human populations," says Jean-Jacques Hublin, a co-author of Pääbo's at Max Planck. In the real world, he says, Mayr's concept doesn't hold up: "There are about 330 closely related species of mammals that interbreed, and at least a third of them can produce fertile hybrids."

There's also no agreed-upon yardstick for how much morphologic or genetic difference separates species. That's why Pääbo's team avoided the species question a second time with respect to the Denisovans. These hominins are known only from a scrap of bone, a single tooth, and their DNA. They are genetically closest to Neandertals. The genetic distance between Denisovans and Neandertals, in fact, is only 9% larger than that between a living Frenchman and a living San Bushman in Africa, both of whom belong to *H. sapiens*. But so far Neandertals seem to have low genetic diversity, based on the DNA of six Neandertals from Russia to Spain. To Pääbo's team, that makes the difference from the Denisovans significant.

Also, the Denisovan tooth doesn't look much like that of a Neandertal. So the team considers them a distinct population but declined to name a new species. "Why take a stand on it when it will only lead to discussions and no one will have the final word?" asks Pääbo.

—A.G.

Yet there were a few dissenting notes. A few studies of individual genes found evidence of migration from Asia into Africa, rather than vice versa. Population geneticists warned that complete replacement was unlikely, given the distribution of alleles in living humans. And a few paleoanthropologists proposed middle-of-the-road models. Smith, a former student of Wolpoff's, suggested that most of our ancestors arose in Africa but interbred with local populations as they spread out around the globe, with archaic people contributing to about 10% of living people's genomes. At the University of Hamburg in Germany, Gunter Brauer similarly proposed replacement with hybridization, but with a trivial amount of interbreeding. But neither model got much traction; they were either ignored or lumped in with multiregionalism. "Assimilation got kicked so much," recalls Smith.

Over time, the two more extreme models moved toward the middle, with most multiregionalists recognizing that the chief ancestors of modern humans arose in Africa. "The broad line of evolution is pretty clear: Our ancestors came out of Africa," says biological anthropologist John Relethford of the State University of New York College at Oneonta. "But what happens next is kind of complex."

Genes from the Past

Then in May 2010 came the Neandertals' complete nuclear genome, sequenced from the bones of three female Neandertals who lived in Croatia more than 38,000 years ago. Pääbo's international team found that a small amount—1% to 4%—of the nuclear DNA of Europeans and Asians, but not of Africans, can be traced to Neandertals. The most likely model to explain this, Pääbo says, was that early modern humans arose in Africa but interbred with Neandertals in the Middle East or Arabia before spreading into Asia and Europe, about 50,000 to 80,000 years ago (*Science*, 7 May 2010, pp. 680, 710).

Seven months later, on 23 December, the team published in *Nature* the complete nuclear genome of a girl's pinky finger from Denisova Cave in the Altai Mountains of southern Siberia. To their surprise, the genome was neither a Neandertal's nor a modern human's, yet the girl was alive at the same time, dating to at least 30,000 years ago and probably older than 50,000 years. Her DNA was most like a Neandertal's, but her people were a distinct group that had long been separated from Neandertals.

By comparing parts of the Denisovan genome directly with the same segments of DNA in 53 populations of living people, the team found that the Denisovans shared 4% to 6% of their DNA with Melanesians from Papua New Guinea and the Bougainville Islands. Those segments were not found in Neandertals or other living humans.

The most likely scenario for how all this happened is that after Neandertal and Denisovan populations split about 200,000 years ago, modern humans interbred with Neandertals as they left Africa in the past 100,000 years. Thus Neandertals left their mark in the genomes of living Asians and Europeans, says co-author Montgomery Slatkin, a population geneticist at the University of California, Berkeley. Later, a subset of this group of moderns—who carried some Neandertal DNA—headed east toward Melanesia and interbred with the Denisovans in Asia on the way. As a result, Melanesians inherited DNA from both Neandertals and Denisovans, with as much as 8% of their DNA coming from archaic people, says co-author David Reich, a population geneticist at Harvard Medical School in Boston.

This means *H. sapiens* mixed it up with at least two different archaic peoples, in at least two distinct times and places. To some, that's starting to sound a lot like multiregionalism. "It's hard to explain how good I feel about this," says Wolpoff, who says that seeing complete replacement falsified twice in 1 year was beyond his wildest expectations. "It was a good year."

And yet the interbreeding with archaic humans seems limited—from 1% to 8% of some living people's genomes. Stringer and many others don't consider it full-scale multiregional continuity. "I think interbreeding was at a low level," says Slatkin, who says that if there had been a great deal of admixture, the genetic data would have revealed it already. Low levels of interbreeding suggest that either archaic people mated with moderns only rarely—or their hybrid offspring had low fitness and so produced few viable offspring, says population geneticist Laurent Excoffier of the University of Bern in Switzerland.

In any case, Reich notes that at least 90% of our genomes are inherited from African ancestors who replaced the archaic people on other continents but hybridized with them around the margins. And that scenario most closely backs the assimilation models proposed by Smith and Brauer.

Of course, it's possible that future data will overturn today's "leaky replacement" model. Slatkin says he cannot rule out an alternative explanation for the data: The "archaic" DNA thought to have come from mating with Neandertals could instead stem from a very ancient ancestor that we shared with Neandertals. Most modern humans retained those archaic sequences, but Africans lost them. But Slatkin says this "doesn't seem very plausible," because it requires modern human populations with the archaic DNA and those without it to have been partially isolated from each other in Africa for hundreds of thousands of years. And it seems even less probable that Melanesians and Denisovans are the only groups that retained a second set of archaic DNA motifs from a common ancestor shared by all modern humans, Neandertals and Denisovans. If those explanations do prove true, replacement would not be falsified.

In the wake of the big genome studies, other researchers such as Hammer are scrutinizing DNA from more living humans to further test the model. Researchers are also trying to pinpoint when admixture happened, which has significant consequences. At just what point did we evolve from archaic humans to become "modern" humans? "There are still archaic [genetic] features floating around until amazingly recently, until 40,000 years ago," says Hammer. He wonders whether the process of becoming modern took longer and was more complex than once thought. "There's no line you can draw and say everything after this is modern. That's the elephant in the room."

Meanwhile, paleoanthropologists are searching for fossils in Asia that might belong to the enigmatic Denisovan population—and might yield more ancient DNA. Paleoanthropologist Russell Ciochon of the University of Iowa in Iowa City and Wolpoff say there are several known, ambiguous fossils in Asia that might be candidates for early Denisovans. "I believe things were going on in Asia that we just don't know about," says Ciochon. "Before this paper on the Denisovans, we didn't have any insight into this. Now, with this nuclear genome, I find myself talking about 'the Denisovans.' It's already had an impact."

As for Stringer and Wolpoff, both now in their 60s, their battle has mellowed. Their views, while still distinct, have converged somewhat, and they shared a beer at a Neandertal meeting last year. "The reason we get on well now," says Stringer, "is we both think we've been proved right."

Critical Thinking

1. Discuss the evidence for the "replacement model" and the "multiregional model" for the origins of modern humans.
2. What evidence is there for a "leaky replacement model"?
3. What is the "species problem" and how does it relate to an understanding of modern human origins?

Article 24

Refuting a Myth about Human Origins

Homo sapiens emerged once, not as modern-looking people first and as modern-behaving people later.

JOHN J. SHEA

For decades, archeologists have believed that modern behaviors emerged among *Homo sapiens* tens of thousands of years after our species first evolved. Archaeologists disagreed over whether this process was gradual or swift, but they assumed that *Homo sapiens* once lived who were very different from us. These people were not "behaviorally modern," meaning they did not routinely use art, symbols and rituals; they did not systematically collect small animals, fish, shellfish and other difficult-to-procure foods; they did not use complex technologies: Traps, nets, projectile weapons and watercraft were unknown to them.

Premodern humans—often described as "archaic *Homo sapiens*"—were thought to have lived in small, vulnerable groups of closely related individuals. They were believed to have been equipped only with simple tools and were likely heavily dependent on hunting large game. Individuals in such groups would have been much less insulated from environmental stresses than are modern humans. In Thomas Hobbes's words, their lives were "solitary, nasty, brutish and short." If you need a mental image here, close your eyes and conjure a picture of a stereotypical caveman. But archaeological evidence now shows that some of the behaviors associated with modern humans, most importantly our capacity for wide behavioral variability, actually did occur among people who lived very long ago, particularly in Africa. And a conviction is growing among some archaeologists that there was no sweeping transformation to "behavioral modernity" in our species' recent past.

As Misia Landau argued nearly a quarter of a century ago in the essay "Human Evolution as Narrative" (*American Scientist,* May–June 1984), prescientific traditions of narrative explanation long encouraged scientists to envision key changes in human evolution as holistic transformations. The idea of an archaic-to-modern human transition in *Homo sapiens* arises, in part, from this narrative tradition. All this makes for a satisfying story, but it is not a realistic framework for understanding the actual, complex and contingent course of human evolution. Most evolutionary changes are relatively minor things whose consequences play out incrementally over thousands of generations.

In order to better understand human prehistory, I recommend another approach, one that focuses on behavioral variability. This trait, easily observed among recent humans, is becoming more apparent in the archaeological record for early *Homo sapiens.* Prehistoric people lived in different ways in different places at different times. We must seek out and explain those differences, for, in evolution, only differences matter. Thinking about prehistoric human behavioral variability in terms of various adaptive strategies offers an attractive way to explain these differences. But first, we need to discard an incorrect and outdated idea about human evolution, the belief that prehistoric *Homo sapiens* can be divided into "archaic" and "modern" humans.

An Idea Is Born

Archaeology's concept of archaic versus modern humans developed as prehistoric archaeological research spread from Europe to other regions. The study of prehistoric people began in Europe during the 19th century in scientific societies, museums and universities. By the 1920s, discoveries made at a number of European archaeological sites had prompted a consensus about the Paleolithic Period, which is now dated from 12,000 to nearly 2.6 million years ago. Archaeologists divided this period into Lower (oldest), Middle, and Upper (youngest) Paleolithic phases. Distinctive stone-tool assemblages—or "industries"—characterized each phase. Archaeologists identified these industries by the presence of diagnostic artifact types, such as Acheulian hand axes (Lower Paleolithic), Mousterian scrapers made of Levallois flakes (Middle Paleolithic), and Aurignacian prismatic blades and carved antler points (Upper Paleolithic). The fact that tools from more recent industries were lighter, smaller and more heavily modified suggested there was a trend toward greater technological and cultural sophistication in the Paleolithic sequence. European Upper Paleolithic industries were associated exclusively with *Homo sapiens* fossils and Lower and Middle Paleolithic industries were associated with earlier hominins (*Homo heidelbergensis* and *Homo neanderthalensis*). This supported the idea that there were important evolutionary differences between modern *Homo sapiens* and earlier archaic hominins.

Early Upper Paleolithic contexts in Europe preserve evidence for prismatic blade production, carved bone tools, projectile weaponry, complex hearths, personal adornments, art, long-distance trade, mortuary rituals, architecture, food storage and specialized big-game hunting, as well as systematic exploitation of smaller prey and aquatic resources. Furthermore, the variability of these behaviors within the Upper Paleolithic is much greater than that seen in earlier periods. In much the same way that anthropologists have documented cultural variability among recent humans, archaeologists can easily tell whether a particular carved bone point or bone bead is from a site in Spain, France or Germany. Not surprisingly, most prehistorians accept that the archaeology of the Upper Paleolithic is, in effect, "the archaeology of us."

Lower and Middle Paleolithic stone tools and other artifacts found in Europe and elsewhere vary within a narrow range of simple forms. Properly equipped and motivated modern-day flintknappers (people who make stone tools) can turn out replicas of any of these tools in minutes, if not seconds. Many of the differences among Lower and Middle Paleolithic artifacts simply reflect variation in rock types and the extent to which tools were resharpened. Geographic and chronological differences among Middle and Lower Paleolithic tools mostly involve differences in relative frequencies of these simple tool types. Nearly the same range of Lower and Middle Paleolithic stone tool types are found throughout much of Europe, Africa and Asia.

The differences between the Lower/Middle and Upper Paleolithic records in Europe are so pronounced that from the 1970s onward prehistorians have described the transition between them as "The Upper Paleolithic Revolution." This regional phenomenon went global in the late 1980s after a conference at Cambridge University entitled "The Human Revolution." This revolution was portrayed as a watershed event that set recent modern humans apart from their archaic predecessors and from other hominins, such as *Homo neanderthalensis.* The causes of this assumed transformation were hotly debated. Scientists such as Richard Klein attributed the changes to the FOXP2 polymorphism, the so-called language gene. But the polymorphism was eventually discovered in Neanderthal DNA too. Many researchers—such as Christopher Henshilwood of the University of Witwatersrand, Curtis Marean of Arizona State University, Paul Mellars of the University of Cambridge, April Nowell of the University of Victoria and Phil Chase of the University of Pennsylvania—continue to see symbolic behavior as a crucial component of behavioral modernity. Yet as João Zilhão of the University of Bristol and Francesco d'Errico of the University of Bordeaux have argued, finds of mineral pigments, perforated beads, burials and artifact-style variation associated with Neanderthals challenge the hypothesis that symbol use, or anything else for that matter, was responsible for a quality of behavioral modernity unique to *Homo sapiens.*

The Missing Revolution

In fact, fossil evidence threatening the Upper Paleolithic revolution hypothesis emerged many decades ago. At about the same time the Paleolithic framework was developed during the 1920s and 1930s, European-trained archaeologists began searching for human fossils and artifacts in the Near East, Africa and Asia. Expatriate and colonial archaeologists such as Dorothy Garrod and Louis Leakey expected that the European archaeological record worked as a global model for human evolution and used the European Paleolithic framework to organize their observations abroad. Very quickly, however, they discovered a mismatch between their expectations and reality when *Homo sapiens* remains outside Europe were found with Lower or Middle Paleolithic artifacts. Archaeologists started assuming then that the remains dated to periods just before the Upper Paleolithic revolution. But in fact, those discoveries, as well as more recent finds, challenge the notion that the revolution ever occurred.

In Europe, the oldest *Homo sapiens* fossils date to only 35,000 years ago. But studies of genetic variation among living humans suggest that our species emerged in Africa as long as 200,000 years ago. Scientists have recovered *Homo sapiens* fossils in contexts dating to 165,000 to 195,000 years ago in Ethiopia's Lower Omo Valley and Middle Awash Valley. Evidence is clear that early humans dispersed out of Africa to southern Asia before 40,000 years ago. Similar modern-looking human fossils found in the Skhul and Qafzeh caves in Israel date to 80,000 to 120,000 years ago. *Homo sapiens* fossils dating to 100,000 years ago have been recovered from Zhiren Cave in China. In Australia, evidence for a human presence dates to at least 42,000 years ago. Nothing like a human revolution precedes *Homo sapiens'* first appearances in any of these regions. And all these *Homo sapiens* fossils were found with either Lower or Middle Paleolithic stone tool industries.

There are differences between the skeletons of these early *Homo sapiens* and Upper Paleolithic Europeans. The best-documented differences involve variation in skull shape. Yet, as Daniel Lieberman of Harvard University writes in the recently published *The Evolution of the Human Head,* we are just beginning to understand the genetic and behavioral basis for variation in human skulls. It makes no sense whatsoever to draw major evolutionary distinctions among humans based on skull shape unless we understand the underlying sources of cranial variation. There is no simple morphological dividing line among these fossil skulls. Most fossils combine "primitive" (ancestral) characteristics as well as "derived" (recently evolved) ones. Even if physical anthropologists divided prehistoric humans into archaic and modern groups, it would be foolish for archaeologists to invoke this difference as an explanation for anything unless we knew how specific skeletal differences related to specific aspects of behavior preserved in the archaeological record.

Early *Homo sapiens* fossils in Africa and Asia are associated with "precocious," or unexpectedly early evidence for modern behaviors such as those seen in the European Upper Paleolithic. They include intensive fish and shellfish exploitation, the production of complex projectile weapons, the use of symbols in the form of mineral pigments and perforated shells, and even rare burials with grave goods in them. But as Erella Hovers and Anna Belfer-Cohen of The Hebrew University of Jerusalem argued in a chapter of *Transitions Before the Transition,* "Now You See It, Now You Don't—Modern Human Behavior in the Middle Paleolithic," much of this evidence is recursive. It is not a consistent feature of the archaeological record. Evidence for one or more of these modern behaviors appears at a few sites or for a few thousand years in one region or another, and then it vanishes. If behavioral modernity were both a derived condition and a landmark development in the course of human history, one would hardly expect it to disappear for prolonged periods in our species' evolutionary history.

For me, the most surprising aspect about the debate regarding when *Homo sapiens* became human is that archaeologists have not tested the core hypothesis that there were significant behavioral differences between the earliest and more recent members of our species. Because modernity is a typological category, it is not easy to test this hypothesis. One is either behaviorally modern or not. And, not all groups classified as behaviorally modern have left clear and unambiguous evidence for that modernity at all times and in all contexts. For example, expedient and opportunistic flintknapping of river pebbles and cobbles by living humans often creates stone tools indistinguishable from the pebble tools knapped by *Homo habilis* or *Homo erectus*. This similarity reflects the nature of the toolmaking strategies, techniques and raw materials, not the evolutionary equivalence of the toolmakers. Thus, the archaeological record abounds in possibilities of false-negative findings about prehistoric human behavioral modernity.

This issue caught my interest in 2002 while I was excavating 195,000-year-old archaeological sites associated with early *Homo sapiens* fossils in the Lower Omo River Valley Kibish Formation in Ethiopia. I am an archaeologist, but I am also a flintknapper. Nothing about the stone tools from Omo Kibish struck me as archaic or primitive. (When I teach flintknapping at my university, I have ample opportunity to see what happens when people with rudimentary skills try to knap stone and how those skills vary with experience and motivation.) The Omo Kibish tools showed that their makers had great versatility in effectively knapping a wide range of rock types. This set me to thinking: Have we been asking the wrong questions about early humans' behavior?

A Better Way

Documenting and analyzing behavioral variability is a more theoretically sound approach to studying differences among prehistoric people than searching for the transition to behavioral modernity. Nearly everything humans do, we do in more than one identifiably different way. As Richard Potts of the Smithsonian Institution argued in *Humanity's Descent* in 1996, our species' capacity for wide behavioral variability appears to be uniquely derived. No other animal has as wide a behavioral repertoire as *Homo sapiens* does. And variability can be investigated empirically, quantitatively, and with fewer problems than occur in ranking prehistoric people in terms of their modernity.

One way to gauge early *Homo sapiens'* behavioral variability is to compare their lithic technologies. Lithics, or stone tools, are nearly indestructible and are found everywhere hominins lived in Pleistocene times. Stone tools do not tell us everything we might wish to know about prehistoric human behavior, but they are no less subject to the selective pressures that create variation in other types of archaeological evidence. Lithic artifacts made by recent humans are more complex and variable than those associated with early hominins. Early Paleolithic stone tools are more complex and variable than those made by nonhuman primates. Thus, there is reason to expect that analysis of these tools will produce a valid signal about early *Homo sapiens'* capacity for behavioral variability. Eastern Africa is an especially good place in which to compare early and later *Homo sapiens'* stone technology because that region preserves our species' longest continuous archaeological record. Restricting this comparison to eastern Africa minimizes the complicating effects of geographic constraints on stone-tool technology.

One of the most popular ways of describing variation among stone-tool industries is a framework that the British archaeologist Grahame Clark proposed in *World Prehistory: A New Synthesis* (1969). This framework describes lithic technological variability in terms of five modes of core technology. (In flintknapping, "cores" are the rocks from which flakes are struck, with the flakes later developed into various kinds of tools.) Variation in core technology is thought to reflect differences in ecological adaptations. Clark's framework is a crude instrument, but it can be made into a reasonably sensitive register of technological variability if we simply note which of these modes are represented in each of a series of lithic assemblages. When it is applied to sites in eastern Africa dating 284,000 to 6,000 years ago, a more complex view of prehistoric life there emerges. One does not see a steady accumulation of novel core technologies since our species first appeared or anything like a "revolution." Instead one sees a persistent pattern of wide technological variability.

What does this variability mean? Archaeologists' understanding of lithic technology continues to grow, from experiments, from studies of recent stone-tool-using groups and from contextual clues in the archaeological record. Our understanding is far from perfect, but we do know enough to make some plausible interpretations. Pebble-core reduction (mode 1 in Clark's framework), in which toolmakers strike flakes opportunistically from rounded pebbles or cobbles, is the simplest way to obtain a cutting edge from stone. Stone tools are still made this way in rural parts of eastern Africa. Its ubiquity in the archaeological assemblages probably reflects a stable strategy of coping expediently with unpredictable needs for cutting edges.

Large bifacial core tools (mode 2) are thought to have been dual-purpose tools. Their heft and long ratting edges make them effective in heavy-duty tasks, such as woodworking or the butchering of large animal carcasses. Thinner flakes knapped from bifacial core tools can be used for lighter-duty cutting or retouched into more functionally specialized forms. In recent archaeological contexts, large bifacial cutting tools are often correlated with people who moved their residences frequently, whereas expedient pebble cores are correlated with more lengthy occupations. High topographic relief and wide seasonal variation in rainfall make residential stability a difficult thing for even recent eastern African pastoralist groups to achieve. The persistence of this technology may reflect relatively high residential mobility among prehistoric eastern Africans.

The behavioral correlates of Levallois prepared-core technology (mode 3) are less clear, if only because the term encompasses so many different core-knapping strategies. Some archaeologists see Levallois prepared cores as reflecting knappers' efforts to obtain desired tool shapes, or to produce relatively broad and thin flakes that efficiently recover cutting edge. These hypotheses are not mutually exclusive, and in the long run, each of them probably explains some part of why people made such cores in eastern Africa for a very long time.

Prismatic-blade core technology (mode 4) involves detaching long rectangular flakes one after another from a cone-shaped core. The most widely repeated hypothesis about the appeal of prismatic-blade production is that it produces greater amounts of ratting edge per unit mass of stone than other strategies. However, recent experiments by Metin Eren at Southern Methodist University and his colleagues have shown that this hypothesis is wrong. A far more likely appeal of this strategy is that the blades' morphological consistency makes them easier to attach to a handle. Attaching a stone tool to a handle vastly increases leverage and mechanical efficiency, but it also restricts the range of tool movement and limits the portion of the tool that can be resharpened. The comings and goings of blade core technology in eastern Africa probably reflect a complex interplay of these strategic considerations.

Differing amounts of geometric microlithic technology (mode 5) are preserved in the most ancient and most recent assemblages in the east African sample. Geometric microliths are small tools made by segmenting blades or flakes and shaping them into triangles, rectangles, crescents and other geometric forms by blunting one or more of their edges. Too small to have been useful while hand-held, geometric microliths were almost certainly used as hafted tools. They are easy to attach to handles, making them suitable for use as projectile armatures, woodworking tools and aids to preparing plant foods. Archaeologists view microlithic stone-tool technology as a strategy for optimizing versatility and minimizing risk. Microlithic technologies first appear and proliferate among African and Eurasian human populations from about 50,000 years ago to around 10,000 years ago. This was a period of hypervariable climate, and it makes a certain amount of sense that humans at that time devised versatile and efficiently transportable stone tools. If, for example, climate change required people to frequently shift from hunting game to reaping grasses and back again, using microlith-barbed arrows and microlith-edged sickles would allow them to do this efficiently, without any major change to their technological strategies. Because microlithic tooks are small, they preserve high ratios of cutting edge to mass. This means that if climate shifts required more seasonal migrations, individuals transporting microliths would be carrying the most cutting edge per unit mass of stone. Variability in the use of microlithic technology in eastern Africa probably reflects strategic responses to environmental unpredictability along with efforts to cope with increased subsistence risk by optimizing versatility in stone-tool technology.

How do the differences between earlier and later eastern African core technologies compare to variation among recent stone-tool-using humans? The range of variability in recent human stone-tool technology is greater than that in the eastern African sample. All five of Clark's modes are to be found among the lithic technology of recent humans. Yet some technologies are not represented in the African sample. For example, more than 30,000 years ago in Australia, and later elsewhere, people began grinding and polishing the edges of stone tools. Such grinding and polishing reduces friction during work, making cutting tools more efficient to use and resharpen. In the New World, ancestral Native American flintknappers deployed a wide range of bifacial-core technologies fundamentally different from those seen in eastern Africa. They used these tools in contexts ranging from hunter-gatherer campsites on the Great Plains to Mesoamerican city-states like Teotihuacan. Differences in recent stone-tool technology reflect variability in adaptive strategies. No anthropologists in their right minds would attribute this variability to evolutionary differences among recent humans. If this kind of explanation makes so little sense in the present, what possible value can it have for explaining past behavioral variability among *Homo sapiens*?

The lithic evidence reviewed here challenges the hypothesis that there were significant behavioral differences between the earliest and more recent members of our species in eastern Africa. Obviously, there is more to human behavioral variability than what is reflected in stone tools. Using Clark's technological modes to capture that variability, as described here, is just a first step. But it is a step forward. This emphasis on variability will gain strength if and when it is supported by more detailed analyses of the stone tools and by other archaeological evidence.

Abandoning a Myth

One could view these findings as just another case of precocious modern behavior by early *Homo sapiens* in Africa, but I think they have a larger lesson to teach us. After all, something is only precocious if it is unexpected. The hypothesis that there were skeletally modern-looking humans whose behavioral capacities differed significantly from our own is not supported by uniformitarian principles (explanations of the past based on studies of the present), by evolutionary theory or by archaeological evidence. There are no known populations of *Homo sapiens* with biologically constrained capacities for behavioral variability. Generations of anthropologists have sought in vain for such primitive people in every corner of the world and have consistently failed to find them. The parsimonious interpretation of this failure is that such humans do not exist.

Nor is there any reason to believe that behaviorally archaic *Homo sapiens* ever did exist. If there ever were significant numbers of *Homo sapiens* individuals with cognitive limitations on their capacity for behavioral variability, natural selection by intraspecific competition and predation would have quickly and ruthlessly winnowed them out. In the unforgiving Pleistocene environments in which our species evolved, reproductive isolation was the penalty for stupidity, and lions and wolves were its cure. In other words: No villages, no village idiots. If any such cognitive "winner take all" wipeout event ever happened, it was probably among earlier hominins (*Homo ergaster/erectus* or

Homo heidelbergensis) or during the evolutionary differentiation of our species from these hominin ancestors.

Dividing *Homo sapiens* into modern and archaic or pre-modern categories and invoking the evolution of behavioral modernity to explain the difference has never been a good idea. Like the now-discredited scientific concept of race, it reflects hierarchical and typological thinking about human variability that has no place in a truly scientific anthropology. Indeed, the concept of behavioral modernity can be said to be worse than wrong, because it is an obstacle to understanding. Time, energy and research funds that could have been spent investigating the sources of variability in particular behavioral strategies and testing hypotheses about them have been wasted arguing about behavioral modernity.

Anthropology has already faced this error. Writing in the early 20th century, the American ethnologist Franz Boas railed against evolutionary anthropologists who ranked living human societies along an evolutionary scale from primitive to advanced. His arguments found an enthusiastic reception among his colleagues, and they remain basic principles of anthropology to this day. A similar change is needed in the archaeology of human origins. We need to stop looking at artifacts as expressions of evolutionary states and start looking at them as byproducts of behavioral strategies.

The differences we discover among those strategies will lead us to new and very different kinds of questions than those we have asked thus far. For instance, do similar environmental circumstances elicit different ranges of behavioral variability? Are there differences in the stability of particular behavioral strategies? Are certain strategies uniquely associated with particular hominin species, and if so, why? By focusing on behavioral variability, archaeologists will move toward a more scientific approach to human-origins research. The concept of behavioral modernity, in contrast, gets us nowhere.

Even today, a caveman remains the popular image of what a prehistoric person looked like. This individual usually is shown with enlarged eyebrows, a projecting face, long hair and a beard. The stereotypical caveman is inarticulate and dim-witted, and possesses a limited capacity for innovation. In 2006, GEICO commercials put an ironic twist on this image. Their cavemen were more intelligent, articulate, creative and culturally sophisticated than many "modern" people. In a striking case of life imitating art, recent archaeological discoveries are overturning long-standing misconceptions about early human behavior.

Bibliography

Bar-Yosef, O. 2002. The Upper Paleolithic revolution. *Annual Review of Anthropology* 31:363–393.

Clark, G. 1969. *World Prehistory: A New Synthesis.* Cambridge: Cambridge University Press.

Klein, R. G. 2009. *The Human Career,* third edition. Chicago: University of Chicago Press.

Landau, M. L. 1984. Human evolution as narrative. *American Scientist* 72:262–268.

McBrearty, S., and A. S. Brooks. 2000. The revolution that wasn't: A new interpretation of the origin of modern human behavior. *Journal of Human Evolution* 39:453–563.

Mellars, P., and C. Stringer. 1989. *The Human Revolution: Behavioural and Biological Perspectives on the Origins of Modern Humans.* Edinburgh: Edinburgh University Press.

Nowell, A. 2010. Defining behavioral modernity in the context of Neandertal and anatomically modern human populations. *Annual Review of Anthropology* 39:437–452.

Potts, R. 1998. Variability selection and hominid evolution. *Evolutionary Anthropology* 7(3):81–96.

Shea, J. J. 2008. The Middle Stone Age archaeology of the Lower Omo Valley Kibish Formation: Excavations, lithic assemblages, and inferred patterns of early *Homo sapiens* behavior. *Journal of Human Evolution* 55(3):448–485.

Shea, J. J. 2011. *Homo sapiens* is as *Homo sapiens* was: Behavioral variability versus "behavioral modernity" in Paleolithic archaeology. *Current Anthropology* 52(1):1–35.

Critical Thinking

1. What is meant by "behaviorally modern" in the context of this article and how were "pre-modern" people presumed to live by most archeologists?
2. How did archeologists perceive the technological stages of the Paleolithic period and their associations with fossil hominin remains?
3. What is meant by the "Upper Paleolithic Revolution" and how is it explained? What kinds of finds associated with Neanderthals challenge this view?
4. In what sense and where has there been a "mismatch" between the fossil record and archeologists' expectations?
5. What is the problem with associating cranial variation among early humans with actual behavior?
6. What are some of the specific kinds of modern behavior found among early modern humans in Africa and Asia? What is the significance of the fact that these behaviors are "not a consistent feature of the archeological record"?
7. Why is it difficult to test the core hypothesis about the presumed relationship between modern technology and modern-looking *Homo sapiens*?
8. What alternative approach does the author propose? Why is eastern Africa an especially good place to compare early and later *Homo sapiens'* technology?
9. Be familiar with Graham Clarke's five modes of core technology and the benefits of each.
10. Why is it that the range of variability in recent human stone tools is greater than that found in just the east African sample? How does this help to invalidate the assumption that stone tool variation in the fossil record reflects stages of human evolution?
11. Why does the author say, "We need to stop looking at artifacts as expressions of evolutionary states and start looking at them as byproducts of behavioral strategies"?

John J. Shea is a professor of anthropology at Stony Brook University and a research associate with the Turkana Basin Institute in Kenya. He earned his PhD at Harvard University in 1991 and has conducted research in Israel, Jordan, Ethiopia, Eritrea, Kenya, and Tanzania. Two of his key scientific articles are "The origins of lithic projectile point technology: Evidence from Africa, the Levant, and Europe"

(*Journal of Archaeological Science,* 2006) and "Stone age visiting cards revisited: A strategic perspective on the lithic technology of early hominin dispersal" (*Vertebrate Paleobiology and Paleoanthropology,* 2010). His forthcoming book will be titled *Paleolithic and Neolithic Stone Tools of the Near East: A Guide*. Shea is a professional flintknapper whose work appears in numerous documentaries and in exhibits at the Smithsonian Institution and the American Museum of Natural History. Address: Anthropology Department, Stony Brook University, Stony Brook, NY 11794-4364. E-mail: john.shea@sunysb.edu.

Article 25

Paleolithic Cave Art in France

JEAN CLOTTES

Introduction

The Bradshaw Foundation presents the recently published paper by Dr. Jean Clottes, French Ministry of Culture. The paper provides a definitive and comprehensive analysis of the Palaeolithic rock art discoveries so far made in France. . . .

European Ice Age rock art, often called 'cave art', is well known all over the world, probably because of the high quality and antiquity of its images. So far, about 350 sites have been discovered, from the southern tip of the Iberian Peninsula to the Urals. Out of them, nearly half (about 160) were found in France. They include some really major caves. When the Abbe Breuil published his big book "Four Hundred Centuries of Cave Art", he pointed out what he called 'The Six Giants', one in Spain (Altamira), the other five in France: Lascaux, Niaux, Les Trois-Freres, Font-de-Gaume and Les Combarelles (Breuil 1952). No doubt that nowadays he would at least add Chauvet (Clottes (ed.) 2001), Cosquer (Clottes & Courtin 1996), Cussac (Aujoulat et al. 2001) and Rouffignac (Plassard 1999) to the list.

Portable art is no less famous for the same periods in France. In the course of the XIXth century, major discoveries were made in several sites such as Le Mas d'Azil, Gourdan, Brassempouy, Laugerie. Other top sites were excavated in the XXth century (Isturitz, La Vache, Enlene, La Marche) with thousands of engraved or carved objects. Mobiliary art is just mentioned here as the purpose of this paper will mainly be rock art (about mobiliary art see Clottes (ed.) 1990).

Geographical Location

Obviously, rock art locations heavily depend upon the presence (or absence) of caves and shelters. However, areas which one might have thought favourable on that account, such as Languedoc, Roussillon, Provence or again the valleys and causses in the south of Quercy and Aveyron have few or no painted or engraved sites. Cultural choices were a determining factor. Differential preservation is another one, as many caves and shelters may have been destroyed by all sorts of phenomena. For example, at the end of the last glaciation, the 115 meters rise of the sea flooded dozens of caves in the Mediterranean. Several could have had wall art. Only one was partly preserved (Cosquer).

Four main areas with Paleolithic rock art stand out. The most important one is that of Perigord, with more than sixty sites, ranging over the twenty thousand years during which wall art was done and including some of the most spectacular caves ever discovered for paintings (Lascaux, Rouffignac, Font-de-Gaume), engravings (Les Combarelles, Cussac) or low-relief sculpture (Le Cap Blanc).

The major ones are Cougnac and Pech-Merle. The Pyrenees constitute a group equivalent to that of Quercy. Its thirty-odd painted or engraved caves are mostly Magdalenian, but a few are older (Gargas, some galleries in Les Trois-Freres and Portel). They are often to be found in small groupings, like the Basque caves in the Arbailles mountains in the west of the chain, the three Volp Caves, and the six caverns in the Tarascon-sur-Ariege Basin. Several are most important (Niaux, Les Trois-Freres, Le Tuc d'Audoubert, Le Portel, Gargas).

The lower valley of the Ardeche used to be considered as a minor group—numbering about twenty caves—before the discovery of the Chauvet Cave, in itself a most exceptional site. The other caves and shelters with rock art are scattered in various places: the Cosquer Cave Provence by the Mediterranean, Pair-non-Pair in the Gironde, Le Placard, La Chaire-a-Calvin, Roc-de-Sers in the Charente, Le Roc-aux-Sorciers and its splendid sculptures in the Vienne, the two caves of Arcy-sur-Cure in Burgundy, the Mayenne Sciences cave in the Mayenne, one or two shelters in the Fontainebleau Forest and two other caves, including Gouy, in Normandy.

Contrary to a well-spread idea, Paleolithic rock art is not merely 'cave art.' In fact, a recent study showed that if the art of 88 sites was to be found in the complete dark, in 65 other cases it was in the daylight (Clottes 1997). Three main cases can be distinguished: the deep caves, for which an artificial light was necessary; the shelters which were more or less lit up by natural light; the open air sites. The latter are essentially known in Spain and Portugal. Only one case has been discovered in France (the engraved rock at Campome in the Pyrenees-Orientales). The art in the light and the art in the dark: those two tendencies have coexisted for all the duration of the Paleolithic. The art in the dark was preferred in certain areas (the Pyrenees) and at certain periods (Middle and Late Magdalenian). The low-relief sculptures are only to be found in shelters. On the other hand, the paintings, which used to exist in shelters, have for the most part eroded away and only very faint traces remain, contrary to engravings which could in many cases be preserved in them.

In the shelters, there have most often been settlements next to the wall art. People lived there and went on with their daily pursuits close to the engravings, the paintings and low-relief sculptures. The case is quite different for the deep caves, which usually remained uninhabited. This must mean that the art of the one and that of the other were probably not considered in the same way: in the deep caves the images were nearly never defaced, destroyed or erased, whereas in the shelters the archaeological layers—i.e. the rubbish thrown away by the group—often ended up by covering up the art on the walls (Gourdan, Le Placard). The art inside the caves was respected, while the art in the shelters eventually lost its interest and protection.

The Themes Chosen

Whether for the art in the dark or for the art in the light, the themes represented are the same. They testify to identical beliefs, even if ritual practices may have varied according to the different locations.

Above all, Paleolithic art, from beginning to end, is an art of animals. In the past few years, some specialists have insisted upon the importance of geometric signs. It is true that those signs and indeterminate traces are numerically more important than the animals and that they constitute one of the major characteristics of the art. Under their most elementary forms, as clouds of dots and small red bars, they can be found from the Aurignacian in Chauvet to the Middle and Late Magdalenian in Niaux. They are the most mysterious images in cave art. Very few caves have none (Mayriere superieure, La Magdelaine) or, on the contrary, have nothing but geometric signs (Cantal and Frayssinet-le-Gelat in the Lot). This means that those signs are practically always associated to animals, either in the same caves and often on the same panels or directly on top of them (G.R.A.P.P. 1993).

However, our first and most durable impression of Paleolithic art is above all that of a bestiary, plentiful and various while remaining typical. Most of the animals represented are big herbivores, those that the people of the Upper Paleolithic could see around them and which they hunted. Those choices were not compulsory. They might have preferred to draw birds, fish or snakes, but they did not do so.

Horses are dominant. Locally they may be outnumbered by bison (the Ariege Pyrenees;) or hinds (Cantabrian Spain), occasionally even by rhinoceroses and lions at the very beginning (Chauvet) or, much later, by mammoths at Rouffignac (Plassard 1999). Nonetheless, they always remain numerous whatever techniques were used at any period and in any region. We might say that the theme of the horse is at the basis of Paleolithic rock art. This is all the more remarkable as that animal, even though present among the cooking debris of Paleolithic living sites, was often less plentifully killed and eaten than reindeer and bison, or again ibex in mountainous rocky areas. This means that it played a major role in the bestiary. The same could be said, even if less so, for the bison, whose images are also found in relatively high numbers from the Aurignacian to the end of the Magdalenian.

The importance of animal themes varies according to the different regions but much more in function of the periods considered. For example, the enormous number of normally rare dangerous animals in the Chauvet Cave created a surprise: rhinoceroses, lions, mammoths and bears represent 63% of the recognisable animal figures (Clottes (ed.) 2001).

However, this is not a unique phenomenon, isolated in time and space. In the Dordogne, at the same epoch, Aurignacians made use of the same themes in their shelters and their caves in much higher proportions than can be found in later art. This would mean that an important thematic change took place in the art of the south of France at the beginning of the Gravettian or at the end of the Aurignacian, when their choices changed from the most fearsome animals to the more hunted ones (Clottes 1996). Human representations can be found, but in far fewer numbers in comparison with the painted and engraved animals. About a hundred have been published, not counting hand stencils and hand prints or isolated female sexual organs. This numerical inferiority, constant at all times during the Upper Paleolithic, is in sharp contrast to what one can see in most forms of rock art all over the world. In addition to their relative scarcity, human representations evidence two main characteristics: they are nearly always incomplete or even reduced to an isolated segment of their body; they are not naturalistic, contrary to the animals.

Whole human representations are exceptional, hardly a score. They may be carved women (La Magdelaine in the Tarn, Le Roc aux Sorciers in the Vienne), or women sketched with a finger or a tool on the soft surface of a wall or ceiling (Pech-Merle, Cussac), or painted (Le Portel) or engraved men (Sous-Grand-Lac, Saint-Cirq, Gabillou in the Dordogne).

Far more numerous are body segments, such as hand stencils and hand prints, heads, female and male genital organs, or again some rather indistinct outlines—which may or may not be human—often called 'ghosts'. Those themes were more or less favoured according to the various cultures (G.R.A.P.P. 1993). Hand stencils and prints can exclusively be found in the earliest periods of the art, probably in the Aurignacian (Chauvet), most certainly in the Gravettian (Cosquer, Pech-Merle, Gargas), roughly between 32,000 and 22,000 BP in uncalibrated radiocarbon years. On the other hand, the female sexes, frequent at the very beginning (Chauvet, Cosquer, several shelters in Dordogne), can also be found in the Solutrean and above all in the Magdalenian (Font-Bargeix, Bedeilhac). That sexual theme is thus a constant of the Upper Paleolithic, with more or less frequent occurrences according to the times and places.

Animals are often drawn without any care for scale, in profile. They can be whole or just represented by their heads or forequarters, which is enough to identify them. Their images are often precise, personalised and identifiable in all their details (sexes, ages, attitudes), whether they be Magdalenian bison in the Ariege or Aurignacian lions and rhinos in the

Chauvet Cave, 18,000 years earlier. Scenes are rare and certain themes are absent, like herds and mating scenes. Paintings and engravings are thus neither faithful copies of the surrounding environment nor stereotypes.

As to humans, whatever the culture and diverse as they may be, they always seem to be uncouth and unsophisticated, mere caricatures. This is also a constant feature that stresses the unity of Paleolithic art.

The artistic abilities of the painters and engravers cannot be questioned. They deliberately chose to represent vague humans, with few details or deformed features.

A particular theme is that of composite creatures, at times called sorcerers. Those beings evidence both human and animal characteristics. This theme is all the more interesting as it departs from normality. It is present as early as the Aurignacian in Chauvet. It can be found in Gabillou and Lascaux 10,000 years later or more and it is still present in the Middle Magdalenian of Les Trois-Freres, nearly 20,000 years after its beginnings.

The Techniques Utilized

In France, only 18 sites are known with sculptures. The most important ones are Cap-Blanc in the Dordogne and the Roc-aux-Sorciers in the Vienne (Lakovieva & Pinion 1997, Airvaux 2001). That technique is the one that required the most work. Some images evidence a 5 cm relief or more. It is present in all the main groups except that of the south-east.

Clay modellings are all dated to the Middle or Late Magdalenian and they are all found within a restricted area, in four caves of the Ariege Pyrenees: Labouiche, Bedeilhac, Montespan and Le Tuc d'Audoubert. Those in the latter two caves are famous, Montespan because of a clay bear which is a real statue, nearly lifesize, and Le Tuc d'Audoubert because of two extraordinary bison following each other in a premating scene. A particularly naturalistic female sex was modelled on the ground in Bedeilhac. It is difficult to understand why other works made with such a simple technique have not been found in other groups and at other periods.

Finger tracings are everywhere. Their presence depends upon the qualities of the walls: when their surface is soft it becomes possible to draw with one's fingers. Finger tracings are often not naturalistic, with volutes and incomprehensible squiggles that occupy many square meters on the walls and ceilings, as in Gargas and Cosquer (Clottes & Courtin 1996). Most frequently they belong to the earliest periods of the art. The engravings on the ground are more frequent in the Pyrenees than anywhere else. For them as for the paintings in the open preservation problems are vital: it is so easy not to notice them and to destroy them by trampling. This must have happened innumerable times.

The engravings on the walls are less famous than the paintings because they are less spectacular, but they probably are more numerous. They were mostly made with a flint and the effects achieved are very diverse. Sometimes, the artists contented themselves with sketching the outlines of animals by means of simple lines, which can be deep and wide or thin and superficial according to the hardness of the surface. The finest ones can only be seen now under a slanting light, but modern experimentation has shown that they must have been far more visible at the time they were made, when they stood out white against the darker colour of the wall; since then they got patinated and their colour is the same as that of their environment. This remark may explain the very numerous superimpositions of motifs that can be found in caves like Les Trois-Freres, Lascaux or Les Combarelles. In other cases, the artists used scraping, which shows white on the wall and enables all sorts of possibilities by playing with the darker hues of the wall and the lighter ones of engravings (Les Trois-Freres, Labastide) (G.R.A.P.P. 1993).

Paintings are generally red or black. The reds are iron oxides, such as hematite. The blacks, either charcoal or manganese dioxide. Sometimes they did real drawings with a chunk of rock or of charcoal held like a pencil. Elsewhere veritable paintings were made. The pigment was then crushed and mixed with a binder to ensure the fluidity of the paint which was then either applied with a finger or with a brush made with animal hair, or blown through the mouth (stencilling).

Modern analyses even revealed that in the Magdalenian of the Pyrenees some paintings (Niaux, Fontanet) had been made according to real recipes by adding an extender, i.e. a powder obtained from the crushing of various stones (biotite, potassium feldspath, talcum). The aims were to save on the pigment, to make the paint stick better to the wall and to avoid its crackling when drying (Clottes, Menu, Walter 1990). Some images evince different techniques for the same subject: bicolour, joint use of engraving and painting.

As early as the Aurignacian, more than 30,000 years ago, the most sophisticated techniques of representation had been discovered and were in use, as can be seen in the Chauvet Cave. Those artists made use of stump drawing in order to shade the inside of the bodies and provide relief. They also used the main two colours (red and black), fine and deep engraving, finger tracing and stencilling.

Chronology

Until the end of the eighties, it was impossible to date paintings directly, as the quantity of pigment necessary for such an analysis was too important. Accelerator mass spectrometry now enables us to obtain a date with less than one milligram of charcoal. Consequently, a number of direct dates are now available for six French caves: Cosquer, Chauvet, Cougnac, Pech-Merle, Niaux, Le Portel. When the caves have only got engravings (Les Combarelles, Cussac) or red paintings, or black paintings made with manganese dioxide (Lascaux, Rouffignac), it remains impossible to get a direct date because of the lack of organic material. Chronological attributions are then made with time-honoured methods, generally by taking advantage of the archaeological context whenever possible or from stylistic comparison with other better-dated sites. For example, when the Cussac cave was discovered in the Dordogne in October 2000, Norbert Aujoulat and Christian Archambeau attributed its engravings to the Gravettian because of the similarities with

Pech-Merle and Gargas (Aujoulat et al. 2001). When, in August 2001, a 25,120 BP ± 120 date was obtained from a human bone in the same cave, it corroborated the initial estimate of those specialists (op. cit.).

Among well-established facts, the most important is the duration of cave art, over at least twenty millenia. The oldest dates are so far those of the Chauvet Cave (between 30,000 and 32,000 BP) and the most recent one that in Le Portel (11,600 ± 150 BP).

Such an immense duration implies several consequences. First, the acknowledgement that in order for such a tradition to persist under such a formalised form for such a long time, it must have meant that a strong compelling form of teaching existed. The fundamental unity of Paleolithic art, obvious as it is in its images and in the activities around it, could not but for that have persisted for so many millenia. It is also a fact that the apparent great number of painted or engraved caves and shelters is not much when compared to the duration of Paleolithic art. This means that there must have been an art in the open which has not been preserved in France, and also that the images, in hundreds of shelters and caves may have been destroyed or buried and concealed for a number of reasons.

Until a rather recent date, the evolution of art was believed to have been gradual, from coarse beginnings in the Aurignacian to the apogee of Lascaux. The recent discoveries of Cosquer, Chauvet and Cussac have shown that that paradigm was wrong, since from as early as the Aurignacian and the Gravettian very sophisticated techniques had already been invented. This means that forms of art evidencing different degrees of mastery must have coexisted in different places and times and also that many artistic discoveries were made and lost and made again thousands of years later. The evolution of Paleolithic art was not in a straight line, but rather as a seesaw.

Human and Animal Activities in the Deep Caves

Paleolithic wall art cannot be dissociated from its archaeological context. This means the traces and remains of human and animal activities in the deep caves, because valuable clues about the actions of their visitors are better preserved in them than in any other milieu.

Bears, particularly cave bears, hibernated in the deepest galleries. Some died and their bones were noticed by Paleolithic people when they went underground. At times they made use of them: they strung them along the way and lifted their impressive canines in Le Tuc d'Audoubert; in Chauvet, they deposited a skull on a big rock in the middle of a chamber and stuck two humerus forcibly into the ground not far from the entrance. Cave bears scratched the walls as bears do trees and their very noticeable scratchings may have spurred people to make finger tracings (Chauvet) or engravings (Le Portel).

Humans left various sorts of traces, whether deliberately or involuntarily. When the ground was soft (sand, wet clay), their naked footprints remained printed in it. (Niaux, Le Reseau Clastres, Le Tuc d'Audoubert, Montespan, Lalbastide, Fontanet, Pech-Merle, L'Aldlene, Chauvet). This enables us to see that children, at times very young ones, accompanied adults when they went underground, and also that the visitors of those deep caves were not very numerous because footprints and more generally human traces and remains, are few.

The charcoal fallen from their torches, their fires, a few objects, bones and flint tools left on the ground are the remains of meals or of sundry activities. They are also part of the documentation unwittingly left by prehistoric people in the caves. From their study, one can say that in most cases painted or engraved caves were not inhabited, at least for long periods. Fires were temporary and remains are relatively scarce. Naturally, there are exceptions (Einlene, Labastide, Le Mas d'Azil, Bdeilhac). In their case, it is often difficult to make out whether those settlements are in relation—as seems likely—or not with the art on the walls. The presence of portable art may be a valuable clue to establish such a relationship.

Among the most mysterious remains are the objects deposited in the cracks of the walls and in particular the bone fragments stuck forcibly into them (see also below). After being noticed in the Ariegie Volp Caves. (Enlene, Les Trois-Freres, Le Tuc d'Audoubert) (Begouen & Clottes 1981), those deposits have been found in numerous other French Paleolithic art caves (Bedeillhaic, Le Portel, Troubat, Erberua, Gargas, etc.). They belong to periods sometimes far apart, which is not the least interesting fact about them because this means that the same gestures were repeated again and again for many thousands of years. Thus, in Gargas, a bone fragment lifted from one of the fissures next to some hand stencils was dated to 26,800 BP, while in other caves they are Magdalenian, i.e. more recent by 13,000 to 14,000 years.

The Gravettian burials very recently discovered in the Cussac cave (Aujoulat et al. 2001) pose a huge problem. It is the first time that human skeletons have been found inside a deep cave with Paleolithic art. Until they have been excavated and studied properly it will be impossible to know whether those people died there by accident (which is most unlikely), whether they were related to those who did the engravings, whether they enjoyed a special status, etc. Their presence just stresses the magic/religious character of art in the deep caves.

Meaning(s)

Ever since the beginning of the XXth century, several attempts have been made to find the meaning(s) of Paleolithic rock art. Art for art's sake, totemism, the Abbe Breuil's hunting magic and Leroi-Gourhan's and Laming-Emperaires's structuralist theories were proposed and then abandoned one after the other (Delporte 1990, Lorblanchet 1995). Since then, most specialists have made up their minds that it would be hopeless to look for the meanings behind the art. They prefer to spend their time and efforts recording it, describing it and dating it, to endeavour to answer the questions 'what?', 'how?' and 'when?', thus carefully avoiding the fundamental question 'why?'. In the course of the past few years, though, a new attempt, spurred by David Lewis-Williams, was made in order to discover an interpretative framework. Shamanism was proposed (Clottes & Lewis-Williams 1998). Considering the fact that shamanism is so widespread among hunter-gatherers and that Upper Paleolithic people were admittedly hunter-gatherers, looking to shamanism as a likely religion for them should have been the first logical step whenever the question of meaning arose.

In addition, shamanic religions evidence several characteristics which can make us understand cave art better. The first one is their concept of a complex cosmos in which at least two worlds—or more—coexist, be they side by side or one above the other. Those worlds interact with one another and in our own world most events are believed to be the consequence of an influence from the other-world(s). The second one is the belief of the group in the ability for certain persons to have at will a direct controlled relationship with the other-world. This is done for very practical purposes: to cure the sick, to maintain a good relationship with the powers in the other-world, to restore an upset harmony, to reclaim a lost soul, to make good hunting possible, to forecast the future, to cast spells, etc. Contact happens in two ways: spirit helpers, very often in animal form, come to the shaman and inhabit him/her when he/she calls on them; the shaman may also send his/her soul to the other-world in order to meet the spirits there and obtain their help and protection. Shamans will do so through trance. A shaman thus has a most important role as a mediator between the real world and the world of the spirits, as well as a social role.

Upper Paleolithic people were *Homo sapiens sapiens* like us and therefore had a nervous system identical to ours. Consequently, some of them must have known altered states of consciousness in their various forms, including hallucinations. This was part of a reality which they had to manage in their own way and according to their own concepts.

This being said, we know as a fact that they kept going into the deep caves for twenty thousand years at the very least in order to draw on the walls, not to live or take shelter there. Everywhere and at all times, the underground has been perceived as being a supernatural world, the realm of the spirits or of the dead, a forbidding gate to the Beyond which people are frightened of and never cross. Going into the subterranean world was thus defying ancestral fears, deliberately venturing into the kingdom of the supernatural powers in order to meet them. The analogy with shamanic mind travels is obvious, but their underground adventure went much beyond a metaphoric equivalent of the shaman's voyage: it made it real in a milieu where one could physically move and in which spirits were literally at hand. When Upper Paleolithic people went into the deeper galleries, they must have been acutely aware that they were in the world of the supernatural powers and they expected to see and find them. Such a state of mind, no doubt reinforced by the teaching they had received, was certain to facilitate the coming of visions that deep caves in any case tend to stir up (as many spelunkers have testified). Deep caves could thus have a double role, the aspects of which were indissolubly linked: to make hallucinations easier; to get in touch with the spirits through the walls.

Wall images are perfectly compatible with the perceptions people could have during their visions, whether one considers their themes, their techniques or their details. The animals, individualised by means of precise details, seem to float on the walls; they are disconnected from reality, without any ground line, often without respect of the laws of gravity, in the absence of any framework or surroundings. Elementary geometric signs are always present and recall those seen in the various stages of trance. As to composite creatures and monsters (i.e. animals with corporal attributes pertaining to various species), we know that they belong to the world of shamanic visions. This does not mean that they would have made their paintings and engravings under a state of trance. The visions could be drawn (much) later.

Trying to get in touch with the spirits believed to live inside the caves, on the other side of the veil that the walls constituted between their reality and ours, is a Paleolithic attitude of mind which has left numerous testimonies, particularly the very frequent use of natural reliefs. When one's mind is full of animal images, a hollow in the rock underlined by a shadow cast by one's torch or grease lamp will evoke a horse's back line or the hump of a bison. How then couldn't one believe that the spirit-animals found in the visions of trance—and that one had expected to find in the other-world which the underground undoubtedly is—are not there on the wall, half emerging through the rock thanks to the magic of the moving light and ready to vanish into it again? In a few lines, they would be made wholly real and their power would then become accessible.

Cracks and hollows, as well as the ends or openings of galleries, must have played a slightly different yet comparable part. They were not the animals themselves but the places whence they came. Those natural features provided a sort of opening into the depths of the rock where the spirits were believed to dwell. This would explain why we find so many examples of animals drawn in function of those natural features (Le Roseau Clastres, Le Travers de Janoye, Chauvet, Le Grand Plafond at Rouffignac).

In addition to the drawings of animals and signs, the intention to get in touch with the powerful spirits in the subterranean world may also be glimpsed through three other categories of testimonies. First, the bone fragments and other remains (teeth, flints) stuck or deposited in the fissures of the walls. Finger tracings and indeterminate lines might stem from the same logic. In their case, the aim was not to recreate a reality as with the animal images but to trail one's fingers and to leave their traces on the wall, wherever this was possible, in order to establish a direct contact with the powers underlying the wall. This might be done by non-initiates who participated in the ritual in their own way and with their own means. Finally, hand stencils enabled them to go further still. When somebody put his or her hand on to the wall and paint was blown all over it, the hand would blend with the wall and take its new colour, be it red or black. Under the power of the sacred paint, the hand would metaphorically vanish into the wall. It would thus, concretely, link its owner to the world of the spirits. This might enable the 'lay people', maybe the sick, to benefit directly from the forces of the world beyond. Seen in that light, the presence of hands belonging to very young children, such as those in Gargas, stops being extraordinary (Clottes & Lewis-Williams 1998, 2001).

Conclusion

In the last ten years, many changes have occurred. New caves of great magnitude (Cosquer, Chauvet, Cussac) have been discovered. Their study has already brought a wealth of information and much is to be expected of the continuation (or the beginning, as in Cussac) of research in them, as well as in half a dozen smaller sites found in various regions of France. AMS radiocarbon dating has proved to be an invaluable tool not only to establish the extreme antiquity of the art in some of the caves but also to help us work out the different periods in their frequentation.

A lot of attention is now being paid to the archaeological context, to its preservation and to its analysis. As a result the activities of Upper Paleolithic people in the caves become more visible and understandable. Finally the new interpretative theories bring another framework in which to study and try to understand the reasons why Upper Paleolithic people went so far underground to leave on the walls their splendid if still mysterious images.

Critical Thinking

1. Why can't we say that Paleolithic rock art is merely "cave art"? What are the three main cases of such art?
2. How does the author contrast the shelters with the deep caves in terms of art and why does he think some of these differences exist?
3. Why does the author claim that, above all, Paleolithic art is an "art of animals"? What kinds of animals are primarily represented?
4. Why is it remarkable that horses are dominant?
5. What was the surprise regarding the kind of animals represented at Chauvet? What thematic change subsequently took place in the art of southern France?
6. How does the Upper Paleolithic contrast with other parts of the world with respect to human representations? What are two main characteristics of such representations?
7. How are animals portrayed? What kinds of things are noticeably absent?
8. How are humans portrayed? Does this reflect artistic abilities? Why are the composite creatures interesting?
9. How does the author assess finger tracings? Engravings?
10. What were the kinds of materials and methods used in paintings?
11. How has it become possible to date the paintings directly?
12. What is the most important fact regarding the dating of the paintings? What are the consequences implied?
13. What is the direct evidence concerning the presence of bears and humans in the caves? Of human activities?
14. How might shamanic religion help us to better understand cave art?

Children of Prehistory

Stone Age kids left their marks on cave art and stone tools.

Bruce Bower

Walk about 300 meters into Rouffignac Cave in southern France, turn left into a dark chamber, raise a lantern, and gaze up at a prehistoric marvel. A welter of undulating, curving, crisscrossing lines blankets the ceiling in abstract abandon. Single, double, and triple sets of lines zigzag and run together in swirls. In other parts of the cave, similarly configured lines appear beside, inside, underneath, and on top of drawings of now-extinct mammoths. Archaeologists refer to such marks as finger flutings, the lines that human fingers leave when drawn over a soft surface. In Rouffignac Cave, finger flutings cut through pliable red clay to expose hard white limestone underneath.

Soon after the discovery of Rouffignac's finger flutings about 50 years ago, researchers started speculating about the mysterious marks. One influential account referred to the decorated ceiling as the "Serpents' Dome." Others interpreted the finger flutings as depictions of mythical creatures or streams of water, symbols from initiation rites into manhood, or shamans' ritual signs.

New evidence, gathered by Kevin Sharpe of the University of Oxford in England and Leslie Van Gelder of Walden University in Minneapolis, challenges those assertions. They argue that 2-to-5-year-old kids generated the bulk of Rouffignac's ancient ceiling designs. Teenagers or adults must have hoisted children so that the youngsters could reach the ceiling and run their fingers across its soft-clay coat.

Sharpe and Van Gelder's study joins a growing number of efforts aimed at illuminating the activities of Stone Age children. Researchers who conduct such studies regard much, but certainly not all, of prehistoric cave art as the product of playful youngsters and graffiti-minded teenagers.

Stone Age adults undoubtedly drew the famous portrayals of bison, mammoths, and other creatures at sites such as France's Lascaux Cave and Spain's Altamira Cave. However, less attention has focused on numerous instances of finger fluting, pigment-stained handprints and hand outlines, and crude drawings of animals and people, all of which may have had youthful originators.

"Kids undoubtedly had access to the deep painted caves [during the Stone Age], and they participated in some of the activities there," says Jean Clottes, a French archaeologist and the current president of the International Federation of Rock Art Organizations. "That's a hard fact."

Moreover, archaeologists suspect that many of the relics found at prehistoric stone-tool sites around the world are the largely unexamined handiwork of children and teenagers who were taking early cracks at learning to chisel rock.

"I suspect that children's products dominate stone-tool remains at some of those sites," remarks archaeologist John J. Shea of Stony Brook (N.Y.) University.

Cave Tots

Sharpe and Van Gelder have long speculated that prehistoric kids created many of the patterned lines that adorn caves such as Rouffignac. Their suspicion was kindled in 1986, when Australian archaeologist Robert G. Bednarik published the first of several papers contending that the walls and ceilings of caves in western Europe and southern Australia contained numerous examples of child-produced grooves as well as some made by adults. He coined the term finger fluting for this practice.

Bednarik, who heads the Australian Rock Art Research Association in Caulfield South, noted that, because of the spacing and width of the marks, a large proportion of the grooves must have been the work of small fingers. "Approximately half the markings were clearly made by children, even infants," he says.

To date, Bednarik has investigated finger fluting in about 70 Australian and European caves. Analyses of wall and ceiling sediment in a portion of these caves indicate that the line designs originated at least 13,000 years ago, and in some cases 30,000 years or more ago.

At Rouffignac, Sharpe and Van Gelder took Bednarik's ideas an empirical step further. First, the researchers asked children and adults to run the fingers of one hand across soft clay. The scientists then measured the width of the impressions of each individual's central three fingers. Participants included 124 pupils and 11 teachers from four schools—three in the United States and one in England. Their ages ranged from 2 to 55. The volunteers held their fingers close together during the exercise, mimicking the fingerfluting style at Rouffignac. Even with adult assistance, 2-to 3-year-olds usually just smacked the clay with an open hand.

Comparisons of modern finger widths with those arrayed on the French cave's ceiling indicate that 2-to-5-year-olds made the vast majority of Rouffignac markings, Sharpe and Van Gelder reported in the December 2006 *Antiquity*. Either teenagers or adults crafted a few finger flutings at the site, since members of these age groups possess similar, larger finger widths than children do. In the modern sample, a 12-year-old girl and a 14-year-old boy displayed wider fingers than any adult did. Hand sizes of late Stone Age people are comparable to those of people today, Sharpe says.

A 5 foot, 10 inch-tall person standing on tiptoes could just reach the ceiling of the Rouffignac chamber, Sharpe notes. Adults must have hoisted children on their shoulders while weaving their way through the inner sanctum, so that their passengers could trace curved, elongated lines. This activity occurred sometime between 27,000 and 13,000 years ago, according to estimates of the extinction dates of animals depicted in drawings in the cave.

Perhaps finger fluting was simply a playful exercise, a form of ancient finger painting, Sharpe suggests.

While Bednarik welcomes the new evidence on youthful finger fluting, he suspects that such marks mimicked visual sensations produced by reactions of the brain in response to prolonged darkness and sensory deprivation deep inside caves. In such situations, people—and especially children, in Bednarik's view—temporarily see wavy lines, points of light, and other geometric shapes.

Stone Age kids at Rouffignac may have translated these visions into finger fluting without adult assistance, Bednarik holds. Since soil movements can alter the height of cave floors, prehistoric children might once have been able to reach the chambers' ceilings on their own, he suggests.

In contrast, Clottes accepts the notion that prehistoric adults lifted young finger fluters at Rouffignac. However, he hypothesizes that ancient people regarded caves as portals to spirit worlds and as places for important rituals. "Children were brought inside the caves to benefit from the supernatural power the caves held by touching the walls, putting or printing their hands on the walls, drawing lines, and perhaps occasionally sketching animals or geometric signs," Clottes says.

Paul Bahn, an independent archaeologist in England, sees no way to confirm Clottes' contention. "Finger fluting may have been deeply significant or may have been almost mindless doodling," Bahn remarks. "The fact that some kids were lifted up by bigger people in no way helps us to decide."

Handy Boys

In September 1940, three teenage boys in rural France set out to find a rumored underground passage to an old manor. Their search led them to a small opening in the ground that had been blocked off to keep away livestock. After returning the next day with a lamp, the boys crawled into the hole and entered the Lascaux cave with its gallery of magnificent Stone Age drawings.

Caves exerted a hypnotic pull on boys long before Lascaux's discovery, says zoologist R. Dale Guthrie of the University of Alaska in Fairbanks. In fact, he contends, teenage boys played a big part in producing the prehistoric cave art, not just in finding it thousands of years later.

Guthrie, who studies the remains of Stone Age animals and is himself an artist, made his case in a 2005 book titled *The Nature of Paleolithic Art* (University of Chicago Press).

Adolescent boys, at times joined by female peers and children, decorated cave walls and ceilings for fun, not to commune with spirits, Guthrie holds. Exploring caves and decorating underground chambers with personal marks provided an outlet for creative play that readied boys for the rigors and challenges of big-game hunting as adults, he suggests.

Youngsters made up a hefty proportion of ancient populations. In a Stone Age band of roughly 35 people, about two dozen individuals were in their twenties or younger, Guthrie estimates. Few elders lived past age 40.

Several European Stone Age caves contain sets of footprints of teens and children, suggesting that prehistoric kids of different ages went exploring together, Guthrie says.

The most extensive evidence of a youth movement in ancient cave art comes from Guthrie's comparison of the size of hand impressions at some sites with corresponding measurements of people's hands today. In at least 30 European caves, ancient visitors rendered hand images by pressing a pigment-covered palm and fingers against a wall or by blowing pigment against an outspread hand held up to a wall to create a stenciled outline.

Guthrie assessed nine different dimensions characterizing each of 201 ancient hand impressions. He obtained the corresponding hand measurements for nearly 700 people, ages 5 to 19, in Fairbanks.

Teenagers ranging in age from 13 to 16 left most of the prehistoric handprints, Guthrie concludes. He classifies 162 prints as those of adult or teenage males, based on traits such as relatively wide palms and thick fingers. The remaining 39 prints belong either to females or to young boys.

Guthrie contends that much Stone Age cave art was concocted hastily, yielding simple, graffitilike images with no deep meaning. For instance, a few caves contain hand outlines with missing fingers or other deformities that teenage boys with normal hands made for fun, in Guthrie's view. He has replicated the "maimed-hand look" by spattering paint around his own bent fingers onto flat surfaces.

Stone Age caves also contain many unfinished or corrected sketches of animals as well as drawings of male and especially female sexual parts. Small groups of boys, flush with puberty but not yet old enough for adult duties, probably invested considerable energy in exploring caves and expressing their hopes and fears on chamber walls, Guthrie proposes.

"Paleolithic art books are really biased in showing only beautiful, finished cave images," he asserts. "The possibility that adolescent giggles and snickers may have echoed in dark cave passages as often as did the rhythm of a shaman's chant demeans neither artists nor art."

Sharpe, a supporter of Guthrie's conclusions, notes that teenage boys apparently jumped up and slapped the walls of chambers in Rouffignac and in a nearby French cave, making hand marks about 2.5 m above the floor.

Clottes, however, doubts that youthful thrill seekers took the lead in generating prehistoric European cave art. "In most caves, images were made by adults" he says. "A majority of those images display both artistic mastery and technical expertise."

Knap Time

Guthrie's labeling of prehistoric teenagers as big-time cave artists stimulated a related insight by John Shea. The Stony Brook researcher realized, after reading Guthrie's book, that nearly every set of stone tools and tool-making debris found at Stone Age sites includes the likely handiwork of children.

"Almost every stone-tool assemblage includes unusually small, simple artifacts, overproduced in an obsessive way, that children could have made," Shea says.

These tiny, rudimentary implements—many dating to hundreds of thousands of years ago—were made from poor-quality rock, an additional sign that they were fashioned by kids taking early whacks at tool production, Shea asserts. Seasoned stone-tool makers used high-quality rock.

Shea teaches a college class in stone-tool making, also known as flint knapping. Observations of novice flint knappers, combined with the likelihood that prehistoric people learned to make stone tools at young ages, bolster his argument—published in the November–December 2006 *Evolutionary Anthropology*—that children produced many previously discovered small stone artifacts. Researchers have already established that modern children can learn to make basic stone tools starting at age 7.

Shea plans to develop criteria to distinguish beginners' stone artifacts from those of experienced flint knappers. For instance, he has noted that beginners create lots of debris as they experiment with tool-making techniques. Also, the shape and quality of their finished products vary greatly from one piece to the next, unlike experts' uniform implements.

As early as 1998, Harvard University archaeologist Ofer BarYosef suggested that Stone Age kids may have watched adults making tools, picked up toolmakers' discarded stones, and tried to imitate what their elders had done. At the time, his suggestion went largely unnoticed.

"Children's activities have been ignored at [Stone Age] sites and at most later archaeological sites as well," remarks archaeologist Steven L. Kuhn of the University of Arizona in Tucson.

Questions remain about whether children and other novices invariably generated smaller stone artifacts than experienced tool makers did, Kuhn says. Research into children's activities in modern hunter-gatherer societies might offer clues to youngsters' behavior long ago, in his view.

Stone Age kids may eventually rewrite what scientists know about ancient stone tools and cave art. It's enough to make a pre-historic parent proud.

Critical Thinking

1. What is "finger fluting" and how has it been variously interpreted?
2. What kinds of cave art did children apparently create? To what extent has it been ignored by researchers?
3. How extensive are these designs geographically and in terms of time?
4. What two theories attempt to explain how children were able to reach the ceilings?
5. What is the evidence for the conclusion that children created much of the art? What was their apparent motivation?
6. How are Paleolithic art books biased?
7. Did children actually take the lead in cave art? Explain.
8. What are the differences between tools made by children and those made by adults?

The Writing on the Cave Wall

KATE RAVILLIOUS

The first intrepid explorers to brave the 7-metre crawl through a perilously narrow tunnel leading to the Chauvet caves in southern France were rewarded with magnificent artwork to rival any modern composition. Stretching a full 3 metres in height, the paintings depict a troupe of majestic horses in deep colours, above a pair of boisterous rhinos in the midst of a fight. To the left, they found the beautiful rendering of a herd of prehistoric cows. "The horse heads just seem to leap out of the wall towards you," says Jean Clottes, former director of scientific research at the caves and one of the few people to see the paintings with his own eyes.

When faced with such spectacular beauty, who could blame the visiting anthropologists for largely ignoring the modest semicircles, lines and zigzags also marked on the walls? Yet dismissing them has proved to be something of a mistake. The latest research has shown that, far from being doodles, the marks are in fact highly symbolic, forming a written "code" that was familiar to all of the prehistoric tribes around France and possibly beyond. Indeed, these unprepossessing shapes may be just as remarkable as the paintings of trotting horses and tussling rhinos, providing a snapshot into humankind's first steps towards symbolism and writing.

Until now, the accepted view has been that our ancestors underwent a "creative explosion" around 30,000 to 40,000 years ago, when they suddenly began to think abstractly and create rock art. This idea is supported by the plethora of stunning cave paintings, like those at Chauvet, which started to proliferate across Europe around this time. Writing, on the other hand, appeared to come much later, with the earliest records of a pictographic writing system dating back to just 5000 years ago.

Few researchers, though, had given any serious thought to the relatively small and inconspicuous marks around the cave paintings. The evidence of humanity's early creativity, they thought, was clearly in the elaborate drawings.

While some scholars like Clottes had recorded the presence of cave signs at individual sites, Genevieve von Petzinger, then a student at the University of Victoria in British Columbia, Canada, was surprised to find that no one had brought all these records together to compare signs from different caves. And so, under the supervision of April Nowell, also at the University of Victoria, she devised an ambitious masters project. She compiled a comprehensive database of all recorded cave signs from 146 sites in France, covering 25,000 years of prehistory from 35,000 to 10,000 years ago.

What emerged was startling: 26 signs, all drawn in the same style, appeared again and again at numerous sites. Admittedly, some of the symbols are pretty basic, like straight lines, circles and triangles, but the fact that many of the more complex designs also appeared in several places hinted to von Petzinger and Nowell that they were meaningful—perhaps even the seeds of written communication.

A closer look confirmed their suspicions. When von Petzinger went back to some of the records of the cave walls, she noticed other, less abstract signs that appeared to represent a single part of a larger figure—like the tusks of a mammoth without an accompanying body. This feature, known as synecdoche, is common in the known pictographic languages. To von Petzinger and Nowell, it demonstrated that our ancestors were indeed considering how to represent ideas symbolically rather than realistically, eventually leading to the abstract symbols that were the basis of the original study.

"It was a way of communicating information in a concise way," says Nowell. "For example, the mammoth tusks may have simply represented a mammoth, or a mammoth hunt, or something that has nothing to do with a literal interpretation of mammoths." Other common forms of synecdoche include two concentric circles or triangles (used as eyes in horse and bison paintings), ibex horns and the hump of a mammoth. The claviform figure—which looks somewhat like a numeral 1—may even be a stylised form of the female figure, she says.

The real clincher came with the observation that certain signs appear repeatedly in pairs. Negative hands and dots tend to be one of the most frequent pairings, for example, especially during a warm climate period known as the Gravettian (28,000 to 22,000 years ago). One site called Les Trois-Frères in the French Pyrenees, even shows four sign types grouped together: negative hands, dots, finger fluting and thumb stencils (a rare subcategory of the negative hands).

Grouping is typically seen in early pictographic languages—the combined symbols representing a new concept—and the researchers suspect that prehistoric Europeans had established a similar system. "The consistency of the pairings indicate that they could really have had a meaning," says Nowell. "We are perhaps seeing the first glimpses of a rudimentary language system."

Lines, Dots and Love Hearts

Von Petzinger caused quite a stir when she presented her preliminary findings last April at the Paleoanthropology Society Meeting in Chicago. She and Nowell have recently submitted a paper to the journal *Antiquity* and they are currently preparing another paper for the *Journal of Human Evolution.* The Smithsonian Institution's National Museum of Natural History in Washington DC plans to include the symbols in a forthcoming exhibition on human evolution.

"This work is really exciting," says Iain Davidson, an Australian rock art specialist at the University of New England in New South Wales. "We can see that these people had a similar convention for representing something."

Suspecting that this was just the beginning of what the symbols could tell us about prehistoric culture, von Petzinger and Nowell's next move was to track where and when they emerged. The line turned out to be the most popular, being present at 70 percent of the sites and appearing across all time periods, from 30,000 to 10,000 years ago.

The next most prolific signs were the open angle symbol and the dots, both appearing at 42 percent of the sites throughout this period. The vast majority of the remaining symbols are each present in around one-fifth of the French caves, the exceptions being the cordiform (roughly a love-heart shape), reniform (kidney shape), scalariform (ladder shape) and spiral, which all turned up in just a handful of sites. "The spiral only appears in two out of the 146 sites throughout the entire time period, which really surprised me as it is a common motif in many later cultures," says von Petzinger.

The Rhone valley and the Dordogne and Lot regions in the south seem to have been the original sites for the symbols in France: most signs seem to appear in these regions before spreading across the rest of the country. Notable exceptions include the zigzag, which first appeared in Provence and is a relative latecomer, debuting around 20,000 years ago.

No signs ever emerged in northern France, though. "For large periods of time the north was uninhabitable because of ice sheets coming and going, so there was less opportunity for culture to develop independently up there," says von Petzinger.

The Ice Age may have hindered the cultural revolution in the north, but elsewhere it could have been instrumental in furthering it. "People were forced to move south and congregate in 'refugia' during the last glacial maximum, 18,000 to 21,000 years ago, and it is at this time when we start to see an explosion in rock art," says Nowell. "One possibility is that they were using the signs to demarcate their territories."

Yet while long winters spent in caves might have induced people to spend time painting wonder walls, there are reasons to think the symbols originated much earlier on. One of the most intriguing facts to emerge from von Petzinger's work is that more than three-quarters of the symbols were present in the very earliest sites, from over 30,000 years ago.

"I was really surprised to discover this," says von Petzinger. If the creative explosion occurred 30,000 to 40,000 years ago, she would have expected to see evidence of symbols being invented and discarded at this early stage, with a long period of time passing before a recognisable system emerged. Instead, it appears that by 30,000 years ago a set of symbols was already well established.

Rewriting Prehistory

That suggests we might need to rethink our ideas about prehistoric people, von Petzinger says. "This incredible diversity and continuity of use suggests that the symbolic revolution may have occurred before the arrival of the first modern humans in Europe." If she is right, it would push back the date of the creative explosion by tens of thousands of years.

The idea would seem to fit with a few tantalising finds that have emerged from Africa and the Middle East over recent years. At Blombos cave on South Africa's southern Cape, for example, archaeologists have recently discovered pieces of haematite (an iron oxide used to make red pigment) engraved with abstract designs that are at least 75,000 years old (*Science,* vol 323, p 569). Meanwhile, at the Skhul rock shelter in Israel, there are shell beads considered by some to be personal ornaments and evidence for symbolic behaviour as far back as 100,000 years ago (*Science,* vol 312, p 1785).

Further evidence may well come from caves elsewhere in the world, and indeed a tentative look at the existing records suggests that many of von Petzinger's symbols crop up in other places. The open angle symbol, for example, can be seen on the engravings at Blombos cave.

Does this suggest that these symbols travelled with prehistoric tribes as they migrated from Africa? Von Petzinger and Nowell think so. Davidson, on the other hand, who has identified 18 of these symbols in Australia, is unconvinced that they have a common origin, maintaining that the creative explosion occurred independently in different parts of the globe around 40,000 years ago. Instead, he thinks the symbols reveal something about a change in the way people thought and viewed their world, which may have emerged around this time. "I believe that there was a cognitive change, which suddenly put art into people's heads," he says.

Clottes, however, thinks they could be on to something. "Language and abstract thought were probably practised long before 35,000 years ago, since 'modern humans' are some 200,000 years old. We shouldn't be surprised by the sophistication of these people's thinking: they were our great-great-grandparents after all," he says.

But if people really did have a symbolic culture this far back, why don't we find more evidence pre-dating 40,000 years ago? "Perhaps the earlier symbols tended to be carved into perishable things such as wood and skins, which have now disintegrated," says von Petzinger. And even if they did paint in caves many of the rock surfaces will have eroded away by now.

Whenever these symbols did emerge, the acceptance of symbolic representation would have been a turning point for these cultures. For one thing, it would have been the first time they could permanently store information. "Symbols enabled people to share information beyond an individual lifespan. It was a watershed moment," says Nowell.

One huge question remains, of course: what did the symbols actually mean? With no Rosetta Stone to act as a key for translation, the best we can do is guess at their purpose. Clottes has a hunch that they were much more than everyday jottings, and could have had spiritual significance. "They may have been a way of relating to supernatural forces. Perhaps they had special symbols for special ceremonies, or they may have been associated with the telling of special myths," he says.

One intriguing aspect is their possible use in deception. "Once symbolic utterances are recognised, communication becomes more flexible," says Davidson. "One result is that ambiguity can be introduced for concealing truths."

With no key to interpret these symbols, though, we can't know whether ancient humans were giving false directions to rival tribes or simply bragging about their hunting prowess. Our ancestor's secrets remain safe—at least for now.

Doodler or da Vinci?

When our ancestors painted beautiful works of art, were they intending them to be viewed by others, or did they just paint for their own pleasure?

The Lascaux caves, in the Dordogne region of France, may have the answer. There you can see a painting of a red cow with a black head high on one of the walls. Up close the cow appears to be stretched from head to toe, but when viewed from the ground the cow regains normal proportions. This technique, known as anamorphosis, is highly advanced, and suggests the painter was considering his audience as he painted the cow.

Our ancestors probably took the quality of their work very seriously. Recent work by Suzanne Villeneuve, from the University of Victoria in British Columbia, Canada, shows that the images painted with the most skill tend to occur in places where large numbers of people would have been able to see them, while poorer-quality images were more likely to be in smaller cubby holes. In most cases it seems that only the "Leonardos" of the day were allowed to paint the big spaces.

Critical Thinking

1. What has been the accepted view regarding our ancestors' "creative explosion" as reflected in their cave paintings?
2. When did writing begin and in what form?
3. What was the ambitious project devised by Genevieve von Petzinger? What emerged from her study?
4. What is the significance of the synecdoche? What are the examples cited?
5. What was the "real clincher" for von Petzinger? What is one of the most frequent pairings? Why is it claimed that this may be one of the first glimpses of a rudimentary language system?
6. What is the time range of the signs and how do they rank in terms of frequency?
7. Where did the signs in France originate? Why do they not show up in the north?
8. Why was von Petzinger surprised to find that more than three quarters of the symbols were present over 30,000 years ago? What does this suggest, according to von Petzinger? What "tantalizing finds" from Africa and the Middle East seem to fit with this idea?
9. What is the significance of the fact that many of the symbols crop up in other parts of the world, according to von Petzinger and Nowell? Why does Davidson disagree? What does he propose as an alternative?
10. Why does Clottes think that von Petzinger and Novell might be "on to something"?
11. If people had symbolic culture before 40,000 years ago, why is there not more evidence for it, according to von Petzinger?
12. What would such symbolic representations enable people to do, according to Nowell?
13. When our ancestors painted beautiful works of art, were they intending them to be viewed by others, or did they just paint them for their own pleasure? What evidence is there that they took their work seriously?

Rethinking the Hobbits of Indonesia

KATE WONG

New analyses reveal the mini human species to be even stranger than previously thought and hint that major tenets of human evolution need revision.

In 2004 a team of Australian and Indonesian scientists who had been excavating a cave called Liang Bua on the Indonesian island of Flores announced that they had unearthed something extraordinary: a partial skeleton of an adult human female who would have stood just over a meter tall and who had a brain a third as large as our own. The specimen, known to scientists as LB1, quickly received a fanciful nickname—the hobbit, after writer J.R.R. Tolkien's fictional creatures. The team proposed that LB1 and the other fragmentary remains they recovered represent a previously unknown human species, *Homo floresiensis*. Their best guess was that *H. floresiensis* was a descendant of *H. erectus*—the first species known to have colonized outside of Africa. The creature evolved its small size, they surmised, as a response to the limited resources available on its island home—a phenomenon that had previously been documented in other mammals, but never humans.

The finding jolted the paleoanthropological community. Not only was *H. floresiensis* being held up as the first example of a human following the so-called island rule, but it also seemed to reverse a trend toward ever larger brain size over the course of human evolution. Furthermore, the same deposits in which the small-bodied, small-brained individuals were found also yielded stone tools for hunting and butchering animals, as well as remainders of fires for cooking them—rather advanced behaviors for a creature with a brain the size of a chimpanzee's. And astonishingly, LB1 lived just 18,000 years ago—thousands of years after our other late-surviving relatives, the Neandertals and *H. erectus,* disappeared [see "The Littlest Human," by Kate Wong; *Scientific American,* February 2005].

Skeptics were quick to dismiss LB1 as nothing more than a modern human with a disease that stunted her growth. And since the announcement of the discovery, they have proposed a number of possible conditions to explain the specimen's peculiar features, from cretinism to Laron syndrome, a genetic disease that causes insensitivity to growth hormone. Their arguments have failed to convince the hobbit proponents, however, who have countered each diagnosis with evidence to the contrary.

A Perplexing Pastiche

Nevertheless, new analyses are causing even the proponents to rethink important aspects of the original interpretation of the discovery. The recent findings are also forcing paleoanthropologists to reconsider established views of such watershed moments in human evolution as the initial migration out of Africa by hominins (the group that includes all the creatures in the human line since it branched away from chimps).

Perhaps the most startling realization to emerge from the latest studies is how very primitive LB1's body is in many respects. (To date, excavators have recovered the bones of an estimated 14 individuals from the site, but LB1 remains the most complete specimen by far.) From the outset, the specimen has invited comparisons to the 3.2-million-year-old Lucy—the best-known representative of a human ancestor called *Australopithecus afarensis*—because they were about the same height and had similarly small brains. But it turns out LB1 has much more than size in common with Lucy and other pre-erectus hominins. And a number of her features are downright apelike.

A particularly striking example of the bizarre morphology of the hobbits surfaced this past May, when researchers led by William L. Jungers of Stony Brook University published their analysis of LB1's foot. The foot has a few modern features—for instance, the big toe is aligned with the other toes, as opposed to splaying out to the side as it does in apes and australopithecines. But by and large, it is old-fashioned. Measuring around 20 centimeters in length, LB1's foot is 70 percent as long as her short thighbone, a ratio unheard of for a member of the human family. The foot of a modern human, in contrast, is on average 55 percent as long as the femur. The closest match to LB1 in this regard, aside from, perhaps, the large-footed hobbits of Tolkien's imagination, is a bonobo. Furthermore, LB1's big toe is short, her other toes are long and slightly curved, and her foot lacks a proper arch—all primitive traits.

"A foot like this one has never been seen before in the human fossil record," Jungers declared in a statement released to the press. It would not have made running easy. Characteristics of the pelvis, leg and foot make clear that the hobbits walked upright. But with their short legs and relatively long feet, they would have had to use a high-stepping gait to avoid dragging their toes on the ground. Thus, although they could probably sprint short distances—say, to avoid becoming dinner for one of the Komodo dragons that patrolled Flores—they would not have won any marathons.

If the foot were the only part of the hobbit to exhibit such primitive traits, scientists might have an easier time upholding the idea that *H. floresiensis* is a dwarfed descendant of *H. erectus* and just chalking the foot morphology up to an evolutionary reversal that occurred as a consequence of dwarfing. But the fact is that archaic features are found throughout the entire skeleton of LB1. A bone in the wrist called the trapezoid, which in our own species is shaped like a boot, is instead shaped like a pyramid, as it is in apes; the clavicle is short and quite curved, in contrast to the longer, straighter clavicle that occurs in hominins of modern body form; the pelvis is basin-shaped, as in australopithecines, rather than funnel-shaped, as in *H. erectus* and other later *Homo* species. The list goes on.

Indeed, from the neck down LB1 looks more like Lucy and the other australopithecines than *Homo*. But then there is the complicated matter of her skull. Although it encased a grapefruit-size brain measuring just 417 cubic centimeters—a volume within the range of chimpanzees and australopithecines—other cranial features, such as the narrow nose and prominent brow arches over each eye socket, mark LB1 as a member of our genus, *Homo*.

Primitive Roots

Fossils that combine *Homo*-like skull characteristics with primitive traits in the trunk and limbs are not unprecedented. The earliest members of our genus, such as *H. habilis*, also exhibit a hodgepodge of old and new. Thus, as details of the hobbits' postcranial skeletons have emerged, researchers have increasingly wondered whether the little Floresians might belong to a primitive *Homo* species, rather than having descended from *H. erectus*, which scientists believe had modern body proportions.

A new analysis conducted by doctoral candidate Debbie Argue of the Australian National University in Canberra and her colleagues bolsters this view. To tackle the problem of how the hobbits are related to other members of the human family, the team employed cladistics—a method that looks at shared, novel traits to work out relationships among organisms—comparing anatomical characteristics of LB1 to those of other members of the human family, as well as apes.

In a paper in press at the *Journal of Human Evolution*, Argue and her collaborators report that their results suggest two possible positions for the *H. floresiensis* branch of the hominin family tree. The first is that *H. floresiensis* evolved after a hominin called *H. rudolfensis*, which arose some 2.3 million years ago but before *H. habilis*, which appeared roughly two million years ago. The second is that it emerged after *H. habilis* but still well before *H. erectus*, which arose around 1.8 million years ago. More important, Argue's team found no support for a close relationship between *H. floresiensis* and *H. erectus*, thereby dealing a blow to the theory that the hobbits were the product of island dwarfing of *H. erectus*. (The study also rejected the hypothesis that hobbits belong to our own species.)

If the hobbits are a very early species of *Homo* that predates *H. erectus*, that positioning on the family tree would go a long way toward accounting for LB1's tiny brain, because the earliest members of our genus had significantly less gray matter than the average *H. erectus* possessed. But Argue's findings do not solve the brain problem entirely. LB1 aside, the smallest known noggin in the genus *Homo* is a *H. habilis* specimen with an estimated cranial capacity of 509 cubic centimeters. LB1's brain was some 20 percent smaller than that.

Could island dwarfing still have played a role in determining the size of the hobbit's brain?

When the discovery team first attributed LB1's wee brain to this phenomenon, critics complained that her brain was far smaller than it should be for a hominin of her body size, based on known scaling relationships. Mammals that undergo dwarfing typically exhibit only moderate reduction in brain size. But study results released this past May suggest that dwarfing of mammals on islands may present a special case. Eleanor Weston and Adrian Lister of the Natural History Museum in London found that in several species of fossil hippopotamus that became dwarfed on the African island nation of Madagascar, brain size shrank significantly more than predicted by standard scaling models. Based on their hippo model, the study authors contend, even an ancestor the size of *H. erectus* could conceivably attain the brain and body proportions of LB1 through island dwarfing.

The work on hippos has impressed researchers such as Harvard University's Daniel Lieberman. In a commentary accompanying Weston and Lister's report in *Nature*, Lieberman wrote that their findings "come to the rescue" in terms of explaining how *H. floresiensis* got such a small brain.

Although some specialists favor the original interpretation of the hobbits, Mike Morwood of the University of Wollongong in Australia, who helps to coordinate the Liang Bua project, now thinks the ancestors of LB1 and the gang were early members of *Homo* who were already small—much smaller than even the tiniest known *H. erectus* individuals—when they arrived on Flores and then "maybe underwent a little insular dwarfing" once they got there.

Artifacts left behind by the hobbits support the claim that *H. floresiensis* is a very primitive hominin. Early reports on the initial discovery focused on the few stone tools found in the hobbit levels at Liang Bua that were surprisingly sophisticated for a such a small-brained creature—an observation that skeptics highlighted to support their contention that the hobbits were modern humans, not a new species. But subsequent analyses led by Mark W. Moore of the University of New England in Australia and Adam R. Brumm of the University of Cambridge have revealed the hobbit toolkit to be overall quite basic and in line with the implements produced by other small-brained hominins. The advanced appearance of a handful of the hobbit tools at Liang Bua, Moore and Brumm concluded, was produced by chance, which is not unexpected considering that the hobbits manufactured thousands of implements.

To make their tools, the hobbits removed large flakes from rocks outside the cave and then struck smaller flakes off the large flakes inside the cave, employing the same simple stone-working techniques favored by humans at another site on Flores 50 kilometers east of Liang Bua called Mata Menge 880,000 years ago—long before modern humans showed up on the island. (The identity of the Mata Menge toolmakers is unknown, because no human remains have turned up there yet, but they conceivably could be the ancestors of the diminutive residents of Liang Bua.) Furthermore, the Liang Bua and Mata Menge tools bear a striking resemblance to artifacts from Olduvai Gorge in Tanzania that date to between 1.2 million and 1.9 million years ago and were probably manufactured by *H. habilis*.

Tiny Trailblazer

In some ways, the latest theory about the enigmatic Flores bones is even more revolutionary than the original claim. "The possibility that a very primitive member of the genus *Homo* left Africa, perhaps roughly two million years ago, and that a descendant population persisted until only several thousand years ago, is one of the more provocative hypotheses to have emerged in paleoanthropology during the past few years," reflects David S. Strait of the University at Albany. Scientists have long believed that *H. erectus* was the first member of the human family to march out of the natal continent and colonize new lands, because that is the hominin whose remains appear outside of Africa earliest in the fossil record. In explanation, it was proposed that humans needed to evolve large brains and long striding limbs and to invent sophisticated technology before they could finally leave their homeland.

Today the oldest unequivocal evidence of humans outside of Africa comes from the Republic of Georgia, where researchers have recovered *H. erectus* remains dating to 1.78 million years ago [see "Stranger in a New Land," by Kate Wong; *Scientific American*, November 2003]. The discovery of the Georgian remains dispelled that notion of a brawny trailblazer with a tricked-out toolkit, because they were on the small side for *H. erectus*, and they made Oldowan tools, rather than the advanced, so-called Acheulean implements experts expected the first pioneers to make. Nevertheless, they were *H. erectus*.

But if proponents of the new view of hobbits are right, the first intercontinental migrations were undertaken hundreds of thousands of years earlier than that—and by a fundamentally different kind of human, one that arguably had more in common with primitive little Lucy than the colonizer paleoanthropologists had envisioned. This scenario implies that scientists could conceivably locate a long-lost chapter of human prehistory in the form of a two-million-year record of this primitive pioneer stretching between Africa and Southeast Asia if they look in the right places.

This suggestion does not sit well with some researchers. "The further back we try to push the divergence of the Flores [hominin], the more difficult it becomes to explain why a [hominin] lineage that must have originated in Africa has left only one trace on the tiny island of Flores," comments primate evolution expert Robert Martin of the Field Museum in Chicago. Martin remains unconvinced that *H. floresiensis* is a legitimate new species. In his view, the possibility that LB1—the only hobbit whose brain size is known—was a modern human with an as yet unidentified disorder that gave rise to a small brain has not been ruled out. The question, he says, is whether such a condition can also explain the australopithecine like body of LB1.

In the meantime, many scientists are welcoming the shakeup. LB1 is "a hominin that no one would be saying anything about if we found it in Africa two million years ago," asserts Matthew W. Tocheri of the Smithsonian Institution, who has analyzed the wrist bones of the hobbits. "The problem is that we're finding it in Indonesia in essentially modern times." The good news, he adds, is that it suggests more such finds remain to be recovered.

"Given how little we know about the Asian hominin record, there is plenty of room for surprises," observes

Digging for Hobbits

Field Notes

Liang Bua is a large limestone cave located in the lush highlands of western Flores. Beyond the remains of some 14 hobbits, excavations there have yielded thousands of stone tools, as well as the bones of Komodo dragons, elephant-like stegodonts, giant rats and a carnivorous bird that stood some three meters high. The hobbits seem to have occupied the cave from around 100,000 to 17,000 years ago. They may have been drawn to Liang Bua because of its proximity to the Wae Racang River, which would have attracted thirsty prey animals. Researchers are now looking for clues to why, after persisting for so long, the hobbits eventually vanished. They are also eager to recover a second small skull. Such a find would establish that LB1 and the other specimens do indeed represent a new species and are not just the remains of diseased modern humans. Bones and teeth containing DNA suitable for analysis would be likewise informative.

Sick Human Hypotheses

Scientists who doubt that LB1 belongs to a new human species argue that she is simply a modern human with a disease resulting in a small body and small brain. Those who think LB1 does represent a new species, however, have presented anatomical evidence against each of the proposed diagnoses, several of which are listed below.

- Laron syndrome, a genetic disease that causes insensitivity to growth hormone.
- Myxoedematous endemic cretinism, a condition that arises from prenatal nutritional deficiencies that hinder the thyroid.
- Microcephalic osteodysplastic primordial dwarfism type II, a genetic disorder whose victims have small bodies and small brains but nearly normal intelligence.

A Mysterious Mosaic

The Evidence

To date, excavators have recovered the remains of about 14 individuals from Liang Bua, a cave site on Flores. The most complete specimen is a nearly complete skeleton called LB1 that dates to 18,000 years ago. Some of its characteristics call to mind those of apes and of australopithecines such as the 3.2-million-year-old Lucy. Other traits, however, are in keeping with those of our own genus, *Homo*. This mélange of primitive features and modern ones has made it difficult to figure out where on the human family tree the hobbits belong.

Homo traits

Thick braincase
Small teeth
Short face

Ape and australopithecine traits

Robust lower jaw
Broad, flaring pelvis
Short thighbone
Short shinbone

BRAIN is the size of a chimpanzee's. But a virtual reconstruction—generated from CT scans of the interior of the braincase—indicates that despite its small size, the organ had a number of advanced features, including an enlarged Broadmann area 10, a part of the brain that has been theorized to play a role in complex cognitive activities. Such features may help explain how a creature with a brain the size of a chimp's was able to make stone tools.

WRIST resembles ape. Of particular called the trapezoid, which has a pyramidal form. Modern humans, in contrast, have a trapezoid shaped like a boot, which facilitates tool manufacture and use by better distributing forces across the hand.

FOOT is exceptionally long compared with the short leg. This relative foot length is comparable to that seen in bonobos, and it suggests the hobbits were inefficient runners. Other apelike traits include long, curved toes and the absence of an arch. Yet the big toe aligns with the rest of the toes, among other modern characteristics.

Did *Homo sapiens* Copy Hobbits?

Analysis of hobbit implements spanning the time from 95,000 to 17,000 years ago indicates that the tiny toolmakers used the same so-called Oldowan techniques that human ancestors in Africa employed nearly two million years ago. The hobbits combined these techniques in distinctive ways, however—a tradition that the modern humans who inhabited Liang Bua starting 11,000 years ago followed, too. This finding raises the intriguing possibility that the two species made contact and that *H. sapiens* copied the hobbits' style of tool manufacture, rather than the other way around.

The Hobbits' Roots

Findings

Researchers originally believed that LB1 and the other hobbits, formally known as *Homo floresiensis,* were descendants of a human ancestor with essentially modern body proportions known as *H. erectus* that shrank dramatically in response to the limited resources available on their island home. But a new analysis suggests *H. floresiensis* is significantly more primitive than *H. erectus* and evolved either right after one of the earliest known members of our genus, *H. habilis* or right before it. Either way, the study implies that *H. floresiensis* evolved in Africa, along with the other early *Homo* species, and was already fairly small when the species reached Flores, although it may have undergone some dwarfing when it got there.

Blazing a Trail

The textbook account of human origins holds that *H. erectus* was the first human ancestor to wander out of Africa and colonize distant lands around 1.8 million years ago. But the evidence from Flores suggests that an older, more primitive forebear was the original pioneer, one who ventured away from the natal continent perhaps around two million years ago. If so, then paleoanthropologists may have missed a significant chunk of the human fossil record spanning nearly two million years and stretching from Africa to Southeast Asia.

Already hobbit hunter Mike Morwood is looking for more remains of *H. floresiensis* and its ancestors at two sites on Sulawesi. And he thinks further excavation at Niah cave in north Borneo could produce evidence of hominins much older than the ones at Liang Bua. The mainland will be harder to comb, because rocks of the right age are rarely exposed there.

Robin W. Dennell of the University of Sheffield in England. Dennell has postulated that even the australopithecines might have left Africa, because the grasslands they had colonized in Africa by three million years ago extended into Asia. "What we need, of course, are more discoveries—from Flores, neighboring islands such as Sulawesi, mainland Southeast Asia or anywhere else in Asia," he says.

Morwood, for his part, is attempting to do just that. In addition to the work at Liang Bua and Mata Menge, he is helping to coordinate two projects on Sulawesi. And he is eyeing Borneo, too. Searching the mainland for the ancestors of the Liang Bua hobbits will be difficult, however, because rocks of the right age are rarely exposed in this part of the world. But with stakes this high, such challenges are unlikely to prevent intrepid fossil hunters from trying. "If we don't find something in the next 15 years or so in that part of the world, I might start wondering whether we got this wrong," Tocheri reflects. "The predictions are that we should find a whole bunch more."

More to Explore

The Primitive Wrist of *Homo floresiensis* and Its Implications for Hominin Evolution. Matthew W. Tocheri et al. in *Science*, Vol. 317, pages 1743–1745; September 21, 2007.

A New Human: The Startling Discovery and Strange Story of the "Hobbits" of Flores, Indonesia. Mike Morwood and Penny van Oosterzee. *Smithsonian*, 2007.

The Foot of *Homo floresiensis*. W. L. Jungers et al. in *Nature*, Vol. 459, pages 81–84; May 7, 2009.

Homo floresiensis and the African Oldowan. Mark W. Moore and Adam R. Brumm in *Interdisciplinary Approaches to the Oldowan*. Edited by Erella Hovers and David R. Braun. Springer, 2009.

Homo floresiensis: A Cladistic Analysis. Debbie Argue et al. in *Journal of Human Evolution* (in press).

LB1's Virtual Endocast, Microcephaly and Hominin Brain Evolution. Dean Falk et al. in *Journal of Human Evolution* (in press).

Critical Thinking

1. Based upon the initial description of *Homo floresiensis,* what was the discoverers' "best guess" about why it looked the way it did?
2. Why did it jolt the anthropological community?
3. How did the skeptics respond?
4. What is it about the foot that is "bizarre"? How would running have been affected?
5. What are some of the other archaic features of the skeleton? What marks it as a member of our genus, *Homo*?
6. What are the two possible positions offered by Debbie Argue and her colleagues? What would this mean with respect to the idea that *H. floresiensis* is a descendant of *H. erectus* and is the result of island dwarfing? In what sense could island dwarfing still play a role and why?
7. What do the artifacts indicate with respect to the claim that *H. floresiensis* is a very primitive hominin? How are the few "sophisticated" tools to be explained?
8. If *H. floresiensis* is a very primitive hominin, how would this idea be even more revolutionary than the original claim?
9. What is the oldest unequivocal evidence of humans outside of Africa? What notion does it dispel and why?
10. What does the new scenario mean and what does it imply? Why does this suggestion not "sit well with some researchers"?
11. What is primate evolution expert Robert Martin's view? What does it perhaps not explain?
12. Why does Robin W. Dennell think that even some australopithecines might have left Africa? What is needed to shed light on the issue? What are the predictions?

UNIT 5

Historical Archaeology

Unit Selections

Learning Outcomes

After reading this Unit, you will be able to:

- Define historical archaeology and discuss examples.
- Summarize the evidence for the early development of medicine.
- Discuss the Sphinx in terms of its importance to understanding the Old Kingdom of Egypt and what ultimately happened to it.
- Discuss the importance of the emperors' villas to the Roman economy and to the ultimate downfall of the Roman Empire.
- Explain why Rome felt it had to destroy Carthage.
- Explain how the Incas become the organizational geniuses of the Americas.
- Explain how the Donner Pass story is an example of cultural/historical reconstruction, even though it is not strictly archaeology.

Student Website

www.mhhe.com/cls

Internet References

NOVA Online/Pyramids—The Inside Story

www.pbs.org/wgbh/nova/pyramid

Society for Historical Archaeology

www.sha.org

How many times have you misplaced your car keys? Locked yourself out of the house? Lost your wallet? Your address book? Eye glasses? Sometimes these artifacts are recovered and brought back into the historical present. Sometimes they are lost forever, becoming part of the garbage of an extinct culture. Have you ever noticed that lost things, when found, are always in the last place you look? Is this a law of science? Be skeptical. Here is an opportunity to practice historical archaeology. You may wish to try this puzzler in order to practice thinking like an archaeologist. (Do not forget to apply the basics discussed in Unit 1.) The incident recounted here is true. Only the names, dates, and places are changed to protect the privacy of the famous personages involved in this highly-charged mystery.

Problem: Dr. Wheeler, a British archaeologist at a large university left his office on Friday December 17, 2003, around 10 P.M. on a cold Friday evening. This was his last night to be at the university because he would not be back again until after the holidays.

Right before he left his office, he placed a thin, reddish, three-ring notebook in an unlocked cupboard.

Dr. Wheeler then proceeded to go directly to his designated campus parking space, got into his Mini Cooper S, and drove directly to his flat in Marshalltown Goldens. When he arrived home, he went straightaway to his study. He remained at his flat with his family and never left his flat during the entire holiday.

Dr. Wheeler and his family had a jolly good holiday, and Dr. Wheeler thought nothing more of his notebook until the university resumed its session on Wednesday, January 5, 2004, at the beginning of the New Year.

Upon returning to his office, Dr. Wheeler could not find his notebook in the cupboard, and he became very agitated. He chased his assistant, Miss Mortimer, around the office, wielding a wicked looking Acheulean hand ax. Poor Miss Mortimer claimed that she had no knowledge of the whereabouts of the notebook.

But Dr. Wheeler had always suspected that Miss Mortimer pinched pens and pencils from his desk, so, naturally. . . . But Miss Mortimer protested so earnestly that Dr. Wheeler eventually settled in, had a cup of tea, and decided that perhaps he had absentmindedly taken the notebook home after all.

However, a thorough search of his flat indicated that the notebook was clearly not there. It was lost! Dr. Wheeler had almost lost himself when his wife, Sophia, caught him excavating her rose garden in the vain hope that Tut, the family dog, had buried the lost article there. It was a professor's nightmare; the notebook contained the only copy of all his class records for the entire term. What could he do? He knew he was in danger of being fired for incompetence.

So, Dr. Wheeler approached the problem in the manner of a proper, eccentric archaeologist. He had another cup of tea and generated several hypotheses about where his notebook might have gone. He tested several hypotheses, but to no avail!

His notebook still remained missing. However, being the good archaeologist he was, he kept on generating hypotheses. But his notebook was still not found. Then he began to wonder if maybe the post-processualists weren't right after all!

© Author's Image/PunchStock

Dr. Wheeler was at his wits' end when, pure luck intervened, as it often does in archaeology. You just get lucky sometimes. Everyone does. His faithful assistant Miss Mortimer received a phone call on January 9, 2004, from a woman who had found the missing notebook on the evening of December 31, 2003. The helpful lady found his notebook in a gutter! To be precise, she found it in a family neighborhood located on the corner of Olduvai Drive and East Turkana Avenue in Hadar Heights, about a mile away from the university. Please note that this area is in the opposite direction from Dr. Wheeler's flat in Marshalltown Goldens. The notebook was wet and muddy, and furthermore, it was wedged down into a gutter grill in the street.

Greatly relieved, the next day, January 10, 2004, Dr. Wheeler had Miss Mortimer run over to the kind woman's flat. It was in this mysterious way that he recouped his class records. Dr. Wheeler was so delighted that when Miss Mortimer returned with the notebook, he invited her to sit and join him for a pot of tea (which was not his habit, being a misogynist). Yet, Dr. Wheeler was not satisfied with merely recovering his notebook. He was curious to know what had happened to it and why! He continued to generate more sophisticated hypotheses to solve the mystery.

Challenge to the Student

Try to place yourself in Dr. Wheeler's position. Attempt to generate your own hypotheses as to the whereabouts of the lost notebook from the night of Friday, December 17, 2003, to the time of its return on January 10, 2004.

How do you go about doing this? First, review everything you "believe" to be true. Be very careful and skeptical about what is true and what is not. Then convert this into your original database. From that point, again set up more hypotheses and/or make alternative hypotheses until you arrive at the simplest possible explanation. The simplest possible explanation is most likely to be the correct answer. Support your answer with your database.

Pretend that you are doing historical archaeology. Ask your living informant(s) for information first. What could you ask Dr. Wheeler? You could ask, "Did you go back to the lavatory before you left the building on December 17, 2003? Are you sure of where your motorcar was parked or could you be mistaken? What was the weather like? Was it raining? Is it possible that you in fact stopped and talked to someone on your way to your motorcar? Are you sure you were home on December 31, 2003 and not out to celebrate the New Year?" Be very precise with your questioning. Also, let your imagination run wild with possibilities. Brainstorm. Sometimes this is when you are most likely to get the answer. Creativity is the essence of all science.

Hints

Dr. Wheeler's university office was never broken into. Poor Miss Mortimer and the kind lady who found the notebook had nothing to do with the disappearance of the notebook. Dr. Wheeler's dog Tut did not bury his notebook. So what did happen? There is, in fact a correct answer that will explain the mystery. Try to find that answer! To do this, you will have to think like an archaeologist. It is a lot of fun, and it will reward you well!

Uncovering Secrets of the Sphinx

Who built it? Why? And how? After decades of research, American archaeologist Mark Lehner has answers.

EVAN HADINGHAM

When Mark Lehner was a teenager in the late 1960s, his parents introduced him to the writings of the famed clairvoyant Edgar Cayce. During one of his trances, Cayce, who died in 1945, saw that refugees from the lost city of Atlantis buried their secrets in a hall of records under the Sphinx and that the hall would be discovered before the end of the 20th century.

In 1971, Lehner, a bored sophomore at the University of North Dakota, wasn't planning to search for lost civilizations, but he was "looking for something, a meaningful involvement." He dropped out of school, began hitchhiking and ended up in Virginia Beach, where he sought out Cayce's son, Hugh Lynn, the head of a holistic medicine and paranormal research foundation his father had started. When the foundation sponsored a group tour of the Giza plateau—the site of the Sphinx and the pyramids on the western outskirts of Cairo—Lehner tagged along. "It was hot and dusty and not very majestic," he remembers.

Still, he returned, finishing his undergraduate education at the American University of Cairo with support from Cayce's foundation. Even as he grew skeptical about a lost hall of records, the site's strange history exerted its pull. "There were thousands of tombs of real people, statues of real people with real names, and none of them figured in the Cayce stories," he says.

Lehner married an Egyptian woman and spent the ensuing years plying his drafting skills to win work mapping archaeological sites all over Egypt. In 1977, he joined Stanford Research Institute scientists using state-of-the-art remote-sensing equipment to analyze the bedrock under the Sphinx. They found only the cracks and fissures expected of ordinary limestone formations. Working closely with a young Egyptian archaeologist named Zahi Hawass, Lehner also explored and mapped a passage in the Sphinx's rump, concluding that treasure hunters likely had dug it after the statue was built.

No human endeavor has been more associated with mystery than the huge, ancient lion that has a human head and is seemingly resting on the rocky plateau a stroll from the great pyramids. Fortunately for Lehner, it wasn't just a metaphor that the Sphinx is a riddle. Little was known for certain about who erected it or when, what it represented and precisely how it related to the pharaonic monuments nearby. So Lehner settled in, working for five years out of a makeshift office between the Sphinx's colossal paws, subsisting on Nescafé and cheese sandwiches while he examined every square inch of the structure. He remembers "climbing all over the Sphinx like the Lilliputians on Gulliver, and mapping it stone by stone." The result was a uniquely detailed picture of the statue's worn, patched surface, which had been subjected to at least five major restoration efforts since 1,400 B.C. The research earned him a doctorate in Egyptology at Yale.

Recognized today as one of the world's leading Egyptologists and Sphinx authorities, Lehner has conducted field research at Giza during most of the 37 years since his first visit. (Hawass, his friend and frequent collaborator, is the secretary general of the Egyptian Supreme Council of Antiquities and controls access to the Sphinx, the pyramids and other government-owned sites and artifacts.) Applying his archaeological sleuthing to the surrounding two-square-mile Giza plateau with its pyramids, temples, quarries and thousands of tombs, Lehner helped confirm what others had speculated—that some parts of the Giza complex, the Sphinx included, make up a vast sacred machine designed to harness the power of the sun to sustain the earthly and divine order. And while he long ago gave up on the fabled library of Atlantis, it's curious, in light of his early wanderings, that he finally did discover a Lost City.

The sphinx was not assembled piece by piece but was carved from a single mass of limestone exposed when workers dug a horseshoe-shaped quarry in the Giza plateau. Approximately 66 feet tall and 240 feet long, it is one of the largest and oldest monolithic statues in the world. None of the photos or sketches I'd seen prepared me for the scale. It was a humbling sensation to stand between the creature's paws, each twice my height and longer than a city bus. I gained sudden empathy for what a mouse must feel like when cornered by a cat.

Nobody knows its original name. Sphinx is the human-headed lion in ancient Greek mythology; the term likely came into use some 2,000 years after the statue was built. There are hundreds of tombs at Giza with hieroglyphic inscriptions dating back some 4,500 years, but not one mentions the statue. "The Egyptians didn't write history," says James Allen, an Egyptologist at Brown University, "so we have no solid evidence for what its builders thought the Sphinx was. . . . Certainly something divine, presumably the image of a king, but beyond that is anyone's guess." Likewise, the statue's symbolism is unclear, though inscriptions from the era refer to Ruti, a double lion god that sat at the entrance to the underworld and guarded the horizon where the sun rose and set.

The face, though better preserved than most of the statue, has been battered by centuries of weathering and vandalism. In 1402, an Arab historian reported that a Sufi zealot had disfigured it "to remedy some religious errors." Yet there are clues to what the face looked like in its prime. Archaeological excavations in the early 19th century found pieces of its carved stone beard and a royal cobra emblem from its headdress. Residues of red pigment are still visible on the face, leading researchers to conclude that at some point, the Sphinx's entire visage was painted red. Traces of blue and yellow paint elsewhere suggest to Lehner that the Sphinx was once decked out in gaudy comic book colors.

For thousands of years, sand buried the colossus up to its shoulders, creating a vast disembodied head atop the eastern edge of the Sahara. Then, in 1817, a Genoese adventurer, Capt. Giovanni Battista Caviglia, led 160 men in the first modern attempt to dig out the Sphinx. They could not hold back the sand, which poured into their excavation pits nearly as fast as they could dig it out. The Egyptian archaeologist Selim Hassan finally freed the statue from the sand in the late 1930s. "The Sphinx has thus emerged into the landscape out of shadows of what seemed to be an impenetrable oblivion," *The New York Times* declared.

The question of who built the Sphinx has long vexed Egyptologists and archaeologists. Lehner, Hawass and others agree it was Pharaoh Khafre, who ruled Egypt during the Old Kingdom, which began around 2,600 B.C. and lasted some 500 years before giving way to civil war and famine. It's known from hieroglyphic texts that Khafre's father, Khufu, built the 481-foot-tall Great Pyramid, a quarter mile from where the Sphinx would later be built. Khafre, following a tough act, constructed his own pyramid, ten feet shorter than his father's, also a quarter of a mile behind the Sphinx. Some of the evidence linking Khafre with the Sphinx comes from Lehner's research, but the idea dates back to 1853.

That's when a French archaeologist named Auguste Mariette unearthed a life-size statue of Khafre, carved with startling realism from black volcanic rock, amid the ruins of a building he discovered adjacent to the Sphinx that would later be called the Valley Temple. What's more, Mariette found the remnants of a stone causeway—a paved, processional road—connecting the Valley Temple to a mortuary temple next to Khafre's pyramid. Then, in 1925, French archaeologist and engineer Emile Baraize probed the sand directly in front of the Sphinx and discovered yet another Old Kingdom building—now called the Sphinx Temple—strikingly similar in its ground plan to the ruins Mariette had already found.

Despite these clues that a single master building plan tied the Sphinx to Khafre's pyramid and his temples, some experts continued to speculate that Khufu or other pharaohs had built the statue. Then, in 1980, Lehner recruited a young German geologist, Tom Aigner, who suggested a novel way of showing that the Sphinx was an integral part of Khafre's larger building complex. Limestone is the result of mud, coral and the shells of plankton-like creatures compressed together over tens of millions of years. Looking at samples from the Sphinx Temple and the Sphinx itself, Aigner and Lehner inventoried the different fossils making up the limestone. The fossil fingerprints showed that the blocks used to build the wall of the temple must have come from the ditch surrounding the Sphinx. Apparently, workmen, probably using ropes and wooden sledges, hauled away the quarried blocks to construct the temple as the Sphinx was being carved out of the stone.

That Khafre arranged for construction of his pyramid, the temples and the Sphinx seems increasingly likely. "Most scholars believe, as I do," Hawass wrote in his 2006 book, *Mountain of the Pharaohs,* "that the Sphinx represents Khafre and forms an integral part of his pyramid complex."

But who carried out the backbreaking work of creating the Sphinx? In 1990, an American tourist was riding in the desert half a mile south of the Sphinx when she was thrown from her horse after it stumbled on a low mud-brick wall. Hawass investigated and discovered an Old Kingdom cemetery. Some 600 people were buried there, with tombs belonging to overseers—identified by inscriptions recording their names and titles—surrounded by the humbler tombs of ordinary laborers.

Near the cemetery, nine years later, Lehner discovered his Lost City. He and Hawass had been aware since the mid-1980s that there were buildings at that site. But it wasn't until they excavated and mapped the area that they realized it was a settlement bigger than ten football fields and dating to Khafre's reign. At its heart were four clusters of eight long mud-brick barracks. Each structure had the elements of an ordinary house—a pillared porch, sleeping platforms and a kitchen—that was enlarged to accommodate around 50 people sleeping side by side. The barracks, Lehner says, could have accommodated between 1,600 to 2,000 workers—or more, if the sleeping quarters were on two levels. The workers' diet indicates they weren't slaves. Lehner's team found remains of mostly male cattle under 2 years old—in other words, prime beef. Lehner thinks ordinary Egyptians may have rotated in and out of the work crew under some sort of national service or feudal obligation to their superiors.

This past fall, at the behest of "Nova" documentary makers, Lehner and Rick Brown, a professor of sculpture at the Massachusetts College of Art, attempted to learn more about construction of the Sphinx by sculpting a scaled-down version of its missing nose from a limestone block, using replicas of ancient tools found on the Giza plateau and depicted in tomb paintings. Forty-five centuries ago, the Egyptians lacked iron or bronze tools. They mainly used stone hammers, along with copper chisels for detailed finished work.

Bashing away in the yard of Brown's studio near Boston, Brown, assisted by art students, found that the copper chisels

The Way it Was?

Egyptologists believe the Sphinx, pyramids and other parts of the two-square-mile Giza complex align with the sun at key times, reinforcing the pharoah's role in sustaining the divine order.

Lehner's vision of the restored Sphinx after the 15th century B.C. includes a statue of Thutmose IV's father, Amenhotep II, atop an engraved granite slab.

became blunt after only a few blows before they had to be resharpened in a forge that Brown constructed out of a charcoal furnace. Lehner and Brown estimate one laborer might carve a cubic foot of stone in a week. At that rate, they say, it would take 100 people three years to complete the Sphinx.

Exactly what Khafre wanted the Sphinx to do for him or his kingdom is a matter of debate, but Lehner has theories about that, too, based partly on his work at the Sphinx Temple. Remnants of the temple walls are visible today in front of the Sphinx. They surround a courtyard enclosed by 24 pillars. The temple plan is laid out on an east-west axis, clearly marked by a pair of small niches or sanctuaries, each about the size of a closet. The Swiss archaeologist Herbert Ricke, who studied the temple in the late 1960s, concluded the axis symbolized the movements of the sun; an east-west line points to where the sun rises and sets twice a year at the equinoxes, halfway between midsummer and midwinter. Ricke further argued that each pillar represented an hour in the sun's daily circuit.

Lehner spotted something perhaps even more remarkable. If you stand in the eastern niche during sunset at the March or September equinoxes, you see a dramatic astronomical event: the sun appears to sink into the shoulder of the Sphinx and, beyond that, into the south side of the Pyramid of Khafre on the horizon. "At the very same moment," Lehner says, "the shadow of the Sphinx and the shadow of the pyramid, both symbols of the king, become merged silhouettes. The Sphinx itself, it seems, symbolized the pharaoh presenting offerings to the sun god in the court of the temple." Hawass concurs, saying the Sphinx represents Khafre as Horus, the Egyptians' revered royal falcon god, "who is giving offerings with his two paws to his father, Khufu, incarnated as the sun god, Ra, who rises and sets in that temple."

Equally intriguing, Lehner discovered that when one stands near the Sphinx during the summer solstice, the sun appears to set midway between the silhouettes of the pyramids of Khafre and Khufu. The scene resembles the hieroglyph *akhet,* which can be translated as "horizon" but also symbolized the cycle of life and rebirth. "Even if coincidental, it is hard to imagine the Egyptians not seeing this ideogram," Lehner wrote in the *Archive of Oriental Research.* "If somehow intentional, it ranks as an example of architectural illusionism on a grand, maybe the grandest, scale."

If Lehner and Hawass are right, Khafre's architects arranged for solar events to link the pyramid, Sphinx and temple. Collectively Lehner describes the complex as a cosmic engine, intended to harness the power of the sun and other gods to resurrect the soul of the pharaoh. This transformation not only guaranteed eternal life for the dead ruler but also sustained the universal natural order, including the passing of the seasons, the annual flooding of the Nile and the daily lives of the people. In this sacred cycle of death and revival, the Sphinx may have stood for many things: as an image of Khafre the dead king, as the sun god incarnated in the living ruler and as guardian of the underworld and the Giza tombs.

But it seems Khafre's vision was never fully realized. There are signs the Sphinx was unfinished. In 1978, in a corner of the statue's quarry, Hawass and Lehner found three stone blocks, abandoned as laborers were dragging them to build the Sphinx Temple. The north edge of the ditch surrounding the Sphinx contains segments of bedrock that are only partially quarried. Here the archaeologists also found the remnants of a workman's lunch and tool kit—fragments of a beer or water jar and stone hammers. Apparently the workers walked off the job.

The enormous temple-and-Sphinx complex might have been the pharaoh's resurrection machine, but, Lehner is fond of saying, "nobody turned the key and switched it on." By the time the Old Kingdom finally broke apart around 2,130 B.C., the desert sands had begun to reclaim the Sphinx. It would sit ignored for the next seven centuries, when it spoke to a young royal.

According to the legend engraved on a pink granite slab between the Sphinx's paws, the Egyptian prince Thutmose went hunting in the desert, grew tired and lay down in the shade of the Sphinx. In a dream, the statue, calling itself Horemakhet—or Horus-in-the-Horizon, the earliest known Egyptian name for the statue—addressed him. It complained about its ruined body and the encroaching sand. Horemakhet then offered Thutmose the throne in exchange for help.

Whether or not the prince actually had this dream is unknown. But when he became Pharaoh Thutmose IV, he helped introduce a Sphinx-worshiping cult to the New Kingdom (1550–1070 B.C.). Across Egypt, sphinxes appeared everywhere in sculptures, reliefs and paintings, often depicted as a potent symbol of royalty and the sacred power of the sun.

Based on Lehner's analysis of the many layers of stone slabs placed like tilework over the Sphinx's crumbling surface, he believes the oldest slabs may date back as far as 3,400 years to Thutmose's time. In keeping with the legend of Horemakhet, Thutmose may well have led the first attempt to restore the Sphinx.

When Lehner is in the United States, typically about six months per year, he works out of an office in Boston, the headquarters of Ancient Egypt Research Associates, a nonprofit organization Lehner directs that excavates the Lost City and trains young Egyptologists. At a meeting with him at his office this past fall, he unrolled one of his countless maps of the Sphinx on a table. Pointing to a section where an old tunnel had cut into the statue, he said the elements had taken a toll on the Sphinx in the first few centuries after it was built. The porous rock soaks up moisture, degrading the limestone. For Lehner, this posed yet another riddle—what was the source of so much moisture in Giza's seemingly bone-dry desert?

The Sahara has not always been a wilderness of sand dunes. German climatologists Rudolph Kuper and Stefan Kröpelin, analyzing the radiocarbon dates of archaeological sites, recently concluded that the region's prevailing climate pattern changed around 8,500 B.C., with the monsoon rains that covered the tropics moving north. The desert sands sprouted rolling grasslands punctuated by verdant valleys, prompting people to begin settling the region in 7,000 B.C. Kuper and Kröpelin say this green Sahara came to an end between 3,500 B.C. and 1,500 B.C., when the monsoon belt returned to the tropics and the desert reemerged. That date range is 500 years later than prevailing theories had suggested.

Further studies led by Kröpelin revealed that the return to a desert climate was a gradual process spanning centuries. This transitional period was characterized by cycles of ever-decreasing rains and extended dry spells. Support for this theory can be found in recent research conducted by Judith Bunbury, a geologist at the University of Cambridge. After studying sediment samples in the Nile Valley, she concluded that climate change in the Giza region began early in the Old Kingdom, with desert sands arriving in force late in the era.

The work helps explain some of Lehner's findings. His investigations at the Lost City revealed that the site had eroded dramatically—with some structures reduced to ankle level over a period of three to four centuries after their construction. "So I had this realization," he says, "Oh my God, this buzz saw that cut our site down is probably what also eroded the Sphinx." In his view of the patterns of erosion on the Sphinx, intermittent wet periods dissolved salt deposits in the limestone, which recrystallized on the surface, causing softer stone to crumble while harder layers formed large flakes that would be blown away by desert winds. The Sphinx, Lehner says, was subjected to constant "scouring" during this transitional era of climate change.

"It's a theory in progress," says Lehner. "If I'm right, this episode could represent a kind of 'tipping point' between different climate states—from the wetter conditions of Khufu and Khafre's era to a much drier environment in the last centuries of the Old Kingdom."

The implication is that the Sphinx and the pyramids, epic feats of engineering and architecture, were built at the end of a special time of more dependable rainfall, when pharaohs could marshal labor forces on an epic scale. But then, over the centuries, the landscape dried out and harvests grew more precarious. The pharaoh's central authority gradually weakened, allowing provincial officials to assert themselves—culminating in an era of civil war.

Today, the Sphinx is still eroding. Three years ago, Egyptian authorities learned that sewage dumped in a nearby canal was causing a rise in the local water table. Moisture was drawn up into the body of the Sphinx and large flakes of limestone were peeling off the statue.

Hawass arranged for workers to drill test holes in the bedrock around the Sphinx. They found the water table was only 15 feet beneath the statue. Pumps have been installed nearby to divert the groundwater. So far, so good. "Never say to anyone that we saved the Sphinx," he says. "The Sphinx is the oldest patient in the world. All of us have to dedicate our lives to nursing the Sphinx all the time."

Critical Thinking

1. In what sense does the Sphinx represent one of the largest and oldest monolithic statues in the world?
2. Why is there no mention of the Sphinx in hieroglyphic inscriptions? What is the significance of Ruti, the double-headed lion?
3. What indications are there that the pharaoh Khafre built the complex including his pyramid, the Sphinx Temple, the Valley Temple, and the Sphinx itself?
4. What can be said about who did the backbreaking work of building the Sphinx? What kinds of tools did they use? What is the estimate regarding the amount of labor involved and for how long?
5. What does Lehner think the pharaoh Khafre had in mind in building the Sphinx and what is his evidence?
6. Why does it seem that Khafre's vision was never fully realized?
7. What is the significance of the fact that the climate in the Sahara was changing from the wetter conditions of Khufu and Khafre's era to a much drier environment in the last centuries of the Old Kingdom?

Evan Hadingham is senior science editor of the PBS series "Nova." Its *"Riddles of the Sphinx"* was to air January 19.

Artful Surgery

Greek archaeologists discover evidence of a skilled surgeon who practiced centuries before Hippocrates.

ANAGNOSTIS P. AGELARAKIS

Sometime before 600 B.C., a surgeon in the settlement of Abdera on the north coast of the Aegean faced a difficult case. Standing back from his patient, a young woman in her late twenties lying on the table before him, he examined the wound cautiously. Normal practice required that the healer ask how an injury occurred, but here it was clear from the broken flesh and hair matted with blood. A stone or lead missile, hurled from a sling by one of the native Thracians intent on the colony's destruction, had hit her on the back of the head. Stepping closer, a grave expression on his face, the surgeon gently explored the wound by hand and with a bronze probe. As he feared, the impact was at a point where the bones came together, joining in a suture—the weakest point of the skull.

Today, most medical students take a solemn vow, repeating the Hippocratic Oath, named for Hippocrates, the ancient Greek physician we call the "Father of Medicine." Although we know little about him—he has been described as the "most famous but least known Greek physician"—in his own day, Hippocrates (ca. 460–370 B.C.) was spoken of with respect by Plato and Aristotle. He was born at the island of Kos, near Ionia (the eastern coast of the Aegean Sea), and after practicing medicine throughout Greece, he devoted considerable time to teaching students.

None of the surviving late fifth- and early fourth-century B.C. Greek medical treatises—numbering about 70 and collectively known as the Hippocratic corpus—can be securely ascribed to the great physician himself. They could have been compiled by his students, who conceivably added to their master's notes, handbooks, and lecture materials. Perhaps in part from a library on Kos, the texts—gathered together in Alexandria at a later date—reflect the rich legacy of the Ionian school of medicine.

Some of the works are instructional, such as *About the Physician* and *In the Surgery.* Others, such as *Fractures* and *On Head Wounds,* appear to have been written as practical handbooks. Of these, the *Oxford Classical Dictionary* notes that, "The directions for bandaging and for diagnosis and treatment of dislocations and fractures, especially of depressed fractures of the skull, are very impressive." And it describes *On Head Wounds* "as a practical work by a highly skilled craftsman, and every sentence suggests experience." Indeed, it was still in use as a medical text in Europe more than two millennia after it was written.

But new evidence, on which the story of the wounded young woman at the head of this article is based, will rewrite our history of the development of ancient medical practice. The patient was among those sent north by Clazomenae, a Greek city in Ionia, to establish a colony at Abdera around 654 B.C. She was successfully treated—a difficult operation performed by a master surgeon saved her—and lived for another 20 years. Her remains, which were excavated at Abdera by Eudokia Skarlatidou of the Greek Archaeological Service and which I have had the privilege to study, provide incontrovertible evidence that two centuries before Hippocrates drew breath, surgical practices described in the treatise *On Head Wounds* were already in use.

According to the historian Herodotus, the Clazomeneans at Abdera were "driven out by the Thracians" who perhaps conducted a war of attrition, contesting the colonists' access to land for agriculture and timber or plundering and destroying their crops. Yet the archaeological record indicates that the Clazomenean settlers persisted for at least eight decades, and excavations have revealed many traces of their colony, including its 13-foot-thick fortification walls and cemeteries. In one burial ground was the grave with the well-preserved skeleton of the woman who had survived the wound and subsequent surgery.

From her bones, I could determine that apart from some dental pathologies and arthritis of the spine and limbs, she had been relatively healthy and quite physically active before she died of an unknown cause. The healed wound itself is dramatic: a hole about the size of a quarter (14.8 by 9.2 mm) on the back right side of her skull is surrounded by a larger oval area (66.4 by 19.9 mm) where the surgeon scraped the bone with a rasp, leaving faintly discernible marks that radiate outward from the opening.

When the young woman was hit, the stone or lead missile crushed the soft tissues of her scalp and caused a serious depressed fracture, possibly with the projectile embedded in the bone. Sharp edges on fissure fractures extending from the wound endangered the dura mater (the fibrous membrane enveloping the brain). Surgery was needed to remove bone splinters and possibly the lodged missile, eliminate fissures, evaluate the condition of the dura mater if exposed, and apply "healing drugs."

To judge by procedures set out in *On Head Wounds,* the surgeon first evaluated the injury without touching the patient, then by touching and subsequently by using a probe to better diagnose the type, extent, and severity of the trauma. He asked about the injury and the patient's physiological responses to it. Then he cut and opened up the soft tissues surrounding the wound for better visual inspection and preparation for surgical intervention before dressing the wound with a paste of fine barley wheat boiled with vinegar. The next day, he further cleaned and dried the soft tissues around the wound and made a final diagnosis of the bone injury. And he might have spread black ink on the cleaned bone; it would seep into and reveal any hairline fissures that might not be visible otherwise.

On Head Wounds sets forth diagnostic procedures for identifying and treating a range of cranial injuries caused by different weapons. In most cases, a wound on the back of the head—"where the bone is thicker and oozing puss will take longer to reach the brain"—was less likely to be fatal than one in the front. But, as in the case of the woman from Abdera, "When a suture shows at the exposed bone area of the wound—of a wound anywhere on the head—the resistance of the bone to the traumatic impact is very weak should the weapon get wedged in the suture." So, according to the Hippocratic text, the case was a serious one. It was made more so because of the nature of the weapon, a missile from a sling, because, "Of those weapons that strike the head and wound close to the cranial bone and the cranium itself, that one that will fall from a highest level rather than from a trajectory parallel to the ground, and being at the same time the hardest, bluntest, and heaviest . . . will crack and compress the cranial bone."

For compressed head fractures, *On Head Wounds* recommends trepanation, removal of a disk of bone from the skull using a drill with a serrated circular bit. This would eliminate the danger of bone splinters and radiating fracture fissures. It would also permit the removal of bone fragments that had been crushed inward, allowing the brain to swell from the contusion without pressing against loose bone fragments with sharp edges that might puncture the dura mater. But there was one cranial area where a scraping approach was strongly recommended instead of trepanation: "It is necessary, if the wound is at the sutures and the weapon penetrated and lodged into the bone, to pay attention for recognizing the kind of injury sustained by the bone. Because . . . he who received the weapon at the sutures will suffer far greater impact at the cranial bone than the one who did not receive it at the sutures. And most of those require trepanation, but you must not trepan the sutures themselves . . . you are required to scrape the surface of the cranial bone with a rasp in depth and length, according to the position of the wound, and then cross-wise to be able to see the hidden breakages and crushes . . . because scraping exposes the harm well, even if those injuries . . . were not otherwise revealed."

Should you determine that the bone is denuded of flesh and that it is not healthy as a consequence of the trauma, it is necessary to carry out a diagnosis of its condition: the extent of the impact and the nature of the surgical intervention required . . . if the wound is at a suture and the weapon penetrated and lodged in the bone, it is necessary to pay attention to recognize the kind of injury sustained by the bone. . . .

— Attributed to Hippocrates

Faced with a compressed fracture with radiating fissure fractures and fearing damage to the dura mater, the surgeon scraped the bone in length, width, and depth, removing fragments and eliminating the fissures through scraping and not trepanation. He then would have tended to any adjacent injured tissues.

While the reconstruction of the patient's treatment is in part conjecture, based on the Hippocratic text itself, the size and shape of the surgical intervention and use of the rasp rather than trepanation is certain from traces on the bone itself. So the surgical procedure matches perfectly what was recommended two centuries later in *On Head Wounds* for this type of injury in this location.

Ancient Greek sources offer little aid in tracing the development of medicine before Hippocrates. It is not surprising that medical historian Guido Majno wrote in *The Healing Hand* that "the beginnings of Greek medicine, which should fill a library, are mostly blank pages." Medical writings from before the Hippocratic corpus have not survived. Moreover, we only know of one real Greek physician before Hippocrates. The historian Herodotus notes that some time after 522 B.C., a Democedes successfully treated the Persian king Darius I for a sprained ankle *after* Egyptian doctors had failed. But that is still a century after the unknown physician of Abdera performed his masterful surgery.

If we look to earlier times, Homer, before 700 B.C., describes more than 140 combat injuries in the *Iliad* and, in a few cases, tells how they were treated—the arrow or spear extracted, ointment applied to reduce the pain and stop the bleeding, and the wounds bound. But in all the Greek army there are only two trained healers, Machaon and Podalirios, both sons of the legendary hero-physician Aesclepius, son of the god Apollo. The healers were highly valued, and when Machaon is wounded, he is rushed off the battlefield in a chariot because, says Homer, "the physician who knows how to extract arrowheads and with herbal ointments to cure the wounds" is worth the lives of many men.

But medicine has an element of the supernatural in Homer. When Machaon and Podalirios are unavailable, it falls to Achilles' comrade Patroclus to treat a wounded warrior. He does so using a method he learned from Achilles. Who taught both Aesclepius and Achilles? According to Homer it was Chiron, the wisest of all the centaurs. And in the *Odyssey,* when the young prince Odysseus is injured by a boar, a charm is recited over the wound to staunch the blood.

Medicine in the *Iliad*, composed just a century before the Clazomenean physician at Abdera, is rather simplistic. Clearly, significant advances in medical thought took place during the eighth and early seventh centuries B.C. Perhaps the sociopolitical changes that occurred with the emergence of city-states favored the rapid evolution of medical practice. While one cannot argue that the Ionian Greeks developed sophisticated medical practices entirely in isolation, there is no strong evidence that they drew on an outside source in making the jump from simple battlefield first aid or reciting a charm over a wound to performing the sophisticated skull surgery exhibited on the young woman from Abdera.

We do not know exactly how the Clazomeneans chose the colonists who sailed to Abdera. Were they an elite group, the less wealthy who were willing to risk the venture, or the politically and socially disfavored? We do know, however, that among them there was a masterful surgeon, Hippocrates' predecessor, who was among the earliest of the Ionian school of medical practitioners.

Critical Thinking

1. Why was Hippocrates considered to be so important to ancient Greek medicine?
2. What is the "incontrovertible evidence" that surgical practices were already in use two centuries before Hippocrates?
3. How did the woman of Abdera probably receive her head wound? How was she treated and why?
4. Why is a wound on the back of the head less likely to be fatal than one on the front?
5. What is trepanation? Why was this not used on the woman of Abdera?
6. What was Greek medicine like at the time of Homer, before 700 B.C.?
7. What probably caused the rapid evolution of medical practice after Homer?

Anagnostis P. Agelarakis is a professor of physical anthropology at Adelphi University; the translations of Hippocratic and Homeric excerpts are his. He would like to thank Evi Skarlatidou, excavator of Abdera cemetery K, and Ntina Kallintzi, head archaeologist of the Museum at Abdera.

Home away from Rome

Excavations of villas where Roman emperors escaped the office are giving archaeologists new insights into the imperial way of life.

Paul Bennett

In A.D 143 or 144, when he was in his early 20s, the future Roman emperor Marcus Aurelius set out for the country estate of his adoptive father, Emperor Antoninus Pius. The property, Villa Magna (Great Estate), boasted hundreds of acres of wheat, grapes and other crops, a grand mansion, baths and temples, as well as rooms for the emperor and his entourage to retreat from the world or curl up with a good book.

Which is just what young Marcus did, as he related in a letter written to his tutor, Fronto, during the excursion. He describes reading Cato's *De agri cultura,* which was to the gentlemanly farmer of the Roman Empire what Henry David Thoreau's *Walden* was to nature lovers in the 19th century. He hunted boar, without success ("We did hear that boars had been captured but saw nothing ourselves"), and climbed a hill. And since the emperor was also the head of the Roman religion, he helped his father with the daily sacrifices—a ritual that made offerings of bread, milk or a slaughtered animal. The father, son and the emperor's retinue dined in a chamber adjacent to the pressing room—where grapes were crushed for making wine—and there enjoyed some kind of show, perhaps a dance performed by the peasant farmworkers or slaves as they stomped the grapes.

We know what became of Marcus Aurelius—considered the last of the "Five Good Emperors." He ruled for nearly two decades from A.D 161 to his death in A.D 180, a tenure marked by wars in Asia and what is now Germany. As for the Villa Magna, it faded into neglect. Documents from the Middle Ages and later mention a church "at Villa Magna" lying southeast of Rome near the town of Anagni, in the region of Lazio. There, on privately owned land, remains of Roman walls are partially covered by a 19th-century farmhouse and a long-ruined medieval monastery. Sections of the complex were half-heartedly excavated in the 18th century by the Scottish painter and amateur treasure hunter Gavin Hamilton, who failed to find marble statues or frescoed rooms and decided that the site held little interest.

As a result, archaeologists mostly ignored the site for 200 years. Then, in 2006, archaeologist Elizabeth Fentress—working under the auspices of the University of Pennsylvania and the British School at Rome—got permission from the property owner and the Italian government to excavate the area and began to make some interesting discoveries. Most important, near the old farmhouse, her team—accompanied by Sandra Gatti from the Italian Archaeological Superintendency—found a marble-paved rectangular room. At one end was a raised platform, and there were circular indentations in the ground where large terra-cotta pots, or *dolia,* would have been set in an ancient Roman *cella vinaria*—a wine pressing room.

The following summer, Fentress and a team discovered a chamber shaped like a semicircular auditorium attached to the pressing room. She was thrilled. Here was the dining area described by Marcus Aurelius where the imperial retinue watched the local workers stomp grapes and, presumably, dance and sing. "If there was any doubt about the villa," says Fentress, "the discovery of the marble-paved *cella vinaria* and the banquet room looking into it sealed it."

In all, roman emperors constructed dozens of villas over the roughly 350-year span of imperial rule, from the rise of Augustus in 27 B.C. to the death of Constantine in A.D 337. Since treasure hunters first discovered the villas in the 18th century (followed by archaeologists in the 19th and 20th), nearly 30 such properties have been documented in the Italian region of Lazio alone. Some, such as Hadrian's, at Tivoli, have yielded marble statues, frescoes and ornate architecture, evidence of the luxuries enjoyed by wealthy, powerful men (and their wives and mistresses). As archaeological investigations continue at several sites throughout the Mediterranean, a more nuanced picture of these properties and the men who built them is emerging. "This idea that the villa is just about conspicuous consumption, that's only the beginning," says Columbia University archaeologist Marco Maiuro, who works with Fentress at Villa Magna.

The villas also point up the sharp contrast between the emperors' official and private lives. "In Rome," says Steven Tuck, a classical art historian at Miami University of Ohio, "you constantly see them through their service to the state—dedications of buildings, triumphal columns and arches and monuments." But battles and bureaucracy are left at the villa's door. Tuck points to his favorite villa—that of Tiberius, Augustus' stepson, son-in-law and successor. It lies at the end of a sandy beach near Sperlonga, a resort between Rome and Naples on the Mediterranean coast. Wedged between a twisting mountain road and crashing waves, the Villa Tiberio features a natural grotto fashioned into a banquet hall. When archaeologists discovered the grotto in the 1950s, the entrance was filled with thousands of marble fragments. Once the pieces were put together, they yielded some of the greatest sculptural groups ever created—enormous statues depicting the sea monster Scylla and the blinding of the Cyclops Polyphemus. Both are characters from Homer's *Odyssey* as retold in Virgil's *Aeneid,* itself a celebration of Rome's mythic founding written just before Tiberius' reign. Both also vividly illustrate man locked in epic battle with primal forces. "We don't see this kind of thing in Rome," says Tuck. It was evocative of a *nymphaeum,* a dark, primeval place supposedly inhabited by nymphs and beloved by the capricious sea god Neptune. Imagine dining here, with the sound of the sea and torchlight flickering off the fish tail of the monster Scylla as she tossed Odysseus' shipmates into the ocean.

If the imperial villa provided opportunities for Roman emperors to experiment with new images and ideas, then the one that Hadrian (A.D 76–138) built at Tivoli in the first decades of the second century may be the ultimate in freewheeling expression. Occupying about 250 acres at the base of the Apennine Hills, Villa Adriana was originally a farm. When Hadrian became emperor in A.D 117, he began renovating the existing structure into something extraordinary. The villa unfolded into a grand interlocking of halls, baths and gathering spaces designed to tantalize and amaze visitors. "This villa has been studied for five centuries, ever since its discovery during the Renaissance," says Marina De Franceschini, an archaeologist working with the University of Trento. "And yet there's still a lot to discover."

Franceschini is especially beguiled by the villa's outlandish architecture. Take the so-called Maritime Theater, where Hadrian designed a villa within a villa. On an island ringed by a water channel, it is reached by a drawbridge and equipped with two sleeping areas, two bathrooms, a dining room, living room and a thermal bath. The circular design and forced perspective make it appear larger than it is. "The emperor was interested in experimental architecture," says Franceschini. "It's an extremely complicated place. Everything is curved. It's unique."

What exact statement Hadrian wanted to make with his villa has been the subject of debate since the Renaissance, when the great artists of Italy—including Raphael and Michelangelo—studied it. Perhaps to a greater extent than any other emperor, Hadrian possessed an aesthetic sensibility, which found expression in the many beautiful statues discovered on the site, some of which now grace the halls of the Vatican museums and the National Museum of Rome, as well as the Metropolitan Museum of Art in New York City and the Louvre in Paris.

Hadrian traveled frequently, and whenever he returned to Italy, Tivoli became his preferred residence, away from the imperial palace on the Palatine Hill. Part business, part pleasure, the villa contains many rooms designed to accommodate large gatherings. One of the most spacious is the *canopus*—a long structure marked by a reflecting pool said to symbolize a canal Hadrian visited in Alexandria, Egypt, in A.D 130, where his lover Antinous drowned that same year. Ringing the pool was a colonnade connected by an elaborate architrave (carved marble connecting the top of each column). At the far end is a grotto, similar to that at Sperlonga but completely man-made, which scholars have named the Temple of Serapis, after a temple originally found at Alexandria.

Today, the canopus and grotto may look austere, but with the emperor seated there with up to 100 other diners around the pool, it must have been something to see. A network of underground tunnels some three miles long trace a labyrinth beneath the villa, which allowed servants to appear, almost magically, to refill a glass or serve a plate of food. The pool on a warm summer night, reflecting the curvilinear architrave, was surely enchanting.

Standing at the grotto today, one can barely see the line made by two small aqueducts running from a hillside behind the grotto to the top of this half-domed pavilion. Water would have entered a series of pipes at its height, run down into walls and eventually exploded from niches into a semi-circular pool and passed under the emperor. Franceschini believes the water was mostly decorative. "It reflected the buildings," he says. "It also ran through fountains and grand waterworks. It was conceived to amaze the visitor. If you came to a banquet in the canopus and saw the water coming, that would have been really spectacular."

Hadrian was not the only emperor to prefer country life to Rome's imperial palace. Several generations earlier, Tiberius had retired to villas constructed by his predecessor Augustus. Installing a regent in Rome, the gloomy and reclusive Tiberius walled himself off from the world at the Villa Jovis, which still stands on the island of Capri, near Neapolis (today's Naples hills). Tiberius' retreat from Rome bred rumor and suspicion. The historian Suetonius, in his epic work *The Lives of the Twelve Caesars,* would later accuse him of setting up a licentious colony where sadomasochism, pederasty and cruelty were practiced. (Most historians believe these accusations to be false.) "Tradition still associates the great villas of Capri with this negative image," says Eduardo Federico, a historian at the University of Naples who grew up on the island. Excavated largely in the 1930s and boasting some of the most spectacular vistas of the Mediterranean Sea of any Roman estate, the Villa Jovis remains a popular tourist destination. "The legend of Tiberius as a tyrant still prevails," says Federico. "Hostile history has made the Villa Jovis a place of cruelty and Tiberian lust."

Perhaps the best-known retirement villa belonged to the emperor Diocletian (A.D 245–316), who ruled at the end of the third century and into the fourth. Besides his tireless persecution of Christians, Diocletian is known for ending a half-century of instability and consolidating the empire—before dividing it into eastern and western halves (thereby setting the stage for the rise of the Byzantine Empire). Much of this work involved quelling rebellions on the perimeter and keeping the ever-agitating senatorial class under control. By A.D 305, at the age of 60, Diocletian had had enough. In a bold, unprecedented move—previous emperors had all died in office—he announced his retirement and sought refuge in a seaside villa on the coast of Dalmatia (today's Croatia).

Now called Diocletian's Palace, the ten-acre complex includes a mausoleum, temples, a residential suite and a magnificent peristyle courtyard complete with a dais and throne. Even out of power, Diocletian remained a force in the empire, and when it fell into chaos in 309, various factions pleaded for him to take up rule again. Diocletian demurred, famously writing that if they could see the incredible cabbages he'd grown with his own hands, they wouldn't ask him to trade the peace and happiness of his palace for the "storms of a never-satisfied greed," as one historian put it. He died there seven years later.

Located in the modern city of Split, Diocletian's Palace is one of the most stunning ancient sites in the world. Most of its walls still stand; and although the villa has been looted for treasure, a surprising number of statues—mostly Egyptian, pillaged during a successful military campaign—still stand. The villa owes its excellent condition to local inhabitants, who moved into the sprawling residence not long after the fall of Rome and whose descendants live there to this day. "Everything is interwoven in Split," says Josko Belamaric, an art historian with the Croatian Ministry of Culture who is responsible for conservation of the palace. "It's so dense. You open a cupboard in someone's apartment, and you're looking at a 1,700-year-old wall."

Belamaric has been measuring and studying Diocletian's Palace for more than a decade, aiming to strike a balance between its 2,000 residents and the needs of preservation. (Wiring high-speed Internet into an ancient villa, for instance, is not done with a staple gun.) Belamaric's studies of the structure have yielded some surprises. Working with local architect Goran Niksic, the art historian realized that the aqueduct to the villa was large enough to supply water to 173,000 people (too big for a residence, but about right for a factory). The local water contains natural sulfur, which can be used to fix dyes. Belamaric concluded that Diocletian's estate included some sort of manufacturing center—probably for textiles, as the surrounding hills were filled with sheep and the region was known for its fabrics.

It's long been thought that Diocletian built his villa here because of the accommodating harbor and beautiful seascape, not to mention his own humble roots in the region. But Belamaric speculates it was also an existing textile plant that drew the emperor here, "and it probably continued during his residence, generating valuable income."

In fact, most imperial Roman villas were likely working farms or factories beneficial to the economy of the empire. "The Roman world was an agriculturally based one," says Fentress. "During the late republic we begin to see small farms replaced by larger villas." Although fish and grains were important, the predominant crop was grapes, and the main product wine. By the first century B.C., wealthy landowners—the emperors among them—were bottling huge amounts of wine and shipping it throughout the Roman Empire. One of the first global export commodities was born.

At Tiberius' villa at Sperlonga, a series of rectangular pools, fed by the ocean nearby, lay in front of the grotto. At first they seem merely decorative. But upon closer inspection, one notices a series of terra-cotta-lined holes, each about six inches in diameter, set into the sides of the pools, just beneath the water's surface. Their likely use? To provide a safe space in which fish could lay their eggs. The villa operated as a fish farm, producing enough fish, Tuck estimates, not only to feed the villa and its guests but also to supply markets in Rome. "It's fantastic to see this dining space that also doubled as a fish farm," says Tuck. "It emphasizes the practical workings of these places."

Maiuro believes that the economic power of the larger villas, which tended to expand as Rome grew more politically unstable, may even have contributed to the empire's decline, by sucking economic—and eventually political—power away from Rome and concentrating it in the hands of wealthy landowners, precursors of the feudal lords who would dominate the medieval period. "Rome was never very well centralized," says Maiuro, "and as the villas grow, Rome fades."

Critical Thinking

1. In what sense do the emperors' villas point up the sharp contrast between their official and private lives?
2. In what respects did the imperial villas reflect the emperors' experimentation with "new images and ideas"?
3. How did Hadrian transform the villa at Tivoli? What evidence is there that he possessed an "aesthetic sensibility"?
4. How and why was Tiberius the object of rumor and suspicion?
5. What was Diocletian known for? In what respects did he remain a "force in the empire"?
6. What was the significance for the Roman Empire that "most imperial Roman villas were likely working farms or factories beneficial to the economy of the empire"? How did this lead to the fading of Rome and the shift to feudalism?

Carthage: The Lost Mediterranean Civilisation

Little remains of the great North African empire that was Rome's most formidable enemy. Because, explains Richard Miles, only its complete annihilation could satisfy its younger rival.

RICHARD MILES

In the spring of 146 B.C. the North African city state of Carthage finally fell. After three years of embarrassing setbacks, the Roman army under their new and relatively inexperienced commander, Scipio Aemilianus, had managed to break through the Carthaginian defences and establish an all-important bridgehead at Carthage's circular war harbour, an engineering masterpiece with capacity for at least 170 ships and ramps to drag the craft from and to the water's edge.

The Roman forces were in a position to launch a final assault on the Byrsa, the citadel of Carthage and the religious and administrative heart of the city. The legionaries were, however, forced to fight every step of the way on the narrow streets that led up the hill as desperate defenders rained missiles down on them. Despite this stiff resistance, it was now a question of when rather than if Carthage would fall.

The Carthaginians who had sought refuge in the tall houses that flanked the city's streets were flushed out by fire and sword. The Greek historian Appian, who is the main surviving source for this episode, wrote of how Scipio employed squads of soldiers to drag burnt and mutilated corpses off the streets so that the progress of his legionaries was impeded no further.

It still took six days and nights to break Carthaginian resolve, with Scipio deploying his forces in rotation to preserve both their strength and sanity for the ghastly work in which they were engaged. On the seventh day a party of Carthaginian elders bearing a peace offering of olive branches from the sacred Temple of Eshmoun, the Carthaginian god of healing, which sat on the highest point of the Byrsa citadel, came to the Roman general begging that their lives and those of their fellow citizens be spared. Scipio acceded to their request and later that day 50,000 men, women and children left the citadel through a narrow gate in the wall.

Although the vast majority of its surviving citizenry had surrendered, a rump consisting of Carthage's commander-in-chief, Hasdrubal, his family and 900 Roman deserters—who could expect no mercy from Scipio—were still holed up in the precinct of the Temple of Eshmoun. Time, however, was on the side of the Romans and eventually this small group of diehards was forced up onto the roof of the building to make a final stand. It was then that Hasdrubal's nerve finally broke. Deserting his wife and children, he went in secret to Scipio and surrendered. It would be left to his wife to deliver a fittingly defiant epitaph for the dying city by throwing herself and her children into the flames of the burning temple after venting scorn at her husband's cowardice.

Although it is a myth that Scipio had the site of Carthage ploughed with salt to ensure that nothing would flourish there again, he was certainly keen to ensure that the city bore the full force of Roman opprobrium. As the fires burnt on the Byrsa Hill, Scipio ordered his troops to demolish the city's walls and ramparts. Following military custom, the Roman general also allowed the soldiers to loot the city and rewards were handed out to those legionaries who had displayed conspicuous bravery during the campaign. Scipio then personally distributed all gold, silver and religious offerings, while other spoils were either sent to Rome or sold to raise funds. The surviving arms, siege engines and warships were burnt as offerings to the gods Mars and Minerva and the city's wretched inhabitants sent to the slave markets, with the exception of a few grandees, including Hasdrubal, who, after being led through Rome as part of Scipio's triumph, was allowed to lead a life of comfortable confinement in various Italian cities.

The brutal destruction of Carthage by the Romans has retained its power to both shock and provoke. When in the 1950s the poet and playwright Bertolt Brecht cast around for a historical metaphor to remind his fellow Germans about the dangers of re-militarisation, he instinctively turned to an event that had taken place over 2,000 years before:

> *Great Carthage drove three wars. After the first one it was still powerful. After the second one it was still inhabitable. After the third one it was no longer possible to find her.*

In recent years the ongoing crisis in Iraq has also afforded political commentators many opportunities to equate the situation in that unfortunate land with what befell Carthage.

The following words by the American sociologist and historian Franz Schurmann are typical of the kind of emotive comparisons that have been drawn:

> *Two thousand years ago the Roman statesman Cato the Elder kept crying out, 'Delenda est Carthago'—Carthage must be destroyed! To Cato it was clear either Rome or Carthage but not both could dominate the western Mediterranean. Rome won and Carthage was levelled to the ground. Iraq is now Washington's Carthage.*

Brecht and Schurmann use the example of Carthage to make seemingly conflicting points: one sees the fall of the city as the result of a hubristic desire for military might; the other views it as the supreme example of destructive bullying by a more powerful and ruthless rival. In fact, whether you view Carthage as villain or victim, those judgments are based almost exclusively on the historical testimony of Carthage's greatest enemy, Rome.

It was not just the physical fabric of Carthage that Scipio sought to obliterate. The learned tomes that graced the shelves of the city's libraries, with the exception of the famous Carthaginian agricultural treatise by Mago which was spirited back to Rome, were dispersed among the local Numidian princes who had aided Rome in their war of extermination against Carthage. Nothing more starkly reflects the success of this Roman project than the fact that less than a couple of thousand words of Punic—the Carthaginian tongue—are known and many of these are proper names. The spoils of war not only included the ownership of Carthage's territory, resources and people but also its past. Destruction did not mean total oblivion. A far worse fate awaited Carthage as a mute, misrepresented ghoul in the historical annals of its enemies.

Both Greek and Latin literature would consistently portray the Carthaginians as mendacious, greedy, untrustworthy, cruel, arrogant and irreligious. Particularly shocking to modern sensibilities are the lurid accounts of hundreds of children being sacrificed by immolation in order to placate Baal Hammon and Tanit, the bloodthirsty chief deities of Carthage. Such was the emphasis placed by the Romans on Carthaginian treachery that the Latin phrase *Fides Punica,* literally 'Punic Faith', became a popular ironic expression denoting gross faithlessness.

Carthage was, of course, not the only city to suffer destruction at the hands of Rome. In the very same year that Scipio's troops were carrying out their grim work in North Africa, the venerable Greek city of Corinth was suffering a similarly traumatic fate at the hands of another Roman army. However, it is Carthage's fate that history remembers. It was not the demolishing of the walls, the burning of the houses or the enslaving and killing of the population that made this episode so infamous but its completeness and the cold-blooded determination with which it was carried out.

Many explanations have been put forward as to why Rome invested so much in the destruction of Carthage. Hatred and vengeance certainly played their part. After all, the two states had fought two of the greatest and bloodiest wars—the Punic Wars—that the ancient world had known. Many Romans considered Carthage to have been their greatest enemy, the 'whetstone' of their greatness. Victory over Carthage in the First Punic War (264–241 B.C.) had demanded that the Romans, who had no previous naval experience, develop their own fleet and defeat the pre-eminent sea power of the ancient world in a period of a little over three decades. In that short time the Mediterranean had been transformed in the Roman mind from a dangerous unknown to *Mare Nostrum,* 'our sea'. For many Romans the final defeat and destruction of Carthage was the great watershed moment of a glorious and eventful history because it marked the transformation of Rome from Italian to 'world' power.

Moreover, Carthage had taken Rome to the brink of total defeat. During the Second Punic War (218–201 B.C.), the great Carthaginian general Hannibal had blazed a trail of devastation across Italy, humiliating a series of Roman armies along the way. It had taken every ounce of Roman resilience and resources to eventually dislodge Hannibal from the Italian peninsula but not before he had come close to capturing Rome itself and, in all likelihood, final victory. Even a century later, the Roman poet Statius was still evoking the ghoulish spectre of 'Libyan hordes' marauding through the Italian countryside.

There was also the question of Rome's ruthless application of realpolitik. By the time of the third and final Punic War (149–146 B.C.), Carthage, despite having made an impressive economic recovery from the disastrous depredations of its defeat in the Second Punic War, was a mere shadow of the power that it had once been. It was really no threat to Rome, who by that time controlled much of the Mediterranean. Despite this, a powerful clique within the Roman senate, led by Cato the Elder of 'Delenda est Carthago' fame, had pushed hard for Carthage to be neutralised permanently. With the argument won, Carthage had been harassed into a foolhardy act of defiance that had at last given the Roman senate the justification to send their legions back to North Africa.

Yet, despite the contemporary emphasis on the destruction of Carthage being the result of the desire for a final settling of accounts, it is clear that more pragmatic considerations were at the fore of Roman thinking on this matter. The sacking of what was still one of the richest port cities in the ancient Mediterranean was unquestionably a hugely profitable business. The slave auctions and the seizure of a large swathe of previous Carthaginian territory which now became public land owned by the Roman state, unequivocally contributed to a massive infusion of wealth into both public and private Roman coffers. At the same time, the conspicuous destruction of such a famous city sent an unequivocal message: dissent from Rome would not be tolerated and past glories counted for nothing in this new world. The destruction of Carthage now stood as a bloody memorial to the cost of resistance to Rome and a suitably apocalyptic fanfare for Rome's coming of age as a new world power.

In the face of such a litany of destruction and misrepresentation both ancient and modern, one might legitimately ask whether it is really possible to write a history of Carthage that is anything more than just another extended essay on victimhood and vilification.

There are some intriguing but equally frustrating clues. Within the burnt-out structure of a temple (thought by its discoverer, the German archaeologist Friedrich Rakob, to have been the Temple of Apollo ransacked by Roman soldiers), were the remains of an archive thought to have contained wills and business contracts, stored there so that their integrity and safekeeping was guaranteed by the sacred authority of the god. The papyrus on which the document was written was rolled up and string wrapped around it before a piece of wet clay was placed on the string to stop the document from unravelling and a personal seal was imprinted upon it. However, in this particular case, the same set of circumstances that ensured the seals were wonderfully preserved because they were fired by the inferno which engulfed the city also meant that the precious documents that they enclosed were burnt to ashes.

When faced with such historical lacunae there is always a temptation to overcompensate when imagining what has actually been lost. However, we should be wary of assuming that the shelves of Carthage's famous libraries groaned under the weight of a vast corpus of Punic and earlier Near Eastern knowledge now destroyed. Although rumours circulated in the ancient world of mysterious sacred parchments which had been hidden away before Carthage fell and there are scattered references in much later Roman literature of Punic histories, it is difficult to gauge whether the city was really a great literary centre comparable with Athens or Alexandria.

At times, researching a history of Carthage is rather like reading a transcript of a conversation in which one interlocutor's contribution has been deleted. However, the responses of the existing protagonists, in this case Greek and Roman writers, allows one to follow the thread of the discussion. Indeed, it is the sheer range and scale of these 'conversations' that allows the historian of Carthage to recreate some of what has been expunged. Ideology and egotism dictate that even historians united in hostility towards their subject still manage vehemently to disagree with one another and it is within the contradictions and differences of opinion that existed between these writers that this heavily biased monologue can be partially overcome.

As regards other material evidence, the ruins of Carthage have always stirred the imagination of those who visited them. Rumours that the Carthaginians had managed to bury their riches in the hope of returning to retrieve them in better times had led the troops of one first-century B.C. Roman general to commence an impromptu treasure hunt. For the modern archaeologist Carthage can resemble a complicated jigsaw of which many pieces have been intentionally thrown away. Yet history tells us that such final solutions are rarely as comprehensive as their perpetrators would have us believe.

Although the religious centre on the Byrsa was completely demolished, many of the outlying districts and, as we have already seen, some parts of the hill itself escaped total destruction. In fact, the Romans inadvertently did much to preserve parts of Punic Carthage by dumping thousands of cubic metres of rubble and debris on top of it. Even the ominous two-foot thick black tide-mark found in the stratigraphy of the western slopes of the Byrsa, the archaeological record of the razing of the city in 146 B.C., is packed full of southern Italian tableware, telling us what pottery styles were in vogue in Carthage at that time.

Then there are the thousands of monuments recording votive offerings made to Baal Hammon and Tanit, which, although extremely formulaic, have furnished invaluable information on Punic religious rites. This is especially so in the case of child sacrifice which is revealed in a different light to the hysterical ritualised savagery found in the historical accounts. There are also a small number of surviving inscriptions relating to other aspects of city life, such as the construction of public monuments and the carrying out of an assortment of religious rituals. This epigraphic evidence has been helpful in aiding understanding not only of Carthage's religious life but also the social hierarchies that existed within the city. It is from the writing on these slabs of stone that we learn of the faceless potters, metal smiths, cloth weavers, fullers, furniture makers, carters, butchers, stonemasons, jewellers, doctors, scribes, interpreters, cloak attendants, surveyors, priests, heralds, furnace workers and merchants who made up the population of the city.

The picture of Carthage that emerges from these very fragmentary glimpses is a strikingly different one from the barbarous, cruel and aggressive city-state found in the Greek and Roman historical canon. Carthage might have been founded by settlers from the Phoenician city of Tyre in what is now southern Lebanon, but it was older (early eighth century B.C.) than any Greek city in the central or western Mediterranean region; so much for their ill-founded reputation as oriental gatecrashers into a pristine Hellenic world. Its Phoenician name, Qart-Hadasht, or 'New City', suggests that Carthage was set up as a colonial settlement and not just as a trading post.

Strategically the site could not have been better chosen, for it stood on the nexus of the two most important trans-Mediterranean trading routes, the east-west route that brought silver from the mines of southern Spain to Tyre and its north-south Tyrrhenian counterpart that linked Greece, Italy, Sicily and North Africa.

It is now thought that Carthage might have actually been established to act as a larger civic centre for other smaller Phoenician colonies in the region. It certainly grew quickly. Although archaeologists are yet to locate any of the important public buildings or harbours from that early period, current evidence indicates that the littoral plain began to fill up with a densely packed network of dwellings made of sun-dried bricks laid out on streets with wells, gardens and squares, all situated on a fairly regular plan that ran parallel to the shoreline. By the early seventh century B.C., the settlement was surrounded by an impressive three-metre wide casement wall. So swift was the development that in the first hundred years of the city's existence there is evidence of some demolition and redevelopment within it's neighbourhoods, including the careful relocation of an early cemetery to make way for metal workshops. Three further large cemeteries ringing the early city indicate that, within a century or so of its foundation, Carthage was home to around 30,000 people, a very considerable number for that period.

Although at first luxury goods were imported from the Levant, Egypt and other areas of the Near East, by the mid-seventh century B.C. Carthage had become a major manufacturer itself through the establishment of an industrial area just outside the city walls, with potter's kilns and workshops for purple-dye production and metalworking. Carthage now became a major manufacturer of terracotta figurines, masks, jewellery, delicately carved ivories and decorated ostrich eggs, which were then exported throughout the western Phoenician colonies.

The decline of Tyre as an economic and political force in the first decades of the sixth century B.C., led to Carthage assuming the leadership of the old Phoenician colonies in the central and western Mediterranean. This was hardly surprising because already Carthage was the most populous and economically powerful member of that grouping. The real source of Carthaginian might was and would remain its fleet, the greatest in the Mediterranean for hundreds of years. A huge mercantile fleet ensured that Carthage was the nexus of a vast trading network, transporting foodstuffs, wine, oil, metals and luxury goods as well as other cargoes across the Mediterranean. If a couple of much later Greek and Roman sources are to be believed then Carthaginian expeditions also made their way into the Atlantic, travelling as far afield as West Africa and Britanny.

With the most feared fleet in the Mediterranean, Carthage remained one of the pacesetters in naval technological innovation. In the fourth century B.C. they were the first to develop the quadrireme, which was both bigger and more powerful than the trireme, the ship that had dominated naval warfare for the previous 200 years. Marine archaeologists who have studied the remains of several Carthaginian ships lying on the sea bed just off Marsala on the west coast of Sicily, were amazed to discover that each piece of the boat was carefully marked with a letter which ensured that the complex design could be easily and swiftly assembled. The Carthaginians had developed what was, in essence, a flatpack warship.

With Carthaginian leadership of the western Phoenician colonies confirmed, we see the growing influence of recognisably Carthaginian cultural traits in other western Phoenician colonies. These included the adoption of Punic, the Levantine dialect spoken in Carthage, as well as a new taste for the luxury goods and religious practices favoured in the city.

Yet the headship of the Phoenician community in the west was not the only source of Carthage's burgeoning power. For the first centuries of its existence the Carthaginians had been hampered by the very limited extent of their hinterland which meant that they had been forced to import much of their food. This began to change in the sixth century B.C. as Carthage sometimes expanded aggressively into the territory of their Libyan neighbours. A whole raft of farmsteads and small towns were developed on this new land with the result that Carthage also became an agricultural powerhouse, producing food and wine not only for its own population but also for export. The Carthaginians were also celebrated for certain technological advances in agriculture, such as the *tribulum plostellum Punicum,* or Punic cart, a primitive but highly effective threshing machine.

Interestingly, this economic and political dominance did not translate into any imperial aspirations until the last decades before the First Punic War. However, the Carthaginian leadership of a Punic bloc that took in North Africa, Sardinia, western Sicily, southern Spain, the Balearics and Malta, did become increasingly involved overseas, politically and militarily. The most significant of these ventures was on Sicily where heavy economic investment and the presence of strategically important Phoenician colonies meant that Carthage quickly became a major player in the highly volatile political landscape that existed there. Over the following two centuries Carthage was obliged to send a number of armies to Sicily in order to defend its own and its allies' interests there, particularly from encroachments by the most powerful Greek city-state on the island, Syracuse. Military action between the two powers and their allies was punctuated by periods of 'cold war' in which each side eyed the other warily.

Despite some Sicilian-Greek historians' claims to the contrary, this was never a straight conflict between the Punic and Greek blocs. Carthage, in particular, often co-operated with Sicilian Greek city-states worried about the growth in Syracusan power. More generally, Greek, Punic and indigenous communities on the island intermarried and worshipped each others' gods and goddesses as well as trading and making war and political alliances with one another. Indeed, it was often the deep and long-standing relationships that existed between supposedly bitter rivals that were the driving force in the creation of a surprisingly cohesive and interconnected central and western Mediterranean.

Politically Carthage was certainly influenced by the Hellenic world, introducing constitutional structures that resembled but did not ape those found in the Greek city-states. Carthage had long been an oligarchy, dominated by a cartel of rich and powerful merchant families represented in a Council of Elders with one dominant clan usually holding the role of first amongst equals. However, over time this led to the introduction of more representative bodies and officials. A body called the Tribunal of One Hundred and Four, made up of members of the aristocratic elite, now oversaw the conduct of officials and military commanders as well as acting as a kind of higher constitutional court. At the head of the Carthaginian state were two annually elected senior executive officers, the Suffetes, as well as a whole range of more junior officials and special commissioners who oversaw different aspects of governmental business such as public works, tax-collecting and the administration of the state treasury. A popular assembly that included all members of the citizen body was also introduced.

However, much to the approval of the Athenian political scientist Aristotle, its powers were strictly limited. In fact, Aristotle thought that the Carthaginian constitution of the fourth century B.C. was the best balanced in the Mediterranean world. Later, however, in line with many Greek states, the powers of the popular assembly increased markedly, leading to charges that Carthage was going down the road of demagogy.

One finds the same mixture of emulation and innovation in Carthage's interactions with Greek culture. There is good evidence for members of the Carthaginian elite being educated in Greek, and Greek artistic and architectural traits were often adopted and adapted for Punic tastes. This familiarity with Greek art, rather than leading to mere mimicry, allowed the Punic population of the island to express themselves in new and powerfully original ways. Traditional Phoenician artforms such as anthropoid sarcophagi, stone coffins whose human heads, arms and feet protruded out from a piece of smooth stone like human pupae, acquired Greek dress and hair decoration. And it was not just one-way traffic. Sicilian Greek art, and architecture in particular, was clearly influenced by the Punic world.

Perhaps the most striking example of Greco-Punic cultural interaction was found by archaeologists excavating on the site of the Punic city of Motya in Sicily in 1979. It was an oversized marble statue of a young man, standing 1.8 metres tall without his missing feet. Although the arms had also gone, it was relatively simple to reconstruct the pose of the left arm, as the hand has been carved resting on the hip. The head was framed by a fringe of curly hair and had once worn a crown or wreath kept in place by rivets. All in all, it appeared to conform to the severe Greek sculptural style of the early fifth century B.C. and, indeed, a very similar statue of an *ephebe,* a young man of military training age, has been discovered on the site of the Sicilian Greek city of Acragas.

It has been argued that only a Greek sculptor could have created such a high quality piece and that the Motya ephebe was a looted Greek work. However, there was a problem. Unlike other statues of ephebes from this period, who are depicted nude, the Motya young man is clothed in a fine long tunic with flowing pleats bounded by a high girdle. Many ingenious solutions have been proposed to explain this anomaly. The strange girdle and hand positions have led to the suggestion that the young man was either a Greek charioteer or a sponsor of a chariot race. However, the Motya figure is very different from other surviving statues of Greek charioteers. In fact, the closest parallels are found within the Punic world. Firstly, despite the clearly Greek sculptural form, the statue follows the Punic convention of not displaying the nude body; second, the clothes and headgear worn by the young man bear a marked resemblance to the ritual garments worn by priests of the cult of the Punic god Melqart, with whom Heracles would enjoy an increasingly close association in Sicily. Neither Greek nor Punic but Sicilian, the Motya ephebe stood as a glittering testament to the cultural syncretism that was such a powerful force in this region.

In such a brief survey it is simply impossible to do justice to all of the different ways that Carthaginian political, economic and cultural dynamism helped to create a western Mediterranean world that existed long before Rome came on the scene. Carthage was, in reality, the bedrock on which much of Rome's success as an imperial power was founded. Rome was not just the destroyer of Carthage but also the inheritor of a politically, economically and culturally joined-up world which was Carthage's greatest achievement. The Romans were always ready, although sometimes grudgingly so, to recognise their debt to the Greeks. However, these had tended to be in cultural fields such as philosophy, art and history that the Romans did not wish, or did not have the confidence, to claim as their own. In fact the creation of what we know as the classical world was founded on the recognition of the complementary nature of Greek and Roman talents. Greek innovation met Roman dynamism. The existence of Carthage, a dynamic Mediterranean power which had also enjoyed a similar complementary relationship with the Greek world, was an inconvenient truth that Rome was simply not willing to acknowledge. Thus Carthage's brutal end might have had as much to do with Roman insecurity about creating its own unique legacy as any desire for vengeance or plunder.

Critical Thinking

1. To what extent was Carthage destroyed by Rome? What was even worse than total destruction, according to the author?
2. How would Carthage be consistently portrayed in Roman and Greek literature? What was meant by "Fides Punica?"
3. Why is the fate of Carthage remembered more than the similar fate of the Greek city of Corinth?
4. Why did Rome invest so much in the destruction of Carthage?
5. What is the nature of the literary and material evidence used by the author to research the history of Carthage? What is the picture of Carthage that emerges?
6. In what respects was Carthage strategically located?
7. Why was Carthage established, according to the author? What evidence is there that it grew rapidly?
8. In what ways did Carthage become a major manufacturing and trade center its own right? How did it also become and "agricultural powerhouse?"
9. How and when did Carthage's imperialistic aspirations develop?
10. Why does the author describe Carthage as part of a "surprisingly cohesive and interconnected central and western Mediterranean?"
11. How is it that Carthage possessed both an oligarchy and constitutional structures?
12. What evidence is there of "Greek-Punic cultural interaction?"
13. Why does the author claim "Carthage was, in reality, the bedrock on which much of Rome's success as an imperial power was founded.?" Why does he say that this was an "inconvenient truth" for Rome?

Richard Miles is a Newton Trust Lecturer in the Faculty of Classics and Fellow and Director of Studies in Classics at Trinity Hall, Cambridge. He is the author of *Carthage Must be Destroyed: The Rise and Fall of an Ancient Mediterranean Civilisation* (Allen Lane, 2010).

Lofty Ambitions of the Inca

Rising from obscurity to the heights of power, a succession of Andean rulers subdued kingdoms, sculpted mountains, and forged a mighty empire.

HEATHER PRINGLE

On the remote Peruvian island of Taquile, in the middle of the great Lake Titicaca, hundreds of people stand in silence on the plaza as a local Roman Catholic priest recites a prayer. Descended in part from Inca colonists sent here more than 500 years ago, the inhabitants of Taquile keep the old ways. They weave brilliantly colored cloth, speak the traditional language of the Inca, and tend their fields as they have for centuries. On festival days they gather in the plaza to dance to the sound of wooden pipes and drums.

Today, on a fine summer afternoon, I watch from the sidelines as they celebrate the fiesta of Santiago, or St. James. In Inca times this would have been the festival of Illapa, the Inca god of lightning. As the prayers draw to a close, four men dressed in black raise a rustic wooden litter holding a painted statue of Santiago. Walking behind the priest in a small procession, the bearers carry the saint for all in the plaza to see, just as the Inca once shouldered the mummies of their revered kings.

The names of those Inca rulers still resonate with power and ambition centuries after their demise: Viracocha Inca (meaning Creator God Ruler), Huascar Inca (Golden Chain Ruler), and Pachacutec Inca Yupanqui (He Who Remakes the World). And remake the world they did. Rising from obscurity in Peru's Cusco Valley during the 13th century, a royal Inca dynasty charmed, bribed, intimidated, or conquered its rivals to create the largest pre-Columbian empire in the New World.

Scholars long possessed few clues about the lives of Inca kings, apart from flattering histories that Inca nobles told soon after the arrival of Spanish conquistadores. The Inca had no system of hieroglyphic writing, as the Maya did, and any portraits that Inca artists may have made of their rulers were lost. The royal palaces of Cusco, the Inca capital, fell swiftly to the European conquerors, and a new Spanish colonial city rose on their ruins, burying or obliterating the Inca past. In more recent times, civil unrest broke out in the Peruvian Andes in the early 1980s, and few archaeologists ventured into the Inca heartland for more than a decade.

Now archaeologists are making up for lost time. Combing rugged mountain slopes near Cusco, they are discovering thousands of previously unknown sites, shedding new light on the origins of the Inca dynasty. Gleaning clues from colonial documents, they are relocating the lost estates of Inca rulers and examining the complex upstairs-and-downstairs lives of imperial households. And on the frontiers of the lost empire, they are piecing together dramatic evidence of the wars Inca kings fought and the psychological battles they waged to forge dozens of fractious ethnic groups into a united realm. Their extraordinary ability to triumph on the battlefield and to build a civilization, brick by brick, sent a clear message, says Dennis Ogburn, an archaeologist at the University of North Carolina at Charlotte: "I think they were saying, We are the most powerful people in the world, so don't even think of messing with us."

On a sun-washed July afternoon, Brian Bauer, an archaeologist from the University of Illinois at Chicago, stands in the plaza of the sprawling Inca ceremonial site of Maukallacta, south of Cusco. He takes a swig of water, then points to a towering outcrop of gray rock just to the east. Carved into its craggy summit are massive steps, part of a major Inca shrine. Some 500 years ago, says Bauer, pilgrims journeyed here to worship at the steep outcrop, once regarded as one of the most sacred places in the empire: the birthplace of the Inca dynasty.

Bauer, a wiry 54-year-old in a battered ball cap and blue jeans, first came to Maukallacta in the early 1980s to uncover the origins of the Inca Empire. At the time most historians and archaeologists believed that a brilliant, young Andean Alexander the Great named Pachacutec became the first Inca king in the early 1400s, transforming a small collection of mud huts into a mighty empire in just one generation. Bauer didn't buy it. He believed the Inca dynasty had far deeper roots, and Maukallacta seemed the logical place to look for them. To his bewilderment, two field seasons of digging turned up no trace of primeval Inca lords. So Bauer shifted north, to the Cusco Valley. With colleague R. Alan Covey, now an archaeologist at Southern Methodist University (SMU) in Dallas, and a team of Peruvian assistants, he marched up and down the steep mountain slopes in straight transect lines for four field seasons, recording every scattering of pottery sherds or toppled stone wall he came across. Persistence paid off. Bauer and his colleagues eventually discovered thousands of previously unknown Inca sites, and the new evidence revealed for the first time how an Inca state had risen much earlier than previously believed—sometime between 1200 and 1300. The ancient rulers of the region, the mighty Wari (Huari) lords who reigned from a capital near modern Ayacucho, had fallen by 1100, in part due to a severe drought that afflicted the Andes for a century or more. In the ensuing turmoil, local chiefs across the Peruvian highlands battled over scarce water and led raiders into neighboring villages in search of food. Hordes of refugees fled to frigid, windswept hideouts above 13,000 feet.

But in the fertile, well-watered valley around Cusco, Inca farmers stood their ground. Instead of splintering apart and warring among themselves, Inca villages united into a small state capable of mounting an organized defense. And between 1150 and 1300, the Inca around Cusco began to capitalize on a major warming trend in the Andes.

As temperatures climbed, Inca farmers moved up the slopes by 800 to 1,000 feet, building tiers of agricultural terraces, irrigating their fields, and reaping record corn harvests. "These surpluses," says Alex Chepstow-Lusty, a paleoecologist at the French Institute for Andean Studies in Lima who has been studying the region's ancient climate, allowed the Inca to "free up many people for other roles, whether building roads or maintaining a large army." In time Inca rulers could call up more conscripts and supply a larger army than any neighboring chief.

With this big stick, Inca kings began eyeing the lands and resources of others. They struck marriage alliances with neighboring lords, taking their daughters as wives, and dispensed generous gifts to new allies. When a rival lord spurned their advances or stirred up trouble, they flexed their military might. In all the surrounding valleys, local lords succumbed one by one, until there was only one mighty state and one capital, the sacred city of Cusco.

Flush with success, Inca kings set their sights farther afield, on the wealthy lands surrounding Lake Titicaca. Sometime after 1400, one of the greatest Inca rulers, Pachacutec Inca Yupanqui, began planning his conquest of the south. It was the dawn of empire.

Massed on a high, cold Peruvian plain north of the great lake in the mid-1400s, the army of the Colla bristled with battle gear, daring the Inca invaders to make war. Pachacutec scanned the enemy ranks in silence, preparing for the great battle ahead. The lords of the Titicaca region were haughty men, ruling as many as 400,000 people in kingdoms arrayed around the lake. Their lands were rich and desirable. Gold and silver veined the mountains, and herds of alpacas and llamas fattened in lush meadows. Military success in the Andes depended on such livestock. A llama, the only draft animal on the continent, could carry 70 pounds of gear on its back. Llamas, along with alpacas, also provided meat, leather, and fiber for clothing. They were jeeps, K rations, and fatigues all rolled into one—crucial military assets. If the Inca king could not conquer the Titicaca lords who owned these vast herds, he would live in fear of the day these lords would come to conquer him. Seated on a shimmering litter, Pachacutec issued the order to attack. Playing panpipes carved from the bones of enemies and war drums fashioned from the flayed skins of dead foes, his soldiers advanced toward the Colla forces, a moving wall of terror and intimidation. Then both sides charged. When the fog of battle lifted, Colla bodies littered the landscape. In the years that followed, Pachacutec and his descendants subdued all the southern lords.

"The conquest of the Titicaca Basin was the jewel in the crown of the Inca Empire," says Charles Stanish, an archaeologist at the University of California, Los Angeles. But military victory was only the first step in the Inca's grand strategy of empire building. Officials next set about establishing civil control.

If provinces mounted resistance, Inca sovereigns reshuffled their populations, deporting restive inhabitants to the Inca heartland and replacing them with loyal subjects. Residents of remote walled villages were moved to new Inca-controlled towns sited along Inca roads—roads that sped the movement of Inca troops. Inca governors ordered the construction of roadside storehouses for those troops and commanded local communities to fill them with provisions. "The Inca were the organizational geniuses of the Americas," says Stanish. Under Inca rule, Andean civilization flowered as never before. Inca engineers transformed fragmentary road networks into interconnected highways. Inca farmers mastered high-altitude agriculture, cultivating some 70 different native crops and often stockpiling three to seven years' worth of food in vast storage complexes. Imperial officials excelled at the art of inventory control, tracking storehouse contents across the realm with an ancient Andean form of computer code—colored and knotted cords known as quipus. And Inca masons raised timeless architectural masterpieces like Machu Picchu, which continues to awe visitors today.

By the time the Inca king Huayna Capac took power around 1493, little seemed beyond the reach of the Inca dynasty. To bring grandeur to his new capital in Ecuador, Huayna Capac put more than 4,500 rebellious subjects to work hauling immense stone blocks all the way from Cusco—a distance of nearly a thousand miles up and down vertiginous mountain roads. And in the Inca heartland, a small army of men and women toiled to construct a royal estate for Huayna Capac and his family. At the king's bidding, they moved the Urubamba River to the southern side of the valley. They leveled hills and drained marshes, then planted corn and other crops such as cotton, peanuts, and hot peppers from far corners of the empire. In the center of the estate, they laid stones and bricks for Huayna Capac's new country palace, Quispiguanca.

As the late afternoon sun slants down, I wander the ruins of Quispiguanca with Alan Covey, the archaeologist from SMU. Situated on the outskirts of the modern town of Urubamba, Quispiguanca basks in one of the warmest and sunniest microclimates in the region, which provided the Inca royal family a welcome escape from the cold of Cusco. The estate's gatehouses now look out on a field of pungent cilantro, and its surviving walls enclose a royal compound that once sprawled over an area equivalent to some seven soccer fields. Encircled by parkland, fields, and gardens, Quispiguanca was an Inca version of Camp David, a retreat from the world, a place for a warrior-king to unwind after military campaigning. Here Huayna Capac entertained guests in the great halls and gambled with courtiers and other favorites, while his queen gardened and tended doves. The grounds boasted a secluded lodge and a forest reserved for hunting deer and other game. In the fields hundreds of workers cleared irrigation channels, raised and mended terrace walls, and sowed corn and a host of exotic crops. These provided Huayna Capac with bountiful harvests and enough corn beer to entertain his subjects royally during Cusco's annual festivals.

Quispiguanca was not the only spectacular estate. Inca kings inherited little more than their titles, so each new sovereign built a city palace and country home for himself and his lineage shortly after assuming power. To date archaeologists and historians have located ruins of roughly a dozen royal estates built by at least six Inca kings.

Even after these kings died, they remained the powers behind the throne. "The ancestors were a key element of Andean life," says Sonia Guillén, director of Peru's Museo Leymebamba. When Huayna Capac perished of a mysterious disease in Ecuador around 1527, retainers mummified his body and carried it back to Cusco. Members of the royal family frequently visited the deceased monarch, asking his advice on vital matters and heeding the replies given by an oracle sitting at his side. Years after his death, Huayna Capac remained the owner of Quispiguanca and the surrounding estate. Indeed, royal tradition dictated that its harvest keep his mummy, servants, wives, and descendants in style for eternity.

It was during the rainy season in 1533, an auspicious time for a coronation, and thousands of people were packed into the main plaza of Cusco to celebrate the arrival of their new teenage king. Two years earlier, amid a civil war, foreign invaders had landed in the north. Metal-clad and bearing lethal new weapons, the Spaniards had journeyed to the northern Inca town of Cajamarca, where they took prisoner the Inca king, Atahuallpa. Eight months later, they executed their royal captive, and in 1533 their leader, Francisco Pizarro, picked a young prince, Manco Inca Yupanqui, to rule as a puppet king.

In the far distance, voices of the young king's bearers echoed through the streets, singing songs of praise. Falling silent, celebrants watched the royal teenager enter the square, accompanied by the mummies of his ancestors, each richly attired and seated on a splendid litter. The wizened kings and their consorts reminded all that Manco Inca descended from a long line of kings. Rulers of other realms might content themselves with displaying carved or painted images of their glorious ancestors. The Inca kings went one better, displaying the expertly preserved bodies of their forefathers.

In the months that followed, the Spanish invaders seized the palaces of Cusco and the spacious country estates and took royal women as mistresses and wives. Incensed, Manco Inca rebelled and in 1536 tried to drive them from the realm. When his army suffered defeat, he fled Cusco for the jungle city of Vilcabamba, from which he launched guerrilla attacks. The Spanish wouldn't subdue the stronghold until 1572.

In the turmoil of those decades, the Inca's sprawling network of roads, storehouses, temples, and estates began slowly falling into ruin. As the empire crumbled, the Inca and their descendants made a valiant attempt to preserve the symbols of imperial authority. Servants collected the precious bodies of the sacred kings and concealed them around Cusco, where they were worshipped in secret—and in defiance of Spanish priests. In 1559 Cusco's chief magistrate, Juan Polo de Ondegardo, resolved to stamp out this idolatry. He launched an official search for the bodies, questioning hundreds. With this information he tracked down and seized the remains of 11 Inca kings and several queens.

For a time colonial officials in Lima displayed the mummies of Pachacutec, Huayna Capac, and two other royals as curiosities in the Hospital of San Andrés in Lima, a facility that admitted only European patients. But the damp coastal climate wreaked havoc with the bodies. So Spanish officials buried the greatest of the Inca kings in secrecy in Lima, far from the Andes and the people who loved and worshipped them.

In 2001 Brian Bauer and two Peruvian colleagues, historian Teodoro Hampe Martínez and archaeologist Antonio Coello Rodríguez, went looking for the mummies of the Inca kings, hoping to right a historic wrong and restore to Peruvians an important part of their cultural heritage. "Can you imagine," Bauer asks, "how American citizens would feel if the British had taken the bodies of the first several presidents back to London during the War of 1812?" For months Bauer and his colleagues pored over old architectural plans of the Hospital of San Andrés, now a girls' school in central Lima. Eventually they identified several possibilities for the burial site of Pachacutec and Huayna Capac. Using ground-penetrating radar, they scanned the likeliest areas, turning up what appeared to be a vaulted underground crypt. Bauer and his Peruvian teammates were thrilled.

When the archaeologists finally dug down and opened the door of the dusty chamber, they were crestfallen. The crypt lay empty. Quite possibly, says Bauer, workmen removed the contents while renovating the hospital after a severe earthquake. Today no one can say where Peru's greatest kings lie. Concludes Bauer sadly, "The fate of the royal Inca mummies remains unknown."

Critical Thinking

1. Why are there so few clues about the lives of Inca kings? In what ways are archaeologists making up for lost time?
2. Until recently, what did most historians and archaeologists believe about the founding of the Inca Empire? What did Brian Bauer find to the contrary?
3. How did the Inca kings of Cuzco come to power?
4. Why did Pachacutec decide that he would have to conquer the Titicaca Basin?
5. In what ways did the Inca become the "organizational geniuses of the Americas"?
6. How did the royal estates function as a retreat for the Inca kings?
7. What did the Spanish do to take control of the Inca? In what ways did the Inca resist?

Living through the Donner Party

The nineteenth-century survivors of the infamous Donner Party told cautionary tales of starvation and cannibalism, greed and self-sacrifice. But not until now are we learning why the survivors survived.

JARED DIAMOND

"Mrs. Fosdick and Mrs. Foster, after eating, returned to the body of [Mr.] Fosdick. There, in spite of the widow's entreaties, Mrs. Foster took out the liver and heart from the body and removed the arms and legs. . . . [Mrs. Fosdick] was forced to see her husband's heart broiled over the fire." "He eat her body and found her flesh the best he had ever tasted! He further stated that he obtained from her body at least four pounds of fat." "Eat baby raw, stewed some of Jake and roasted his head, not good meat, taste like sheep with the rot."

—George Stewart,
Ordeal by *Hunger: The Story of the Donner Party*

Nearly a century and a half after it happened, the story of the Donner Party remains one of the most riveting tragedies in U.S. history. Partly that's because of its lurid elements: almost half the party died, and many of their bodies were defiled in an orgy of cannibalism. Partly, too, it's because of the human drama of noble self-sacrifice and base murder juxtaposed. The Donner Party began as just another nameless pioneer trek to California, but it came to symbolize the Great American Dream gone awry.

By now the tale of that disastrous journey has been told so often that seemingly nothing else remains to be said—or so I thought, until my friend Donald Grayson at the University of Washington sent me an analysis that he had published in the *Journal of Anthropological Research.* By comparing the fates of all Donner Party members, Grayson identified striking differences between those who came through the ordeal alive and those who were not so lucky. In doing so he has made the lessons of the Donner Party universal. Under more mundane life-threatening situations, who among us too will be "lucky"?

Grayson's insights did not depend on new discoveries about the ill-fated pioneers nor on new analytical techniques, but on that most elusive ingredient of great science: a new idea about an old problem. Given the same information, any of you could extract the same conclusions. In fact, on page 163 you'll find the roster of the Donner Party members along with a few personal details about each of them and their fate. If you like, you can try to figure out for yourself some general rules about who is most likely to die when the going gets tough.

The Lewis and Clark Expedition of 1804 to 1806 was the first to cross the continent, but they didn't take along ox-drawn wagons, which were a requirement for pioneer settlement. Clearing a wagon route through the West's unmapped deserts and mountains proved far more difficult than finding a footpath. Not until 1841 was the first attempt made to haul wagons and settlers overland to California, and only in 1844 did the effort succeed. Until the Gold Rush of 1848 unleashed a flood of emigrants, wagon traffic to California remained a trickle.

As of 1846, when the Donner Party set out, the usual wagon route headed west from St. Louis to Fort Bridger in Wyoming, then northwest into Idaho before turning southwest through Nevada and on to California. However, at that time a popular guidebook author named Lansford Hastings was touting a shortcut that purported to cut many miles from the long trek. Hastings's route continued west from Fort Bridger through the Wasatch mountain range, then south of Utah's Great Salt Lake across the Salt Lake Desert, and finally rejoined the usual California Trail in Nevada.

In the summer of 1846 a number of wagon parties set out for California from Fort Bridger. One, which left shortly before the Donner Party, was guided by Hastings himself. Using his shortcut, the party would eventually make it to California, albeit with great difficulty.

The pioneers who would become the members of the Donner Party were in fact all headed for Fort Bridger to join the Hastings expedition, but they arrived too late. With Hastings thus unavailable to serve as a guide, some of these California-bound emigrants opted for the usual route instead. Others, however, decided to try the Hastings Cutoff anyway. In all, 87 people in 23 wagons chose the cutoff. They consisted of 10 unrelated families and 16 lone individuals, most of them well-to-do midwestern farmers and townspeople who had met by chance and joined forces for protection. None had had any real experience of the western mountains or Indians. They became known as the Donner Party because they elected an elderly Illinois farmer named George Donner as their captain. They left Fort Bridger on July 31, one of the last parties of that summer to begin the long haul to California.

Within a fortnight the Donner Party suffered their first crushing setback, when they reached Utah's steep, brush-covered Wasatch Mountains. The terrain was so wild that, in order to cross, the men had first to build a wagon road. It took 16 backbreaking days to cover just 36 miles, and afterward the people and draft animals were worn out. A second blow followed almost immediately thereafter, west of the Great Salt Lake, when the party ran into an 80-mile stretch of desert. To save themselves from death by thirst, some of the pioneers were forced to unhitch their wagons, rush ahead with their precious animals to the next spring, and return to retrieve the wagons. The rush became a disorganized panic, and many of the animals died, wandered off, or were killed by Indians. Four wagons and large quantities of supplies had to be abandoned. Not until September 30—two full months after leaving Fort Bridger—did the Donner Party emerge from their fatal shortcut to rejoin the California Trail.

By November 1 they had struggled up to Truckee Lake—later renamed Donner Lake—at an elevation of 6,000 feet on the eastern flank of the Sierra Nevada, west of the present-day California-Nevada border. Snow had already begun to fall during the last days of October, and now a fierce snowstorm defeated the exhausted party as they attempted to cross a 7,200-foot pass just west of the lake. With that storm, a trap snapped shut around them: they had set out just a little too late and proceeded just a little too slowly. They now faced a long winter at the lake, with very little food.

Death had come to the Donner Party even before it reached the lake. There were five casualties: on August 29 Luke Halloran died of "consumption" (presumably tuberculosis); on October 5 James Reed knifed John Snyder in self-defense, during a fight that broke out when two teams of oxen became entangled; three days later Lewis Keseberg abandoned an old man named Hardkoop who had been riding in Keseberg's wagon, and most of the party refused to stop and search for him; sometime after October 13 two German emigrants, Joseph Reinhardt and Augustus Spitzer, murdered a rich German named Wolfinger while ostensibly helping him to cache his property; and on October 20 William Pike was shot as he and his brother-in-law were cleaning a pistol.

They cut off and roasted flesh from the corpses, restrained only by the rule that no one partook of his or her relative's body.

In addition, four party members had decided earlier to walk out ahead to Sutter's Fort (now Sacramento) to bring back supplies and help. One of those four, Charles Stanton, rejoined the party on October 19, bringing food and two Indians sent by Sutter. Thus, of the 87 original members of the Donner Party, 79—plus the two Indians—were pinned down in the winter camp at Donner Lake.

The trapped pioneers lay freezing inside crude tents and cabins. They quickly exhausted their little remaining food, then killed and ate their pack animals. Then they ate their dogs. Finally they boiled hides and blankets to make a glue-like soup. Gross selfishness became rampant, as families with food refused to share it with destitute families or demanded exorbitant payment. On December 16 the first death came to the winter camp when 24-year-old Baylis Williams succumbed to starvation. On that same day 15 of the strongest people—5 women and 10 men, including Charles Stanton and the two Indians—set out across the pass on homemade snowshoes, virtually without food and in appallingly cold and stormy weather, in the hope of reaching outside help. Four of the men left behind their families; three of the women left behind their children.

On the sixth morning an exhausted Stanton let the others go on ahead of him; he remained behind to die. On the ninth day the remaining 14 for the first time openly broached the subject of cannibalism which had already been on their minds. They debated drawing lots as to who should be eaten, or letting two people shoot it out until one was killed and could be eaten. Both proposals were rejected in favor of waiting for someone to die naturally.

Such opportunities soon arose. On Christmas Eve, as a 23-year-old man named Antoine, a bachelor, slept in a heavy stupor, he stretched out his arm such that his hand fell into the fire. A companion pulled it out at once. When it fell in a second time, however, no one intervened—they simply let it burn. Antoine died, then Franklin Graves, then Patrick Dolan, then Lemuel Murphy. The others cut off and roasted flesh from the corpses, restrained only by the rule that no one would partake of his or her own relative's body. When the corpses were consumed, the survivors began eating old shoes.

On January 5, 23-year-old Jay Fosdick died, only to be cut up and boiled by Mrs. Foster over the protests of Mrs. Fosdick. Soon after, the frenzied Mr. Foster chased down, shot, and killed the two Indians to eat them. That left 7 of the original 15 snowshoers to stagger into the first white settlement in California, after a midwinter trek of 33 days through the snow.

On January 31 the first rescue team set out from the settlement for Donner Lake. It would take three more teams and two and a half months before the ordeal was all over. During that time many more people died, either in the winter camp or while fighting their way out with the rescue teams. There was never enough food, and by the end of February, cannibalism had established itself at the lake.

When William Eddy and William Foster, who had gotten out with the snowshoers, reached the lake with the third rescue team on March 13, they found that Keseberg had eaten their sons. The Foster child's grandmother accused the starving Keseberg of having taken the child to bed with him one night, strangling him, and hanging the corpse on the wall before eating it. Keseberg, in his defense, claimed the children had died naturally. When the rescuers left the lake the next day to return to California, they left Keseberg behind with just four others: the elderly Lavina Murphy, the badly injured George Donner, his 4-year-old nephew Samuel and his healthy wife Tamsen, who could have traveled but insisted on staying with her dying husband.

The fourth and last rescue team reached the lake on April 17 to find Keseberg alone, surrounded by indescribable filth and mutilated corpses. George Donner's body lay with his skull split open to permit the extraction of his brains. Three frozen ox legs lay in plain view almost uneaten beside a kettle of cut-up human flesh. Near Keseberg sat two kettles of blood and a large pan full of fresh human liver and lungs. He alleged that his four companions had died natural deaths, but he was frank about having eaten them. As to why he had not eaten ox leg instead, he explained that it was too dry: human liver and lungs tasted better, and human brains made a good soup. As for Tamsen Donner, Keseberg noted that she tasted the best, being well endowed with fat. In a bundle held by Keseberg the rescuers found silk, jewelry, pistols, and money that had belonged to George Donner.

After returning to Sutter's Fort, one of the rescuers accused Keseberg of having murdered his companions, prompting Keseberg to sue for defamation of character. In the absence of legal proof of murder the court verdict was equivocal, and the issue of Keseberg's guilt remains disputed to this day. However, Tamsen Donner's death is especially suspicious since she had been in strong physical condition when last seen by the third rescue team.

Experience has taught us that the youngest and oldest people are the most vulnerable even under normal conditions, and their vulnerability increases under stress.

Thus, out of 87 Donner Party members, 40 died: 5 before reaching Donner Lake, 22 in their winter camp at the lake, and 13 (plus the two Indians) during or just after efforts to leave the lake. Why those particular 40? From the facts given in the roster, can you draw conclusions, as Grayson did, as to who was in fact the most likely to die?

As a simple first test, compare the fates of Donner Party males and females irrespective of age. Most of the males (30 out of 53) died; most of the females (24 out of 34) survived. The 57 percent death rate among males was nearly double the 29 percent death rate among females.

Next, consider the effect of age irrespective of sex. The worst toll was among the young and the old. Without exception, everyone over the age of 50 died, as did most of the children below the age of 5. Surprisingly, children and teenagers between the ages of 5 and 19 fared better than did adults in their prime (age 20 to 39): half the latter, but less than one-fifth of the former, died.

By looking at the effects of age and sex simultaneously, the advantage the women had over the men becomes even more striking. Most of the female deaths were among the youngest and oldest, who were already doomed by their age. Among those party members aged 5 to 39—the ones whose ages left them some reasonable chance of survival—half the men but only 5 percent of the women died.

The dates of death provide deeper insight. Of the 35 unfortunates who died after reaching the lake, 14 men but not a single woman had died by the end of January. Only in February did women begin to buckle under. From February onward the death toll was essentially equal by sex—11 men, 10 women. The differences in dates of death simply underscore the lesson of the death rates themselves: the Donner Party women were far hardier than the men.

Thus, sex and age considered together account for much of the luck of the survivors. Most of those who died (39 of the 40 victims) had the misfortune to be of the wrong sex, or the wrong age, or both.

Experience has taught us that the youngest and oldest people are the most vulnerable even under normal conditions, and their vulnerability increases under stress. In many natural disasters, those under 10 or over 50 suffered the highest mortality. For instance, children under 10 accounted for over half the 240,000 deaths in the 1970 Bangladesh cyclone, though they constituted only one-third of the exposed population.

Much of the vulnerability of the old and young under stress is simply a matter of insufficient physical strength: these people are less able to walk out through deep snow (in the case of the Donner Party) or to cling to trees above the height of flood waters (in the case of the Bangladesh cyclone). Babies have special problems. Per pound of body weight a baby has twice an adult's surface area, which means double the area across which body heat can escape. To maintain body temperature, babies have to increase their metabolic rate when air temperature drops only a few degrees below body temperature, whereas adults don't have to do so until a drop of 20 to 35 degrees. At cold temperatures the factor by which babies must increase their metabolism to stay warm is several times that for adults. These considerations place even well-fed babies at risk under cold conditions. And the Donner Party babies were at a crippling further disadvantage because they had so little food to fuel their metabolism. They literally froze to death.

But what gave the women such an edge over the men? Were the pioneers practicing the noble motto "women and children first" when it came to dividing food? Unfortunately, "women and children last" is a more accurate description of how most men behave under stress. As the *Titanic* sank, male crew members

Manifest of a Tragic Journey

Donner Family

Name	Sex	Age	Notes
Jacob Donner	M	65	died in Nov. in winter camp
George Donner	M	62	died in Apr. in winter camp
Elizabeth Donner	F	45	died in Mar. in winter camp
Tamsen Donner	F	45	died in Apr. in winter camp
Elitha Donner	F	14	
Solomon Hook	M	14	
William Hook	M	12	died Feb. 28 with first rescue team
Leanna Donner	F	12	
George Donner	M	9	
Mary Donner	F	7	
Frances Donner	F	6	
Isaac Donner	M	5	died Mar. 7 with second rescue team
Georgia Donner	F	4	
Samuel Donner	M	4	died in Apr. in winter camp
Lewis Donner	M	3	died Mar. 7 or 8 in winter camp
Eliza Donner	F	3	

Murphy-Foster-Pike Family

Name	Sex	Age	Notes
Lavina Murphy	F	50	died around Mar. 19 in winter camp
William Foster	M	28	
William Pike	M	25	died Oct. 20 by gunshot
Sara Foster	F	23	
Harriet Pike	F	21	
John Landrum Murphy	M	15	died Jan. 31 in winter camp
Mary Murphy	F	13	
Lemuel Murphy	M	12	died Dec. 27 with snowshoers
William Murphy	M	11	
Simon Murphy	M	10	
George Foster	M	4	died in early Mar. in winter camp
Naomi Pike	F	3	
Catherine Pike	F	1	died Feb. 20 in winter camp

Graves-Fosdick Family

Name	Sex	Age	Notes
Franklin Graves	M	57	died Dec 24. with snowshoers
Elizabeth Graves	F	47	died Mar. 8 with second rescue team
Jay Fosdick	M	23	died Jan. 5 with snowshoers
Sarah Fosdick	F	22	
William Graves	M	18	
Eleanor Graves	F	15	
Lavina Graves	F	13	
Nancy Graves	F	9	
Jonathan Graves	M	7	
Franklin Graves Jr.	M	5	died Mar. 8 with second rescue team
Elizabeth Graves	F	1	died soon after rescue by second team

Breen Family

Name	Sex	Age	Notes
Patrick Breen	M	40	
Mary Breen	F	40	
John Breen	M	14	
Edward Breen	M	13	
Patrick Breen Jr.	M	11	
Simon Breen	M	9	
Peter Breen	M	7	
James Breen	M	4	
Isabella Breen	F	1	

Reed Family

Name	Sex	Age	Notes
James Reed	M	46	
Margaret Reed	F	32	
Virginia Reed	F	12	
Patty Reed	F	8	
James Reed Jr.	M	5	
Thomas Reed	M	3	

Eddy Family

Name	Sex	Age	Notes
William Eddy	M	28	
Eleanor Eddy	F	25	died Feb. 7 in winter camp
James Eddy	M	3	died in early Mar. in winter camp
Margaret Eddy	F	1	died Feb. 4 in winter camp

Keseberg Family

Name	Sex	Age	Notes
Lewis Keseberg	M	32	
Phillipine Keseberg	F	32	
Ada Keseberg	F	3	died Feb. 24 with first rescue team
Lewis Keseberg Jr.	M	1	died Jan. 24 in winter camp

McCutchen Family

Name	Sex	Age	Notes
William McCutchen	M	30	
Amanda McCutchen	F	24	
Harriet McCutchen	F	1	died Feb. 2 in winter camp

Williams Family

Name	Sex	Age	Notes
Eliza Williams	F	25	
Baylis Williams	M	24	died Dec. 16 in winter camp

Wolfinger Family

Name	Sex	Age	Notes
Mr. Wolfingter	M	?	killed around Oct. 13 by Reinhardt and Spitzer
Mrs. Wolfinger	F	?	

Unrelated Individuals

Name	Sex	Age	Notes
Mr. Hardkoop	M	60	died around Oct. 8, abandoned by Lewis Keseberg
Patrick Dolan	M	40	died Dec. 25 with snowshoers
Charles Stanton	M	35	died around Dec. 21 with snowshoers
Charles Burger	M	30	died Dec. 29 in winter camp
Joseph Reinhardt	M	30	died in Nov. or early Dec. in winter camp
Augustus Spitzer	M	30	died Feb. 7 in winter camp
John Denton	M	28	died Feb. 24 with first rescue team
Milton Elliot	M	28	died Feb. 9 in winter camp
Luke Halloran	M	25	died Aug. 29 of consumption
William Herron	M	25	
Samuel Shoemaker	M	25	died in Nov. or early Dec. in winter camp
James Smith	M	25	died in Nov. or early Dec. in winter camp
James Smith	M	25	died in Nov. or early Dec. in winter camp
John Snyder	M	25	killed Oct. 5 by James Reed
Jean Baptiste Trubode	M	23	
Antoine	M	23	died Dec. 24 with snowshoers
Noah James	M	20	

took many places in lifeboats while leaving women and children of steerage class below decks to drown. Much grosser male behavior emerged when the steamship *Atlantic* sank in 1879: the death toll included 294 of the 295 women and children on board, but only 187 of the 636 men. In the Biafran famine of the late 1960s, when relief agencies tried to distribute food to youngsters under 10 and to pregnant and nursing women, Biafran men gave a brutally frank response: "Stop all this rubbish, it is we men who shall have the food, let the children die, we will make new children after the war." Similarly, accounts by Donner Party members yield no evidence of hungry men deferring to women, and babies fared especially poorly.

Instead, we must seek some cause other than male self-sacrifice to account for the survival of Donner Party women. One contributing factor is that the men were busy killing each other. Four of the five deaths before the pioneers reached the lake, plus the deaths of the two Indians, involved male victims of male violence, a pattern that fits widespread human experience.

However, invoking male violence still leaves 26 of 30 Donner Party male deaths unexplained. It also fails to explain why men began starving and freezing to death nearly two months before women did. Evidently the women had a big physiological advantage. This could be an extreme expression of the fact that, at every age and for all leading causes of death—from cancer and car accidents to heart disease and suicide—the death rate is far higher for men than for women. While the reasons for this ubiquitous male vulnerability remain debated, there are several compelling reasons why men are more likely than women to die under the extreme conditions the Donner Party faced.

The Donner Party records make it vividly clear that family members stuck together and helped one another at the expense of the others.

First, men are bigger than women. Typical body weights for the world as a whole are about 140 pounds for men and only 120 pounds for women. Hence, even while lying down and doing nothing, men need more food to support their basal metabolism. They also need more energy than women do for equivalent physical activity. Even for sedentary people, the typical metabolic rate for an average-size woman is 25 percent lower than an average-size man's. Under conditions of cold temperatures and heavy physical activity, such as were faced by the Donner Party men when doing the backbreaking work of cutting the wagon road or hunting for food, men's metabolic rates can be double those of women.

To top it all off, women have more fat reserves than men: fat makes up 22 percent of the body weight of an average non-obese, well-nourished woman, but only 16 percent of a similar man. More of the man's weight is instead made up of muscle, which gets burned up much more quickly than does fat. Thus, when there simply was no more food left, the Donner Party men burned up their body reserves much faster than did the women. Furthermore, much of women's fat is distributed under the skin and acts as heat insulation, so that they can withstand cold temperatures better than men can. Women don't have to raise their metabolic rate to stay warm as soon as men do.

These physiological factors easily surpass male murderousness in accounting for all those extra male deaths in the Donner Party. Indeed, a microcosm of the whole disaster was the escape attempt by 15 people on snowshoes, lasting 33 days in midwinter. Of the ten men who set out, two were murdered by another man, six starved or froze to death, and only two survived. Not a single one of the five women with them died.

Even with all these explanations, there is still one puzzling finding to consider: the unexpectedly high death toll of people in their prime, age 20 to 39. That toll proves to be almost entirely of the men: 67 percent of the men in that age range (14 out of 21) died, a much higher proportion than among the teenage boys (only 20 percent). Closer scrutiny shows why most of those men were so unlucky.

Most of the Donner Party consisted of large families, but there were also 16 individuals traveling without any relatives. All those 16 happened to be men, and all but two were between 20 and 39. Those 16 unfortunates bore the brunt of the prime-age mortality. Thirteen of them died, and most of them died long before any of the women. Of the survivors, one—William Herron—reached California in October, so in reality only 2 survived the winter at the lake.

Of the 7 men in their prime who survived, 4 were family men. Only 3 of the 14 dead were. The prime-age women fared similarly: the 8 survivors belonged to families with an average size of 12 people, while Eleanor Eddy, the only woman to die in this age group, had no adult support. Her husband had escaped with the snowshoers, leaving her alone with their two small children.

The Donner Party records make it vividly clear that family members stuck together and helped one another at the expense of the others. A notorious example was the Breen family of nine, every one of whom (even two small children) survived through the luck of retaining their wagons and some pack animals much longer than the others, and through their considerable selfishness toward others. Compare this with the old bachelor Hardkoop, who was ordered out of the Keseberg family wagon and abandoned to die, or the fate of the young bachelor Antoine, whom none of the hungry snowshoers bothered to awaken when his hand fell into the fire.

Family ties can be a matter of life and death even under normal conditions. Married people, it turns out, have lower death rates than single, widowed, or divorced people. And marriage's life-promoting benefits have been found to be shared by all sorts of social ties, such as friendships and membership in social groups. Regardless of age or sex or initial health status, socially isolated individuals have well over twice the death rate of socially connected people.

For reasons about which we can only speculate, the lethal effects of social isolation are more marked for men than for women. It's clear, though, why social contacts are important for both sexes. They provide concrete help in case of need. They're our source of advice and shared information. They provide a sense of belonging and self-worth, and the courage to face tomorrow. They make stress more bearable.

All those benefits of social contact applied as well to the Donner Party members, who differed only in that their risk of death was much greater and their likely circumstances of death more grotesque than yours and mine. In that sense too, the harrowing story of the Donner Party grips us because it was ordinary life writ large.

Critical Thinking

1. Why was the Donner Party so late in getting to the eastern flank of the Sierra Nevada?
2. Why had death come to the Donner Party even before reaching Truckee Lake?
3. What did the trapped pioneers do once they exhausted their little remaining food?
4. Once the subject of cannibalism had been broached, how did they decide to go about it? What was the one rule that would restrain them?
5. What conclusions can we draw from the roster of the Donner Party with respect to gender and age? How does Jared Diamond explain these differences in death rate?
6. How important to survival are family ties and membership in social groups? Explain.

Jared Diamond is a contributing editor of *Discover,* a professor of physiology at UCLA School of Medicine, a recipient of a MacArthur genius award, and the author of *The Third Chimpanzee.*

UNIT 6

Contemporary Archaeology

Unit Selections

Learning Outcomes

After reading this Unit, you will be able to:

- Discuss the pros and cons of describing the Amazon rainforest as a "counterfeit paradise."
- Explain Betty Meggers thinking when she accuses some archaeologists as endangering the rainforest.
- Discuss the evidence for regional integration of agricultural communities in the Amazon.
- Identify the links between the archaeological evidence and the present-day customs of the Kuikuro of the Amazon.
- Did Brazil's rain forest once support an ancient civilization? Support your position.
- Discuss the ways in which the Nazis used prehistoric archaeology to further their political goals.
- Discuss the motivations of German archaeologists that went along with the Nazi Party's use of archaeology to further its own ends. Discuss what you would do and why.
- Review the effects of climate change on archaeological sites around the world.

Student Website

www.mhhe.com/cls

Internet References

Al Mashriq-Archaeology in Beirut
http://almashriq.hiof.no/base/archaeology.html

American Indian Ritual Object Repatriation Foundation
www.repatriationfoundation.org

Archaeology and Anthropology: The Australian National University
http://online.anu.edu.au/AandA

ArchNet—WWW Virtual Library
http://archnet.asu.edu/archnet

Current Archaeology
www.archaeology.co.uk

National Archaeological DataBase
www.cast.uark.edu/other/nps/nagpra/nagpra.html

Past Horizons
www.pasthorizonspr.com

Society for Archaeological Sciences
www.socarchsci.org

WWW Classical Archaeology
www.archaeology.org/wwwarky/classical.html

The origins of contemporary archaeology may be traced back to the nineteenth century. Several currents of thought and beliefs coalesced in that unique century. Some say it started with a Frenchman named Boucher de Perthes who found odd shaped stones on his property, stones that could comfortably be held by a human hand. Undoubtedly, thousands of other people made such finds throughout history. But to Monsieur de Perthes, these stones suggested a novel meaning. He wondered if these odd rocks might be tools made by humans long lost in the mists before history.

Other exciting changes were occurring in the epistemology of the nineteenth century that would soon lend credibility to this hypothesis. In 1859, there was the publication of "On the Origin of Species" by Charles Darwin. In this book (which, by the way, never mentioned humans or any implied relationship they might have to apes), Darwin suggested a general process that became known as natural selection. The theory suggested that species could change gradually in response to the environment. This was an idea counterintuitive to scientific thought. Even biologists believed that species were immutable. But this theory changed forever the way human beings regarded their place in nature. If species could change, then the implication was—so could humans. And that idea knocked humankind down from the loft and into the archaeological record.

There was the concurrent emergence of uniformitarianism, which implied that the Earth was old, very old. (It is, in fact, about 5 billion years old.) But with this idea, the revolutionary possibility that human beings could have existed before history became more plausible. Such a serious challenge to the established wisdom that the Earth was only about 6,000 years old additionally contributed to the new age speculation about the meaning of being human.

The newly emerging science of paleontology, and the discovery and recognition of extinct fossil species seriously challenged the traditional, elevated status of human beings. Nineteenth-century philosophers were forced to reexamine the nature of humanity. Among the intellectuals of the Western world, the essential anthropocentrism of the Christian view gradually shifted to a more secular view of humankind as a part and parcel of nature. Therefore, humans became subject to the rules of nature and natural events, without reference to theology.

So, it was within this new nineteenth-century enlightenment that Boucher de Perthes suggested his hypothesis regarding the antiquity of his stone tools. The time had come, and others came forward saying that they too had found these same, odd shaped stones, and had thought similar thoughts. The study of archaeology had begun.

As a science evolves, it naturally diversifies. In fact, because mainstream archaeology is being pulled in different directions, some have had concerns that archaeologists will specialize themselves right out of the mainstream of anthropology. The other side of the coin, however, is that our shared cultural concept and holistic approach should help us to maintain our traditional relationships with each other, and with the field of anthropology.

Current economic climate presents challenges in yet another realm, that of financing future archaeological endeavors and finding additional sources of labor. And then, there are the ethical questions that archaeologists must consider. Because an archaeological site is a nonrenewable resource, excavation results in the systematic destruction of the site and its ecological context. Anything overlooked, mislaid, not measured, or in some way not observed is a lost piece of the past, and if the information that is retrieved is never shared with an audience, it is a complete loss. Yet, as the world population continues to expand, we are destined to impact this scarce and valuable resource. The applied field of archaeology, commonly referred to as Cultural Resource Management (CRM), deals with the complex needs of developers and state and federal agencies. Its practitioners derive their livelihood from this work, even if it means physically destroying archaeological sites. They do so while striving to mitigate adverse impact, and collect data in a way that will enable the archaeological community of the future to answer questions that have yet to be asked.

One saving grace in the field may be found in the current trend toward a more "public archaeology." There is awareness that archaeologists should present their findings in a more palatable, story format. Now is the time for the archaeological community to start a give-and-take dialogue with the public; by portraying their projects within the larger picture that expresses more than a set of tedious details in archaeological lingo. It is for these reasons that the articles presented in this section deal with the archaeological community's current interest in the preservation, conservation, and reconstruction of archaeological sites, and their educational and aesthetic value.

Earth Movers

Archaeologists say Brazil's rain forest, once thought to be inhospitable to humans, fostered huge ancient civilizations. The proof is in the dirt.

MARION LLOYD

High along bluffs overlooking the confluence of the mighty Negro and Solimões Rivers here, supersize eggplants, papayas, and cassava spring from the ground.

Their exuberance defies a long-held belief about the Amazon. For much of the last half century, archaeologists viewed the South American rain forest as a "counterfeit paradise," a region whose inhospitable environment precluded the development of complex societies. But new research suggests that prehistoric man found ways to overcome the jungle's natural limitations—and to thrive in this environment in large numbers.

The secret, says James B. Petersen, an archaeologist at the University of Vermont who has spent the past decade working in the Brazilian Amazon, is found in the ground beneath his feet. It is a highly fertile soil called *terra preta do indio,* which is Portuguese for "Indian black earth." By some estimates, this specially modified soil covers as much as 10 percent of Amazonia, the immense jungle region that straddles the Amazon River. And much of that area is packed with potsherds and other signs of human habitation.

"This was one of the last archaeological frontiers on the planet. It's as if we know nothing about it," says Mr. Petersen, as he analyzes the discovery of the day, a series of circular carbon deposits that might indicate the outline of a prehistoric house.

Scientists are now working to determine whether *terra preta,* which contains high levels of organic matter and carbon, was deliberately created by pre-Columbian civilizations to improve upon the notoriously poor rain-forest soil, or whether the modified earth was an accidental byproduct of sustained habitation by large groups of people.

Either way, Mr. Petersen believes it likely that pre-Columbian societies in the Amazon were not the primitive tribal societies they were once thought to be, but highly complex chiefdoms.

"We're providing the proof," he says during a several-week-long dig in August near the Brazilian jungle city of Manaus. His team of American and Brazilian archaeologists, who call themselves the Central Amazon Project, have excavated more than 60 sites rich in *terra preta* near where the Negro and Solimões Rivers merge to form the Amazon River proper.

One of the group's founders, Michael J. Heckenberger of the University of Florida, is bolstering the new findings with research on large prehistoric earthworks farther east along the upper Xingu River. Studying this area, which now is inhabited by the Kuikuru Indians, has allowed him to compare data of prehistoric land management with modern ethnographic studies.

On some pre-Columbian sites explored by Mr. Petersen and his team, several miles of earth are packed with millions of potsherds. The archaeologists have also found evidence that they say points to the existence of giant plazas, bridges, and roads, complete with curbs, and defensive ditches that would have taken armies of workers to construct.

Intriguingly, the earliest evidence of large, sedentary populations appears to coincide with the beginnings of *terra preta.*

"Something happened 2,500 years ago, and we don't know what," says Eduardo Góes Neves, a Brazilian archaeologist at the Federal University of São Paulo, who is co-director of the Central Amazon Project. He dusts off the flanged edge of a bowl from around 400 B.C. that one of his Brazilian graduate students pulled from a layer of *terra preta* eight feet down. The team got lucky when the landowner at Açutuba, the largest of their excavation sites, bulldozed a huge pit in one of his fields. The "swimming pool," as the team jokingly calls the 15-yard-wide hole, is giving them a rare chance to compare levels of *terra preta* over a large area.

The research has implications not only for history, but also for the future of the Amazon rain forest. If scientists could discover how the Amerindians transformed the soil, farmers could use the technology to maximize smaller plots of land, rather than cutting down ever larger swaths of jungle. The benefits of what Mr. Petersen calls this "gift from the past" are already well known to farmers in the area, who plant their crops wherever they find *terra preta.*

Rich in Controversy

The claims made for *terra preta* extend far beyond a legacy passed down from farmer to farmer. The archaeologists now reject the idea that pre-contact Amerindians were—as one team member says, ironically—"Stone Age primitives frozen at the dawn of time."

"It's made by pre-Columbian Indians and it's still fertile," says Bruno Glaser, a soil chemist from the University of Bayreuth, in Germany, who was taking samples of *terra preta* from another site discovered by Mr. Petersen's team. "If we knew how to do this, it would be a model for agriculture in the whole region."

It's made by pre-Columbian Indians and it's still fertile. If we knew how to do this, it would be a model for agriculture in the whole region.

Ideally what researchers dub "slash and char" agriculture, the indigenous technique that returns nutrients to the soil by mixing in organic waste and carbon, could replace slash-and-burn, a contemporary technique that consumes tens of thousands of acres of rain forest every year. Mr. Glaser is part of an international team of scientists studying the chemical composition of *terra preta* in an effort to recreate it.

The research into *terra preta* fuels a revisionist school of scientists who argue that pre-Columbian Amazonia was not a pristine wilderness, but rather a heavily managed forest teeming with human beings. They believe that advanced societies existed in the Amazon from before the time of Christ until a century after the European conquest in the 1500s decimated Amerindian populations through exploitation and disease. The theory is also supported by the accounts of the first Europeans to travel the length of the Amazon in 1542. They reported human settlements with tens of thousands of people stretching for many miles along the river banks.

But not everyone working in the field of Amazonian research buys the new theory.

"The idea that the indigenous population has secrets that we don't know about is not supported by anything except wishful thinking and the myth of El Dorado," says the archaeologist Betty J. Meggers, who is the main defender of the idea that only small, tribal societies ever inhabited the Amazon. "This myth just keeps going on and on and on. It's amazing."

Ms. Meggers, director of the Latin American Archaeology Program at the Smithsonian Institution's Museum of Natural History, in Washington, has spent her life trying to prove that Amazonia is a uniquely untrammeled and hostile wilderness. Now 82, Ms. Meggers has been working in the field since the late 1940s, when she and her husband, Clifford Evans, now deceased, began pioneering fieldwork on Marajó Island, at the mouth of the Amazon. She summarized their findings in a seminal 1954 article, "Environmental Limitation on the Development of Culture," which was published in *American Anthropologist.*

Ms. Meggers's 1971 book, *Amazonia: Man and Culture in a Counterfeit Paradise* (Aldine-Atherton), converted her views into gospel for a generation of Amazonian archaeologists. In it, she argued that modern Amerindian groups, generally composed of a few hundred people, follow ancient practices of infanticide and other population-control measures to exist in a hostile environment.

"It had a huge impact," says Susanna B. Hecht, a geographer at the University of California at Los Angeles who has spent three decades studying traditional farming practices in Amazonia. "Virtually every Anthropology I class read that book." Ms. Hecht's most recent research is with the Kayapó Indians in the upper Xingu River, the same region where Mr. Heckenberger is working. To her surprise, she discovered the Indians were creating a version of *terra preta* by burning excess vegetation and weeds and mixing the charcoal into the soil.

"One of the things we found rather unusual was how much burning was going on all the time," she says. "It wasn't catastrophic burning. It was that the whole landscape was smoldering all the time."

Ms. Hecht says the technique was probably more widespread before Indian societies were devastated by the arrival of the Europeans, who introduced measles, typhoid, and other diseases to which the Indians had no resistance. By some estimates, 95 percent of the Amerindians died within the first 130 years of contact. While their numbers were once estimated in the millions, there are now roughly 250,000 Amerindians living in Brazil.

"I think you could have had very dense populations, and what you had was a real holocaust in various forms," she says. However, Ms. Hecht notes, little was known about the impact of those epidemics when Ms. Meggers was first writing, and her persuasive arguments against large civilizations discouraged archaeologists from probing deeper into the Amazon. "Everyone said, 'Nobody was there anyway. Why bother?'" says Ms. Hecht.

The difficulty and dangers of conducting research in the Amazon also played a part. The region was largely impassible until the 1960s, when the Brazilian government began encouraging settlement in the jungle's interior.

A few researchers did challenge Ms. Meggers's theories early on. The most outspoken figure was Donald Lathrap, a University of Illinois archaeologist who worked in the Peruvian Amazon in the 1950s. He argued that Amazonia could and did support complex societies with advanced technology, and that the cradle of those civilizations was very likely in the central Amazon, where Mr. Petersen is working.

Another pioneer was William M. Denevan, a geographer emeritus at the University of Wisconsin, whose discovery of huge earthworks in lowland Bolivia in the early 1960s suggested that pre-Columbian peoples modified their environment for large-scale agriculture. In a 1992 article, "The Pristine Myth: The Landscape of the Americas in 1492," he argued that the modern Amazon rain forest was the result of human management over millennia, not a virgin wilderness.

"The key issue here can be summed up in two words: environmental determinism," he says, referring to the once-popular school of thought, favored by Ms. Meggers, that says environment dictates man's ability to progress. "We are saying people always have options," he says. "We can farm in outer space. And we can farm in the Antarctic. Or we can crop in the driest part of the Sahara Desert. It may be very expensive, but that's a different issue."

Building a Mystery

Other researchers working in Amazonia go even further. They suggest that prehistoric man may have created cities that rivaled those of the Aztecs and Maya. Again, they say, the proof is in the dirt.

William I. Woods, a geographer at Southern Illinois University at Edwardsville, has been studying *terra preta* deposits extending over 100,000 acres around the Brazilian jungle city of Santarém, where the Tapajós River meets the Amazon. He believes as many as 500,000 people might once have inhabited the area, implying a civilization larger than the Aztec capital of Tenochtitlán, once the largest city in the Americas.

"There is some fussing about the magnitude, from" he says. "But I don't think there are too many scholars who have any problems with chiefdoms existing and lots of people being supported for long times in various places in the Amazon."

Ms. Meggers has not taken challenges to her life's work lying down. In a 2001 article in *Latin American Antiquity,* she accuses the revisionist camp of endangering the rain forest by suggesting that large-scale farming was feasible in the region. Her view is shared by some biologists and environmentalists.

"Adherence to 'the lingering myth of Amazonian empires' not only prevents archaeologists from reconstructing the prehistory of Amazonia, but makes us accomplices in the accelerating pace of environmental degradation," she writes.

Mr. Neves, the Brazilian archaeologist, disagrees. "It's not like loggers are revving up the chainsaws after reading our articles," he says as he walks along a winding dirt road littered with pre-Columbian potsherds on his way to the dig site at Açutuba, a jungle-shrouded stretch of farmland overlooking the Negro River. "Deforestation through ranching isn't how the Amerindian interacted with the landscape," he says. "The Amerindians weren't destroying the environment. They were enriching it."

The rain forest is not inherently hostile to man, says Mr. Neves. He argues that pre-Columbian peoples knew how to use the huge diversity of species to their advantage, through a combination of farming, fishing, and managed tree harvesting. Cassava, a starchy root that grows well in the acidic rain-forest soil, was probably the Amerindians' main food source, which the Indians could have supplemented with corn and other vegetables grown on *terra preta.* But they also relied heavily on fish and turtles for protein, he says.

Blowing Dust from the Pages

Terra preta proponents also argue that historical accounts support their theories. The Rev. Gaspar de Carvajal, a Spanish priest who accompanied the first exploratory expedition down the Amazon in 1542, reported seeing hundreds of tortoises kept in corrals and "an abundance of meat and fish . . . that would have fed 1,000 men for a year." The friar also recounts an ambush by more than 10,000 Indians at a point in the river just west of modern-day Manaus, suggesting that the area was heavily populated as recently as the 16th century. He also describes armies of Indians who repelled attempts by the Spaniards to come ashore near modern-day Santarém.

Ms. Meggers is skeptical. "How could these people, when they're fleeing, count 10,000 warriors?" she says. "It's silly." She notes that other portions of Father Carvajal's account, in particular his description of female Amazon warriors, which gave the river its name, have since been dismissed by historians as inventions to impress the Spanish crown.

They have not done enough work to establish whether it was a single large settlement or a result of intermittent occupation over longer periods of time.

She also challenges estimates by the Central Amazon Project that between 5,000 and 10,000 people may have once inhabited Açutuba, possibly the largest site under excavation in the Brazilian Amazon. "They have not done enough work to establish whether it was a single large settlement or a result of intermittent occupation over longer periods of time," she says. She also accuses the group of ignoring the results of surveys in the region backed by the Smithsonian Institution over several decades.

Mr. Petersen shrugs off the criticism. "We're not here to fight Betty Meggers," he says, while taking a break from digging under the broiling jungle sun. "We're here to build on her work and refine it." He says that Ms. Meggers made a major contribution to the field by highlighting the enormous challenges involved in inhabiting the Amazon rain forest, even if he argues that later research shows that pre-Columbian peoples found ways of overcoming those natural limitations.

His team has several dozen radiocarbon dates from potsherds and carbon deposits collected throughout Açutuba, which they say show that the entire site was continuously inhabited during two waves from about 360 B.C. to as late as 1440 A.D. The evidence also supports the existence of stratified societies, says Mr. Petersen. He picks up an ornate, white- and black-painted potsherd from the *terra preta* under a field of glistening eggplants. "This is probably from about A.D. 800, and look how sophisticated it is. It's like fine dinnerware," he says, comparing the sherd with that from a coarser vessel from about the same period, which he calls "everyday china." His team has unearthed more than 100,000 potsherds dating from 500 B.C. to about A.D. 1500 at the three-square-mile site, including roughly a dozen burial urns.

Digging through earth packed with tons of pottery is slow going. Particularly when you only have about eight pairs of hands.

"We've been working here nine years, and we've barely scratched the surface," says Mr. Neves, who has raised the bulk of the money from his university and the São Paulo state government. He estimates that there are at least 100 unexcavated sites within their research area, which extends over 40 square miles around the town of Iranduba. Some of the sites might be even larger than Açutuba.

Ecological Edge

Unlike the Maya in northern Central America, the inhabitants of the Amazon lacked stone for building. So they had to resort to organic and man-made materials. As a result there are few permanent markers of earlier civilizations, forcing archaeologists to extrapolate from small scraps of evidence.

"The only reason that everyone accepts large, socially complex societies in Maya land is that they have surviving pyramids and stelae," says Mr. Petersen. "If the Maya and others had used mostly organic perishables in their architecture, like the Amazon people, then I would bet there would be much more mystery and debate about the nature of pre-Columbian Amerindians in Central America, too."

At a nearby site, called Hatahara, the team recently excavated 11 human skeletons dating to about A.D. 800 from one nine-yard trench dug into a large burial mound. Believing it unlikely that they would have stumbled upon the only evidence in the mound, they estimate there may be hundreds more bodies buried there, suggesting a population of at least a few thousand people.

The skeletons provided the team with other insights into the previous inhabitants. "These were not famine-stricken people," Mr. Neves says, noting that the skeletons measured about 5-foot-7. In contrast, modern indigenous inhabitants often do not grow taller than five feet, a fact used by earlier archaeologists to argue that the jungle was unsuited for human habitation. "I don't think there were ever severe limitations here," says Mr. Neves.

He points at the acres of glistening vegetables that seem to grow effortlessly throughout the Açutuba site. Settlers throughout the Iranduba area take advantage of the abundant *terra preta* deposits to grow vegetables and fruit for the nearby city of Manaus, supplying much of the produce consumed by its 1.4 million people.

"I know *terra preta* is very good and that it was made by the Indians," says Edson Azevedo Santos, a 48-year-old farmer drenched in sweat from weeding his zucchini patch. Unlike the acidic soil found in most of the rain forest, which can only sustain crops for a three-year period, *terra preta* plots can withstand constant farming for decades, if properly managed.

Even more striking, *terra preta* may have the capacity to regenerate itself, says Mr. Woods, the Southern Illinois geographer. He recently tested that possibility by removing a large section of *terra preta* on a plot near Santarem. To his amazement, the soil grew back within three years. "I suggested that the soil should be treated as living organism and that microorganisms are the secret," he says, adding that more research is needed to allow scientists to repeat the process. "This is very sophisticated stuff."

Critical Thinking

1. Why was the South American rain forest referred to as a "counterfeit paradise" for much of the last half century? What does new research suggest?
2. Where is the "secret" found? Explain. What are the alternatives for explaining the *terra preta do indio*?
3. What evidence is there that the appearance of the *terra preta* coincides with the earliest evidence of large, sedentary populations?
4. In what sense does this history have implications for the future?
5. Discuss the claims as well as the evidence put forth by the "revisionist school of scientists" versus the views of Betty J. Meggers.
6. Why does Meggers accuse the revisionist camp of endangering the rain forest? How does Eduardo Góes Neves respond?
7. What historical accounts seem to support the *terra preta* proponents? How does Meggers respond?
8. What are the claims and counter claims regarding Açutuba?
9. Why might there be fewer markers of earlier civilization in the Amazon?
10. What do the 11 human skeletons of Hatahara reveal? What about the acres of "glistening vegetables"?
11. What beneficial qualities does the *terra preta* exhibit?

Lost Cities of the Amazon

The Amazon tropical forest is not as wild as it looks.

MICHAEL J. HECKENBERGER

When Brazil established the Xingu Indigenous Park in 1961, the reserve was far from modern civilization, nestled deep in the southern reaches of the vast Amazon forest. When I first went to live with the Kuikuro, one of the reserve's principal indigenous groups, in 1992, the park's boundaries were still largely hidden in thick forest, little more than lines on a map. Today the park is surrounded by a patchwork of farmland, its borders often marked by a wall of trees. For many outsiders, this towering green threshold is a portal, like the massive gates of Jurassic Park, between the present—the dynamic modern world of soy fields, irrigation systems and 18-wheelers—and the past, a timeless world of primordial nature and society.

Long before taking center stage in the world's environmental crisis as the giant green jewel of global ecology, the Amazon held a special place in the Western imagination. Mere mention of its name conjures images of dripping, vegetation-choked jungles; cryptic, colorful and often dangerous wildlife; endlessly convoluted river networks; and Stone Age tribes. To Westerners, Amazonian peoples are quintessential simple societies, small groups that merely make do with what nature provides. They have complex knowledge about the natural world but lack the hallmarks of civilization: centralized government, urban settlements and economic production beyond subsistence. In 1690 John Locke famously proclaimed, "In the beginning all the World was America." More than three centuries later the Amazon still grips the popular imagination as nature at its purest, home to native peoples who, in the words of *Rolling Stone* editor Sean Woods in October 2007, preserve "a way of life unchanged since the dawn of time."

Looks can be deceiving. Hidden under the forest canopy are the remnants of a complex pre-Columbian society. Working with the Kuikuro, I have excavated a network of ancestral towns, villages and roads that once supported a population perhaps 20 times its present size. Huge swaths of forest have grown over the ancient settlements, gardens, fields and orchards, which fell into disuse when epidemics brought by European explorers and colonists decimated the native peoples. The region's rich biodiversity reflects past human intervention. By developing a mix of land uses, soil-enrichment techniques and long crop rotation cycles, the ancestors of the Kuikuro thrived in the Amazon despite its infertile natural soils. Their accomplishments could inform efforts to reconcile the environmental and development goals of this region and other parts of the Amazon.

"Nature Folk"

The most famous person to go looking for lost civilizations in the southern Amazon was Percy Harrison Fawcett. The British adventurer scoured what he called the "uncharted jungles" for an ancient city, Atlantis in the Amazon, replete with stone pyramids, cobbled streets and alphabetic writing. His tales inspired Conan Doyle's *The Lost World* and perhaps the Indiana Jones movies. David Grann's gripping recent book, *The Lost City of Z,* retraced Fawcett's path before his disappearance in the Xingu in 1925.

Actually, five German expeditions had already visited the Xinguano people and lands. In 1894 Karl von den Steinen's book *Unter den Naturvölkern Zentral Brasiliens,* which described the earliest expeditions, became an instant classic in the fledgling discipline of anthropology. The book set the tone for 20th-century studies of Amazonian peoples as small, isolated groups living in a delicate balance with the tropical forest: "nature folk." Later anthropologists often viewed the forest environment as uniformly inimical to agriculture; the soil's poor fertility seemed to preclude large settlements or dense regional populations. By this reasoning, the Amazon of the past must have looked much like the Amazon in recent times.

But this view began to erode in the 1970s as scholars revisited early European accounts of the region, which talked not of small tribes but of dense populations. As Charles Mann's bestselling book *1491* has eloquently described, the Americas were heavily populated on the eve of the European landings, and the Amazon was no exception. Gaspar de Carvajal, the missionary who chronicled the first Spanish expedition down the river, noted fortified towns, broad, well-kept roads and large numbers of people. Carvajal wrote on June 25, 1542:

> We went among some islands which we thought uninhabited, but after we got to be in among them, so numerous were the settlements which came into sight . . . that we grieved . . . and, when they saw us, there came out to meet us on the river over two hundred pirogues [canoes],

> that each one carries twenty or thirty Indians and some forty . . . they were colorfully decorated with various emblems, and they had with them many trumpets and drums . . . and on land a marvelous thing to see were the squadron formations that were in the villages, all playing instruments and dancing about, manifesting great joy upon seeing that we were passing beyond their villages.

Archaeological research in several areas along the Amazon River, such as Marajó Island at the mouth of the river and sites near the modern cities of Santarèm and Manaus, has confirmed these accounts. These societies interacted in far-flung systems of trade. Less is known about the southern peripheries of the Amazon, but recent work in Llanos de Mojos in lowland Bolivia and in the Brazilian state of Acre suggests that they, too, supported complex societies. In 1720 Brazilian frontiersman António Pires de Campos described a densely settled landscape in the headwaters of the Tapajós River, just west of the Xingu:

> These people exist in such vast quantity, that it is not possible to count their settlements or villages, [and] many times in one day's march one passes ten or twelve villages, and in each one of them there are ten to thirty houses, and in these houses there are some that are thirty to forty paces across . . . even their roads they make very straight and wide, and they keep them so clean that one finds not even a fallen leaf. . . .

An Ancient Walled Town

When I ventured to Brazil in the early 1990s to study the deep history of the Xingu, lost cities were the furthest things from my mind. I had read Steinen but had barely heard of Fawcett. Although much of the vast Amazon basin was archaeological terra incognito, it was unlikely that ethnographers, much less local Xinguanos, had missed a large monolithic center towering over the tropical forests.

Nevertheless, signs of something more elaborate than present-day settlements were all around. Robert Carneiro of the American Museum of Natural History in New York City, who lived with the Kuikuro in the 1950s, had suggested that their settled way of life and productive agricultural and fishing economy could support communities 1,000 to 2,000 strong—several times the contemporary population of a few hundred. He also cited evidence that indeed it once had: a prehistoric site (designated "X11" in our archaeological survey) that was surrounded by extensive ditches. The Villas Boas brothers—Brazilian *indigenistas* who were nominated for a Nobel Peace Prize for their part in creating the Xingu park—had reported such earthworks near many villages.

In January 1993, soon after I arrived in the Kuikuro village, the principal hereditary chief, Afukaka, took me to one of the ditches at a site (X6) they call Nokugu, named for the jaguar spirit being thought to live there. We passed local men who were raising a huge fish weir across the Angahuku River, which was already swelling from the seasonal rains. The ditch, which runs over two kilometers, was two to three meters deep and more than 10 meters wide. Even though I had expected to find an archaeological landscape different from today's, the scale of these ancient communities and their constructions surprised me. Kuikuro research assistants and I spent the following months mapping it and other earthworks at the 45-hectare site.

Since that time, our team has studied numerous other sites in the area, hacking more than 30 kilometers of line-of-sight transects through the forest to map, examine and excavate the sites. Many Kuikuro helped in one way or another, and some became well versed in archaeology.

At the end of 1993, Afukaka and I went back to Nokugu so I could tell him what I had learned. We followed the contour of the site's outer ditch and stopped at an earthen bridge, where a major road we had uncovered passed over it. I pointed down the arrow-straight ancient dirt road, which was 10 to 20 meters wide and led to another ancient site, Heulugihïtï (X13), about five kilometers away. We crossed the bridge and entered Nokugu.

The road, defined by low earthen curbs, widened to 40 meters—the size of a modern four-lane highway. After a couple of hundred meters, we passed over the inner ditch and stopped to look at our recently finished excavation trench, where we had found a funnel-shaped footing for a tree-trunk palisade. Afukaka told me a story of palisaded villages and raids in his people's distant past.

As we moved farther into the ancient town, we passed through patches of forest, scrub and open areas that now cover the site—the footprints of diverse past activities. We emerged into a grassy glade of towering palms marking the former plaza. I slowly spun and pointed along the perfectly circular edge of the plaza, marked by a meter-high mound. The tall palms, I told him, had colonized the plaza centuries ago from compost gardens in domestic areas.

Leaving the plaza to explore the surrounding neighborhoods, we came across large refuse middens that closely resembled the one behind Afukaka's own house. They were filled with broken pots that he noted were exactly like those his wives used to process and cook manioc, down to minute details. On a later visit, when we were excavating a pre-Columbian house, the chief bent down in the central kitchen area, popped out a big hunk of pottery, and corroborated my sense that the daily life of the ancient society was much like today's. "You're right!" Afukaka exclaimed. "Look here, a pot support"—an *undagi,* as the Kuikuro call it, used to cook manioc.

These connections are what make the Xinguano sites so fascinating. They are among the few pre-Columbian settlements in the Amazon where archaeological evidence can be linked directly to present-day customs. Elsewhere, the indigenous culture was completely wiped out, or the archaeological record is spotty. The ancient walled town I showed Afukaka was much like his current village, with its central plaza and radial roads, only it was 10 times larger.

From House to Polity

"Palatial" is not the word that usually comes to mind to describe a pole-and-thatch house. Most Westerners think "hut." But the house that the Kuikuro were building for the chief when I arrived in 1993 was massive: well over 1,000 square meters.

Xingu History

Radiocarbon dating indicates that people have lived in the Upper Xingu for at least 1,500 years.

6th century. The ancestors of today's inhabitants moved in from the west.

13th century. Groups organized themselves into integrated clusters with a regional population estimated at 30,000 to 50,000.

1542. Spanish conquistador Francisco de Orellana led the first European expedition down the Amazon, as chronicled by Gaspar de Carvajal.

18th century. Slave raids further decimated the Xinguano people.

1884. German anthropologist Karl von den Steinen visited the Xingu and estimated a population of 3,500.

1950s. Orlando, Cláudio and Leonardo Villas Boas led a campaign to found the Xingu reserve. The Xinguano population was about 500.

It is hard to imagine that a house built like a giant, overturned basket without stone, mortar or nails could get any bigger. Even the average Xinguano house, at 250 square meters, is as big as the average American home.

What makes the chief's house stand out is not just size but also its position, located on the southern point of the central circular plaza. As one enters the village along the formal entry road, high-ranking families live to the right (south) and left (north). The arrangement reproduces, on a larger scale, the layout of an individual house, whose highest-ranking occupant hangs his hammock to the right, along the long axis of the house. The entry road runs approximately east-west; in the chief's house, his hammock is oriented in the same direction. When a chief dies, he is also laid to rest in a hammock with his head to the west.

This basic corporeal calculus applies on all scales, from houses to the entire Upper Xingu basin. Ancient towns are distributed across the region and interconnected by a lattice of precisely aligned roads. When I first arrived in the area, it took weeks to map the ditches, plazas and roads using standard archaeological techniques. Beginning in 2002, we began using precise GPS, enabling us to map major earthworks in a matter of days. What we have found is an impressive degree of regional integration. The landscape planning seems almost overdetermined, with a specific place for everything. Yet it was based on the same basic principles of the current village. Main roads run east-west, secondary roads radiate out to the north and south, and smaller roads proliferate in other directions.

We mapped two hierarchical clusters of towns and villages in our study area. Each consists of a major ceremonial center and several large satellite towns in precise orientations relative to the center. These towns likely held 1,000 or more inhabitants. Smaller villages are located farther from the center. The northern cluster is centered on X13, which is not a town so much as a ritual center, rather like a fairground. Two large walled settlements lie equidistant to the north and south of X13, and two medium-size walled towns lie equidistant to the northeast and southwest. The southern cluster is slightly different. It is centered on X11, which is both a ritual center and a town, around which are medium- and small-size plaza settlements.

In land area, each cluster was more than 250 square kilometers, of which about a fifth was the built-up core area, making it roughly equivalent in size to a small modern city. Today most of the ancient landscape is overgrown, but forests in the core areas have distinctive concentrations of certain plants, animals, soils and archaeological artifacts, such as prolific ceramics. Land use was more intensive in the past, but the remains suggest that many practices were similar to those of the Kuikuro: manioc plots, small orchards of pequi fruit trees and fields of *sapé* grass, the preferred material for house thatch. The countryside was a patchy landscape interspersed with secondary forests that invaded fallow agricultural areas. Wetlands, which today are choked with Buriti palm, the most important industrial crop, preserve diverse evidence of fish farming, such as artificial ponds, raised causeways and weir footings. Outside the core areas was a more lightly populated green belt and even deeper forest wilderness between clusters. This forest, too, had its uses for animals, medicinal plants and certain trees, and it was considered the home of diverse forest spirits.

The areas in and around residential sites are marked by dark earth, which the Kuikuro call *egepe,* a highly fertile soil that has been enriched by household refuse and specialized soil-management activities, such as controlled burning of vegetation cover. People have altered soils the world over, making them darker, more loamy and richer in certain chemicals. In the Amazon these changes are particularly important for agriculture in many areas because the natural soil is so poor. In the Xingu, the dark earth is less prevalent than some areas, because local populations depend mostly on manioc and orchards, which do not require high-fertility soils.

Identification of large walled settlements over an area about the size of Vermont suggests that at least 15 clusters were spread across the Upper Xingu. But most of the region is unstudied, so the true number could have been much higher. Radiocarbon dating of our excavated sites suggests that ancestors of the Xinguanos settled the area, most likely from the west, and began to mold the forests and wetlands to their design about 1,500 years ago or before. In the centuries before Europeans first discovered the Americas, the communities were re-formed into hierarchical clusters. Records date back only to 1884, so the settlement patterns are our only way of estimating the pre-Columbian population; the scale of the clusters suggests a regional population many times larger than today, perhaps numbering 30,000 to 50,000.

Garden Cities of the Amazon

A century ago Ebenezer Howard's *Garden Cities of To-morrow* proposed a model for low-density, sustainable urban growth. A forerunner of today's green movement, Howard envisioned networked towns as an alternative to an industrial world filling with high-rise cities. Ten towns with tens of thousands of people, he suggested, could have the same functional and administrative capacity of a single megacity.

The ancient Xinguanos built such a system, a flat, green style of urbanism or proto-urbanism: an inchoate garden city. Perhaps Percy Fawcett was in the right place but looking for the wrong thing: stone cities. What the small-scale centers lacked in size and elaborate structures, they made up for in numbers and integration. Had Howard known of them, he might have devoted a passage to the "Garden Cities of Yesterday." The common conception of the city as a dense grid of masonry buildings dates to early desert oasis civilizations such as Mesopotamia but was uncharacteristic of many other environments. Not only the Amazon's tropical forests but also temperate forest landscapes throughout much of medieval Europe were dotted with towns and villages of similar size to those in the Xingu.

These insights are especially important today as the southern Amazon is redeveloped, this time by Western civilization. The transitional forest of the southern Amazon is being quickly converted into farmland and pasture. At the present rate, it will be reduced to 20 percent of its original size over the next decade. Much of what is left will be restricted to reserves, such as the Xingu, where indigenous people are the stewards of the remaining biodiversity. In these areas, saving tropical forests and protecting indigenous cultural heritage are, in many respects, one and the same thing.

At the present rate, the southern Amazon forest will be reduced to 20 percent of its original size over the next decade. Indigenous people are the stewards of the remaining biodiversity.

Critical Thinking

1. What kind of sites has Michael Heckenberger excavated in the Amazon? Why are they now overgrown?
2. How did the people thrive in spite of the infertile natural soils?
3. Why did anthropologists at one time view the forest environment as "inimical to agriculture"? How and why did this view begin to erode in the 1970s?
4. In what ways has the author been able to see links between the archaeological evidence and present-day customs? Why is this possible with the Kuikuro?
5. How is the ancient walled town similar to Afukaka's current village?
6. What makes the chief's house stand out?
7. How does the arrangement of the village reproduce, on a large scale, the layout of an individual house?
8. Why is the degree of regional integration impressive?
9. How was the land being used?
10. What is the significance of the dark earth in and around the settlements?
11. What does radiocarbon dating indicate?
12. What does the scale of the clusters suggest?
13. Where does the common conception of the city as a dense grid of masonry buildings come from? Why does it not apply in the Amazon?
14. At what rate is the Amazon forest being reduced in size?
15. Why is it that saving tropical forests and protecting indigenous cultural heritage are, in many respects, one and the same thing?

Michael J. Heckenberger has done archaeology in the Xingu region and elsewhere in the Brazilian Amazon since 1992, most recently as a professor at the University of Florida. His work focuses on the social and political organization and historical ecology of late prehistoric complex societies in the region, as well as changes in indigenous societies following European colonization not just in Brazil but also in northeastern South America, the Caribbean and northeastern North America. At home, he relaxes by cultivating bonsai.

Germany's Nazi Past

The Past as Propaganda

How Hitler's archaeologists distorted European prehistory to justify racist and territorial goals.

Bettina Arnold

The manipulation of the past for political purposes has been a common theme in history. Consider Darius I (521–486 B.C.), one of the most powerful rulers of the Achaemenid, or Persian, empire. The details of his accession to power, which resulted in the elimination of the senior branch of his family, are obscured by the fact that we have only his side of the story, carved on the cliff face of Behistun in Iran. The list of his victories, and by association his right to rule, are the only remaining version of the truth. Lesson number one: If you are going to twist the past for political ends, eliminate rival interpretations.

The use of the past for propaganda is also well documented in more recent contexts. The first-century Roman historian Tacitus produced an essay titled "On the Origin and Geography of Germany." It is less a history or ethnography of the German tribes than a moral tract or political treatise. The essay was intended to contrast the debauched and degenerate Roman Empire with the virtuous German people, who embodied the uncorrupted morals of old Rome. Objective reporting was not the goal of Tacitus's *Germania*; the manipulation of the facts was considered justified if it had the desired effect of contrasting past Roman glory with present Roman decline. Ironically, this particular piece of historical propaganda was eventually appropriated by a regime notorious for its use and abuse of the past for political, imperialist, and racist purposes: the Third Reich.

The National Socialist regime in Germany fully appreciated the propaganda value of the past, particularly of prehistoric archaeology, and exploited it with characteristic efficiency. The fact that German prehistoric archaeology had been largely ignored before Hitler's rise to power in 1933 made the appropriation of the past for propaganda that much easier. The concept of the *Kulturkreis,* pioneered by the linguist turned-prehistorian Gustav Kossinna in the 1920s and defined as the identification of ethnic regions on the basis of excavated material culture, lent theoretical support to Nazi expansionist aims in central and eastern Europe. Wherever an artifact of a type designated as "Germanic" was found, the land was declared to be ancient Germanic territory. Applied to prehistoric archaeology, this perspective resulted in the neglect or distortion of data that did not directly apply to Germanic peoples. During the 1930s scholars whose specialty was provincial Roman archaeology were labeled *Römlinge* by the extremists and considered anti-German. The Römisch Germanische Kommission in Mainz, founded in 1907, was the object of numerous defamatory attacks, first by Kossinna and later by Alfred Rosenberg and his organization. Rosenberg, a Nazi ideologue, directed the Amt Rosenberg, which conducted ethnic, cultural, and racial research.

Altered prehistory also played an important role in rehabilitating German self-respect after the humiliating defeat of 1918. The dedication of the 1921 edition of Kossinna's seminal work *German Prehistory: A Preeminently National Discipline* reads: "To the German people, as a building block in the reconstruction of the externally as well as internally disintegrated fatherland."

According to Nazi doctrine, the Germanic culture of northern Europe was responsible for virtually all major intellectual and technological achievements of Western civilization. Maps that appeared in archaeological publications between 1933 and 1945 invariably showed the Germanic homeland as the center of diffusionary waves, bringing civilization to less developed cultures to the south, west, and east. Hitler presented his own views on this subject in a dinner-table monologue in which he referred to the Greeks as Germans who had survived a northern natural catastrophe and evolved a highly developed culture in southern contexts. Such wishful thinking was supported by otherwise reputable archaeologists. The *Research Report of the Reichsbund for German Prehistory,* July to December 1941, for example, reported the nine-week expedition of the archaeologist Hans Reinerth and a few colleagues to Greece, where they claimed to have discovered major new evidence of Indogermanic migration to Greece during Neolithic times.

This perspective was ethnocentric, racist, and genocidal. Slavic peoples occupying what had once been, on the basis of the distribution of archaeological remains, Germanic territory, were to be relocated or exterminated to supply true Germans with *Lebensraum* (living space). When the new Polish state was created in 1919, Kossinna published an article, "The German Ostmark, Home Territory of the Germans," which used archaeological evidence to support Germany's claim to the area. Viewed as only temporarily occupied by racially inferior "squatters," Poland and Czechoslovakia could be reclaimed for "racially pure" Germans.

Prehistoric archaeologists in Germany who felt they had been ignored, poorly funded, and treated as second-class citizens by colleagues specializing in the more honored disciplines of classical and Near Eastern archaeology now seemed to have everything to gain by an association with the rising Nazi party. Between 1933, the year of Hitler's accession to power, and 1935, eight new chairs were created in German prehistory and funding became available for prehistoric excavations across Germany and eastern Europe on an unprecedented scale. Numerous institutes came into being during this time, such as the Institute for Prehisitory in Bonn in 1938. Museums for protohistory were established, and prehistoric collections were brought out of storage and exhibited, in many cases for the first time. Institutes for rune research were created to study the *futhark,* or runic alphabet in use in northern Europe from about the third to the thirteenth centuries A.D. Meanwhile, the Römisch Germanisches Zentral Museum in Mainz became the Zentral Museum für Deutsche Vor- und Frühgeschichte in 1939. (Today it has its pre-war title once again.)

Open-air museums like the reconstructed Neolithic and Bronze Age lake settlements at Unteruhldingen on Lake Constanz were intended to popularize prehistory. An archaeological film series, produced and directed by the prehistorian Lothar Zotz, included titles like *Threatened by the Steam Plow, Germany's Bronze Age, The Flames of Prehistory* and *On the Trail of the Eastern Germans.* The popular journals such as *Die Kunde (The Message),* and *Germanen-Erbe (Germanic Heritage)* proliferated. The latter publication was produced by the Ahnenerbe ("Ancestor History") organization, run as a personal project of Reichsführer-SS and chief of police Heinrich Himmler and funded by interested Germans to research, excavate, and restore real and imagined Germanic cultural relics. Himmler's interests in mysticism and the occult extended to archaeology; SS archaeologists were sent out in the wake of invading German forces to track down important archaeological finds and antiquities to be transported back to the Reich. It was this activity that inspired Steven Spielberg's *Raiders of the Lost Ark.*

The popular journals contained abundant visual material. One advertisement shows the reconstruction of a Neolithic drum from a pile of meaningless sherds. The text exhorts readers to "keep your eyes open, for every *Volksgenosse* [fellow German] can contribute to this important national project! Do not assume that a ceramic vessel is useless because it falls apart during excavation. Carefully preserve even the smallest fragment!" An underlined sentence emphasizes the principal message: "Every single find is important because it represents a document of our ancestors!"

Amateur organizations were actively recruited by appeals to patriotism. The membership flyer for the official National Confederation for German Prehistory (*Reichsbund für Deutsche Vorgeschichte*), under the direction of Hans Reinerth of the Amt Rosenberg, proclaimed: "Responsibility with respect to our indigenous prehistory must again fill every German with pride!" The organization stated its goals as "the interpretation and dissemination of unfalsified knowledge regarding the history and cultural achievements of our northern Germanic ancestors on German and foreign soil."

For Himmler objective science was not the aim of German prehistoric archaeology. Hermann Rauschning, an early party member who became disillusioned with the Nazis and left Germany before the war, quotes Himmler as saying: "The one and only thing that matters to us, and the thing these people are paid for by the State, is to have ideas of history that strengthen our people in their necessary national pride. In all this troublesome business we are only interested in one thing—to project into the dim and distant past the picture of our nation as we envisage it for the future. Every bit of Tacitus in his *Germania* is tendentious stuff. Our teaching of German origins has depended for centuries on a falsification. We are entitled to impose one of our own at any time."

Meanwhile archaeological evidence that did not conform to Nazi dogma was ignored or suppressed. A good example is the controversy surrounding the Externsteine, a natural sandstone formation near Horn in northern Germany. In the twelfth century Benedictine monks from the monastery in nearby Paderborn carved a system of chambers into the rock faces of the Externsteine. In the mid-1930s a contingent of SS Ahnenerbe researchers excavated at the site in an attempt to prove its significance as the center of the Germanic universe, a kind of Teutonic mecca. The excavators, led by Julius Andree, an archaeologist with questionable credentials and supported by Hermann Wirth, one of the founders of the SS Ahnenerbe, were looking for the remains of an early Germanic temple at the Externsteine, where they claimed a cult of solar worshipers had once flourished. The site was described in numerous publications as a monument to German unity and the glorious Germanic past, despite the fact that no convincing evidence of a temple or Germanic occupation of the site was ever found.

So preposterous were the claims made by Andree, Wirth, and their associates that numerous mainstream archaeologists openly questioned the findings of the investigators who became popularly known as *German omanen* or "Germanomaniacs." Eventually Himmler and the Ahnenerbe organization disowned the project, but not before several hundred books and pamphlets on the alleged cult site had been published.

By 1933 the Nazis had gone a step further, initiating a movement whose goal was to replace all existing religious denominations with a new pseudopagan state religion based loosely on Germanic mythology, solar worship, nature cults, and a Scandinavian people's assembly or *thing,* from which the new movement derived its name. Central to the movement were open-air theaters or *Thingstätten,* where festivals, military ceremonies, and morality plays, known as *Thingspiele,* were to be staged. To qualify as a Thingstätte, evidence of significant Germanic occupation of the site had to be documented. There was considerable competition among municipalities throughout Germany for this honor. Twelve Thingstätten had been dedicated by September 1935, including one on the summit of the Heiligenberg in Heidelberg.

The Heiligenberg was visited sporadically during the Neolithic, possibly for ritual purposes; there is no evidence of permanent occupation. It was densely settled during the Late Bronze Age (1200–750 B.C.), and a double wall-and-ditch system was built there in the Late Iron Age (200 B.C. to the Roman occupation), when it was a hillfort settlement. Two provincial Roman watchtowers, as well as several Roman dedicatory inscriptions, statue bases, and votive stones, have been found at the site.

When excavations in the 1930s failed to produce evidence of Germanic occupation the Heiligenberg was granted Thingstätte status on the basis of fabricated evidence in the published excavation reports. Ironically, most of the summit's prehistoric deposits were destroyed in the course of building the open-air arena. The Heiligenberg Thingstätte actually held only one Thingspiel before the Thing movement was terminated. Sensing the potential for resistance from German Christians, the Ministry of Propaganda abandoned the whole concept in 1935. Today the amphitheater is used for rock concerts.

Beyond its convenience for propaganda and as justification for expansion into countries like Czechoslovakia and Poland, the archaeological activities of the Amt Rosenberg and Himmler's Ahnenerbe were just so much window dressing for the upper echelons of the party. There was no real respect for the past or its remains. While party prehistorians like Reinerth and Andree distorted the facts, the SS destroyed archaeological sites like Biskupin in Poland. Until Germany's fortunes on the eastern front suffered a reversal in 1944, the SS Abhenerbe conducted excavations at Biskupin, one of the best-preserved Early Iron Age (600–400 B.C.) sites in all of central Europe. As the troops retreated, they were ordered to demolish as much of the site's preserved wooden fortifications and structures as possible.

Not even Hitler was totally enthusiastic about Himmler's activities. He is quoted by Albert Speer, his chief architect, as complaining: "Why do we call the whole world's attention to the fact that we have no past? It's bad enough that the Romans were erecting great buildings when our forefathers were still living in mud huts; now Himmler is starting to dig up these villages of mud huts and enthusing over every potsherd and stone axe he finds. All we prove by that is that we were still throwing stone hatchets and crouching around open fires when Greece and Rome had already reached the highest stage of culture. We should really do our best to keep quiet about this past. Instead Himmler makes a great fuss about it all. The present-day Romans must be having a laugh at these revelations."

"Official" involvement in archaeology consisted of visits by Himmler and various SS officers to SS-funded and staffed excavations, like the one on the Erdenburg in the Rhineland, or press shots of Hitler and Goebbels viewing a reconstructed "Germanic" Late Bronze Age burial in its tree-trunk coffin, part of the 1934 "Deutsches Volk—Deutsche Arbeit" exhibition in Berlin. Party appropriation of prehistoric data was evident in the use of Indo-European and Germanic design symbols in Nazi uniforms and regalia. The double lightning bolt, symbol of Himmler's SS organization, was adapted from a Germanic rune. The swastika is an Indo-European sun symbol which appears in ceramic designs as early as the Neolithic in western Europe and continues well into early medieval times.

German archaeologists during this period fall into three general categories: those who were either true believers or self-serving opportunists; those (the vast majority) who accepted without criticism the appropriation and distortion of prehistoric archaeology; and those who openly opposed these practices.

Victims of the regime were persecuted on the basis of race or political views, and occasionally both. Gerhard Bersu, who had trained a generation of post–World War I archaeologists in the field techniques of settlement archaeology, was prematurely retired from the directorship of the Römisch Germanische Kommission in 1935. His refusal to condone or conduct research tailored to Nazi ideological requirements, in addition to his rejection of the racist Kossinna school, ended his career as a prehistonian until after World War II. The official reason given for the witchhunt, led by Hans Reinerth under the auspices of the Amt Rosenberg, was Bersu's Jewish heritage. By 1950 Bersu was back in Germany, again directing the Römisch Germanische Kommission.

It should be noted that some sound work was accomplished during this period despite political interference. The vocabulary of field reports carefully conformed to the dictates of funding sources, but the methodology was usually unaffected. Given time this would have changed as politically motivated terms and concepts altered the intellectual vocabulary of the discipline. In 1935, for example, the entire prehistoric and early historic chronologies were officially renamed: the Bronze and pre-Roman Iron Ages became the "Early Germanic period," the Roman Iron Age the "Climax Germanic period," the Migration period the "Late Germanic period," and everything from the Carolingians to the thirteenth century the "German Middle Ages."

It is easy to condemn the men and women who were part of the events that transformed the German archaeological community between 1933 and 1945. It is much more difficult to understand the choices they made or avoided in the social and political contexts of the time. Many researchers who began as advocates of Reinerth's policies in the Amt Rosenberg and Himmler's Ahnenerbe organization later became disenchanted. Others, who saw the system as a way to develop and support prehistory as a discipline, were willing to accept the costs of the Faustian bargain it offered. The benefits were real, and continue to be felt to this day in the institutions and programs founded between 1933 and 1945.

The paralysis felt by many scholars from 1933 to 1945 continued to affect research in the decades after the war. Most scholars who were graduate students during the 12-year period had to grapple with a double burden: a humiliating defeat and the disorienting experience of being methodologically "deprogrammed." Initially there was neither time nor desire to examine the reasons for the Nazi prostitution of archaeology. Unfortunately prehistoric archaeology is the only German social-science discipline that has still to publish a self-critical study of its role in the events of the 1930s and 1940s.

The reluctance of German archaeologists to come to terms with the past is a complex issue. German prehistoric archaeology is still a young discipline, and first came into its own as a result of Nazi patronage. There is therefore a certain feeling that any critical analysis of the motives and actions of the generation and the regime that engendered the discipline would be ungrateful at best and at worst a betrayal of trust. The vast majority of senior German archaeologists, graduate students immediately after the war, went straight from the front lines to the universities, and their dissertation advisers were men whose careers had been determined by their connections within the Nazi party.

The reluctance of German archaeologists to come to terms with the past is a complex issue.

The German system of higher education is built upon close bonds of dependence and an almost medieval fealty between a graduate student and his or her dissertation advisor. These bonds are maintained even after the graduate student has embarked on an academic career. Whistle-blowers are rare, since such action would amount to professional suicide. But in the past decade or so, most of the generation actively involved in archaeological research and teaching between 1933 and 1945 have died. Their knowledge of the personal intrigues and alliances that allowed the Nazi party machine to function has died with them. Nonetheless, there are indications that the current generation of graduate students is beginning to penetrate the wall of silence that has surrounded this subject since 1945. The remaining official documents and publications may allow at least a partial reconstruction of the role of archaeology in the rise and fall of the Nazi regime.

The future of prehistoric archaeology in the recently unified Germany will depend on an open confrontation with the past. Archaeologists in the former East Germany must struggle with the legacy of both Nazi and Communist manipulation of their discipline. Meanwhile, the legacy of the Faustian bargain struck by German archaeologists with the Nazi regime should serve as a cautionary tale beyond the borders of a unified Germany: Archaeological research funded wholly or in part by the state is vulnerable to state manipulation. The potential for political exploitation of the past seems to be greatest in countries experiencing internal instability. Germany in the years following World War I was a country searching for its own twentieth-century identity. Prehistoric archaeology was one means to that end.

Critical Thinking

1. What is lesson number one of this article? What example is used? What is the irony of this particular piece of historical propaganda?
2. What is Kulturkreis? How did it lend theoretical support to Nazi expansionism?
3. What was the attitude towards scholars who specialized in provincial Roman archaeology?
4. What role did "altered history" play for the Germans? What were the primary claims of the Nazi doctrine regarding Germanic culture?
5. How did German prehistoric archaeologists benefit by their association with the rising Nazi party?
6. What was Heinrich Himmler's role in promoting German prehistoric archaeology? Was there any attempt to be objective? Explain.
7. Who coined the term "Germanomaniacs" and why?
8. In what sense was Nazi archaeology just "so much window dressing"? Why was even Hitler not totally enthusiastic?
9. How was party appropriation of prehistoric data evident?
10. In what three categories did German archaeologists fall?
11. How does the author describe German archaeology during this period?
12. Why was there a continued "paralysis" after the war?
13. Why are German archaeologists still reluctant to come to terms with the past? How does this fit in with the German system of higher education?
14. What is the "cautionary tale" here?

Climate Change: Sites in Peril

ANDREW CURRY

Rising sea levels are eating away at coastal sites, increased rainfall is eroding mud-brick ruins, creeping desert sands are blasting the traces of ancient civilizations, and the melting of ice is causing millennia-old organic remains to rot. "With climate change, we're feeling a sense of urgency," says University of Northern Colorado anthropologist Michael Kimball, who organized a panel discussion on climate change and archaeology at the World Archaeology Congress in Dublin last year. "It definitely focuses the mind."

For countless communities, archaeology can be a source of local identity, pride, and even income. "It may be intangible, but when a community loses its connection to history it loses something pretty important," says Kimball.

The International Panel on Climate Change (IPCC), a group of more than 1,000 experts on climate science convened by the United Nations, estimates that the world's temperature has risen about two degrees in the past century, thanks in part to an increase in carbon dioxide that traps heat in the earth's atmosphere. The consequences have already been dramatic. The world's oceans have risen four inches in that time. Weather patterns have also gotten less predictable and more extreme.

Over the next hundred years, the IPCC predicts that sea levels will rise at least another four inches. The worst-case scenario is truly frightening: a 10-degree rise in global temperatures, causing ice caps to melt and sea levels around the world to rise more than three feet.

Archaeologists can't stop global warming, but they can make dealing with it a priority. That may mean documenting sites before they disappear; in some places, simple steps like putting roofs over melting or rain-threatened areas are ways to preserve them. Action, however, must be taken soon. "Our job is not so much to talk about how to get climate change to stop," says Giovanni Boccardi, the chief of UNESCO's Asia and Pacific Unit. "While climate change is global, lots of solutions are local—and within our reach." What follows is a look at some of the threats facing archaeological sites around the world.

Retreating Swiss Glaciers

The summer of 2003 was a scorcher in Europe, setting record temperatures across the continent and contributing to the deaths of more than 30,000 people. High in the Swiss Alps, the heat wave melted glaciers and snow, causing severe floods in the valleys below.

On September 17, a hiker named Ursula Leuenberger was crossing an iced-over pass near the Schnidejoch glacier when something odd caught her eye—a leather quiver that had been left high in the Alps by a Neolithic hunter around 2800 B.C.

The following summer, University of Bern archaeologist Albert Hafner organized a team of glaciologists and archaeologists to follow Leuenberger back up the mountain. There they found a five-foot-thick ice patch 260 feet long and 100 feet wide. In just one sunny week, the edges of the ice patch shrank 20 feet. Over the course of two summers, archaeologists found in it everything from prehistoric leather pants and shoes to nails from Roman sandals.

The finds revealed that people have climbed high in the Alps for millennia, despite its harsh conditions. (At Schnidejoch's altitude, the ground is covered in snow nine months out of the year.) "This was just the quickest way from one valley to another," says Hafner. His work also showed that 1,000-year gaps in the ages of the artifacts corresponded with cold periods when glacial ice would have blocked the pass. The fact that fragile organic materials were preserved near Schnidejoch for more than 5,000 years means the ice cover hasn't been this small since the Stone Age. "I think in the next years if there is a hot summer, the ice will disappear completely," says Hafner. "It's obviously related to climate change."

For archaeologists, the melting ice is both a crisis and an opportunity: the artifacts at Schnidejoch never would have been found without climate change, but as more and more alpine ice fields thaw and vanish, countless more artifacts may rot away and disappear forever, along with the icy glaciers and snowfields that define the Alps. Hafner says he has his eye on other sites that are on the verge of thawing. "I'm very happy to find the objects because they will give us new inputs, but I am not happy about the climate change," he says. "I'm an archaeologist, but I'm also an alpinist."

Peru's Rainstorms

The civilizations that rose and fell in the bone-dry deserts of coastal Peru knew the signs well. When Spanish conquistadors arrived, they noticed its effects around Christmas, and named the phenomenon El Niño, or little boy, after the Christ child. Every seven to ten years, currents in the Pacific Ocean shift, changing weather patterns from Australia to California. In Peru, El Niño means warmer water, and heavy rainfall along the coast.

The difference between a normal and a bad El Niño year can be tremendous. Peru's deserts typically get just over an inch of rain per year. In 1998, the last severe El Niño season, the region was doused with 120 inches, which caused serious flooding. Water takes a heavy toll on exposed archaeological sites, many of which are located along rivers or on easily eroded slopes.

Ironically, archaeologists have made the problem worse. "If we don't mess with the sites, water runs off without doing too much damage," says University of Maine archaeologist Dan Sandweiss. "But if you excavate, that's the end of them, basically." Holes made by looters also channel and trap moisture, doing more damage.

Take Chan Chan, an elaborately planned city eight miles square that dates back 1,000 years. Made of unfired mud brick, Chan Chan's pyramids and palaces were put on UNESCO's list of World Heritage Sites in Danger in 1986 because they were threatened by erosion. Over the past two decades, the site has deteriorated steadily. Researchers are investigating whether global warming could make El Niño occur more frequently. "There's the potential for greater destruction if the pace of El Niño events increases," says Sandweiss.

So far, climatologists can't say for sure what climate change will do to the powerful weather phenomenon. "The models are all over the place," says National Oceanic and Atmospheric Administration climatologist David Enfield. "We're up against a huge uncertainty at present." As climate experts work to refine their predictions, archaeologists anxiously await the arrival of the next El Niño.

Greenland's Melting Sea Ice

In a normal summer, Greenland's northern and eastern coasts should be ringed by an ice belt 30 to 40 miles wide. The drifting ice acts like a shock absorber, dampening the strength of the North Atlantic. "It takes a lot of wave energy to move the ice, and normally water along the coast is very calm," says Danish archaeologist Bjarne Gronnow, of the National Museum in Copenhagen.

But in the past five years, the sea ice has all but disappeared. Without its floating frozen shield, Greenland's coast is being pummeled by storm surges originating hundreds of miles away. When Gronnow visited the region last summer, his team was barely able to land their Zodiac rafts on the beaches because of waves almost 10 feet high.

The effect on the island's heritage has been catastrophic. Hardest hit have been sites associated with the Thule culture, people closely related to the Inuit of northern Canada who first migrated to Greenland around 2,000 years ago. The Thule were formidable hunters and whalers, and their villages were built close to the shore. Today, Thule houses—made of stone and turf with whale-bone rafters—are disappearing quickly, along with buried tools and artifacts. "A meter per season will be tumbled down to the beach and washed away," Gronnow says. "It's not a slow process."

Older sites along the coast are also in danger. As the Arctic warms up, archaeologists fear the frozen turf that covers Qeqertasussuk, a 4,500-year-old settlement where evidence for the earliest settlement of Greenland was found, may be melting. Gronnow—who excavated the remote site for the first time in the 1980s—is headed back this summer, and he is not optimistic. "I've been working in Greenland for 30 years now," he says. "I can see with my own eyes how it has changed."

Thawing Scythian Tombs

Three thousand years ago, Scythian nomads ruled the Eurasian steppes from the edges of the Black Sea in the west to China in the east. The Greek historian Herodotus reported their exploits as warriors and their drug-fueled religious rituals. The Scythians buried their dead in huge grave mounds that have been rich resources for archaeologists studying how this nomadic culture spread, thrived, and ultimately faded away around 200 B.C.

Though the burial mounds—called kurgans—are found everywhere from Ukraine to Kazakhstan, few are as spectacularly preserved as those in the Altai Mountains on the edge of the vast Siberian permafrost region. Many of these graves have been on ice for millennia, sandwiched between a frozen layer of earth and the insulating grave mound above.

Beginning with Soviet excavations in the 1940s and '50s, archaeologists have found amazingly well-preserved mummies in the tombs, often with their clothing, burial goods, horses, and even stomach contents intact. "Instead of archaeology, the material culture is so well preserved it's almost a kind of ethnography," says Hermann Parzinger, who discovered the tomb of a mummified Scythian warrior in Mongolia in 2006 and now directs the Prussian Cultural Heritage Foundation in Berlin.

But scientists say the Altai Mountains aren't as cold as they used to be. The glaciers that covered the slopes of the Altai are receding and even disappearing. And for the first time since their occupants were buried 3,000 years ago, the Scythian tombs are in danger of thawing out and rotting away. "These tombs are all in an area where the permafrost is just at an equilibrium," says Jean Bourgeois, an archaeologist at Ghent University who works on sites in Russia and Kazakhstan. "Just a degree or two can be enough to [destroy] frozen contents."

Mapping and listing all the region's kurgans using old spy satellite photos and old-fashioned ground surveys is the first phase of an international effort to save the frozen tombs. Bourgeois says the first priority is identifying kurgans that may still have permafrost underneath.

Archaeologists are scrambling to figure out the next step: how to keep the grave mounds cool. Instead of emergency excavations, Bourgeois hopes to work with engineers to find low-cost solutions to preserve the kurgans intact for future researchers. Proposals range from reflecting sunlight away from the kurgans by painting them white to stabilizing the underground temperature by installing "thermo-pumps." But after seeing the region's climate change with his own eyes over the past decade, Bourgeois has come to realize that even in a best-case scenario, archaeologists cannot preserve all of them. "They will have to choose."

Channel Islands Erosion

The Channel Islands off the coast of California are a critical link in the study of how humans settled the Americas. For decades, the consensus has been simple: America's first immigrants crossed the Bering Strait on foot and made their way south, over land through what is now Canada. Many researchers now believe, however, that the first people came to America by boat, island-hopping from Siberia all the way down to the California coast.

Some of the best evidence for this comes from the Channel Islands. "We have in excess of 10,000 years of human occupation," says Channel Islands National Park Archaeologist Kelly Minas. Evidence from shell middens, rock shelters, and other settlement sites supports the idea that early Americans were good sailors who reached the islands more than 13,000 years ago, hunting pygmy mammoths, elephant seals, and sea lions. Human bones found on Santa Rosa Island in 1959 have been radiocarbon-dated to 13,000 years ago, making them the oldest human bones found in the Americas.

Back then, the world was much colder, and the oceans much lower—low enough that four of the Channel Islands were connected by dry land. Now, rising sea levels are threatening some of the last coastal rock shelters left on the islands. "Erosion is a problem on the islands," Minas says. Coastal winds, waves, storm surges, and even seals hauling out of the water can damage or destroy coastal sites on the islands.

Rising seas now threaten to wipe out clues to how early humans made their way into the Americas just as researchers are beginning to look into the possibility of coastal migration. At Daisy Cave, a sea-side site on San Miguel Island, University of Oregon archaeologist Jon Erlandson has spent a decade excavating a 65-foot-wide midden that the island's prehistoric residents built up over thousands of years. Excavators have found the remains of tools, beads, and even baskets.

But, their work is becoming a race against time. Erlandson says the midden has shrunk by about three feet in the past decade. "If we've lost a meter in 10 years, how much will we lose in 50 or 100?" Erlandson asks. "If this keeps up, we're going to lose an incredible amount of archaeological sites."

Sudan Desertification

Local nomads call the ruins Musawwarat es-Sufra, or "Yellow Pictures." More than 2,000 years ago, the kings of the Meroites—a desert kingdom closely linked to ancient Egypt—built a temple complex 20 miles east of the Nile Valley, in what is today Sudan. Built of soft yellow sandstone, the walls and columns of the complex were decorated with hieroglyphs and elaborate reliefs, covered in mortar and colorfully painted. "It was probably the most important pilgrimage site of the Meroitic kingdom," says Claudia Naeser, an archaeologist at Humboldt University in Berlin who is excavating the site's reservoirs and temples.

Musawwarat's centerpiece was the 50-foot-long Temple of the Lion God, carved inside and out with reliefs dedicated to the Meroitic god of fertility, Apedemak. The lion god's temple was once in the middle of a grassland. But warming temperatures and overuse have killed off the area's vegetation, and the Sahara's sands are creeping ever closer. In the 1960s, an earlier Humboldt University mission uncovered and reconstructed the temple's collapsed walls—in retrospect, a mistake. "The reliefs suffer heavily from wind erosion," Naeser says. "The sandstone is relatively soft, and it just abrades."

Musawwarat is far from alone. Desertification is an often-overlooked problem because shifting dunes and blowing sand cover archaeological remains—leading to a misperception that the ruins are being shielded from further damage. "There's this belief that sand is protective. It's not," says Henri-Paul Francfort, a director of research at the French National Center for Scientific Research. "Sand can quickly destroy remains, both because of the weight of dunes and because of terrible winds that erase everything."

The scale of the problem is overwhelming, and solutions—from hardening stone with special chemicals to erecting protective walls or planting trees as windbreaks—are either prohibitively expensive or impossible because of a lack of water. UNESCO is now considering an application to have Musawwarat listed as a World Heritage Site. Soon, however, there may be no more "yellow pictures" to be seen.

Critical Thinking

1. What are some of the dramatic consequences of climate change that can already be seen?
2. What does the International Panel on Climate Change estimate with regard to the world's temperature in the past century and what does it predict with respect to sea levels? What is the "worst case scenario"?
3. What are some of the things that archaeologists can do about the effect of climate change on archaeological sites?
4. In what respects have the retreating Swiss glaciers been shown to be both "a crisis and an opportunity" to archaeologists?
5. What is *El Niño*? How has it affected archaeological sites in Peru? How have archaeologists and looters made the problem worse? What do climatologists say so far as to what global climate change will do to El Niño?
6. Why has Greenland's northern and eastern coasts been recently pummeled by storm surges? What has been the effect on the island's Thule heritage?
7. How is it that the Scythian burial mounds, or kurgans, have been preserved for so many millennia?
8. How well have the mummies and the material culture been preserved?
9. Why are the tombs in danger of rotting away?

10. What is the first phase of the international effort to save the tombs? What have been the proposals to keep the grave mounds cool? What is the "best case scenario"?
11. In contrast to what was once believed, what is the archaeological evidence now telling us about how humans settled the Americas?
12. What were climatic conditions like back then? How is climate change affecting archaeologists' ability to research the coastal migration theory?
13. How have warming temperatures and overuse of the local vegetation endangered the ruins of Musawwarat es-Sufra in Sudan?

Test-Your-Knowledge Form

We encourage you to photocopy and use this page as a tool to assess how the articles in *Annual Editions* expand on the information in your textbook. By reflecting on the articles you will gain enhanced text information. You can also access this useful form on a product's book support website at *www.mhhe.com/cls*.

NAME: DATE:

TITLE AND NUMBER OF ARTICLE:

BRIEFLY STATE THE MAIN IDEA OF THIS ARTICLE:

LIST THREE IMPORTANT FACTS THAT THE AUTHOR USES TO SUPPORT THE MAIN IDEA:

WHAT INFORMATION OR IDEAS DISCUSSED IN THIS ARTICLE ARE ALSO DISCUSSED IN YOUR TEXTBOOK OR OTHER READINGS THAT YOU HAVE DONE? LIST THE TEXTBOOK CHAPTERS AND PAGE NUMBERS:

LIST ANY EXAMPLES OF BIAS OR FAULTY REASONING THAT YOU FOUND IN THE ARTICLE:

LIST ANY NEW TERMS/CONCEPTS THAT WERE DISCUSSED IN THE ARTICLE, AND WRITE A SHORT DEFINITION: